W9-BBE-461

PHILOSOPHY
AS SOCIAL
EXPRESSION

Descartes at the Court of Queen Christina. Detail of the painting *Queen Christina of Sweden Surrounded by Scholars of Her Time* by Dumesnil at Versailles.

Albert William Levi

PHILOSOPHY AS SOCIAL EXPRESSION

The University of Chicago Press
Chicago and London

ALBERT WILLIAM LEVI is David May Distinguished
University Professor of the Humanities at Washington University
in St. Louis. His publications include *Philosophy and the Modern
World, Literature, Philosophy and the Imagination,* and
Humanism and Politics.
1974

THE UNIVERSITY OF CHICAGO PRESS, CHICAGO 60637
THE UNIVERSITY OF CHICAGO PRESS, LTD., LONDON

International Standard Book Number: 0-226-47389-9 (clothbound)
Library of Congress Catalog Card Number: 73-84191

For Estelle and Sasha and their three young ladies,
Tita, Michélle, and Nina

Was das Individuum betrifft, so ist ohnehin jedes ein *Sohn seiner Zeit*; so ist auch die Philosophie *ihre Zeit in Gedanken erfasst*. Es ist ebenso töricht zu wähnen, irgendeine Philosophie gehe über ihre gegenwärtige Welt hinaus, als, ein Individuum überspringe seine Zeit, springe über Rhodus hinaus.

Hegel

CONTENTS

ILLUSTRATIONS

PREFACE

For some time now the conviction has grown upon me that the relationship between philosophizing and the history of philosophy is in need of reexamination. Partly this has come about because so much of contemporary philosophy (following Carnap and Wittgenstein) ignores the rich resources of the philosophic tradition. But I have also been distressed by a narrow intellectualism in the treatment of the history of ideas itself — a narrowness which forgets the way ideas arise in historical context and take on the individual color of the lives and genius of their creators. Knowing, however, that less can be accomplished by precept than by example, instead of chiefly demonstrating how others have done it wrong, I have attempted the far riskier enterprise of using exemplary figures to show the way I think the job ought to be done. I make no claim to having succeeded. It is the new direction and the general principles upon which it rests that count, and these should appear here cleanly and clearly.

Philosophy as Social Expression is thus frankly a work in the reinterpretation of the history of philosophy, and although it had its origins in a series of lectures delivered at the University of Notre Dame in 1969, it is basically the product of many years of interest in teaching in this field. Although I should think it would be of primary interest to philosophers, I hope it might also appeal to historians whose field is the history of ideas and to sociologists specializing in the sociology of knowledge.

Philosophy as Social Expression has in no sense been written as a textbook, but is intended as a contribution to the philosophy of culture and the history of ideas. Yet because my scholarly work is never far from the atmosphere of teaching and learning, nothing would please me more than for it to find use as a basic text in courses in philosophical classics or introductory history of philosophy. Used in conjunction with, say, Plato's *Republic*, selections from Saint Thomas, Descartes's *Discourse on Method* or his *Meditations*, and G. E. Moore's *Principia Ethica* (or his little *Ethics*), it might make some modest contribution in opposing our age's rampant professionalism, and in shifting the center of philosophic instruction away from the merely technical toward the humane.

I would like to express my indebtedness to several of my colleagues at Washington University. To Professor Richard Watson, who permitted me to give the course in seventeenth-century rationalists which he usually teaches, while I was working on Descartes. To Professor Herbert Spiegelberg for some suggestions concerning the Cartesianism of Edmund Husserl which limitations of space prevented me from utilizing as they deserved. To Professor Carl Wellman for some useful hints on how an analytic philosopher might approach the history of philosophy. And to Professor Norris K. Smith of the Department of Art and Archaeology for help in selecting and reproducing the pictures of the philosophers which appear in this book.

For information about G. E. Moore, given during a delightful luncheon in Graz, I am indebted to Gilbert Ryle, as I am to Casimir Lewy for his infinite patience and good nature during a visit to Cambridge, seat of Moore's activity for so many years.

1

INTRODUCTION
Method in the History of Ideas
Philosophy, Logic, and Time

Crisis in the History of Philosophy

It is the case, I think, that at present the field we call the history of philosophy is in a state of crisis. It is not that the historian's skill has been lost, or that all the information about the life and times of the great classical philosophers has been discovered and all interpretive novelty exhausted. The crisis lies rather in an impoverishment of interest and a serious loss of the sense of relevance. The *history of ideas* does indeed flourish, but it has been taken out of the hands of philosophers proper and placed in the hands of historians — not as an act of violence, but as a permitted appropriation in the face of philosophic indifference and unconcern.

Nor is it merely that the great specialized histories of the nineteenth century — of Erdmann and Ueberweg, or of Victor Cousin and Kuno Fischer — are now extinct species: post-Hegelian dinosaurs whose bodies are too large for our heads. Even the more modest efforts of the earlier years of this century — the problem-oriented unification of Windelband and the elegant and focused (and typically Gallic) overview of Bréhier — have some difficulty in finding their contemporary successors. But even more crucial, that intimate link between philosophizing and thinking within the boundaries of a tradition, of intimately conversing (and arguing) with the intellectual giants of the past, so that speculative philosophy and the history of philosophy mutually interpenetrate, seems to have all but disappeared.

In *The Quest for Certainty* Dewey put forward a defense of the practical uses of philosophy, but his recommendation of the arts of control and an instrumental theory of the good was grounded in a thoroughgoing examination and, finally, a negative critique of Plato, Aristotle, and the aristocratic bias of the ancient world. In part 1 of *Process and Reality* Whitehead presents the enduring categories of his own speculative cosmology, but the whole of part 2 uses the history of philosophy (chiefly from Descartes to Kant) to ground and substantiate his own theoretical position. But Wittgenstein's *Tractatus* seems unaware that there were philosophers on earth before the birth of Bertrand Russell, and the now enormously popular work of J. L. Austin stands or falls not on the tradition of the *philosophia perennis*, but ostensibly upon the authority of the *Oxford English Dictionary*.

It is true that for Dewey "ideas" meant conceptions historically anchored, playing their appropriate roles in the ebb and flow of historical circumstance; for if ideas in general are primarily to be conceived as instruments of adaptation and adjustment, then philosophic ideas too must be examined in the light of the social needs they were meant to fulfill, and the class structure of the society whose tensions they were originated to explode or adjust. Somewhere in *Reconstruction in Philosophy* Dewey remarks that philosophies are more effectively refuted by exposing the conditions of their origin than by any battery of arguments by which they might be logically opposed, and although this is somewhat less than congenial to that philosophic temper whose criterion of intellectual validity is logical rather than historical and pragmatic, yet for such a pragmatic mentality the history of philosophy is indeed important. Even if the doctrines of Plato and Descartes, of Aquinas and Kant, of Aristotle and Hume had a local significance for their own times which they cannot possibly retain for ours their continual inspection and reexamination is a permanent necessity if we wish to understand the rhythms of intellectual history—how the genesis, decline, and fall of ideas is a function of temporality and social circumstance.

One might, of course, object that such an interest in the history of philosophy, although it might be "historical" or even "sociological," is certainly not "philosophical." But this is surely to beg the issue of what constitutes a philosophical interest, and it is at least clear that Dewey's conception of the role ideas play in the history of civilization rests upon an appeal to certain principles of judgment which make philosophical criticism of socially grounded classical philosophical systems possible.

The attitude of Whitehead (and even of so minimally historical-minded a position as that of Viennese Logical Empiricism) is quite different. For to Whitehead, who has characterized the entire Western philosophical tradition as "a series of footnotes to Plato," the continuity of the philosophical generations is an article of faith, and he knows that however much he may disagree with some of his predecessors, every original and constructive philosopher must honor his philosophic forebears and acknowledge his conceptual debts. Thus, however strongly he urges his objections against Aristotle's subject-predicate logic, Descartes's theory of substance, and Hume's "unbelievable" doctrines about causality and personal identity, Plato is his ultimate hero, Locke (however mistakenly) is the source of his doctrine of "actual occasions," and the British Empiricists (as well as Bradley and Spinoza), he thinks, anticipate some of the most characteristic components of the Philosophy of Organism. To read that great trilogy beginning with *Science and the Modern World* and ending with *Adventures of Ideas* is to sense the cumulative effect of the entire Western philosophic tradition.

It may seem strange to compare Whitehead with Viennese Logical Empiricism in this respect, but I think that they share a certain dependence upon the infinite subject matter of the history of philosophy, although for Whitehead (as for a sculptor in clay or plaster) the technique is one of adding to and building up — that is to say, of maximum incorporation — whereas for modern Positivism (as for a carver in wood or stone) the technique is one of carving out a narrowly restricted tradition — of cutting away, of paring down to size. A position like Quine's or Carnap's which tries to free philosophy from the bondage of its metaphysical past in order to make it increasingly scientific — that is, more logical and mathematical — and to purge it of the ghosts of former theological (and teleological) systems, is not notable for its references to the history of philosophy. Yet a work like Hans Reichenbach's *The Rise of Scientific Philosophy* or Phillip Frank's *Modern Science and Its Philosophy* spends no little time in expunging the dangerous traces of Platonic realism and the sinister implications of Kant's synthetic a priori. For, true to its Comtian origins, Positivism is not merely a timeless philosophy of scientific method, but is also a doctrine of historical progress, envisaging the ultimate triumph of scientific rationality. As such it cannot be totally indifferent to the processes of time and history.

Positivism too has its philosophic heroes and its villains. It approves the Aristotelian empiricism as it scorns the Platonic metaphysics of Being. It values the Baconian temper as it is impatient with the transcendentalism of Kant. Hume is perhaps its most admirable philosophic figure. And it despises Hegel. It too partly values the history of philosophy, although less as a reservoir of currently usable principles and formulae than as a kind of necessary morality play in the realm of ideas. It has some mild ancestral piety for the primitive origins of what is most

modern in its logical method and verification theory and at
the same time its historical memory constructs a kind of cham-
ber of horrors against the possibility of theological and metaphysical relapse. Thus for Positivism the history of philosophy
is without theoretical significance, although of considerable
moral use.

The great modern speculative systems of Dewey and Whitehead, as well as the historically conscious logical empiricism of
Frank and Reichenbach, utilized the history of philosophy to
acknowledge their debts of appropriation, to refute false doctrine,
and to place themselves within the continuity of the intellectual
history of Western culture. But they belong to a previous generation. Their powerful thrusts have been lost or absorbed, and they
have been replaced by an analytic and linguistic orientation whose
obsessive concentration on specific philosophic problems in isolation from any determinate cultural context gives to philosophizing
in the modern world an abstractness and an ahistoricity hardly
matched throughout its long development.

The Cambridge Philosophy of Analysis (drawing its inspiration
from G. E. Moore) and the Oxford Philosophy of Language
(based primarily upon Wittgenstein and Austin) pursue their
narrow investigations in a technical and exclusive sense, largely
outside the consciousness of time, and with a concept of mental
space which makes the arena of philosophic controversy into a
kind of neutral vacuum. And this is productive of a historical
absentmindedness (or purposive neglect) which allows its practitioners to pursue their specialized researches into the nature of
adverbs and "perception words" or of promises and "mental acts"
as if in some permanently enduring present without pressure and
without limit. In such an atmosphere (quite in opposition to
Dewey), the philosophically essential questions are independent of
their cultural history, and questions of social stratification, cultural period, and *date* are irrelevant to philosophical *speculation*,
however much a part of historical *scholarship*. Whitehead's loose
distinction has here been elevated into a watertight compartment-
alization of intellectual fields.

I do not wish to do an injustice to the analytic and linguistic
point of view. And perhaps the way I have just stated it is literally
(if not in spirit) an exaggeration. Surely the Analytic philosophers
know, for example, that Descartes existed; in fact, it is almost
possible to say that they have contributed prominently to a new

wave of Cartesian studies. But the kind of Cartesian studies they have undertaken (as illustrated, for example, in the book of essays collected by Willis Doney, or in Anthony Kenney's *Descartes*) would be largely unrecognizable by a previous generation of Cartesian scholars: men like Gilson or Brunschvicg, Gouhier or Guéroult. They are interested in a narrow logical analysis of the proposition *Cogito ergo sum*. They are concerned to show the errors in Descartes's account of dreaming. They reenact the battles over the ontological argument in linguistic terms. Above all, they are impatient to demonstrate why Wittgenstein's denial of the possibility of a private language invalidates Descartes's subjectivist claims. But these abstract and isolated bits of analysis typically fail to consider what role the immediacy of self-consciousness, the reference to dreaming, the ontological argument, and the claims of Cartesian privacy make in the Cartesian philosophy *as a whole, as an integral position*. Nor, needless to say, do they recognize the position seventeenth-century thinking occupies with reference to the problems set by medieval thought (Anselm and Aquinas), and the distinctive contribution of the French renaissance (Montaigne) in their solution. "Descartes" therefore ceases to be a *man*, living in a specific *period*, and becomes a *text* from whose complicated internal structure *arguments* may be isolated and lifted for philosophic purposes having little to do with those of Descartes himself. It is occasionally interesting and even (for its limited relevance) impressive stuff, but as critical work it is far from unprejudiced. For its criteria necessarily lie outside of time, and even for the establishment of meaning, it systematically neglects those contextual resources provided by the historical categories of time and place.

What is at issue here, and why it constitutes a crisis for the history of philosophy, can be better seen, I think, if we put ourselves in the position of the Analytic philosopher and try to formulate, as he himself would, his objections to the history of philosophy as customarily presented, and as embodying the claims of essential temporality. "Why should I," he might ask, "as a philosopher, concern myself with the history of philosophy?" And he might answer as follows: "We as philosophers, trying to answer philosophic questions, or solve certain metaphysical or epistemological puzzles, or [if he is a Wittgensteinian] dissolve certain tormenting philosophical problems, do indeed find it useful to study the history of philosophy. And the reason is this. By seeing our problem through the eyes of others we may understand it better. But above all, from the history of philosophy we may come to acquire *a battery of technical concepts* that may be useful in our thinking; we discover *a repository of arguments* that we must consider in dealing with the problem ourselves, and we find *an array of possible solutions* from which we may find clues toward our own answer. In all this it does not really seem to matter *who* said what, or in answer to *whom*, much less *why* he said it at a certain point in history. What I as a problem-solving philosopher want from the history of philosophy is not history as such, but logical possibilities to think about. And for this purpose 'bad' history may even be more useful than 'good.' For if the history of philosophy is to speak to *my* problems, it may need to be history distorted and misinterpreted precisely because it is put in the idiom of *my* thinking and *my* times rather than that appropriate to the personalities and culture of its own historical setting. To repeat: the working philosopher does not need accurate or explanatory history of philosophy, but rather a panorama of logically possible positions, and a suggestive historical falsification may be philosophically preferable to a correct interpretation which does not happen to speak to the issue with which the philosopher may currently be wrestling. More, there is even a positive danger that specifically historical concern with some of the greatest works in the history of philosophy may actually tend to draw one away from philosophy by substituting dramatic biography or absorbing sociological comment for true philosophical thinking."

If this is a fair statement of the analytic position, it is now possible to see more clearly what is basically at stake. And I think it can be stated rather simply in two dichotomies, one expressed in terms of competing subject matters, the other in terms of the prime categories which govern their definition. It is the issue of "philosophy" versus "history" or, better, the issue of the competing claims within our philosophical cognition of "logic" and of "time."

It is clear from the imaginarily constructed statement above that what the analytic philosopher really needs is a catalog of arguments or a prospectus of positions, anonymous, dateless, and placeless, a universal index of logical possibilities totally abstracted from all tincture of *particularity*, of individual origination, or of social grounding—in short, of all *historicity*—and that to the extent that he turns to the history of philosophy at all, he uses it in this perverse and intrinsically inappropriate fashion. For the philosophers who are most characteristic of the age dominated by the influence of G. E. Moore and Wittgenstein would agree, I think, that the history of philosophy is really of little importance to philosophy and to speculation, however interesting it may be to history and to scholarship. And the reason for this assessment seems to lie in some tacit acknowledgment that the temporal element, so fundamental in Hegel's assertion that philosophy itself is only the progressive realization of man's self-consciousness in time, has been eliminated and superseded by Russell's dictum that "logic is the essence of philosophy."

Logic, like mathematics, is notoriously atemporal and Platonic. A proposition once true is held to be true forever, and meanings remain permanently stable in that frozen conceptual space from which they from time to time ingress and inhabit our consciousness. The quarrels between philosophers are therefore governed by this essential property of propositions and meanings, so that it inevitably follows that philosophy as a discipline is dependent upon logical rules and principles whose validity is unaffected by time, and the historical conditions and consequences of whose discovery and statement are not at bottom *philosophically* important.

In such a climate of prevailing opinion, it is little wonder that the role and prestige of the history of philosophy is in a state of crisis, and that we need to examine its presuppositions and conditions in order to ask ourselves what we need to do to guarantee its legitimate future. For, although since the time of Plato logic and temporality have been legislated into different realms, and although there is surely a valid conceptual distinction between philosophy and history as separate disciplines within the humanities, the degree to which these disjunctions dominate our thinking today is neither healthy nor inevitable.

Kant himself in his *Introduction to Logic* clearly distinguished "rational" from "historical" knowledge, the former being derived from *principles*, the latter from *empirical data*. But he admitted that knowledge may originate in reason and yet be historical, and his own "Short Sketch of a History of Philosophy" was meant to illustrate the truth that "he who desires to learn to philosophize must regard all systems of philosophy only a a *history of the use of reason.*" And indeed, it is upon this seminal idea that the Hegelian theory of the history of philosophy as a revelation of the development of the rational idea in time is securely founded.

Whether, therefore, the disjunction between philosophy and history is as absolute as is claimed by the philosophical analysts and whether also the philosopher is obliged to commit himself to the choice of logic over time are questions worthy of our further examination.

The Opposition of Logic and Time

In the preceding section I have been speaking as if the distinctions between philosophy and history, and between rational principles and their temporal qualifications, were an invention of analytic philosophy and hence a threat to the history of philosophy launched *from outside*. But this is only half the story. For long before these distinctions had become the basis of analytic arguments they had been points of open dissension between two factions of those clearly sympathetic with the history of philosophy, and they remain so to this day. This dissension concerns both the normative question of how the history of philosophy ought to be written and the prior technical questions upon which it hinges: of how philosophical texts are to be read, their meanings established, and their interpretations validated. We are therefore thrown back upon the somewhat professional issues concerning method in the history of ideas and of styles of philosophical controversy.

The dimension of philosophy that constitutes its temporal side is, of course, its participation in the processes of history. Texts are written, and they are our chief philosophical data; but behind every text stands a man, and behind every man lies a social order in which he has been educated and intellectually nourished. The *Phaedrus,* the *Summa contra gentiles*, the *Discourse on Method,* and the *Principia Ethica* are all crucial philosophical texts with which we moderns must reckon, but the first was written by a Greek aristocrat and disciple of Socrates, the second by a south Italian dialectician who studied liberal arts at medieval Naples and theology under Albert the Great, the third by a seventeenth-century French gentleman who, however much he tried, could not clear his mind of the Jesuit lessons of La Flèche, and the last by an almost contemporary Englishman who went up to Trinity College, Cambridge, ten years before the death of Queen Victoria. Is there no intrinsic (and philosophical) tie between these texts and the historical situations of these agents who produced them?

There is one school of theorists of the history of ideas which denies it, or at least claims that if there is such a tie, although it may be of historical interest, it is philosophically of no importance. What counts philosophically, they claim, is simply the text itself. Every philosophical work is a unique entity—a kind of Kantian *Ding-an-sich,* outside space and time—and it is the logical independence of the text, its intellectual autonomy, which is the exclusive presupposition of its meaning. We can thus examine the *Phaedrus* and the *Summa contra gentiles,* the *Discourse on Method* and the *Principia Ethica* and understand each solely within the terms of its own compositional boundaries, without reference to the peculiar and highly individual historical situations of Plato or Saint Thomas, of Descartes or G. E. Moore. For we must assume that these texts were written by reasonable men, and rationality is a generic quality which we share with them and which, in fact, guarantees our communication across the centuries. Whatever the accidental causes of the *posing* of philosophical problems in the details of personal biography or social circumstance, *the questions themselves* are eternal; the *concepts* through which they are formulated are common, and the *answers* which are given speak to all men because they presuppose a permanent intelligibility in rational discourse. Behind this theory of the history of ideas lies the Platonic faith in the permanence of reason and Frege's belief in the immutability of logic—in short, the fundamental assumption that all intensional meaning is timeless and eternal.

It is for these reasons that, the partisans of this theory believe, Saint Thomas could understand Aristotle almost better than he understood himself, that Descartes could support Saint Augustine across the ages, that Hobbes could resurrect the position of Greek sophistry without doing it violence, and that Hume would have felt a special blood brotherhood with Sextus Empiricus. All of this is possible precisely because in all thinking there are "timeless elements," because philosophy itself is but a system of "universal ideas" in pursuit of a "dateless wisdom," and because the subject matter of intellectual history is a series of "perennial problems" with their "solutions."

It is with these presuppositions that Hutchins and Adler taught "the great books" at Chicago, that Jacques Maritain found the relevance of the Thomistic wisdom throughout the history of philosophy, and that Leo Strauss investigated the political "messages" of Hobbes, Spinoza, and Machiavelli. Yet perhaps none of

these has expressed the underlying assumption of this position as
clearly as Karl Jaspers in the introduction to his book *The Great
Philosophers:*

The great philosophers are best approached as contemporaries
in the realm of a single, unbroken present, comprising three
millenia—that is, in a timeless area of human kinship. We shall
understand them best by questioning them, side by side, without regard for history and their place in it.

It is clear that to view the history of philosophy in this fashion
has certain very real pedagogical advantages, and that it provides
just those conditions for the establishment of a universal intellectual community which are so conspicuously missing in the fragmentation of our contemporary world. Yet in fact it constitutes a
high abstraction from the historical nature of intellectual communication, and it does a doubtful service to the cause of a full
and accurate comprehension of the basic historical texts. For to
postulate the temporal coexistence of vastly separated historical
positions is to *assume* the conditions of simultaneous discourse—
that is, to impose the forms of dialogue and dialectic (with their
plural modes of agreement and conflict) upon a factual situation
of great semantic uncertainty.

It is true that one can find a certain curious continuity between
Plato and G. E. Moore. The doctrine of "organic wholes" put
forward in *Principia Ethica* is not unlike the attribution of value
to the "composite mixture" of the *Philebus*, and both *Principia
Ethica* and the *Phaedrus* seem to underwrite the same ultimate
values of "friendship" and "the experience of the beautiful." Yet
the perplexities about identity of meaning stretch much further
than the mere problem of translation from Greek to English. If
concepts are the end product of a process of abstraction from
particulars (as classical epistemology from Aristotle to Kant
asserts), and if, therefore, intensional meaning is always originated within a range of denotation, can general ideas avoid
infection and coloration by historical particularity? Can ideas any
more than propositions resist the inevitability of dates? And can
"friendship" and "aesthetic experience" conceivably be *identical*
to a twentieth-century Englishman and a fourth-century Greek?
To say so is to assume an unconscionably heavy burden of proof.

It is also true that the Cartesian strategy with respect to argument for the existence of God is in profound opposition to that of
Saint Thomas in the *Summa theologica* and the *Summa contra
gentiles*. For Saint Thomas consciously rejected the very ontolog-

ical proof which Descartes reintroduces. Is this a clear case of ideological disagreement? Yes, in a certain sense—yet only if the concept of "God" is identical in meaning and function for the two philosophers. But "God" obviously operates differently as an object of adoration and as a cosmological explanation, as a locus of emotion and as a rational principle. Can it be said in this respect that what is referred to in the *Summa theologica* and in the *Meditations* is precisely identical? What semantic faith entitles us to assert that "God" *means* the same to a pious medieval saint and to a sophisticated Renaissance gentleman?

Moreover, although it is obvious that the terms "liberty," "justice," and "democracy" occur in a vast series of philosophic texts from Plato and Aristotle to Hobbes and Rousseau, and from Hobbes and Rousseau to Karl Marx and John Stuart Mill, yet the historic necessities which have given them thrust and relevance their political milieu and sociological contexts—have expressed profoundly different cultural realities. To hold therefore to the constancy and immutability of their "meaning" is to subscribe in the most unsophisticated fashion to the illusion of permanent and unambiguous communication.

To the doctrine outlined above, that every philosophical work is an autonomous entity capable of self-interpretation, and that as a consequence, as Jaspers says, the history of philosophy is best defined as a "single unbroken present" and best understood as one great dialectic of ideas where individual philosophers may be interrogated "without regard for history and their place in it," the historicist position stands directly opposed. For it insists upon *the doctrine of essential temporality,* where the very meaning of texts hinges upon the historical questions they were designed to answer, and where, since "meaning" and "social context" are dependent variables, much attention must be paid by the historian of ideas to historical milieu, social structure, and epochal description. Here the general presupposition of a shared rationality making for interpretive unity is supplanted by the claims of an individuality and particularity so extreme as almost to shatter completely the possibility of dialectical confrontation in the history of philosophy. Thus, the extreme timelessness of Jaspers's *The Great Philosophers* is confronted by the extreme historicism of R. G. Collingwood, expressed to perfection in his *Autobiography.* "You cannot," says Collingwood,

find out what a man means by simply studying his spoken or

written statements, even though he has spoken or written with
perfect command of language and perfectly truthful intention.
In order to find out his meaning, you must also know what the
question was . . . to which the thing he has said or written was
meant as an answer.

The "realists" thought that the problems with which philos-
sophy is concerned were unchanging. They thought that Plato,
Aristotle, the Epicureans, the Stoics, the Schoolmen, the Car-
tesians, etc., had all asked themselves the same set of questions,
and had given different answers to them.

If there were a permanent problem P, we could ask, "What
did Kant, or Leibniz, or Berkeley, think about P?," and if that
question could be answered, we could then go on to ask "Was
Kant, or Leibniz, or Berkeley, right in what he thought about
P?" But what is thought to be a permanent problem P is really
a number of transitory problems p1, p2, p3 . . . whose individual peculiarities are blurred by the historical myopia of the
person who lumps them together under the one name P.

Collingwood's profound skepticism with regard to the historical
continuity of meaning is surely a welcome antidote to the high
abstraction of Jasper's assumption of a permanence of meaning
outside of time, and its implied emphasis upon cultural factors in
the history of philosophy (say, the Greekness of Plato, or the
gentlemanliness of Descartes, or the Britishness of Hume, or the
middle-class rectitude of Kant) is a useful guideline for method in
the history of ideas, but it too is extreme and unbelievable in its
exaggeration of the total incommensurability of philosophical
meanings. Every historical epoch does indeed have its individual
peculiarities, but "human nature" has a high degree of stability,
and "mind" has its sets and its intellectual habits persisting
through the mutability of circumstance. New problems arise, but
older problems persist, and it is generally possible in the history of
philosophy to recognize and to discriminate the individual twists
from the ancient residues. Absolute variability in the theory of
meaning is no more satisfactory than absolute permanence. The
trick is to recognize both the Britishness of Hume and how it expresses itself in the permanent dilemma of the causal nexus, and the
middle-class rectitude of Kant and the way it provided him with a
new approach to the persistent perplexity concerning moral value.

The unitary and atemporal interpretation of the history of ideas
works best as these ideas themselves approach the limits of abstract universality — when it is chiefly a question of such ultimate
logical principles or metaphysical categories or epistemic concepts

as appear in philosophical treatises like Plato's *Parmenides* or Saint Thomas's *De ente et essentia* or Descartes's *Rules for the Direction of the Mind*. But when, for example, we read in the *Timaeus* that God created the liver in man to temper his cheerfulness with the restraining bitterness of gall (71b), or in the *Summa theologica* that the female sex is defective and "misbegotten" and occurs only through some external influence like a moist south wind (i.qu.92.3), or in the *Meditations* that insanity in man is caused by the clouding of the cerebellum by violent vapors of black bile (sec. 1), then the insistence upon a common abstract rationality is clearly compromised by the influence of external and empirical factors (such as the state of religious superstition or scientific knowledge at the time). These indiscreet reminders of a frequently impure mixture of metaphysical principles and accidental knowledge end by forcing us to supply for these speculations a *date*, and thus inexorably to recognize the inconvenient errors of temporal knowledge within the magnificent eternity of the principles of logic and mathematics.

If one objects that to abandon the doctrine of a logic of permanent ideas for a doctrine of essential temporality indicates a lack of interest in philosophy proper and a turn toward an interest in the history of culture for its own sake, this would again sharpen unprofitably the history/philosophy dichotomy. For the argument in favor of contextualism implies that the very nature of a philosophy as such is that to discuss it apart from its author and its age is to falsify and misunderstand it. Two things are at stake here. One is a theory of what constitutes intellectual history. The other is a theory of essential meaning. And they are closely related.

If, with Whitehead, we ask: What is the sort of history which ideas can have in the life of humanity? and if we answer this question as he did in *Adventures of Ideas* (and as Plato in the *Timaeus* did before him), then we should indeed say that there is an eternal pattern of *ideas* (such as "freedom," "progress," "justice," and the like) and that these timeless notions find their temporal exemplification in the thought of historical epochs (the ancient world, the Middle Ages, the Renaissance) and in the texts of specific philosophical thinkers within them. These abstract ideas "ingress" into history, and what we call "the history of ideas" is nothing but the description of their historical emergence. But if, on the other hand, we answer Whitehead's question not in terms of Plato's *Timaeus* but according to the theory of Aristotle's

Physics (and his own practice in such a work as *The Constitution of Athens*), then there are no "ideas" apart from human "propositions" or "statements" consciously entertained. The universe is here a world of individual primary *substances,* of moral *agents,* of thinking *persons,* all subject to strict causal agency. And the implication for the history of ideas is clear. There are no archetypal ideas which individual philosophers have intuited and sought to approximate and embody in their works. Instead, there are only a plurality of *agents* with a plurality of intensions and expressive modes, and our intellectual history must focus not upon the abstract ideas but upon the individual philosophers who have created the ideas in response to the challenge of their time and its range of historical problems. These two different versions of the nature of intellectual history might be called respectively a *Platonic* and an *Aristotelian* theory of the history of ideas, and our choice about which we are committed to will determine, for example, whether our subject matter is such topics as "the history of freedom," or "the idea of progress," or "the development of the concept of justice in the late Middle Ages," on the one hand, or "the philosophy of Aristotle and the Hellenic-Macedonian policy," or "Hegel and the rise of social theory," or "the role of the causal nexus in the philosophies of Aristotle and Hume" on the other.

But to these respective theories of the history of ideas belong also two diverse theories of essential meaning. One claims that intellectual understanding is a product of the activities of *isolating* and of *bracketing*; the other believes it is a consequence of *relating* and *embedding*. The one find its chief exemplification in the atomistic methods of Locke, Hume, and the British analytical tradition, the other in the insistent contextualism of Hegel, Bradley, and the procedures of idealistic logic.

The atomistic theory, as we have seen before, holds to a passionate belief in the autonomy of the text—to the notion that Aristotle's *Metaphysics* or Locke's *Essay* or Kant's *Critique of Pure Reason* are best understood as self-contained bodies of logically interrelated concepts and ideas, divorced from any extraneous facts concerning Aristotle's relationship to Athens, or Locke's links with the Earl of Shaftesbury and the Earl of Pembroke, or Kant's umbilical ties to Königsberg. "Understanding" these works requires an intense effort, to be sure, but the effort must be given to concentrated contemplation of the structure of ideas they contain, without elaborations of meaning or principles of interpretation drawn from the life of the author, the society in which he lived, or the specific audience for which he wrote. The only meaningful and philosophically responsible statements to be made are about the logical texture of the individual treatise. All that is relevant to the given work lies in the work itself.

The contextual position combats this atomism with an alternative theory of knowledge. It holds that knowledge itself is no absolute, but can be hierarchically graded as to its adequacy, scope, depth, and finality. A decade ago a German literary critic, Clemens Heselhaus, wrote an article "Auslegung und Erkenntnis" (in *Gestaltprobleme der Dichtung,* Bonn, 1957) in which he distinguished between two ambitions of literary scholarship: that of achieving "mere understanding" (*Verstehen*) and that of "full comprehension" (*Erkennen*). The terminology may be special to Heselhaus, but the idea it expresses is as old as Dilthey, or Hegel, or perhaps even Plato, and it represents in essence the answer which contextualism urges against semantic atomism. The doctrine of textual autonomy, it says, may indeed produce a "mere understanding" of philosophical works, but "full comprehension" is a goal never fully realized but only relatively approximated, and the degree of its successful accomplishment hinges squarely upon the scope and adequacy of its contextual analysis. The more we know of Kant's life, of his relationship to Königsberg, of his predecessors in the history of philosophy (like Hume and Leibniz and Rousseau) to whom he was intellectually indebted, and the more comprehensive our investigations of how the Critical Philosophy evolved, of the relationship of the First Critique to the Inaugural Dissertation which came before and the Second Critique and Third Critique which followed — indeed of the role it played within the total context of the Kantian intellectual effort — and, finally, the more persistent our attempts to fit this total intellectual effort into the ideals of the Enlightenment and the very special conditions of the German eighteenth century, the "fuller" our comprehension of the *Critique of Pure Reason.* Atomism sharpens the outline of the text to its utmost logical purity. Contextualism enlarges these outlines until they include all that the broadest canons of cultural relevance will permit.

I do not wish to force an exclusive choice between atomism and contextualism with respect to method in the history of ideas. For, as I shall try to show in the next section, actual practice in the writing of the history of philosophy paradoxically seems to require

both. But I do wish to maintain that wisdom in these matters
backs up practice, and our strategy should indeed be that of
"both...and" rather than "either...or." But if by some misfortune
of intellectual exclusiveness one were forced to choose between
logic and time, or between the isolated text and its cultural
context, I should unhesitatingly cast my lot with time and cultural
context. All three things exist: ideas, agents, and social contexts,
and the best history of philosophy is, I believe, constituted by the
careful consideration of the interrelationships between them. Indeed, it is primarily to illustrate this proposition that I have
written this book.

Texts, I think, do not exhaust their own meanings. There is
always a historical grounding and a web of personal and social
events that give them wider and deeper significance. And this is
precisely why we must ask such questions as: What sort of society
was the author writing for and trying to persuade? What were the
conventions of communication and the literary forms of discourse
current at the time? What was the author's class affiliation, his
place in the social hierarchy of his age? And perhaps above all:
What were his moral commitments, the structure of his ideals?
These questions are *not* philosophically irrelevant. They are the
very vehicles which lead us from the lean subsistence of "mere
understanding" *toward* the more generous nourishment of a
"fuller comprehension" of the great philosophers and their classic
texts.

Method in the History of Philosophy

To attribute the crisis in the history of philosophy to the opposition of logic and time or of philosophy and history is, I believe,
justified, but it does make the issue unnecessarily abstract. What
we need here is not the theory of those who are little practiced in
writing the history of philosophy, but the guiding principles of
those who have made substantial contributions to the field. For
this reason I should like to turn to two historians of philosophy—
one German, Wilhelm Windelband, and one French, Emile
Bréhier—whose histories have perhaps been the most influential
and widely read among philosophers themselves for the last fifty
years. Such examination will reveal, I think, the curious paradox
that, even among the most illuminating of the historians of philosophy in the great tradition since Hegel, the methodological prin-

ciples they announce in their preliminary remarks are almost
entirely ignored in the body of their work which follows. So
persuasive has been "the rationalistic fallacy" in the history of
ideas that it has infected practice even when it has been
recognized and opposed in theory.

It is certainly true that both Windelband and Bréhier would
have thought of themselves as "philosophers" and not merely as
"historians." Windelband indeed made impressive and original
contributions to value theory and the philosophy of the *Geistes-*
wissenschaften, and Bréhier taught philosophy for many years. In
writing their histories, each would have thought of himself as
"thinking philosophically"—of utilizing canons of critical judgment which had been learned through philosophical training
and not in seminars in historiography. For the separation of philosophy and history in current analytic theory is only a curious
consequence of our own cultural situation. There is certainly a
natural tendency of some philosophers—Descartes and Wittgenstein are perhaps paradigmatic—to begin from scratch, to
disregard the past, to espouse parochialism in time as a kind of
guarantee of philosophical originality. But it is no accident that
Descartes was a great mathematician and that Wittgenstein was
nourished on *Principia Mathematica*, for the more philosophy is
assimilated to the model of logic, mathematics, and the natural
sciences, and the less to the model of literature and the arts, the
wider will be the separation between philosophy and its history.
Neither Windelband nor Bréhier would have been guilty of this
mistake.

Windelband begins broadly enough: for him the history of
philosophy "is the process in which European humanity has
embodied in scientific conceptions, its views of the world, and its
judgments of life." We may neglect the Ptolemaic provincialism
of "European" humanity and the boundless optimism of "scientific conceptions" to turn, as Windelband himself does, to the
methodological factors by means of which these "views of the
world" and "judgments of life" are to be elucidated.

Investigation in the history of philosophy has accordingly the
following tasks to accomplish: (1) To establish with precision
what may be derived from the available sources as to the circumstances in life, the mental development, and the doctrines
of individual philosophers; (2) from these facts to reconstruct

the genetic process in such a way that *in the case of every philosopher we may understand how his doctrines depend in part upon those of his precedessors, in part upon the general ideas of his time, and in part upon his own nature and the course of his education*; (3) from the consideration of the whole to estimate what value for the total result of the history of philosophy belongs to the theories thus established and explained as regards their origin. [Italics added]

Of these three tasks, it is the second which is basic. For in writing the history of philosophy, judgments of value cannot hope to be so objective as to make the claim of indubitability, and using sources with precision to establish biographical fact and philosophic doctrine is only a specialized adaptation of historiographic techniques. But in (2) is comprehended the threefold factorial account which is crucial to constructing a successfully comprehensive history of philosophy.

Windelband's first factor is *logical*. It is the intellectual response which a given philosophy makes to the claims of its significant predecessors or contemporaries, where the very *problems taken as central* have somehow been *given* by the climate of controversy. Thus many of the details of Aristotle's political, ethical, and metaphysical system arise in arguments directed against Platonic statements and principles; much of Locke's *Treatise* is directed against current Cartesian presuppositions; and Leibniz's *New Essays on the Human Understanding* is in turn directed against Locke. This is not to deny that philosophical problems *can* arise in the antinomies of ordinary thinking or in the perplexities of immediate experience, but only to recognize that perhaps for most philosophers the sense of urgency is more often contributed by the mistakes of their predecessors or immediate contemporaries. There is no more candid expression of this fact than G. E. Moore's famous: "I do not think that the world or the sciences would ever have suggested to me any philosophical problems. What have suggested philosophical problems to me are things which other philosophers have said about the world or the sciences."

In speaking of Windelband's first factor as logical, there is no intention to deny that in any polemical atmosphere rhetorical considerations enter in, but neither does this mean that considerations of courtesy and intellectual generosity are abandoned. In this respect Leibniz's introductory statement about Locke in the *New Essays* is exemplary:

Since the *Essay on the Human Understanding*, by a famous Englishman, is one of the finest and most highly esteemed works of our time, I have resolved to make some remarks on it, because, having long meditated on the same subject and on the greater part of the matters therein contained, I thought this would be a good opportunity for publishing something under the title of *New Essays on the Human Understanding*, and for securing a favorable reception for my reflections by putting them in such good company. I further thought that I might profit by someone else's labor not only to diminish my own (since in fact it is less trouble to follow the thread of a good author than to work at everything afresh), but also to add something to what he has given us, which is always an easier task than making a start, for I think I have removed certain difficulties which he had left entirely to one side. . . . It is true that I am often of another opinion from him, but, far from denying the merit of famous writers, we bear witness to it by showing wherein and wherefore we differ from them, since we deem it necessary to prevent their authority from prevailing against reason in certain important points; besides the fact that, in convincing such excellent men, we make the truth more acceptable, and it is to be supposed that it is chiefly for truth's sake that they are laboring.

The logical factor does indeed attest the desire to "prevent authority from prevailing against reason," and to emphasize that "it is chiefly for truth's sake" that we are all laboring, and that the methods of argument and refutation with their essential timelessness are *the* methods of philosophy. But philosophical controversies nonetheless are always *dated* controversies with an anchorage in history and the context of social institutions, and this leads Windelband to his second factor: *that contributed by the history of civilization.* This is the factor which in the modern writing of the history of philosophy is the legacy of Hegel — the recognition that although on the surface it seems as if philosophers receive their problems from one another, yet more deeply considered it is clear that typical problems (and the materials for their solution) arise out of the general consciousness of the time and spring from the needs of society as expressed in that latent unease which attests to serious, perhaps even insoluble, problems of social conflict. "We have," says Windelband, in a characteristically Hegelian passage, "under certain circumstances a philosophical system appearing, that represents exactly the knowledge which a definite age has of itself; or we may have the oppositions in the general culture of the age finding their expression in the strife of philosophical systems."

Although this cultural factor was first elaborated by Hegel as an axiom of his historical dialectic, and in a later generation was adopted by Kuno Fischer, in the modern world it is most closely associated with Marxism, and particularly with certain philosophical Marxists of real speculative brilliance like Lukács and Sartre. For the ultimate failure of both Windelband and Bréhier to do justice to this factor — a failure shared by most contemporary historians of philosophy — has given the Marxists carte blanche to use it for their own partisan ideological purposes. And it may be rewarding to turn for a moment to a consideration of this use.

The Lukács of *Geschichte und Klassenbewusstsein* had insisted that the Hegelian notion of of "cultural self-consciousness" needed to be changed into the notion of "class-consciousness," and by this transformation he had established a new interpretive canon for the writing of the history of philosophy: the idea that the alienation implicit in the system of capitalist production would express itself in a series of philosophic oppositions which he called "the antinomies of bourgeois thought." With this as his chief conceptual tool, he has explored in some detail how, out of the reified structure of the modern consciousness, has grown the whole of Western philosophy since Descartes.

That Descartes is "the father of modern philosophy" is thus, according to Lukács, no accident. Nor is it fortuitous that his frank dualism and subjectivism have served as the classic statement for every subsequent philosophy to either embellish or overcome. For his central intuition of subjectivity, with its related yet opposed counterclaim that the geometric method is the proper means for establishing philosophic generality, provided a dichotomy which was to haunt both the eighteenth and nineteenth centuries. The conflicts of rationalism and empiricism (which seemed to find their resolution in Kant, only to give way to an even deeper split between the phenomenal and the noumenal world, between knowing and doing, and between the theoretical and the practical reason) predetermine the fate of all modern philosophizing, since they suggest an eternal dialectic of thought (the rationality of *form* against the sheer irrational immediacy of *content*, and the insurmountable *necessity* of nature against the moral consciousness and its *freedom*) which is rooted both in the nature of things and in the structure of the human mind. It is Lukács's peculiar Marxist originality that he finds them rooted in neither, but rather in the *sociologically given frame*, so that the philosophical separation of mind and nature is less an ontological truth than a historical necessity — the simple epistemic correlate of the acute internal problems confronting modern bourgeois society.

In this perspective, Kant becomes "the great philosopher of capitalism" not because he was in any serious sense its apologist, or indeed even conscious of it as a philosophically productive force, but because he made no attempt to disguise the fatal split between appearance and reality or between liberty and necessity, but asserted them (and the insoluble character of the problems they raise) vigorously, even brutally, and thereby perfectly symbolized the ultimate dilemma of the bourgeois consciousness.

The situation of bourgeois man in this, the final phase of advanced industrial capitalism, confronts him with what he takes to be the permanent and unalterable opposition of nature — of an essence strange to him, but to whose laws he is delivered without possibility of resistance. And since as a result of this reification he is compelled to experience his own powerlessness, to be the *object* and not the *subject* of historical change, the field of his proper activity is turned totally inward — toward *subjectivity*.

It is an exquisite irony that Sartre, whose existentialism is the very epitome of this bourgeois subjectivity and whose philosophy Lukács himself characterized in a hostile work (*Existentialisme ou Marxisme?*) as "ontological solipsism," should yet be the most renowned appropriator of Lukács's Marxist method. For he too, particularly in his "Marxisme et existentialisme: Questions de méthode" (*Les temps modernes,* 1957), denies the logical independence of philosophic thought and fully accepts instead the characteristic Marxist claim that philosophy is only an expression of the particular way in which a dominant class becomes conscious of itself as it faces the historical tasks set for it by its sociological location. Much more crudely than Lukács, Sartre establishes philosophy's *ideological* function.

At the time of the *noblesse de robe* and of mercantile capitalism, a bourgeoisie of lawyers, merchants, and bankers gained a

certain self-awareness through Cartesianism: a century and a
half later, in the primitive stage of industrialization, a bourgeoisie of manufacturers, engineers and scientists dimly discovered itself in the image of universal man which Kantianism
offered to it.

It is clear that Sartre's treatment of the history of modern
philosophy is more orthodox (in the Marxist sense) than Lukács's,
and more grossly and unimaginatively conceived, for it emphasizes the *use* to which the ideology may be put rather than the
detailed way in which it *reflects* the given social reality. And this is
because he is basically less interested in the conception of "reification" than in that of "social dynamism": less interested, that is, in
the mechanisms of intellectual life than in the politics of revolution. His account of the nature of philosophy continues:

> *Born from the movement of society*, it is itself a movement and
> acts upon the future. This concrete totalization is at the same
> time the abstract project of pursuing the unification up to its
> final limits. In this sense philosophy is characterized as a meth-
> od of investigation and application. The confidence which it
> has in itself and in its future development merely reproduces
> the certitude of the class which supports it. Every philosophy
> is practical, even the one which at first appears to be most con-
> templative. Its method is a social and political weapon. [Italics
> added]

Where Sartre deals explicitly with the history of philosophy, it is
in the vein of Lukács, but indirectly — less because he has been
reading Lukács than because he has read his well-known French
followers. It is no accident that the two figures in the history of
philosophy who are the objects of his constant attention are
Descartes and Kant. Knowing readers will find that Sartre has
constantly borrowed (and without acknowledgment) from Henri
Lefebvre's *Descartes* of 1947 and from Lucien Goldmann's *La
communauté humaine et l'universe chez Kant* of 1948. Lefebvre
has learned much from Lukács. Goldmann has been his chief
disciple in France.

I have inserted this very brief account of typical Marxist treatments of the history of modern philosophy as a footnote illustrating the use to which Windelband's second factor has been put
precisely because it has never been independently developed in an
objective writing of the history of philosophy. Excessive rationalism (Philosophical Analysis) emphasizes the logical relationships

of philosophical doctrines apart from their social role. Excessive politicization of ideas (Marxism) distorts this social role by grossly exaggerating its materialistic roots and class anchorage. What seems to me to be needed is a treatment of *philosophy as social expression* which avoids the abstractness of the one and the over-zealous political partisanship of the other. To the concrete attempt at this mediation my next four chapters on Plato, Saint Thomas, Descartes, and G. E. Moore will be devoted.

Although the historical process presents its own necessities, and although the philosophical theories in which these necessities are mirrored may be formed into abstract conceptions according to logical rules, the *act* of philosophizing is accomplished only *in the thinking of individual personalities* who, as Windelband says, "although rooted ever so deeply with their thought in the logical connection and prevalent ideas of a historical period, always add a particular element by their own individuality and conduct of life."

This distinctly *individual* or *biographical* third factor in the development of the history of philosophy Windelband saw primarily in aesthetic terms. Socrates, Abelard, Descartes, Spinoza, Kant, and Hegel are men of unusual and independent personality whose systems (in the case of Socrates and Abelard "philosophic preoccupations" is perhaps the better term) bear the mark of their originators. And since there is no philosophic contribution entirely free of the influence of the personality of its founder, their individual creations, both in form and in content, as in expression and in style, bear a certain resemblance to works of art. Here the universality or generality or objectivity associated with the first two factors often disappears, and we are left with something like uniqueness or aesthetic charm. As Windelband puts it:

The elements of every philosopher's *Weltanschauung* grow out of the problems of reality which are ever the same, and out of the reason as it is directed to their solution, but besides this out of the views and ideals of his people and his time; the form and arrangement, however, the connection and valuation which they find in the system, are conditioned by his birth and education, his activity and his lot in life, his character and his experience. Here, accordingly, the universality which belongs to the other two factors is often wanting. In the case of these purely individual creations, aesthetic charm must take the place of the worth of abiding knowledge, and the impressiveness of many phenomena of the history of philosophy rests, in fact, only upon the magic of their "poetry of ideas" (*Begriffsdichtung*).

The historian of ideas, however, who takes Windelband's third factor seriously will be less impressed by the aesthetic criterion than by certain problems of causal influence or determination set for the content and development of ideas by the striking character of biographical considerations. It is a preoccupation easy to caricature. I agree that to know that the philosopher Abelard was enamored of Héloïse is not particularly relevant to his attempted solution of the problem of universals (although I can imagine him telling her in all seriousness that he loved her not only for her unique, individual self, but also for the way in which she expressed so perfectly the essence of all femininity). Yet modified Platonists perhaps make very good lovers, and eros is certainly not irrelevant to Platonism, although it is an old story that the logical validity of philosophical ideas is independent of the conditions of their origin (much as in the special theory of relativity, the velocity of light is independent of the motion of its source). Yet to know of Kant that his own life was strict and rule-laden, that the Königsbergers set their watches by his daily walk, and that he could not break a glass at the table without rushing out at once to bury the broken pieces deep in the garden is surely to illuminate both the *Foundation of the Metaphysics of Morals* and the *Critique of Practical Reason*. For it is no accident that one of the most anxious and compulsive personalities in the history of modern philosophy should be an advocate of conscience and the father of the categorical imperative.

Such considerations set with amazing regularity problems of the interpretation of ideas in the philosophy of the nineteenth century. That crucial turning point in Mill's ethics away from Bentham and toward Aristotle, and in his social theory away from Ricardo and James Mill and toward the Utopian Socialists and Auguste Comte, is triggered by the neurotic breakdown he suffered in his early manhood. The exact point in Nietzsche's later writings where a caveat must be entered against the paranoid delusions of organic illness is of some importance for our just estimate of *Der Antichrist, Ecce Homo*, and the scattered fragments of *Der Wille zur Macht*. And in the case of Auguste Comte, if not that of Abelard, the element of love does much to explain the extraordinary duality of his mature system.

The riddle of the early and the later Comte is no less intriguing than that of the early and later Wittgenstein, but for reasons which are more human and less mysterious. His great *Cours du philosophie positive* (1840-42) with its emphasis upon the scientific apparatus of "intelligence" and "general law" and its famous "*savoir pour prevoir*," is followed ten years later by the equally remarkable (if now neglected) *Système de politique positive* (1851-54) with its new emphasis upon the affective principle of "feeling" (*sentiment*) and its "religion of humanity." But whereas the difference between the *Tractatus* and the *Philosophical Investigations* is due to the fact that Wittgenstein had been reading Gödel and was thereby forced into pondering the foundations of mathematics anew, the difference between Comte's earlier and his later masterpiece is that he had become enamoured of Clothilde de Vaux. In a letter of 1845 he writes to her: "I rejoice in the happy coincidence of the sweet re-animation of my moral nature due to you with the dawning elaboration of my second great book." But is is no coincidence — it is a real causal connection. Windelband, who so clearly enunciated the principle of biographical interpretation, in this case, as usual, does not think of applying it. He speaks of Comte as of one "whose thought passed through an extremely peculiar course of development." To bring his own principle to bear on the riddle never seems to have crossed his mind.

I have stressed Windelband's third factor because, like his second, it is a generally neglected principle of interpretation in the history of ideas. Yet there *is* a tradition which attends to it. Nietzsche, always quick in his precocious psychologizing to see nonrational factors behind the cool facade of reason, was perhaps the first (long before Stevenson) to insist that ethics itself is generally the expression of a deep emotional partisanship. In his *Jenseits von Gut und Böse* appears a relevant aphorism: *Die Moralen sind auch nur eine Zeichensprache der Affekte* ("Systems of morals are also only a sign-language of the emotions"). Perhaps this is no less true of "logical" commitments and metaphysical constructions!

Explanation of facts in the history of philosophy is, as Windelband contended, either *logical, sociological* (in his terms "based on the history of civilization"), or *psychological*, but he is singularly unenlightening about the interrelations between them and, indeed, upon what shall govern their application in any particular case. Thus, although Beck provides us with a logical

interpretation of Descartes, Lukács with a sociological interpretation of Kant, and Littré with a psychological interpretation of
Comte, it is not clear from Windelband's description of factors
alone how we ought to judge the adequacy of these treatments.

Explanation of facts in the history of philosophy is either logical, or based upon the history of civilization, or psychological,
corresponding to the three factors which we have set forth
above as determining the movement of thought. Which of these
three modes of explanation is to be applied to individual cases
depends solely upon the state of the facts with regard to the
transmission of material. It is then incorrect to make either one
the sole principle of treatment.

That it is incorrect to make any single one the sole principle of
treatment is useful to know, to be sure, but to say that which of the
three modes of explanation is to be appealed to in a given case
"depends solely upon the state of the facts with regard to the
transmission of material" is surely an ambiguous suggestion. It is
not clear whether "the state of the facts" mentioned refers to an
incompleteness in the historical record, or to some intrinsic
appropriateness in the use of any single one to the nature of the
doctrines or doctrinal changes to be explained. And since Windelband himself, after having in his theory outlined three factors, in
his *History of Philosophy* almost entirely neglected the second and
third while confining himself to the first, it is impossible to infer
the intricate implications of his theory from an examination of his
practice.

A generation separates the work of Windelband from that of
Bréhier. And as Windelband expressed for the decade before the
turn of the century the entire thrust of historical interest originating in the German eighteenth century and culminating in Hegel,
so Bréhier has felt the influence of the later, but comparable,
thrust of the French impulse toward clarity, system, and classification as expressed in the histories of Victor Cousin and Renouvier.
One consequence of Bréhier's greater modernity is that he finds it
necessary to counteract the exclusiveness of the logical factor in
the interpretation of the history of philosophy illustrated in
Windelband's practice. He says:

If the history of philosophy is to be accurate, it cannot be an
abstract history of ideas and systems, separated from the intentions of their authors and from the moral and social atmosphere in which they were born. It is impossible to deny that,

in different periods, philosophy has occupied very different places in what we call the intellectual climate of the time.

The matter of an author's "intentions" mentioned here is of some importance, for Bréhier is not speaking with that narrow usage which requires the reader to infer meaning with respect to a mere word or a passage isolated within a text, but rather has in mind some estimate of the *ultimate purpose or meaning* of the philosopher's work as a whole. The question is: What was Plato, or Aquinas, or Descartes, or G. E. Moore ultimately trying to do? And it is a relevant question, because some philosophers have been scholars like Cassirer, some have been conscious social reformers like Marx, some have been moralists or preachers like Spinoza or Bonaventura. And the question whether a philosopher is also a professional of speculative thought like Kant or G. E. Moore, or one who aims at immediate practical influence like Fichte or Sartre, or one who bewilderingly combines the two like John Stuart Mill or Bertrand Russell is of more than passing interpretive importance.

It is also characteristic that Bréhier should combine the subjective factor of intention with the objective factor of moral and social atmosphere, for they may well be related according to the now classic historical model of challenge and response. There is certainly a sense in which every cultural period sets its own philosophical requirements for its major thinkers, and it is precisely to this consideration that I will return in the next four chapters of this book to indicate: how Plato is the conservative response to the challenge of an aristocratic culture in extremis in the cumulative unrest of fourth-century Athens; how Aquinas devoted himself to rationalizing medieval order and to the institutional task of strengthening the Roman church against both the pagan and internal challenges of the thirteenth century; how in the seventeenth century Descartes, gentleman and solitary meditator, became the fashionable mirror of a courtly age; and how, finally, the philosophy of G. E. Moore reflects the increasing narrowness and isolation required by philosophic professionalism in the modern world. The social anchorage of philosophy in any epoch gives the clue to the intentions of its major practitioners. This is why the attempts so often made to treat Locke and Hume, Descartes and Kant in an abstract "introduction to epistemology" as "mistaken" or partially misguided answerers of the epistemic questions exercising us today, without making specific reference to the questions they set themselves and thought they were answering, can so often seem to be examples of Whitehead's "fallacy of misplaced concreteness" which obscure rather than reveal the meaning of the sources.

Bréhier in his theory also tried manfully to escape the temptation of the historian of philosophy toward abstraction. A philosophy, he asserts, is not merely the sum of the doctrines it maintains. "It is much more important to see the spirit inspiring them and the intellectual realm in which they are situated." And he concludes by stating as an axiom of method that the historian of ideas must constantly strive to remain in contact with the facts of political and social history and with the development of the cultural disciplines like art and literature, so as not to isolate philosophy as a special and a separate technique without regard to its political implications and its cultural relevance.

In this respect Bréhier's practice is certainly more satisfactory than Windelband's, but even in his case, his axioms of method are honored rather in the breach than in the observance. Instead, in his introduction he turns to the problem which has exercised historians of philosophy since Hegel and which is of particular concern to an Alexandrian age — the plotting of tendency and the rationalizing of plurality.

Does philosophizing have an immanent law of development, or is the succession of systems radically contingent — dependent simply upon the accidents of social history and individual temperament? Is the history of philosophy susceptible to interpretation by permanent categories which permit a systematic classification of doctrines? — for example, monism, dualism, pluralism in metaphysics; skepticism, subjectivism, realism in epistemology; hedonism, deontology, self-realization in ethics? Or is the eternal recurrence this suggests inadequate as a model for the real internal development which an organicist might discern? Hegel's famous statement in the introduction to the *Encyclopedia*, "The history of philosophy makes clear that there is only a single philosophy in different stages of development; the particular principles on which a system is built are only divisions of a single whole," is a classic statement of the organicist thesis. But Renouvier, in his less well known "Esquisse d'une classification systématique des doctrines philosophiques," denies this Hegelian assertion. He too is a dialectician — but of another sort. For him the human mind is antinomic by nature, and it expresses itself in the central controversy between the doctrine of freedom and that of determinism. Since all other philosophic issues reduce to this, the model for the history of philosophy is indeed that of eternal recurrence, and it hardens into a timeless dialogue between two contradictory and forever reviving theses.

The alternative readings of the total course of the history of philosophy in the West by Hegel and Renouvier are paradigms of two classic forms of an application of the principle of internal unity to philosophy's history. The principle enunciated by Hegel (in which he would be joined by Comte, **Lukács**, and Sartre) envisages a process of gradual development, with each divergent type forming an essential moment in the process. The principle enunciated by Renouvier (in which he would be joined by Cousin, Dilthey, Jaspers, Scheler, and McKeon) involves a classification which reduces all philosophical possibilities to a limited number of forms inherent in mind and its activity. The critical differ-ence between the two is the same as that between Windelband's first factor and his second and third; namely, in the *relevance of time*. The distinctions which Renouvier, Dilthey, and McKeon wish to celebrate lie outside of time, as the principles of logic themselves lie outside of time; in the systems of Hegel, Comte, and Lukács, real time provides the matrix of the distinctions, and historicity is of their essence.

In the end Bréhier, like Windelband before him, is skeptical about the formulation of anything like a law of the development of philosophic thought, and I have not appealed to them with this possibility in mind. For ultimately the history of philosophy, true to its Aristotelian origins (and like the dominant trait of our liter-ary criticism which emphasizes the "original" and the "unique") must concentrate upon *individuals* — must see the past not as a congeries of "sects" or "systems" or "collective mentalities," but as *persons* in all the richness of their intelligence and moral char-acters engaging in philosophic reflection and producing philo-sophic works. Plato, Aquinas, Descartes, and G. E. Moore are not therefore simply expressions of their culture or of the historic moments in which they lived, but real philosophic creators whose philosophies, like the works of our greatest writers and dramatists, are also original and unique. Windelband was of the same opinion. "In truth," he said, "the picture of the historical move-ment of philosophy . . . depends not solely upon the thinking of 'humanity' or even of the '*Weltgeist*,' but just as truly upon the reflections, the needs of mind and heart, the presaging thought and sudden flashes of insight of *philosophizing individuals*" (italics added).

And this is why the logical consideration of doctrine, Windelband's first factor, is not historically enough, and why his third factor is so important; why, in short, however critical we must be of the biographical source material, we must yet be eternally in its debt. No historian of ideas who considers Plato can afford to neglect Diogenes Laërtius and the *Epistles*, however unreliable the first and however problematic the second. No historian of philosophy who deals with Saint Thomas can afford to neglect the *Life* by William of Tocco, despite the exaggeration of saintliness understandable in a work prepared to further his canonization. No historian of ideas who seeks the meaning of Descartes can afford to neglect the monumental *Life of Descartes* by Adrien Baillet, although it too was written a generation after his death and softens somewhat the harsh outlines of his skepticism and materialism in order to reconcile him (unsuccessfully) with the suspicious reservations of the Catholic church.

Biographical sources immeasurably aid the historian's task, for philosophic doctrines, as Windelband saw, in the end are the product of "the needs of mind and heart." No methodology for writing the history of philosophy can responsibly neglect any resources which bring us closer to a valid perception of these needs.

Wholeness: Philosophy as Culture

In turning to the theories of Windelband and Bréhier for method in the history of philosophy, I have been aware that although they too have in practice concentrated very largely on the logical presentation and comparison of philosophic doctrines, their conceptual apparatus is fully adequate to the needs of a holistically conceived history of philosophy. Windelband's three factors of logical content, sociological grounding, and personal situation could hardly be improved, and Bréhier's contribution of the relation of author's intention to moral and social atmosphere and insistence upon the uniqueness and originality of individual philosophic creation only broaden and relate Windelband's second and third factors. And the consequence is that the sharp dichotomy of logic versus temporality and of philosophy versus history which so concerned us in the first two sections of this chapter now finds its resolution in a totality sufficiently comprehensive to include them both.

The logic of philosophic doctrines is no longer artifically separated from the persons and social contexts which mark their temporal emergence and characterize their factual reality, but becomes an ingredient in that single whole which includes selves in time, their cultural motivations, and their intellectual products. And thus the subject we call "the history of philosophy," less attuned to sharp logical separations than to the making of connections, sees itself finally as philosophy *and* history at once, since it is not so clear that history must be only one kind of thing and philosophy another, and since no ironclad categories of the mind or understanding rule out a sympathy for that kind of historiography which is most philosophical, on the one hand, or of that kind of philosophizing which is most historical on the other.

In the chapters on Plato, Aquinas, Descartes, and G. E. Moore which follow, I shall attempt in part to embody the theory which Windelband presents but does not himself adequately follow. And yet, in titling this book *Philosophy as Social Expression* I have meant to place particular emphasis upon Windelband's second factor, that contributed by the history of civilization in its impact upon the creation and statement of philosophic doctrines. For I think that the Marxist appropriation of this factor (as exemplified in the work of Lukács and Sartre), as well as the attention paid it in the more suggestive works of *Wissensoziologie* of Max Weber, Max Scheler, and their contemporary followers, tend to *oversociologize* the possibilities inherent in this mode of interpretation. Of course, the types of questions I presented at the end of the second section (What sort of society was the given author writing for and trying to persuade? What were the conventions of communication, the literary forms of discourse current at the time? What was the author's class affiliation, his place in the social hierarchy of his age?) are those which the historian of philosophy ought certainly to pose, however much he shares them with the proponents of the sociology of knowledge and with the Marxist critics of intellectual history. But in the latter's hands there lies the ever present danger of the peculiar abuse of exclusively materialistic grounding of all individual and social values. To convert all cultural consciousness into class consciousness (as Lukács does) and therefore to find all oppositions between form and content,

subjectivity and objectivity, necessity and freedom to be simply
"the antinomies of bourgeois thought," or to see Descartes merely
as the "self-awareness of mercantile capitalism" or Kant simply as
"the producer of an image of man with which the bourgeoisie of
early industrialization can identify" (as does Sartre), is, I think, to
unnecessarily coarsen, oversimplify, and trivialize the structure of
general ideas and the creative systems of the great philosophers.

For there is another important alternative. To interpret philosophy as a mode of social expression (surely a rather neglected
factor in the customary history of philosophy), one does not need
to concentrate exclusively upon the merely economic aspects of
society. The materialistic interpretation can easily be supple-
mented by a principle of social idealism. For whole social epochs
have dominating *values* as well as characteristic stages of production, and it is by no means true that it is the economic
necessities which must validate the ideal ends. Fact and value here
constitute a sort of productive duality, a kind of "two sides of the
same coin" relationship, so that for every configuration of social
structure there is an analogue of valuational achievement and
concern. The Greek city-state is governed through its aristocratic
families at just that moment when the four cardinal virtues prevail
as ideal ends. The feudal hierarchy of the Middle Ages is
paralleled by the hierarchy of the Roman church, and in the
ascendency of purity, spirituality, and self-denial the virtues of the
pagans, as Augustine said, have become as "gilded vices." The city
life of seventeenth-century Holland is commercial, orderly,
middle-class, and thrifty to its very core, and the modesty of
Spinoza, Grotius's love of freedom, and the Dutch cleanliness in
the art of Jan Vermeer are ideal expressions of that same strong
bourgeois feeling for reality which they draw upon for their
support.

Moral ideals are expressed less in philosopher's quarrels about
"ethical language" or their debates over "the objectivity of moral
judgments" than in those concrete images of a preferred way of
life or of an accredited style of behavior presented for emulation
which are precipitated out of the indeterminate matrix of sociological situation and historical need. We learn more about the
reality of moral aspiration in Seneca's portrayal of "the Stoic
sage," in the "saintliness" of the life of Saint Francis, in Castiglione's presentation of "the courtier" (or Polonius's advice to his
son Laertes, which is its Elizabethan translation), or in Oliver

Goldsmith's or Lord Chesterfield's eighteenth-century picture of "the cosmopolitan man of the world" than in all the currently esteemed ethical treatises of Ross or Pritchard, of Toulmin, Hart, or Hare!

Seen in this light, the entire cultural history of the West since the Greeks can be visualized as the continuity of a succession of moral ideals or norms of social aspiration belonging at once to moral philosophy and to social history, which I would designate as "The Seven Ethical Ages of Western Man." And the nodes of this moral succession could be identified respectively as: (1) the age of the politically responsible aristocrat (Hellenic); (2) the age of the Stoic sage (Hellenistic); (3) the age of the saint (medieval); (4) the age of the gentleman (Renaissance); (5) the age of the cosmopolitan man of the world (eighteenth century); (6) the age of the merchant prince (19th century); and (7) the age of the professional (contemporary). And it would, I think, follow that the characteristics of philosophizing — its questions and its answers, its basic concepts and its preoccupations, its functions and its form — would vary not merely, as the Marxists would maintain, according to the material interests of its ruling class, but in some measure also according to the ideal nature and moral quality of the age of which it was a chosen form of social expression. In the four chapters which follow I shall attempt to explore this thesis, not throughout the entire spectrum of historical succession, but in four important ages, using in each case the single example of an important and, I believe, characteristic philosophic representative. Thus my subject becomes the nature of philosophy in (1) The Age of the Aristocrat: Plato; (2) The Age of the Saint: Aquinas; (3) The Age of the Gentleman: Descartes; and (4) The Age of the Professional: G. E. Moore.

To construe the history of philosophy in this way is in no sense to depart completely from a utilization of the three factors enunciated by Windelband and Bréhier. The assemblage of philosophic doctrines, reference to the cultural requirement of the age, and attention to the peculiar genius and personal circumstance of the individual philosopher are still relevant elements of interpretation, but the second factor becomes a favored lever of understanding for the other two. Philosophic reflection and social milieu are now related through the instrument of societal evaluation, the systematic study of "forms of life" becomes philosophically relevant, and the concept of the *cognitive life-style* can be removed from the mists of Spenglerian mysticism to become a norm of criticism in the examination of our major philosophic thinkers.

To be sure, to regard the history of philosophy from this perspective requires something a little different from the usual archival or linguistic skills. For to "rethink" selected phases in the history of philosophy in the light of the society in which they originated, with attention to its dominant social ideal, is indeed to depend to some degree upon sympathetic reconstruction, aesthetic intuition, and a certain "sensing the atmosphere" and "getting the feel." In one of his late essays ("Of the Art of Discussion"), Montaigne speaks of the nature of his voluminous and serious reading in this fashion:

My humor is to consider the form as much as the substance, the advocate as much as the cause. And everyday I amuse myself reading authors without any care for their learning, looking for their style, not their subject.

It might seem like a merely aesthetic preoccupation; but I think it is considerably more than that. In rereading Plato, Aquinas, Descartes, and G. E. Moore for my present purposes, it would be false to say that I had been completely careless of their arguments, looking only for their "style" and not at all noting the internal logic of their philosophical doctrines, and yet I do think that I have been newly forced to consider in their philosophic expressiveness "the form as much as the substance, the advocate as much as the cause." This is turn has required me to ask some new questions. What does it mean to philosophize like an aristocrat? Like a saint? Like a gentleman? Like a professional? And the answers have suggested aspects of Plato, of Saint Thomas, of Descartes, and of Moore which had been unavailable to me before.

Another consequence of this perspective is its entailment of a unified and holistic rather than a fragmented or piecemeal point of view, for, quite in line with Windelband's third factor and the Aristotelian emphasis upon the personal subject of philosophizing, the philosopher himself here becomes the center of the activity, since he is the bearer or exemplification of the social requirement. "Philosophy," Whitehead somewhere says, "is the attempt to clarify the fundamental beliefs which finally determine the emphasis of attention that lies at the base of character." Three things are related here in the philosophic activity: fundamental personal beliefs, the act of individual attention, and a moral self. When the character of the moral self is concerned, the chief thrust is always toward avoiding incoherence. Thus, although internal division and inconsistency are versions of the human possibility, the works of a great thinker are *generally* the expression of a single *Weltanschauung,* or vision of the world, and to infer this unity and to place within it each personal trait, each classic work, even each individual idiosyncrasy, is a serious imperative for the historian of philosophy. To find the fundamental themes which unify the philosophy and render it coherent is perhaps his basic task.

Plato wrote both the *Phaedrus* and the *Parmenides,* the *Symposium* and the *Sophist,* and one can learn to recognize that in him logic and the love of beauty combine in a single aristocratic vision of the world. Saint Thomas produced the *Summa theologica,* a commentary on Aristotle's *Physics,* devout sermons for the Feast of Saint Martin and All Saints' Day, and a divine service for Corpus Christi, and one can see in him how logical analysis and mystic devotion combine in a single unswerving commitment to the Christian message and to the Holy Roman church which he took to be its eternal bearer. Descartes wrote the *Discourse on Method* and the *Principles of Philosophy,* but also treatises on music and on fencing and elevated letters on the conduct of life to important royal personnages of his time, and it is possible to recognize in all this a gentlemanly decorum of the mind — that mathematical rationality which elevates "form" and "order" into a veritable sense of life. G. E. Moore wrote widely on the status of "sense-data" and "judgments of perception" and "the principles of ethics," and he operated a vigorous method of logical analysis; but he also loved to sing Brahms and Schubert *Lieder* and he thought that personal affections and aesthetic enjoyments include all the greatest goods we can imagine. And to see in this passion of the amateur the complete underpinning and support of the philosophic professional also requires a necessary integrative effort.

An emphasis upon the philosophizing individual, rather than on the hermetically sealed and fully abstracted text, also entails a new concern with the philosophic *process,* with the ever-relevant problems about the matrix of philosophic communication. Questions like: For what audience was the author writing, and whom was he trying to persuade? What were the conventions of discourse, the literary and rhetorical forms of dialectical exchange of the age in which he lived? become vehicles for a more adequate appreciation of philosophy's inevitable grounding in its social context. One reads a Platonic dialogue like the *Euthydemus* and "sees" Plato in a "classroom" of the Academy discussing with the aristocratic youth of the classical world and attempting to recreate the dialectical community of Socratic memory. One reads an article from the *Disputed Questions on Truth* and imagines the learned monk Thomas Aquinas holding public disputation in the largest courtyard of the University of Paris, surrounded by masters and bachelors of arts and of theology intent upon the outcome. One reads a treatise of Descartes and visualizes how it was lovingly composed during the late afternoon in the sunny study of some Dutch house in the tranquil countryside near Utrecht or the Hague, and then anxiously sent to a few well-born and intellectual friends for concentrated perusal and comment. Or, finally, one reads Moore's "The Status of Sense-Data," and imagines its delivery by the professor to his peers—the careful attention with which it was received and the uncompromising vigor (and modesty) with which it was defended at that meeting of the Aristotelian Society in London almost on the eve of the outbreak of the First World War, at the very moment when Lord Grey was remarking that the lights were going out all over the world. Here becomes possible a new *sense of the concrete* of which current philosophizing seems to me very much in need.

Two important limitations of *Philosophy as Social Expression* should be candidly noted. First, there is a discrepancy between my notion of the *seven* ages of Western man and the mere *four* which will be treated in what follows. I have not dealt with every period in the history of philosophy. The Hellenistic age, the Enlightenment, and the nineteenth century are not to be found here. This I regret, for I should have enjoyed completing the panorama with further studies of Seneca or Epictetus, of Hume or Shaftesbury or Montesquieu, of Hegel or Marx or John Stuart Mill. But if the gap between Plato and Aquinas seems wide, and that between Descartes and G. E. Moore even wider, I have provided for the latter a brief consideration of the intermediate figure of Kant, and it can at least be said that the four ages I have chosen do in large part express the social conditions of ancient, medieval, modern and contemporary philosophy. What is contained here, at least in capsule form, is the underlying spirit of the history of Western philosophy in the four periods into which we customarily divide it.

The second difficulty has to do with the choices of Plato, Saint Thomas, Descartes, and G. E. Moore to exemplify the periods chosen. For although I have used the image of the aristocrat and the saint, the gentleman and the professional to characterize a series of philosophic modes of perception, no one should be misled into thinking that I have merely dealt with four miscellaneous figures in the development of philosophic thought. Probably other philosophers of each period might have been equally representative, and would have done just as well. Aristotle could perhaps have been substituted for Plato (although his being a scientist and a foreigner in Athens makes less immediate his political and social involvement); and Bonaventura or Scotus could be substituted for Saint Thomas, Bacon, Spinoza, or Hobbes for Descartes, and Broad, C. I. Lewis, or Carnap for G. E. Moore. But whomever I should have chosen, it would not have been merely for the abstraction of "the ideal type," but always with specific reference to the details of his philosophic individuality and personal uniqueness. For my chief point is to emphasize how social necessity and personal identity interact in producing notable philosophic achievement.

I am sure that this book could have been better—more complete in its treatment; possibly more specific and detailed in its consideration of the figures chosen, surely more imaginative in its conception of their achievement and their role. But perhaps, nonetheless, it can serve as a token of the more comprehensive and better work which ought to come—as a pilot study in its emphasis upon social factors and upon philosophy as an exemplification of human culture—perhaps, I hope, as the signal of a new direction in the writing of the history of philosophy.

Plato. Detail of the painting *The School of Athens* by Raphael in the Stanza della Segnatura, the Vatican.

2

ANCIENT PHILOSOPHY
The Age of the Aristocrat
Plato

Introduction

The most profound danger in considering the philosophy of Plato
is anachronism. For us who live this side of the French Revolution,
the true meaning of aristocracy has been decisively lost. For
classical bourgeois thought, whether in the case of Locke or
Hume, Bentham or John Stuart Mill, the basic values are "the
individual" and "liberty." Empiricism with its sensationalist base
has served as an admirable foundation for a doctrine of legal
equality, and Bentham's proposed reform of the law was therefore
no accident. Where man's sensory equipment is relatively equal,
and sensitivity to pain and pleasure "normal," why should the laws
favor upper class privilege? But even rationalism since the seventeenth century has served to underwrite democratic values. In
Descartes it signified a certain freedom from authority and external institutional constraint, and in Leibniz it signified an ultimate
reliance upon the metaphysical individualism of the monad. Thus
even the rapport between philosophy and mathematics suggested
by the rebirth of Platonism in the Renaissance ultimately served
social aims quite foreign to those espoused by Plato himself.

But both rationalism and empiricism signify the rupture of
intimate relations with the human community. Each individual
possesses the criteria of decision within himself. Each social atom
decides autonomously, independently, and alone. Thus both the
natural universe and the human community have become *external realities* from which man is basically estranged. They are the
object of his study but not of his existential concern. It is easier to
consider them scientifically than to relate to them. In such a
climate of belief the liberty and autonomy of the individual operates in opposition to the human community, the universe, and *the
whole*. Estrangement is a common consequence. Meaninglessness

English translations for passages from the works of Plato have been taken primarily
from the editions of Plato in the Loeb Classical Library (Harvard University Press)
or from the admirable edition *Plato: The Collected Dialogues,* edited by Edith
Hamilton and Huntington Cairns (Pantheon Books). Very occasionally, I have
slightly modified a translation for the sake of simplicity or clarity. Other works
used are listed in the Bibliography.

and isolation are common psychic symptoms. Nostalgia for real
community infects all the privileges of freedom. And in such a
universe Platonism, with its aristocratic presupposition and its
architecture of the organic community, returns once more to
claim attention as ideal possibility. But this revival is only the
child of historicism and regret. Its *conditions* can never return. Its
philosophy is time-bound and institution-attached. Its perpetual
lure is that of an aristocratic nostalgia. But it is eminently worthy
of our attention, for it is a prime example of how a philosophy
incorporates the defining relations of the social forms it serves.

The Platonic Sources

When Paul Shorey wrote *What Plato Said* in 1933 he caricatured
the possibilities which might lie open to a modern imaginative
biographer of Plato. Such a writer could (1) enliven his sketch by
all the legends and anecdotes that have gathered about Plato's
name since his death. He could (2) expand the life of Plato by
narrating it in connection with the history of his time, describing
in detail all that Plato must have witnessed, experienced, and felt.
Or (3):

On the supposition that the chronology of Plato's writings is
determined and that the mainly spurious letters are genuine,
he could attempt to trace the necessary sequence and evolution
of Plato's thought from his Socratic discipleship and the youthful exuberance of his satires on Periclean society to the logical
aridity of the so-called dialectical dialogues and the disillusionment of the *Laws*; and he could exercise the sympathetic historical imagination by divining the occasion and the motive of
each one of Plato's principal works, and the mood or emotional
crisis which it expresses.

These possibilities do in fact represent the options chosen respectively by Diogenes Laërtius in his *Life of Plato*, G. C. Field in
Plato and His Contemporaries, and Ulrich von Wilamowitz-
Moellendorff in his great two-volume *Platon*. It was the latter
work for which Shorey reserved some of his choicest irony. "It is,"
he said,

if we regard it as a historical novel, deserving of all praise. But
a historical novel it essentially remains. How could Professor
Wilamowitz or anybody else possibly know that the *Phaedrus*
represents a happy picnic day to celebrate the completion of the
Republic, that Plato never read the extant work of Thucydides

but had read the lost writings of Thrasymachus, that Plato
could never have written the *Laws* if he had ever visited Sparta,
that the *Theaetetus* originally contained no dramatic Introduction, that Plato lectured without manuscript, that Eudoxus was
rector of the Academy in Plato's absence, that Plato began to
write a dialogue entitled *Thrasymachus* but threw it aside and
wrote the *Gorgias* instead and later re-wrote the unfinished
Thrasymachus as the first book of the *Republic*, that Plato
brought home from his travels the plan to found a school, that
the *Laches, Charmides, Euthyphro,* and an omitted dialogue
on justice were written solely to exhibit Socrates as a type of the
cardinal virtues and have no philosophical significance. Divinatory biographers affirm or suggest scores of propositions more
fanciful than these, for which there is no evidence, except the
feeling of their authors that they are plausible.

And in refutation Shorey proceeded to cite as an axiom of method
the judicious observation of Lewis Campbell: "The less known
cannot throw light on the more known: and Plato's thoughts are
better known to us than the particular incidents of Athenian life
which gave occasion to them."

The axiom is admirable. Unfortunately, when Shorey himself
comes to deal with Plato's life and character he slips no less easily
into "divinatory" biography. For a few pages later he tells us of the
youthful Plato:

He witnessed the dismay of Athens and heard the comments of
his relatives when in 413 the news arrived of the defeat and
destruction of the magnificent Armada, whose spectacular embarkation at the Peiraeus he may have seen two years before.
He shared the discomforts and distress caused by the virtual
state of seige to which the Spartan occupation subjected the city
in the next few years. . . . He may have fought in an undeter-
mined battle of Megara, in which, in the *Republic*, he says
that his brothers, Glaucon and Adeimantus, distinguished
themselves. He may have served in the fleet at the battle of
Arginusae, where the Athenian victory was marred by the failure to recover the bodies of the dead in the storm that followed. He probably was a witness of the scene in the Assembly
when Socrates as president, as he ironically puts it in the *Gorgias*, "did not know how to put the vote" the unjust motion to
condemn the negligent generals by one sweeping decree without allowing them the separate trials that the law prescribed.
He shared the alternations of hope and fear in the next few
years.

It is difficult to see that Shorey's conjecture about Plato's wit-
nessing the embarkation of the ill-fated Sicilian expedition is any
better founded than Wilamowitz's that Plato had not read Thucydides, his assurance that Plato was in the Assembly on the day of
Socrates' presidency more dependable than Wilamowitz's that
Plato lectured without manuscript, his conviction about Plato's
inner states "of hope and fear" more firmly evidenced than Wilamowitz's that the *Phaedrus* represents a happy day in the country
to celebrate the completion of the *Republic.* Nor do the qualifications of "may" and "probably" do more than hedge against the
worst accusations of dogmatism. For Shorey himself goes on to tell
us that Plato "doubtless" *did* read Thucydides, that we must
"obviously" consider the Platonic Socrates as the embodiment of
Plato's ideal of the philosopher and the mouthpiece of Plato's
ideas, and, steeped as he was in the best of Victorian culture (to
which on almost every page his great edition of the *Republic*
provides anachronistic evidence), he ends with the charming nineteenth-century insight that "the mature Plato was obviously, apart
from his philosophy and mathematics, a scholar in Emerson's and
Pater's sense of the word!"

There is perhaps little but personal inclination to cause us to
make a choice when Wilamowitz transforms Plato into a meticulous Prussian schoolmaster and Shorey makes him into an erudite
Victorian gentleman, but in any case what I want to do is to
defend the principle of imaginative method against the rigorous
canons of evidence which Shorey asserts, but which he himself
finds it impossible to follow. For in matters of Platonic scholarship
there are no unimpeachable witnesses, no unshakable platforms of
fact, no bulwarks of evidence so stout as to withstand all assaults of
skepticism and denial. Of Plato we possess all the writings attributed to him in antiquity, including some which even the ancients
rejected as spurious, and, as for biographical detail, we "know"
more about him perhaps than about any other philosopher of
antiquity. Yet twenty-four hundred years after his death each
scholar constructs a different Plato, and bitter controversy rages
over the believability of such evidence as survives.

Our three chief sources are singularly unreliable and problematic. Aristotle, who, if we believe the tradition, entered the Platonic Academy in 367 and remained there as Plato's pupil until
Plato's death twenty years later, is in his own works curiously
laconic about the personality and scholarly deportment of his

great teacher. Perhaps this is simply the good manners of a proper scholarly impersonality, but it is curious that in whatever Aristotle says of Plato's doctrines in the *Rhetoric,* the *Metaphysics,* and the *Politics,* there is no echo of Plato's authentic voice, no clue to his personality, no indication of his humor, his method of instruction, or his behavior within the Academy. As Gilbert Ryle so rightly said in *Plato's Progress*: "It is as if Aristotle knew as a reader many, though not all of Plato's dialogues; knew as a listener Plato's *Lecture on the Good*; but did not know Plato the man." And from the pedagogical reverence which we have come to expect through Plato's own brilliant portrayals of his beloved master Socrates, Aristotle's comparable references to Plato are singularly disappointing.

Even where Aristotle deals directly with Platonic doctrine, we seem to be in the presence of a certain distorting reluctance. As a historian of the philosophic doctrines of his predecessors, Aristotle always seems less concerned with a literal transcription of their beliefs than with the fashion in which they rightly or wrongly anticipate his own philosophic dogmas. Already in 1935 Cherniss established conclusively that the interpretations of the pre-Socratic philosophers which appear in such works as the *Physics, Metaphysics,* and *De anima* are assimilated to the problems and indeed to the solutions of Aristotle's elaborate system. And in Cherniss's *The Riddle of the Early Academy* (University of California Press, 1945), in showing some of the paradoxes which follow if we expand our evidence of Plato's lecturing within the Academy into an inflated doctrine of basic oral teaching, he demonstrated the discrepancies between what Aristotle asserted about the Platonic theory of ideas in the first book of the *Metaphysics* and that doctrine as we usually find it in the *Phaedo* and the *Republic,* the *Parmenides, Theaetetus,* and *Sophist.* Such reticences and discrepancies appearing in the surviving works of Plato's most illustrious pupil hardly sustain confidence in the contemporary reconstruction of an intellectual biography beyond dispute.

Our other two chief sources are even more heavily suspect. The real foundation for everything that we know of Plato's life as a whole comes from Diogenes Laërtius, the Hellenistic editor and compiler and the contemporary of such authors as Lucian, Galen, Philostratus, and Clement of Alexandria, whose *Life of Plato* is written therefore at least *six hundred years* after Plato's death.

And it is as if our sole information about Saint Thomas Aquinas
or Dante were to be obtained from a single biography written by
some Pre-Raphaelite enthusiast in Victorian England.

Diogenes Laërtius is clearly not writing from personal knowledge, but is copying, borrowing, making excerpts and citations,
and appropriating interesting stories and legends. But if he is
multifarious in his reading, amazing in his industry, and insatiable in his curiosity, he is at the same time pedantic, vain, and
hopelessly credulous. The Hellenistic tradition in these matters
favored personal anecdote, surprising episode, and dramatic
detail, and Diogenes Laërtius, its child, seems to have ransacked
earlier literature to appropriate the novel and the startling twist,
the unusual or the bizarre detail. He was an uncritical writer,
writing for an uncritical and legend-hungry age, and the Platonic
biography he presents suffers severely from the intrusion of irrelevant and untrustworthy detail. Yet the *Life of Plato* is even today
indispensable, and its importance is little the less because it
represents a kind of summation of the indiscipline of Hellenistic
biography. As the only complete exemplar of early Platonic biography in our possession, its value is unique.

From Diogenes Laërtius we learn the facts of Plato's ancestry
and early education: that he wrestled, applied himself to painting, and wrote poems; first dithyrambs, afterward lyrics and tragedies. But an event like his Socratic conversion, for example, is
treated dramatically and with mystic intent.

It is stated that Socrates in a dream saw a cygnet on his knees,
which all at once put forth plumage, and flew away after utter-
ing a loud sweet note. And the next day Plato was introduced
as a pupil, and thereupon he recognized in him the swan of his
dream. At first he used to study philosophy in the garden of
Colonus as a follower of Heracleitus. Afterwards, when he was
about to compete for the prize with a tragedy, he listened to
Socrates in front of the theater of Dionysus, and then consign-
ed his poems to the flames.

Diogenes tells us that Plato was six years younger than Isocrates,
that he acted as choragus at Athens, that when Socrates was gone
he attached himself to Cratylus the Heracleitean, and that he
travelled to Italy to see the Pythagorean philosophers. But he also
tells us that he received the name of Plato because of his broad
shoulders, that he had a weak voice, that he traveled to Egypt in

the company of Euripides, that he was the first to engage in argument by means of question and answer, and that he died in his eighty-first year at a wedding feast. In every case fact and fiction, justifiable inference and painted legend seem inextricably intermingled, and no nicety of logical deduction or classical scholarship has conclusively effected their separation. Platonic scholars have plundered and mined Diogenes Laërtius, taking what they needed and rejecting what they must, but every account of Plato's life from the sixteenth century onward is utterly dependent upon him for its material.

Our last basic source is, perhaps, the most controversial of all. It is the series of thirteen Platonic "letters" which appears in all our manuscripts of Plato at the end, just before the spurious dialogues. The median position is symbolic, for Platonic scholars are in complete disagreement about whether their authority belongs with the genuine and accredited dialogues or with the other *dubia* and *spuria* of the Platonic collection. A part of this collection since the time when (during the reign of the Emperor Tiberius) Thrasyllus arranged the Platonic writings into "tetralogies" and placed the *Epistles* in his last tetralogy, the letters have a limited and restricted subject matter. Eight out of the thirteen are concerned with contemporary Sicilian politics: with the rulers Dion and Dionysius and with the causes and occasions of Plato's three trips to that confused and turbulent kingdom. The other five — supposedly written to various rulers and statesmen of the time — recommend political principles which are themselves a product of the Sicilian experience. Their chief utility, therefore, is that they "explain" Plato's political principles and ambitions, and that they provide a brilliant clue to the fashion in which his political disillusionment expresses itself in the serial passage from the early and idealistic *Republic* through the later and transitional *Statesman* to the late and final "political realism" of the *Laws*.

Whether the *Epistles* are authentic or not, they represent an ancient tradition. "If then, said John Burnet in his *Greek Philosophy: Thales to Plato,* "the *Epistles* are forgeries, they are at least the work of a sober and well-informed writer, whose use of the Attic dialect proves him to have been Plato's contemporary." And he went on to express his confidence in the availability of the most important of the collection:

We may, indeed, go so far as to say that the supposed forger of
the *Epistles* must have been a man of almost unparalleled literary skill, or he could not have reproduced so many of the
little peculiarities that marked Plato's style at the very time of
his life to which the *Epistles* profess to belong, though with
just those shades of difference we should expect to find in letters as contrasted with more elaborate literary work. I believe
that all the letters of any importance are Plato's, and I shall
therefore make use of them.

Burnet's optimism is shared by A. E. Taylor, who in his *Plato:
The Man and His Work*, after having disposed of numbers 1 and
12, is even more dogmatic. "No grounds," he says, "have ever
been produced for questioning the authenticity of the rest which
will bear examination." Unfortunately, some very great classical
scholars *have* thought otherwise. Although in the nineteenth century both Grote and Eduard Meyer believed in their authenticity,
both Ast and Zeller, on the other hand, unhesitatingly proclaimed the entire collection spurious. An important middle ground
was taken by Wilamowitz in his *Platon* in deciding for the genu-
ineness of the most important of the thirteen: 6, 8, and above all
7. Since then have come the dogmatic affirmative positions of
Burnet and Taylor and the more moderate affirmation of G. C.
Field, although elaborate arguments against the *Epistles* have
also been presented by H. Richards and especially by Constantin
Ritter in his *Neue Untersuchungen über Platon*. R. Hackforth is
also critical, and a good part of the bizarre, although original,
reinterpretation of Plato presented in Gilbert Ryle's *Plato's Progress* hinges upon his finding the *Epistles* to be rank forgeries and
the traditional story about Plato, Dion, and Dionysius to be mere
political propaganda without factual foundation.

The chief external evidence *for* authenticity was given by
Grote: that since the *Epistles* are part of the collection of the
authentic Platonic dialogues after Plato's death, it must be that
they too were cherished and preserved intact within the Platonic
Academy, whence, untampered with, they passed into the hands
of the Alexandrian libraries. The chief external argument *against*
authenticity is equally cogent: the inherent improbability that
any ancient collection of letters would be systematically preserved,
combined with the undeniable fact (attested by Galen) that high
prices were customarily paid by these same libraries for letters
signed with illustrious names, so that it was to the material advan-
tage of some skilled forger or unscrupulous man of letters to study

the style of a celebrated author like Plato with the express intent of personally profiting from foisting upon the learned world a plausible fabrication. So the argument over the *Epistles* rages from age to age. The classical philologists disagree. There is no definitive settlement.

Here again, as in the case of Diogenes Laërtius, it seems that we are constrained by what we cannot do without. The seventh letter too is indispensible. Largely autobiographical, supposedly dating from 353, when Plato was seventy-three or seventy-four, and vastly concerned with providing justification for the role he played in the internal affairs of Sicily and in the struggle between the rival leaders Dion and Dionysius, it both recapitulates all the political wisdom which we have grown to associate with the *Republic* and once more reaffirms the indispensible role of philosophy in the political process which is of the very essence of Platonism. An "open" or "public" letter, probably never meant for Sicily at all, but rather for the general public of his own malicious Athens, it constitutes a kind of *Apologia pro vita sua* or self-justification, in which Plato, withdrawn into the solitude of the Academy, ventures forth only to counteract the damaging misrepresentations current in an Athens he has practically forsaken, although never really abandoned in his ideal imagination. As evidence for the course of his early life, of the meaning to him of the Socratic martyrdom, and of the progress of his political hopes and aspirations, it is too "meaningful" to be relinquished.

Interpretive Method

I have lingered over the paradoxes and the difficulties, the perplexities and the uncertainties of our chief extrinsic sources for an interpretation of the life and work of Plato — Aristotle, Diogenes Laërtius, and the *Epistles* — not out of any love for the strategies of debate of the classical philologists, but in order to show that the strictness of the interpretative criterion which Shorey invokes is impossible of adoption, even by Shorey himself, and that he too relies upon both Diogenes Laërtius and the *Epistles* without that rigid skepticism which complete purity in the matter of interpretative methodology requires. And all this only reinforces that need for a principle of "imaginative" method which shall seek to understand and elucidate the inner formative forces which are at the heart of Platonism.

It is true, of course, that there is a preordained congruence

between choice of sources and interpretive bent. Those who follow
Aristotle are naturally those most interested in Plato the logician,
metaphysician, and scientist. Aristotle devotes particular attention to a critique of the theory of ideas, and throughout his works
he draws more heavily upon, and quotes more frequently from,
the *Timaeus* than any other Platonic dialogue. This may well be
because, as Ryle says, Plato, while in Sicily, had studied the
physical and physiological doctrines of Archytas of Tarentum and
Philistion, and, returning to Athens with this scientific harvest,
then wrote the *Timaeus* not for popular consumption, but as a
basic text for students within the Academy.

In the same way, those who follow Diogenes Laërtius cannot fail
to be impressed by the account of Plato the artist who was choragus, wrote lyrics and dithyrambs, and was the first to bring the
mimes of Sophron to Athens. These are the ones who concentrate
upon Plato the dramatist and stylist, the creator of the *Phaedrus*
and *Symposium,* who sympathized with that form of madness of
which the Muses are the source, and found that every discourse
should be constructed like a living creature, organically whole and
inwardly alive.

And, finally, those who draw heavily upon the *Epistles* are
concerned largely with Plato the political reformer, the author of
the *Republic* and the *Laws*, who, having rejected a political career
because of the corruption he found in every breed of statesman
and every political party in Athens, turned to the substitute consolations of political philosophy, forsaking his teaching career in
middle life, only at the moment when he was persuaded that his
dream of an aristocratically governed community might be accomplished. These expectations cruelly disappointed, he returns
at last to Athens, disillusioned by his Sicilian adventure; again
content to reenter the Academy and now to advocate the rationality of the written law rather than the administrative discretion of
fallible and impure human statesmen. For every predominantly
political age — whether that of Machiavelli, or Hobbes, or Ranke,
or Friederich Meinecke — this is the essential Plato.

Despite the difficulties in constructing our Platonic picture out
of materials provided by Aristotle, Diogenes Laërtius, and the
Epistles, there is one basic resource which transcends them all —
the corpus of the authentic dialogues, the impressive body of
Plato's works. What Plato said is infinitely more important than
what anyone else, even Aristotle, said about Plato. Yet the interpretation of this body of work as a whole is also not without its

difficulties. To be sure, in the matter of arrangement, the great
Platonic scholars like Arnim, Lutoslawski, Ritter, and Wilamowitz (to say nothing of the later generation of Shorey, Burnet, and
Taylor) have come to a broad consensus. With respect to chronology, as Shorey says:

> There is now general agreement upon the broad division into
> three groups: the earlier, minor, "Socratic" dialogues; the ar-
> tistic masterpieces of Plato's maturity; the less dramatic and
> more technical works of his old age. It is generally agreed that
> the dramatic, minor, "Socratic" dialogues are for the most part
> early; that the *Laws* is the latest of Plato's works; that the
> more arid, undramatic, dogmatic, elaborately metaphysical,
> dialectical dialogues form a later group preceding or perhaps
> partly contemporary with the composition of the *Laws*; and
> that such artistic masterpieces as the *Symposium*, the *Phaedo*,
> the *Phaedrus*, and the *Republic* belong to the period of Plato's
> full maturity.

It is true that even within this consensus there are important
divergences. But these lie largely in the matter of the ordering of
the early or "Socratic" dialogues. Whereas Lutoslawski, Ritter,
and Wilamowitz differ in toto on the serial order of such dialogues
as the *Euthyphro, Crito,* and *Apology,* the *Charmides, Euthydemus,* and *Protagoras,* nevertheless as regards the later dialogues
from the *Republic* on—the *Theaetetus, Parmenides, Sophist,
Statesman, Philebus, Timaeus,* and the *Laws*—the agreement is
almost complete. This is because whereas the ordering of the early
dialogues is based for the most part upon "subjective" theories
about the development of Plato's thought, hinging upon the
question of the relation of "essentially Socratic" to "essentially
Platonic" conceptions, the ordering of the late dialogues is primarily based on the relatively stable ground of the persuasive styl-
ometric tests initiated by that same Lewis Campbell whose axiom
of interpretive method Shorey approved.

But underlying the issue of the serial ordering of the dialogues
in time lies a larger and more philosophical problem of interpretation: whether the model of the Platonic mentality shall be constructed according to a picture of growth, evolution, and development or according to an image of basic fixity with endless
elaboration. It is the same issue that divided Richard McKeon and
Werner Jaeger on the interpretation of Aristotle. In the dialogues
Plato appears to address himself to a series of particular topics:

piety, temperance, courage, sense perception, categories, knowledge, pleasure, political arrangements, theory of ideas, cosmology. Nowhere (with the possible exception of the cosmology of the
Timaeus) does he provide a complete and systematic philosophy.
In the nineteenth century especially (in any case dominated by the
evolutionary point of view) this circumstance led to the notion
that, beginning tentatively and hesitantly, Plato gradually
thought his way into a definite philosophical position which solidified in the form of the later dialogues. The early questioning
"dialogues of search" turn, therefore, into the later, more dogmatic "dialogues of seizure." This position has been fortified by
careful examination of the literary form in which the dialogues
have been cast. In practically all the earlier dialogues through the
Theaetetus Socrates is the chief speaker, but, although he leads
and controls the discussion, other speakers contribute opinions
and objections, so that the dialogue proceeds as a real conversational interchange. But in the first part of the *Parmenides* he is
not the chief speaker, and in the second part he is a silent listener.
The *Sophist* and the *Statesman* have him appear early only to be
virtually supplanted by an "Eleatic Stranger." The *Timaeus* and
the *Critias* are practically monologues by the persons after whom
these dialogues are named. In the *Laws* Socrates does not appear
at all; the dialogue is conducted by the "Athenian Stranger." The
more dogmatic and assured temper of the later Platonic content is
thus underscored by two elements of formal composition: the
later works lack the element of lively dialogue, and now Socrates
has ceased to be the principal speaker.

Already in 1904 Shorey countered the prevailing evolutionary
interpretation with his formula (also the title of his book) *The
Unity of Plato's Thought*. Here he not only categorically rejected
the attempt to date the dialogues by the evolution and sequence of
Plato's thoughts, but suggested the untenability of the hope that
any critic could discern how the variations of the Platonic mood
and emphasis were determined by definite incidents in contemporary Greek history or by inferences about the transformations of
Plato's own personal experiences. He directed attention back exclusively to Plato's text, with the suggestion that careful examination will reveal it to be consistent throughout. For in the dialogues
the same fundamental concepts appear again and again, differently stated, perhaps, and surely with different emphases in vary-
ing contexts, but always expressing a certain limited number of

basic ideas. The Platonic dialogues deal with increasingly abstract and difficult philosophic problems, but there is no dramatic shift in Plato's deepest convictions. The same first principles are appealed to throughout. The same basic insights recur. And, as Shorey pointed out, this is because, although the Platonic method, unlike that of Aristotle, does not proceed formally to construct a coherent system, nonetheless when the dialogues are taken as a whole the world view they reveal is clear and consistent. If not stated once and for all and with strict deductive elaboration, it is at least presented dialectically—its implications gradually unfolded and its consequences explained. The center of Shorey's insistence is that only the total body of the Platonic writings—the dialogues as a whole—present the true statement of his philosophy.

I believe that Shorey's position is fundamentally correct, and that he has presented a principle of interpretation which is completely congruent with the essentials of Platonism. Those who are primarily influenced by the practice of Aristotle—and it is indeed the method of an analyzing and distinction-making science—have a tendency to separate the areas of human philosophic preoccupation: logic from aesthetics, ethics from metaphysics, science from politics; but this tendency is itself diametrically opposed to the organic unity of all philosophic areas which is the implied consequence of Plato's holistic logic. No better proof of this can be found than the *Republic*, the central masterpiece of the Platonic system, not only because it reveals his creative powers at their most brilliant, but because it is a perfect example of the philosophy of organic wholeness. "Who is the just man?" that dialogue asks at the outset, and true to Greek presuppositions in the fifth and fourth centuries it answers: "The man who lives in a just state." "But what is a just state?" the inquiry continues, only to reply: "The just state is that one which possesses wise rulers." "But how are rulers made wise?" "Through education." "What kind of education?" "That kind which instructs us in that which is most real." "But what things then are most real?" we persist. And the answer is brilliantly set forth: "The forms, the ideas, the eternal archetypes of our impermanent, changing, temporal experience." From ethics to politics to educational theory to epistemology to metaphysics: the passage is the closely reasoned entailment of a progressive implication.

Those who read the Platonic dialogues piecemeal, like those

who read Shakespeare's historical plays in the same fashion, fail to discern the integral logic which binds together the body of the work. And there is indeed a temptation to note slight discrepancies from dialogue to dialogue. Obviously we must make congruent the attitude toward pleasure in the *Gorgias*, the *Protagoras*, and the *Philebus*, reconcile the political principles of the *Republic*, the *Statesman*, and the *Laws*, derive one unified theory of forms or ideas from the *Meno, Phaedo, Republic, Theaetetus, Parmenides*, and *Timaeus*. But with careful attention to variable problems and shifting contexts this presents no insuperable difficulties. For the presupposition is always in favor of one complex but comprehensive doctrine, one moral philosophy, one vision of the world. Those whose bias is toward separateness, distinctness, and atomicity will never master the strategies of Platonism, but those sympathetic to a "philosophy of organism" (in a sense analogous to, but not quite the same as, Whitehead's use of this phrase) will find no difficulty in seeing the Platonic politics intimately related to the Platonic insistence upon self-cultivation and the transformation of the soul; the Platonic dialectic as a consummation of the Platonic mathematics in the direction of self-cultivation; and all four related to a perception of the nature of ultimate reality as forbidding any ultimate separation.

Shorey's insistence upon a return to the Platonic text, and upon "the unity of Plato's thought," is unexceptionable, but his refusal to relate that thought to the circumstances of Plato's life and the sociology of contemporary Athens is an unnecessary limitation and impoverishment. And it proves only that with respect to the interpretation of a great philosopher no principle proposed by Greek scholar or classical philologist in his professional capacity is authoritative enough. What one requires is a general theory of philosophical interpretation, based upon a deeper understanding of what it means to philosophize, and of the source conditions of the philosophic impulse. Shorey's strictures against a Platonism which is incoherent and irrelevant are surely right, but those very factors which make for coherence and relevance are, I think, best discovered in the motivations of personal biography and in the crucial problems posed by the social order in which the philosophy arises.

Our primary concern here is to examine the different relations between philosophy and the social forms it serves, and our master assumption is that philosophy is most significantly conceived as a conceptual response to the fundamental human problems posed in any given society in any given epoch. It is only *déformation professionnelle,* which causes one to view philosophy as an isolated set of response to a series of merely professional problems. On the contrary, it must be conceived as a segment of general culture like literature, politics, and the arts, so that, as John Dewey once said, its connection with social history and with civilization is intrinsic.

It was Dilthey, I think, who first noted that the works of any thinker are the expression of a single, comprehensive vision of the world—a *Weltanschauung*—and that the interpretive task is to understand the structure of the whole and see each individual segment as part of a totality in which it has its definite function and precise importance. It is in this sense that Shorey's thesis of the unity of Plato's thought is valid, and that to find the fundamental themes which unify the philosophy and render it coherent remains the first task of the student of Plato. This task does not depend upon principles which are isolated or unique. Whether it is true or not, as Dilthey believed, that there are a limited number of typical visions of the world, there *are* a limited number of problems which any age faces, and whose interrelated answers do, in fact, constitute its essential *Weltanschauung*: Where should political power lie? What are the ingredients of wisdom? In whose hands lies the governance of the cosmos? What are the compelling and authoritative values? Through which individual faculties and social agencies are they known and guaranteed? How ought their rightful claims to be sustained and perpetuated from generation to generation?

These questions are enduring, and they appear in Plato as in any great philosopher whose ideas are a landmark in the world-orientation of his time. It is thus an important function of the historian of philosophy to note the Platonic answers, establish the coherent totality of the body of thought in which they appear, and to note also how these answers constitute a mode of social response. This requires an effort to ground them in the facts of Greek culture, to recognize them as efforts to eliminate the paradoxes and conflicts within the social reality out of which they were generated, and perhaps even to explore the intrinsic limitations which such a time-bound vision of the world necessarily implies. To this task of Platonic interpretation I should now like to turn.

Plato and Athens

No one who reads the great documents of Greek cultural history, whether the epics of Homer, the tragedies of Aeschylus and Sophocles, Thucydides' *History* or Aristotle's *Constitution of Athens*, can doubt that the chief crises of the Greek world center on the claims, the moral dilemmas, and the political validity of an aristocratic system of values. In the *Iliad* and the *Odyssey*, *agathos*— the principal term of moral approbation— is applied to strength, military prowess, and the skills that promote success in war. But in addition *agathos* is used to characterize high social position and a place in the ruling hierarchy. In a heroic age the two usages are not distinct, but parts of a single world-view. In *Merit and Responsibility: A Study in Greek Values* Arthur Adkins says:

Agathos commends the most admired type of man: and he is the man who possesses the skills and qualities of the warrior-chieftain in war and, as will be seen, in peace, together with the social advantages which such a chieftain possessed. To be *agathos*, one must be brave, skillful, and successful in war and in peace; and one must possess the wealth and (in peace) the leisure which are at once the necessary conditions for the development of these skills and the natural reward of their successful employment.

If we examine the culture in which these values predominate, we discover a society patterned upon an aristocratic model, a model from which later Greek society sometimes seems to depart, but whose traditional excellences are never far from its deepest memory. The kings and chieftains of Homer are in some respects primitive, but they are all members of a royal house, rich in valor as in armor and inherited wealth, and possessed of a place in the chain of command as is their right. And, although they mirror the force of elementary need (for Homeric society does value most highly that class which guarantees its preservation), this functionalism does finally give a permanent stamp to the class structure of Greek society. *Agathoi* comes to denote *a social class*, and there is an inevitable tendency for the word finally to denote social position alone, irrespective of the characteristics of high moral quality. It is this ambiguity which clogs the pages of any history of European morals and is to haunt even the dialogues of Plato.

Seven hundred years later—in Periclean Athens—the situation has changed. In a city-state, the rise of commerce and a more settled form of life, the concentration of population and the invention of coined money all signify that wealth may be earned as

well as inherited, and that prosperity and success require the
security of codified laws rather than the talent for unmitigated
aggression. This strains the ancient system of values. Men of low
birth acquire great wealth and high-born men may sink to a
position of questionable prosperity. In a situation of such social,
economic, and moral ambiguity the conflict between the old and
the new is a center of ethical focus. Solon and Cleisthenes wrestle
with the same problems which two thousand years later faced
Western Europe with the breakup of the feudal pattern, the rise of
the towns, and the emergence of a prosperous urban bourgeoisie.
The manliness and good birth of Homeric times are compromised. What a man *has* becomes as important as what he *is* and
does. Wealth has thrown lineage into confusion.

But by the same token "moral virtue" has now become separated from the intrinsic desirability of birth and valor. In a famous
couplet, cited by Aristotle in the *Nicomachean Ethics,* Theognis
proclaimed: "The whole of virtue is summarized by justice; any
man, Cyrnus, is morally good if he is just." This, as Adkins says,
smashes the whole framework of Homeric values. But it heralds
the democratic revolution in Athens.

In the newer situation of increasing democratization where both
rich and poor, aristocrats and tradesmen participate in defense
and deliberation, the "good" no longer is a term denoting and
commending a higher social class: instead it will denote men of all
social classes among the citizenry if they possess those specific
attributes which make them valuable to the state. To discover
what is expected of a man by the Athenian democracy in order
that he may be termed *agathos polites* — a good citizen — one has
only to turn to the speeches delivered in the assembly and the law
courts. The conception is embedded and enshrined in the masterpieces of Greek rhetoric. The democratic thrust turns against the
traditional values of wealth and good family, and it redefines
virtue in terms of man's actual behavior rather than his name and
lineage.

But the crisis in values of the fifth century is attested by a
curious paradox of Greek social history: the contradiction between the undeniable facts of aristocratic prestige and the new
belief in the *teachability* of political skills represented by the rise
of the sophistic movement in Athens. The finances of Athens did
not in fact permit the state to underwrite all military and cultural
expense. To outfit a trireme or to serve as choragus, one must be a
man of substance, and probably an aristocrat with inherited

wealth. Thus the financing of the Athenian navy and the Athenian drama work against the pretensions of democracy. And since
good citizenship is clearly related to the promotion of civic wel-
fare, even the *agathos polites* retains about it an aura of aristocratic competency. But at the same moment when it is clear that
only the upper classes—the traditional *agathoi*—can perform the
services required, the Sophists and rhetoricians (often indistin-
guishable) are insisting that the political skills of everyday life are
both indispensible and *teachable*. Not to underwrite civic costs,
but to become a politician skilled in word and deed is, according
to them, the real means of promoting the prosperity of the city.
This is the insistent message of Hippias and Prodicus, of Gorgias,
and above all of Protagoras. Almost the very raison d'être of Greek
Sophistry was to allow those with the requisite rhetorical mastery
to make instantaneously available to any who could pay that
political knowledge which is indispensable for civic success. And
that is why the Sophistic movement was itself the child and the
servicing technical resource of the new Athenian democracy.
When in the *Protagoras* of Plato the elderly Sophist is induced by
Socrates to define the nature of his teaching, he slyly distinguishes
it from the customary Sophistic irrelevance and comes straight to
the point:

> Protagorus heard me out and said You put your questions well,
> and I enjoy answering good questioners. When he comes to me,
> Hippocrates will not be put through the same things that an-
> other Sophist would inflict on him. The others treat their pupils
> badly; these young men, who have deliberately turned their
> backs on specialization, they take and plunge into special stud-
> ies again, teaching them arithmetic and astronomy and geom-
> etry and music—here he glanced at Hippas—but from me he
> will learn only what he has come to learn. What is that subject?
> The proper care of his personal affairs, so that he may best
> manage his own household, and also of the state's affairs, so as
> to become a real power in the city, both as speaker and man
> of action. [318e]

In this dialogue, set in the Periclean Age, when the Athenian
democracy is at the very height of its opulence and glory, Plato
pokes a certain amount of good-natured fun at the elderly Sophist, showing up his pretentiousness and vanity, his pedantic distinctions and preposterous claims. And, although Protagoras is
treated with considerable respect as the dialogue proceeds, there is
little doubt about Plato's attitude toward Protagoras's profession.

Plato's antagonism toward the entire Sophistic movement is not simply because of its vaunted professionalism and the hollowness of its pedagogical claims; it is also the instinctive response of the Athenian aristocrat to the effectiveness of a leveling and a democratizing civic force.

And yet despite his antagonism Plato has learned from the Sophists. For he too is finally willing to admit that the virtue of the good man and the good citizen is a skill, a *techne* which can be taught. From the time of the composition of his earliest dialogues Plato has insisted that virtue is teachable as knowledge is teachable, and the adjective *phronimos* (which may be translated "intelligent in practical matters") is used over and over again in connection with the words denoting courage, manliness, temperance, high-mindedness, and the excellencies of social position. In fact it hardly goes too far to say that the chief thrust of the Platonic ethics is to take those value terms of the Greek tradition which have been constantly refined from the Homeric Age to the fifth century and pin them securely to the concept of the *kalos kathagos* — the noble spirit, or aristocrat or "gentleman." In this effort he is but recapitulating an aristocratic tendency permanently enshrined in the Greek consciousness.

Despite the enthusiasm with which the popular mind associates the structure of Periclean Athens with "democracy," there is little doubt that the preeminent Greek value pattern is the enthronement of nobility and the pursuit of excellence. From the *aristeus* of Homer (the best man, or the noblest chief) to the *aristokratia* of Plato (the rule of the noblest or the best-born) the moral quality of the *agathos bios* (the good life) had been identified with those who had become *aristoi* (preeminent) in war, in philosophy, and in social life.

The history of Athens from the seventh century to the fourth illustrates the fluctuating fortunes of the well-born — that permanent repository of moral virtue and superior quality (as it was believed) — in the eternal struggle for supreme political power. The sharp division between the small number of land-owning noble families (with their enormous wealth, elegance, and good breeding) and the great mass of poor and underprivileged citizens was the evil which Solon attempted to remedy at the close of the seventh century, and his distrust of private political organization in Athens (which at certain times made it an offense to join a *hetaireia* or political club) was soundly based, since these clubs

were often the chief refuge and agency of aristocratic and virulently antidemocratic elements within the polis.

The Periclean miracle created and maintained a broad balance
of political rights within a class structure of extreme economic
inequality, but the later years of the fifth century witnessed a
profound reaction against the democratic idea which was to have
an insistent impact on the direction of Plato's own thought.
Athenian misfortune in the Peloponnesian War is probably the
determining influence here, since throughout that war the extreme
democracy was always the war party and the richer and more
conservative citizens the peace party. Political policy thus became
consolidated upon class lines, and with this development came a
more sustained and concentrated conservative attack upon democracy. The end of the fifth century found not only violent antidemocratic counterrevolutions actually led by Plato's close relatives, but the creation of an established body of virulently antidemocratic theory and ideology. A small treatise by an unknown
aristocrat called the "Old Oligarch" (dating probably from the
earlier years of the war) states openly and ill-naturedly the same
bias which was to underlie and animate the entire subtle web of
the Platonic philosophy.

Plato himself was a born aristocrat, "an Attic Tory" of distinguished lineage, naturally destined for membership in the ruling
class of Athens. Son of Ariston and Perictione, his family was one
of the most illustrious in the Periclean age. His father's lineage
went back to the first kings of Athens, and ultimately (it was held)
to the god Poseidon. His stepfather, Prilampes, was known as an
intimate friend of Pericles. But much more important in explain-
ing his political bias, Plato's mother was the sister of Charmides
and the cousin of Critias, both leaders of the antidemocratic
revolution which followed the collapse of Athens at the end of the
Peloponnesian War. As a youth of twenty-three (as Shorey imagines it) Plato "was doubtless invited to share the counsels of his
uncle Charmides, and his mother's cousin Critias, and of the
sincere conservatives or unscrupulous oligarchs who were planning
with Spartan aid to restore the good old constitution of the fathers
and do away with the acknowledged folly of democracy once and
for all." With this background and these early experiences, it is
not difficult to understand why Plato remained his whole life an
irreconcilable aristocrat, constantly proposing rule by a cultured
elite, and a permanent opponent of every democratizing tendency.

Whatever their generating causes, a passion for excellence and an eternal mistrust of the many are Plato's enduring presuppositions, and this, I think, provides all the explanatory hypotheses which are needed to answer the complex questions to which his life and philosophy give rise, such as the meaning of his trips to Syracuse; the nature and the purpose of the Academy he founded between his first and second visits; the attitude he adopts toward Socrates (and toward the Sophists and rhetoricians of the fifth century); the role the dialogues play in the public life of Athens; and even the problem of the relationship within the dialogues themselves of the aristocratic ethics and politics they assert and Plato's more theoretical metaphysics and epistemology.

In light of an enormous diversity of directions and intentions, then, one must always ask: What was Plato's ultimate commitment, and how did he define his essential task? And here the answer is, I think, clear. *He was the great philosophic spokesman for, and the lifelong educator toward, an aristocratic restoration in the Greek world.*

Plato as *theorist*, Plato as *educator*: these are the primary poles of Platonic achievement; and from this two directions of Platonic interpretation clearly emerge. (1) That Plato's philosophy as a whole (like the *Republic* itself as this total philosophy "writ small") is to be read as a double demonstration: positively as the reasoned presentation of a system of ideal aristocratic values through the medium of the metaphysics in which they are grounded, the epistemology by which they are known, the ethics to which they point, and the ideal political system in which they might be realized, and negatively as a sustained attack upon the Athenian city-state which has so disastrously departed from these values, together with its debased culture, its democratic political system, and above all its corrupt and misguided "educators"—rhapsodes, poets, Sophists, or rhetoricians, as the case may be. (2) That the founding of the Academy is the culmination of Plato's life, since its groundplan and structure, its functioning and operation were to be the illustration and the proving ground for the principles presented in those dialogues which preceded its creation, as well as those dialogues specifically written to serve as its educational manuals or as explanations of its rationale within the wider context of the contemporary Greek world.

At one point these two directions of Platonic interpretation clearly merge, for they show us that theory and practice, philosophizing and teaching are intimately related in the Platonic vision of the world. This is why Eric Havelock in his *Preface to Plato* is so correct in asserting "that the *Republic* sets itself a problem which is not philosophical in the specialized sense of that term, but rather social and cultural. It questions the Greek tradition as such and the foundations on which it has been built. Crucial to this tradition is the condition and the quality of Greek education. That process, whatever it is, by which the mind and attitude of the young are formed lies at the heart of Plato's problem."

But Havelock could have gone further, for this is not only the problem of the *Republic*, but of the entire Platonic philosophy. The fundamental thrust of Platonism is, as we have said, the move toward a restoration of aristocratic values in the Greek world. It was with this intent that the dialogues with their insistent message were written, that the trips to Syracuse with their hope of turning a Sicilian tyrant into an aristocratically motivated philosopher-king were undertaken, and that after this latter venture had ignominiously failed, Plato founded the Academy to begin again from scratch and instruct a new generation to become the legislators and the aristocratic statesmen of a future world.

Plato's background at first caused him to view the task of an aristocratic restoration in merely political terms. But his life experience transformed his early hopes of direct action into the slower, but more realistic channels of an educational solution. Thus the restoration of values is in the end conceived primarily as a pedagogical problem. Teaching is at its center, and the form of teaching and the content of what is taught become issues of overwhelming importance. But this insight had never been far from Plato's deepest perceptions at every stage of his life. Thus the dramatic attention focused upon "Socrates as teacher" in the early *Euthyphro, Charmides, Lysis, Laches,* and *Meno.* Thus the *itinerarium studii* of the ideal education in the *Republic* and the *Laws.* Thus the metaphysical grounding of knowledge in apprehension of the permanent forms in the *Theaetetus, Parmenides, Timaeus,* and *Sophist.* Thus the persistent attacks upon those customary educators who had persistently led Athens astray. For if the Academy was to have recruits, and if its preeminence as an agency for the true aristocratic education was to be established, a systematic attack upon its chief competitors was clearly in order. The *Ion* and books 2 and 10 of the *Republic* mount this attack against the rhapsodes and the poets. The *Gorgias* and to some extent the *Phaedrus* attack the rhetoricians. The *Euthydemus, Cratylus, Protagoras,* and to some extent the *Theaetetus* attack the Sophists.

Althought the Sophists flourished in the Periclean Age, a full generation before the time of Plato's maturity, their successors and their influence must have made themselves felt during his lifetime. Without doubt he thinks they constitute the chief threat against the aristocratic vision of the world. For intellectually they formed a truly revolutionary and disturbing element in what was essentially a conservative Athenian milieu. Rootless foreigners in their origins; skeptical, nominalistic, subjectivistic, and relativistic thinkers in their point of view, as new "visiting intellectuals" during the Periclean Age, they created a critical tension against the ancient, traditional, rooted values of a settled, landed aristocracy. In the great antithesis between *phusis* and *nomos* ("nature" and "convention") which was a permanent source of controversy within Greek thought, the Sophists were always on the side of *nomos*, or convention. They had no axioms, no epistemic certainties, no fixed axes of value, no ancestral pieties. Everything for them could be an object of doubt and criticism, and their philology, epistemology, and ethics were tempered by an almost Heracleitean sense of relativity and temporal flux. Plato's abiding opposition to them can be reconstituted in the message of a series of important dialogues: he argues against their ethical doctrines, based upon the contingent variability of pleasure in the *Protagoras*, against their conventionalist theory of language in the *Cratylus*, and most important of all, against their relativistic theories of sense perception, which he found to be the denial of all true knowledge in the *Theaetetus*.

A generation after the Sophistic triumphs of the Periclean Age, the Platonic Academy (and the whole of the Platonic philosophy with it) met their continuing challenge in a typically aristocratic fashion: with a secure sense of the metaphysically and morally anchored, as opposed to the changing and restless universe; as a manifestation of the opposition of a true *Gemeinschaft* of the intellect as against the mere *Gesellschaft* — the stipulative, contractual, conventional dimensions of the mind.

This, I think, is the ultimate significance of the theory of forms or "ideas" in the later Platonic dialogues, whether appearing in

the *Timaeus*, the *Sophist*, or the *Parmenides*, although its characteristic use has already shown itself in an epistemological dialogue like the *Theaetetus*, where knowledge itself is validated only
in terms of its object and true knowledge is that whose object is
Being, reality and eternal immutability. In a famous passage of
the *Theaetetus* Plato distinguishes between "the river gods" and
"the pillar gods"—between the tradition of Heraclitus where
Ocean and Tethys are the source of all things, are flowing streams
and nothing is at rest, and that of Parmenides, the partisan of the
immovable whole, where eternity and constancy rules. And his
own invariant appeal to the pillar gods—to a rooted and a
grounded and a timeless order which at once invalidates moral
conventionalism and perceptual relativism—shows the ultimate
metaphysical strategy of philosophy in an aristocratic age. The
meaning of aristocracy is the reliance upon the tradition of excellence, and the meaning of tradition is an implicit equation of
endurance and value. Since the time of Plato, Western thinking
has held fast to the principle that the more real, steadfast, and
eternal a thing was, the greater its goodness and perfection, and
philosophy has habitually deduced the meaning of the transitory
from the permanent. This is the eternal legacy of Platonic conservatism, and its fruits can be discovered once again resurrected
in the great doctors of the Middle Ages.

Plato as Aristocrat

The chief thesis of this chapter is that since philosophy in general
should be conceived of primarily as the conceptual response to
those basic problems faced by any given society at a particular
moment in its history, therefore the philosophy of Plato can be
seen as the characteristic product of an aristocratic age and sensibility, weaving together its political, moral, educational, and
metaphysical themes to constitute an aristocratic value configuration and vision of the world. In this light Platonism may be
conceived as the inevitable product and the quintessential expression of the entire Greek valuational consciousness as expressed in
that broad expanse of cultural experience between Homer and
Pericles and, more particularly, between Pericles and Philip of
Macedon.

But in characterizing Platonism as aristocratic, one meets at
once the objection of those partisans for whom Plato can do no

wrong, and who see, or fancy that they see, in this assertion of an upper-class affiliation a Marxist or quasi-Marxist form of personal denigration. The objection is without merit. For to interpret philosophy as a mode of social expression does not require one to concentrate merely upon its economic aspects. Class struggle and the genesis of ideas as rationalizations of property relations, ideas as ideological or utopian weapons in the struggle for the minds of men, are concepts which may have considerable appeal to one kind of interpretive mentality, and may even be useful in the limited areas of social dialectics or *Wissensoziologie*; but they do not exhaust the fruitful possibilities. And even when Sartre in the best orthodox Marxist fashion speaks of philosophy as "a partic ular way in which a ruling class becomes conscious of itself," he quite unwittingly suggests a strategy for the history of philosophy in which not Hegel, but Marx, may be stood upon his head, and where the materialistic interpretation of history may be supplant- ed by a principle of social idealism.

Even a materialist like Santayana was interested to discover what wisdom is possible for an animal who possesses a mind which is from beginning to end poetic, even religious, and the strategy of his naturalism was ever to oscillate between the grounding of experience in the necessities of natural fact and its constant struggle to realize ideal ends. The Marxist perspective is always focused upon the economic necessities, but there is no reason to neglect the ideal ends. If, therefore, philosophy were simply the particular way in which a dominant class exhibited its self-aware- ness, this self-awareness might equally consist in the cognitive projection of an ethical ideal. This is the position I wish to adopt in treating the philosophy of Plato.

And yet, with respect to Plato's aristocratic bias, there *is* a problem which must be faced: that of the consequences in terms of valuational objectivity and philosophic impartiality of a pos- ition which combines intimately and without the possibility of separation a passion for excellence with an eternal contempt for the multitude. Even so perceptive a critic as Huntington Cairns, in his introduction to *The Collected Dialogues* (Pantheon Books, 1961), attempts in his enthusiasm to gloss over the seriousness of the difficulty. "In several senses Plato was an aristocrat," he says, "but not in the opprobrious sense of some of his critics." And he continues:

In Plato's hands aristocracy meant the rule of the best, from
whatever class they came. The able were to receive special
training for the responsibilities requiring great ability, the less
able were to perform the tasks suitable to their ability. Plato's
political theory is an implication of the system of nature, and
to call this philosophy aristocratic is meaningful only in the
sense that nature is itself aristocratic. But to call any philosophy aristocratic in the sense of class interest is meaningless;
preoccupation with the interests of one class to the detriment
of others is not philosophy. Philosophy is disinterested or it is
not philosophy. When ideas are manipulated for personal ends,
for class or group interests, the name for this in Plato's day was
sophistry. It was against this that his dialogues were directed.
To accuse Plato of being in league with the sophistic forces that
undermined the classical world is an instance of the more subtle
misrepresentation of his position. Plato's disinterested pursuit
of knowledge has not only made the word *Platonism* synonymous with the word *philosophy*, it has marked him as the aristocrat of aristocrats, the paragon of excellence emulated by
high-minded men for over two thousand years.

This argument is itself both disingenuous and biased — and it is
false. For to say that Plato's political system is "an implication of
the system of nature" so that Plato "is aristocratic only as nature is
herself aristocratic" is to succumb to the worst excesses of an
untenable doctrine of natural law. One other age, the Elizabethan, was also fond of analogizing the conventions of kingship and
class power to the central position of the sun and the necessities of
natural operation, and in *Troilus and Cressida*, Shakespeare puts
into the mouth of Ulysses a famous speech which shows that
nature "observes degree" as do the social arrangements of men.
But it has long been known that this is but a feudal survival, a part
of "the Tudor myth" which no modern man could possibly take
seriously.

But further, even those who call Plato's philosophy a function of
his class position hardly maintain that his bias was consciously
Machiavellian and that he "manipulated ideas for personal ends
or group interests." They claim only that, born an aristocrat and
raised an aristocrat, it would be curious if the biases he had quite
naturally absorbed from family and cultural background would
not color, however unconsciously, his outlook upon Athenian
politics and his view of the world. Plato was surely not "in league
with Sophistic forces," and as a philosopher he, like his master

Socrates, was surely willing to follow the argument wherever it should lead; but who can deny that those basic premises, those unacknowledged presuppositions which always haunt the life of the mind, however immediately noble seeming and disinterested, do not play their part here also? He is the critic of his age; his dominant aim is to combat that democratic disintegration which he discerned alike in the poets, the rhetoricians, and the Sophists, and to promote the restoration of that essentially Greek view of life which from Homeric times is associated with the *aristoi*. But his contempt for the many constantly recurs in the body of his work, and his scorn for inferiority reaches proportions which can only be an embarrassment for his partisans and disciples.

We can be clearest in this whole matter if we state explicitly what we mean by calling the Platonic philosophy "aristocratic." There are, I think, three ingredients which make it so: (1) an unwavering preference for excellence; (2) a profound belief in the principle of hierarchy; (3) a constantly reiterated belief in the supreme value of the few. No one can criticize an aristocratic bias in the first sense. But a belief in the principle of hierarchy is more ambiguous, and when belief in the supreme value of the few is stated in reverse — as a persistent distrust, contempt, and even fear of the many, then there is much to be explained — and excused. The difficulty is that a man's virtues and his vices generally spring from precisely the same source. The great problem for any contemporary democratic admirer of Plato is always how to remain sensitive to the Platonic feeling for excellence without succumbing to Plato's contempt for the multitude which is its reverse side.

All the evidence we have indicates that Plato was a politican manqué. It is true that Diogenes Laërtius shows him at first as the budding poet and dramatist, coming with Socrates under the spell of a rational dialectic, but the seventh epistle presents a picture which is of considerable importance for interpreting that strain of Plato's political doctrine in which the theory of aristocracy is constantly reiterated and developed, and Diogenes Laërtius himself accepts the story epistle 7 tells. "In the days of my youth," says the aged Plato (324c), "my experience was the same as that of many others. I thought that as soon as I should become my own master I would immediately enter into public life. But it so happened, I found, that the following changes occurred in the political situation." And he then relates the circumstances of the aristocratic plot in which in 404 at the end of the Peloponnesian War the Thirty, including his uncle Charmides and his cousin Critias, seize power.

> In the government then existing [a democratic government, Plato might have added, the last poor remnant of the Periclean heritage], reviled as it was by many, a revolution took place . . . and Thirty were established as irresponsible rulers of all, of whom some were actually relatives of mine; and indeed they invited me at once to join their administration, thinking it would be congenial. The feelings I then experienced, owing to my youth, were in no way surprising: for I imagined that they would administer the State by leading it out of an unjust way of life, into a just way, and consequently I gave my mind to them very diligently to see what they would do.

The disillusionment is fearful and wonderful to behold. As Plato says, within a short time these men caused all to look back on the former government as a golden age. But the crucial point for Plato — and perhaps the only one which would have definitively turned him against his close relatives, whose upper-class opinions he shared — was that they treated his revered Socrates badly, trying to force him (although unsuccessfully) to act unjustly and thus share in their own iniquities. "So," says Plato, "seeing all this, I was indignant and withdrew." Soon afterward the Thirty were in turn overthrown and the moderate democracy restored. "Then once again," says Plato, "I was really, though less urgently, impelled with a desire to take part in public and political affairs." But again disillusionment ensued. One of the first acts of the restored democracy was to charge Socrates with impiety and corrupting the youth. And it thereupon condemned and executed the very man who, when the democratic leaders were in exile, had refused to proceed unjustly against one of their number. The irony was not lost on Plato, and the general political injustice and corruption, both upper class and lower class, both aristocratic and democratic, permanently affected his enthusiasm for a political career and sublimated his inherent political interest into a lifelong concern with theory and the philosophical establishment of the principles of the just society. What (if the seventh epistle is authentic) are presumably his own words are of the greatest interest.

When, therefore, I considered all this, and the type of men

who were administering the affairs of State, with their laws too
and their customs, the more I considered them and the more I
advanced in years myself, the more difficult appeared to me the
task of managing affairs of State rightly. For it was impossible
to take action without friends and trusted companions; and
these were not easy to find, *since our State was no longer managed according to the principles and institutions of our forefathers.* . . . Moreover, both the written laws and the customs
were being corrupted, and that with surprising rapidity. Consequently, although at first I was filled with an ardent desire
to engage in public affairs, I finally became dizzy; and although I continued to consider by what means some betterment
could be brought about, yet as regards political action I kept
constantly waiting for an opportune moment; until finally,
looking at all the States which now exist, I perceived that one
and all they are badly governed; for the state of their laws is
such as to be almost incurable without some enormous over-
hauling and good luck to boot. [Italics added]

Three things, I think, are worthy of note in the account of the
political disillusionment which epistle 7 details. In the first place,
Plato's repugnance for the Thirty and for the restored democracy
which followed, rests largely upon the way both treated Socrates.
Here is not only the fruit of personal admiration for an adored
teacher, but a lure away from the practical and toward the
philosophic life. Second is the clear evidence of aristocratic nostalgia — "since our State was no longer managed according to the
principles and institutions of our forefathers" — of that backward
looking to a set of prior values which is to make the Platonic
lifework into the instrument for an aristocratic restoration. And
third, there is the paradoxical consequence that although *both* a
corrupt aristocracy and a corrupt democracy are here the objects
of reproach, *only the latter* continues to be the lifelong target of
his political contempt.

This is indicated both theoretically and historically. In the
Republic is set forth as if in some mathematical demonstration "the
inevitableness of the degeneracy of the majority." It is unnecessary
to repeat the detailed presentation in book 8 of "democracy" and
"the democratic man." Democracy grows out of oligarchy by the
insatiable greed for wealth, and it eventuates in a state where such
negligence and encouragement of licentiousness obtain that civil
war breaks out, and the poor, winning the victory, initiate the
reign of a lawless equality. Absolute license holds sway; men

submit to rule or keep the peace only at will; there are no qualifications of excellence for the holding of public office; noble ideals are trampled underfoot, and anarchy sweeps all before it. And the characteristic type, the typical man produced by this madness of a false equality, is also licentious in his inner nature — subject to no rule of reason, teeming with appetites, and interested only in their satisfaction, with no concern at all about the true excellences of the soul and their proper nurture.

In the *Statesman* the strategy is even more shamefully biased, although the philosophic framework makes its own kind of aristocratic sense. Plato wishes to assert that there must be an intimate relationship between power and intellectual capacity, that "royal" power is itself one of the sciences — is indeed, as he puts it (292b), "a science of judgment and command." This is fundamentally to intellectualize politics, for the true king "is more akin to the intellectual than to the manual or the practical in general" (259d). And the net result is to effect the virtual identity of royal rulership and political wisdom. "Shall we, therefore, put all these together as one — the political art and the statesman, the royal art and the king?" "Obviously."

But the consequence of this identification of the political art with the intellect and its separation from "the manual and the practical" becomes all too plain when we come to the negative demonstration: to the identification of those classes whose position and functions completely disqualify them for statesmanship and should therefore cut them off from the exercise of political power. These are (1) slaves and servants in general, (2) those free men who hire themselves out in menial capacities, or who engage in any form of commercial transaction (such as brokers, masters of commercial ships, and peddlers), (3) hired workmen or laborers, and (4) "that troop of charlatans," the Sophists, who claim political wisdom and the ability to sell it to the unwary. It is clear that Plato's passion for excellence never deserts him, but it is equally clear that the prejudices of an Athenian aristocrat are no less ubiquitous.

Even where this prejudice is not expressed as an element of Platonic theory, it shines forth in the very characterizations and dramatic settings of the dialogues. It is no accident that Charmides, brother of Plato's mother and of noble birth, later to become ultraconservative and antidemocratic, is presented in the *Charmides* as a young man typifying that balance, self-discipline, and wholesomeness of mind which the Greeks called *sophrosyne* and we translate "temperance." On the other hand, Callicles appears in the *Gorgias* as not unintelligent, but self-assertive and "pushy" — a prime example of the ambitious man of inferior birth who advocates political opportunism, the unrestrained use of power, and in general that "going beyond the limit" which the *Charmides* protests. The contrast between the aristocratic Charmides, fountainhead of decency and moral virtue, and the commoner Callicles, opportunist, careerist and political immoralist, haunts Plato's social theory. For the presupposition is always that it is impossible to find political judgment or moral virtue in any person in a servile position. For Plato the relation between mental power, decency, and superior position within the social hierarchy seems to be intrinsic.

But this bias has even further ramifications. In the *Statesman* (as in the *Republic*) Plato recognizes that the rule of one and the rule of the few have both admirable and degenerate forms: monarchy can be either tyrannical or "truly royal" rule; government by the few can be either oligarchical or "truly aristocratic." But in the single case of rule by the many, issues of the distribution of wealth, or of violence or persuasion, or of a written constitution and careful observance of laws or their absence *make no difference*: as Plato disingenuously observes, in this one form "no one habitually changes the name." And the consequence is that for the rule by the multitude there is no truly admirable form as there is in the case of aristocracy and royalty. Why this should be so soon becomes apparent. The science of ruling men — the highest science and the most dificult to acquire — is one which is simply beyond the grasp of the multitude. This is the prerogative only of "the wise and kingly nature." "No great number of men, *whoever they may be*," says Plato (297c), "could ever acquire political science and be able to administer a state with wisdom, but our one right form of government must be sought in some small number or one person."

The State recommended in the *Laws*, the work of Plato's old age, is a moderate oligarchy, with the average citizen given but little freedom, except the freedom to obey. Plato's political idealism — his dream of what is politically both ideal and possible — has become progressively attenuated, and he depends heavily upon the explicitness of written laws and upon the supervisory functions of his Nocturnal Council of old men whose primary responsibility

is the strict preservation of the status quo. But with respect to his
major bias, nothing in Plato has changed. As the editor of the
Loeb edition of the *Laws* so rightly says: "The 'Athenian Stranger'
of the *Laws* is no less of an anti-democrat than the 'Socrates'
of the *Republic*: and his conviction of the natural perversity and
stupidity of the average man has increased with the passing of the
years."

Plato's persistent bias against democracy is not only expressed
theoretically in his chief political works, the *Republic*, the *Statesman*, and the *Laws*, but also makes its appearance in those bits of
social commentary, scattered throughout the dialogues, in which
the events of Athenian history are subjected to a political critique.
Two examples will serve. In the third book of the *Laws* Plato
constructs a historical survey of the origin and development of
civic communities in order to show how the extremes of liberty
and tyranny are both disastrous. He examines in turn the Doric
confederacy, the Persian empire, and the Athenian democracy.
His chief point is that there are two "mother-forms" of constitution from which all the rest are derived. Of these one is properly
termed monarchy and the other democracy, the extreme case of
the former being the Persian polity, and of the latter the Athenian. Plato's critique of historic Athens is also aristocratic and
reactionary. Its "present" shows a polity of "freedom unmixed and
in excess," without measure and without "reverence" (*aidos*). The
very old days were better, for the common people had no political
voice, but were voluntary slaves to the laws. But now all this has
been lost in a democratic frenzy.

> We ought to examine next, in like manner, the Attic polity,
> and show how complete liberty, unfettered by any authority, is
> vastly inferior to a moderate form of constitution under elected
> magistrates. At the time when the Persians made their on-
> slaught upon the Greeks, we Athenians had an ancient constitu-
> tion (the Solonian), and magistrates based on a fourfold grad-
> ing; and we had Reverence, which acted as a kind of queen,
> causing us to live as the willing slaves of the existing laws.
> [698b]

Corruption set in, Plato very quaintly says, when the arts became democratized, when music began to be considered as a thing
without intrinsic standards of correctness, of which the only criterion is the pleasure of the auditor. Then there arose "leaders of
unmusical illegality," poets who, "ignorant of what was just and

lawful in music," mixed dirges with hymns and paeans with dithyrambs, and in their frenzy to promote pleasure bred in the populace a spirit of lawlessness and the effrontery of supposing themselves capable of judgment. "In place of an aristocracy in music," says Plato, "there sprang up a kind of base theaterocracy." A conceit of universal wisdom and a contempt for law originated in the music, and on the heels of these came license, the absence of respect, and the withdrawal of submission to the rightful sources of authority: parents and elders, the laws, oaths, pledges, and divinities.

It is of course necessary to make allowances for the Platonic overemphasis upon the political and social efficacy of the arts, and for the backward looking tendencies of an elderly man, but the adverse judgment upon the Athenian democracy was abiding in Plato. He had also made it as a younger man—in the *Gorgias*. The *Gorgias* is roughly contemporary with the *Republic* and the founding of the Academy, probably written when Plato is around forty as an antidemocratic manifesto and a tacit explanation of why he is undertaking his new and revolutionary experiment in philosophic education. As the *Apology* supplied the meaning of the life of Socrates, so the *Gorgias*, through the mouth of Socrates, explains the rationale of Plato's own educational attempt, and especially why he has turned to it after abandoning the life of politics. It is to explain his purpose in founding the Academy that the critique of Athenian statesmen past and present is relevant, and that his harshness toward them becomes more than the mere ill nature of a man disappointed in his own political ambitions. As in his future *Laws* Plato is to censure the musicians because they humored the multitude instead of providing them with the music which would promote their virtue, so now in the *Gorgias* he censures the leaders of the great days of the Athenian democracy because they too have given the people great material rewards and advantages without at the same time training them in obedience, in temperance, and in justice. If the test of statesmanship is the making of good citizens, then the famous men of the fifth century—Cimon and Miltiades, Themistocles and Pericles—have failed to meet the test. And here, through the person of Socrates, Plato purposely libels the greatest statesman of the democratic golden age.

But tell me one thing in addition, Callicles, whether the Athen-

ians are said to have become better because of Pericles, or
quite the contrary, to have been corrupted by him. What I,
for my part, hear is that Pericles has made the Athenians idle,
cowardly, talkative, and avaricious, by starting the system of
public payment for jury duty. [515e]

And a moment later:

And you now, Callicles, you praise men who have regaled the
citizens with all the good things they desired. People do say that
they have made the city great; but that it is with the inflation of
a tumor, caused by these men of a former time, this they do
not perceive. For with no regard for temperance and justice
they have stuffed the city with harbors and arsenals and walls
and tribute and such trash: so that when the final reckoning
of weakness comes they will blame their advisors, but will praise
Themistocles and Cimon and Pericles who caused all the
trouble. [519a]

It is true that in Plato it is always difficult to distinguish true
history from philosophic theory. The theoretical account of the
degeneration of states in the *Republic* reeks of historicity and the
actualities of the Greek historical experience, whereas the pur-
ported historical account of the Greek commonwealth in the *Laws*
and the strictures against the actualities of the Periclean age in the
Gorgias are thoroughly infected with Platonic presuppositions
concerning the effectiveness of the arts in transforming character
and the power of the statesman to produce moral virtue. Yet this
too is but further evidence of "the unity of Plato's thought." If, as
I have suggested, Platonism is the characteristic consequence of
an aristocratic sensibility in an aristocratic age, then its antidemocratic vision of the world will express itself equally as historical critique and as assertion of ideal value, and the two will
mingle in one unified product of the aristocratic imagination.

The Academy

The more one considers the unitary message of the dialogues, and
the light it throws upon the character of Plato's lifework, the
more probable becomes the inference that the establishment of
the Academy was the crowning event of his total career and its
philosophical endeavors. And it can only be a probably inference,
since we have absolutely no firm evidence concerning the date of
its founding, its organization, course of studies, or pedagogical
methods. The seventh epistle does not mention the Academy, and

Diogenes Laërtius simply reports that after the death of Socrates and a subsequent visit which Plato, along with certain other Socratic disciples, made to Euclides of Megara, he proceeded on a series of travels: to Cyrene to visit Theodorus the mathematician, and to Italy to speak with the Pythagorean philosophers Philolaus and Eurytus. Upon his return to Athens, says Diogenes Laërtius, he lived in the Academy, which was a gymnasium outside the walls in a grove named after the hero Hecademus. And in reporting Plato's death he further notes: "He was buried in the Academy, where he spent the greatest part of his life in philosophical study. And hence the school which he founded was called the Academic school. And all the students there joined in the funeral procession."

It is generally supposed that the visits to Theodorus the mathematician at Cyrene and to the Pythagorean philosophers in Italy were preparatory to the founding of the Academy, but if so opinions continue to differ as to the basic model Plato followed — whether that of the pure mathematical research of Theodorus or the more comprehensive and life-engaged philosophizing of the Pythagoreans. A. E. Taylor espouses the first alternative. "The founding of the Academy," he says, "is the turning point in Plato's life, and in some ways the most memorable event in the history of Western European science. For Plato it meant that, after long waiting, he had found his true work in life. He was henceforth to be the first president of a permanent institution for the prosecution of science by original research."

But there is something intrinsically unpersuasive about the assumption that the chief purpose of the Platonic Academy was the furtherance of merely scientific study. The sharp separation of the intellectual and the moral virtues is an Aristotelian, not a Platonic, invention. And although it is true that in Plato *episteme* (knowledge) and *sophia* (wisdom) are always aristocratically separated from *cheirotechnike* (manual skill) and *praktike* (practical skill in general), it is equally true that their association with *phronesis* (intelligence in practical matters of action) is constant and close. Indeed, the basic educational message of the *Republic* is that mathematical knowledge is the chief road of access to "the good," and that dialectical inquiry into the "essence of reality" is propaedeutic to the legislative and administrative capabilities of the philosopher-kings. That holistic temper of mind which insists upon the role of pure intellect in practical judgment and sees no essential incompatibility, but rather an analogous performance, in the activities of the mathematician and the legislator must surely have framed the Academy after its basic intuition.

Anyone who takes the *Republic* and the seventh epistle seriously will see the Academy neither as the monument of an ambitious teacher nor as a fortuitous pedagogical enterprise, but as the specific consequence of Plato's political disillusionment and an attempt to personify his aristocratic counterclaim to the critique of the decadence of that democratic Athenian society which the dialogues present. It is the institutional embodiment of that little band of educated and educating men which the *Republic* portrays, and whose opposite the *Gorgias* and the *Euthydemus* satirically caricature. The condemnation of Socrates has proved once and for all that the truly good man and the philosophic life no longer have their rightful place in an Athens of lower-class citizens, ambitious and inflated politicians, conventional poets, opportunistic and commercially oriented Sophists and teachers. On the other hand, the early Socratic dialogues picture in imagination what it means to be one of a community of men who are "good," if for no other reason than that they are "engaged in seeking out the good," and who do so in the presence and under the guidance of a noble teacher who is an inspiration to all because of his own reverent loyalty to a sought-for truth. The Socratic "myth" which the earlier dialogues construct is *the myth of the existence of the dialectical community*, a myth no less outside time and space than the ideal city of the *Republic*. The essence of Plato's problem is this: how in a corrupt, commercial, and democratically minded Athens to service and retain the philosophic temper—in short, *how to re-create the dialectical community in actuality*. The founding of the Academy has this as its primary purpose.

This at least in part accounts for Taylor's opinion, and for the reputation the Academy later acquired as a scientific institution and as a gathering place for the greatest mathematicians of the Hellenic world. The concept of scientific research under the conditions of a common life has had an immense and continuous appeal to the Western mind. Plato has been celebrated as its originator and Aristotle as the agent of its consolidation, and the Academy and the Lyceum have been conceived thus as originating models of the technical institutes of the modern university. It is, of course, true that the mathematical contributions of the

Academy were enormous. Theaetetus (hero of the dialogue and actual member of Plato's Academy) practically invented solid geometry. Eudoxus originated the theory of proportion. Menaechmus is the discoverer of conic sections. The whole of book 13 of Euclid is, as Burnet says, in a preeminent sense the work of the Academy. And although this is a hotly disputed point there is some evidence that biological studies were also pursued within the Academy. Speusippus, Plato's nephew and successor as head of the Academy, wrote on the classification of plants and animals, and the biological works of Aristotle are commonly thought to have had their origins during his residence in the Academy. The fantasy of modern scholars (Burnet and others) also represents the Academy as well provided with scientific apparatus and natural history collections as well as a magnificent research library.

But, unless one completely disregards the evidence of epistle 7 and the *Laws* (which show that politics retains its lure for Plato even in old age), the thesis of an Academy which is merely a research institute for pure science seems like a nineteenth- or twentieth-century invention. It is true that every humanist has felt the magnetic attraction of political involvement as a fatefully ambiguous force. Petrarch and Dante, Montaigne and Erasmus, Goethe and Schiller, Burckhardt and Ranke have reacted in diametrically opposed fashions. The ballet of political advance and political withdrawal remains as a permanent dilemma for the intellectual life. Plato's political disillusionment is real enough, but that its response should have been a retreat into pure science squares neither with the autobiographical evidence, the later writings, nor the total thrust of the Platonic philosophy. The retreat— if retreat it can be called—was from the hope of a life as active politician to one as political theorist and teacher, as preparer for the ideal aristocratic world of the future, when intellectual capacity should be recognized as political qualification, when those who are right and true philosophers attain political supremacy, or, as the seventh epistle has it, when "the class of those who hold power in the State become, by some dispensation of Heaven, really philosophic."

Burnet's account, therefore (in *Greek Philosophy: Thales to Plato*), seems more plausible than Taylor's. The Academy was no doubt suggested by the schools of Euclides at Megara and Theodorus at Cyrene, and by the Pythagorean societies in southern Italy, but it is the last which provide the basic model. The Academy thus was probably organized as a quasi-religious guild. It had its deities among the Muses, its sacrifices at stated times, and its members for the most part lived a common life. It attracted a group of aristocratic young men from all over Greece who came to sit at the feet of Plato as they had been coming for some time previously to sit at the feet of Isocrates. Both Plato and Isocrates believed that the only hope for a corrupt Athens was intellectual enlightenment, and they were both committed to the restoration of monarchy or rule by the few. But whereas Isocrates was the heir of a rhetorical and, in some sense, a humanistic tradition, Plato saw mathematics and dialectic rather than literature and the speech arts as the key to political wisdom. There is little reason to doubt that the education prescribed in *Republic* 7 was central in the mind which conceived and founded the Academy, and that it had been formed under the influence of the Pythagorean conviction that philosophy means "science in the service of society," or "rational belief as the foundation of a way of life." Burnet has insisted that Plato regarded philosophy under two different aspects: as the spiritual conversion of a self, and as the service of mankind; and this is surely essentially Pythagorean, since the two aspects are not irreconcilably distinct, but rather form two branches of a single enduring impulse. Isocrates turned out rhetoricians, and rhetorically minded historians, whereas the Academy produced statesmen and men of science. But if a distinction is to be made, in an important sense the latter are rather a by-product and the former closest to Plato's motivational center. As Burnet says: "The Academy was first and foremost, then, an institution for training rulers and legislators, and it was extremely successful in its task."

This follows logically if the chief aim of Platonism is seen to be the effectuation of an aristocratic restoration. For here the details of the course of study presented in *Republic* 7 are no more crucial than the presuppositions of that course of study presented in *Republic* 6. For the Aristotle of the *Politics*, "the range of democracy is the range of the orator's voice"; but for Plato, and particularly the Plato of the *Republic* and the Academy, the range of aristocracy is not the roar of the public assembly, or even the wide compass of the circulated written word, but rather the narrow confines of the spoken word imparted to the little coterie of philosophic friends and disciples.

Why, when, I said, the multitude are seated together in
assemblies or in court-rooms or theaters or camps or any other
public gathering of a crowd, and with loud uproar censure
some of the things that are said and done and approve others,
both in excess, with full-throated clamor and clapping of
hands, and thereto the rocks and the regions round about re-
echo double the noise of the censure and the praise. In such
case how do you think the young man's heart, as the saying
goes, is moved within him? What private teaching do you think
will hold out against this rather than be swept away in the tor-
rent of censure or applause, and carried off in its current, so
that he will hold the same things as they do to be honorable
and base, and will do as they do, and be as they are? [429b]

But the danger is compounded when it is at once seen that to
assert that what the multitude likes is really good and honorable,
or that what it prizes is really valuable, is simply ridiculous. For
the many are drenched in sensation and a prey to the lure of particularity; they have no ability to generalize or to appreciate essences, and thus for them the true love of wisdom is impossible. Plato then offers gratuitous insult to the metics and citizen artisans.

Just as men escape from prison to take sanctuary in temples,
so these gentlemen joyously bound away from the mechanical
arts to philosophy, those that are most cunning in their little
craft. For in comparison with the other arts the prestige of philosophy even in her present low estate retains a superior dig-
nity; and this is the ambition and aspiration of that multitude
of pretenders unfit by nature, whose souls are bowed and mut-
ilated by their vulgar occupations even as their bodies are de-
formed by their arts and crafts. [495d]

The multitude are clearly unfit for culture, and when they approach philosophy, they consort with her unworthily, and the
ideas they conceive are Sophisms and impure, and have no affinity
with that which partakes of true intelligence. It would not be these
for whom the Academy was established, but rather for the "happy
few."

There is a very small remnant, then, Adeimantus, I said, of
those who consort worthily with philosophy, *those well-born and
well-bred natures*, it may be, held in check by exile, and so
in the absence of corruptors remaining true to philosophy as
its quality bids. [496b; italics added]

It is these who are the ideal members of the Platonic Academy, the remnants of the Socratic circle, that *jeunesse dorée* of Athens who have experienced the true pleasures of the search for wisdom and with the death of Socrates have seen the last hope for the achievement of the good life in the corrupted democratic city fade: "those who have been of this little company and have tasted the sweetness and blessedness of this possession *and who have also come to understand the madness of the multitude sufficiently and have seen that there is nothing sound or right in any present politics* [italics added]." In this passage from the *Republic*, Plato is, I think, addressing himself directly to a prophetic statement of the recruitment policy of the Academy which would require not only the philosophic and the theoretic appetite, but a clear willingness to hold aloof from the political arena, to go into social retreat with other companions who also seek a cloistered isolation out of the firm conviction that "no present government is suitable for philosophy, no contemporary polity worthy of the philosophic nature." From such passages we may well infer that the Academy, established in the very center of the Athenian city-state, is nonetheless a product of alienation and disgust.

The Academy was not only a course of studies (to some extent foreshadowed in *Republic* 7), but a retreat from the world of current Athenian politics, and this is directly related to the fate of Socrates. After Socrates' execution, Plato becomes the educator of Athens in his place, but purposely cuts off his school from the body of the *polis*. The death of Socrates created a permanent rift between the State and the Socratic disciples, and for Plato, his chief follower, whose instincts were Pythagorean in any case, there remained two basic tasks: to forge the Socratic myth and to create the Academy. They were parts of a single enterprise, for by the creation of the myth the community of Socratic memory becomes the cornerstone of Platonic education. The early Socratic dialogues: *Euthyphro, Laches, Apology, Crito, Phaedo,* and *Symposium* are devoted to this task.

This is not to say that the only function of the early dialogues is to create a personal mystique. The Socratic charisma is not only bound up with irony (*Protagoras*) and courage (*Apology*) and a temperate fortitude before hardship and wine (*Symposium*) and an insuperable honesty (*Crito*), but it personifies also the life of reason, the search for permanent and unambiguous meanings, and an attempted codification of values which are essentially aristocratic. And this is why Plato can afford to forget (as Nietzsche could not) that the Socratic background is artisan and far from highborn. For the Socratic investigation into truth is itself a principle of social selection, naturally and intrinsically aristocratic. The loving search for truth in a leisurely atmosphere where time and labor and economic necessity hardly count is the prerogative only of the favored few, and the rationality it presupposes (as the "natural light of reason" is to be for Descartes two thousand years later) is thus a socially favored and aristocratic trait. The function of the early dialogues is to show that the center of the Socratic teaching is no fixed body of principles, no dogma, but a magnetic personality whose lure is simply that of rationality itself. Pythagoras built his fellowship otherwise. But Plato, whose instincts were Pythagorean, yet utilizes the dynamic of Socratic memory to found a school where a distinct sense of serial curriculum can be used in producing true aristocratic leaders.

There is one area, however, in which the Socratic and the Pythagorean impulses are clearly cognate. Socrates was the son of a stonemason, himself began as one, and only continued by transferring his loving concern to human rather than inanimate materials. As a "sculptor of men," personality became the "matter" from which he drew out the forms of beauty and virtue implicit in its nature. And the Pythagorean "science" was also no merely theoretical construction, but the wisdom which might cause a man to regulate and change his life. That principle of harmony, measure, and congruence of the inner and the outer man which Socrates asserts at the end of the *Phaedrus* and in the fourth book of the *Republic* is Pythagorean through and through, and if the Academy draws upon both the Pythagorean science and its ethics of proportion, it is presumably not simply for the creation of the community of reason, but also for the transformation of souls who, in their conversion to the good, have felt the power of a common psychic impulse. It is for this reason that so much of the controversy of modern scholars over the pedagogical methods of the Academy and its precise curriculum seems formalistic and of minor relevance.

It is true, of course, that there are two serious problems here. The matter of a serial curriculum is of some importance if the purpose of the Academy is to be interpreted in terms drawn from the suggested education of the guardian class in *Republic* 7. For if

80 — CHAPTER TWO

the basic Platonic intention is to turn out ideal rulers—fit instruments of an aristocratic restoration— then the intimate relation suggested in the *Republic* between theoretical and practical wisdom links politics, mathematics, dialectic, and the theory of ideas in such a way that it had to be taken seriously within the Academy itself. That pure mathematics was a central presupposition of the Academy is clear from external evidence. But was dialectic its next step, and was it used by Plato to present the theory of ideas as absolute presupposition for all work within the Academy? Here the first unsettled question arises and controversy rages.

And this is closely related to the second problem. For if the Academy is indeed a "school" rather than a mere "research institute," its methods must have included those types of intimate communication which we know as small lectures and seminar presentations. What was the nature of the Platonic instruction? What doctrines were propounded? The same as in the written dialogues as we know them, or others more private, more hermetic, as would perhaps be fitting for the intimate communication of an elite philosophical fellowship? Aristotle's reference to Plato's "unwritten doctrines" (*agrapha dogmata*) only piques our curiosity and poses with renewed urgency the second problem— the relation of the teachings of the Academy to the published Platonic dialogues and the use for which the latter were intended by Plato himself.

The conventional position on the first problem is held by Burnet. "It is of the utmost importance to remember that Plato's real teaching was given in the Academy, and that even his later dialogues only contain what he thought fit to give to a wider public in order to define his attitude to other schools of philosophy." Although there is no direct evidence, we must suppose that Plato gave regular lectures in the Academy without notes, and that his hearers took down what they could. This, together with the setting of "scientific" problems and attention to their solution, was the method of instruction. The curriculum was the ascending serial progression we have learned to expect from the *Republic*: arithmetic, plane and solid geometry, astronomy, and harmonics, after which we come to the keystone of the entire edifice, dialectic—that science of question and answer which permits us to define terms, clarify minds, and finally discover the real truth about things, enabling us at last to ascend to that first principle which is no longer a postulate: the supreme Form of the Good.

But Cherniss, in *The Riddle of the Early Academy*, has taken great pains to deny this earlier account and to argue otherwise. He holds that although mathematics, the preliminary study in the *Republic*, was here the basis of the curriculum, the great mathematicians who joined the Academy and pursued their investigations in common were not themselves compelled to subscribe to any fixed metaphysical position. Indeed, he considers it very improbable that Plato gave any lectures on the theory of ideas or tried to "teach" it in any formal sense at all. Thus not only is formal instruction in the Academy confined to geometry, but Plato did not even present any natural philosophy beyond what he set down in the *Timaeus*, nor did he give to his students or associates any private exegesis of the doctrines which appear in his other dialogues. Even the question of his systematic lecturing within the Academy becomes a matter of extreme doubt.

Since "hard" evidence does not exist, I see no way of conclusively adjudicating between these contrary claims, although I have a great deal of sympathy for Sir David Ross's impatience with Cherniss as expressed in chapter 9 of his *Plato's Theory of Ideas*: "Is it likely, then, that Plato declined all conversation with the members of his school, in which he might have elucidated what he had written, and have expounded ideas which he had not yet committed, or was never to commit, to paper? It is really unthinkable." In one sense the issue really hinges upon the prior question of whether the Academy was primarily a school or a research institute, a fellowship to train aristocratic political leaders or an association of professional mathematicians; whether, as was previously suggested, the model of Theodorus or of the Pythagoreans was decisive. Burnet's account fits in best with the Pythagorean picture; Cherniss takes more seriously the tradition which considers the Academy an association of mathematical experts. Yet it is perhaps not necessary to decide exclusively between the two alternatives. Plato's Academy existed for forty years during his own lifetime, and over such an extended period it is no unusual thing for educational institutions to alter their organization and structure, to change their purposes, even to modify their original aims. I think that inferences from the dialogues and from the whole meaning of Plato's philosophical experience indicate unmistakably that the original Academy was a quasi-Pythagorean fellowship, and that its purpose was to train political leaders for the new aristocratic world of the future. But the central role of mathematics in that transformation not only made Plato hospitable to professional mathematicians, but in turn drew them to the peace and isolation of the Academic establishment. Plato may well have begun by lecturing, proceeding dialectically where possible, indeed attempting to institute the ideal curriculum the *Republic* details. But as the complexion of his professional associates slowly changed, it may have become increasingly clear that the intimacy between mathematical discipline and political wisdom which he had presupposed existed only in his own perceptions and not in those of his mathematical associates. Then the political and the mathematical interests may have slowly become two independent centers within the Academy (we know that it was celebrated among his contemporaries for its production of mathematics *and* legislators, or constitutional experts), and Plato's metaphysical demands may have relaxed as his role became increasingly less that of teacher and more that of chief administrator of a growing educational institution.

There is a famous metaphor in the *Statesman* in which Plato analogizes the kingly art of the statesman to "the royal art of weaving," where the test of success is the manner in which it combines the threads and the kind of web it produces. For the statesman too is a weaver of an integrated web of men, and the threads with which he has to work are the various human temperaments—the passionate who tend toward courage and the quieter who tend toward decorum.

> This, then, is the end, let us declare, of the web of the statesman's activity, the direct interweaving of the characters of restrained and courageous men, when the kingly science has drawn them together by friendship and community of sentiment into a common life, and having perfected the most glorious and best of all textures, clothes with it all the inhabitants of the state, both slaves and freemen, holds them together by this fabric, and omitting nothing which ought to belong to a happy state, rules and watches over them all. [311c]

I have often thought that this passage may well have unconsciously described the role Plato himself played within the later Academy, watching over and harmonizing that little band "drawn together by friendship and community of sentiment into a common life." And if the mathematically and the politically minded

(like the passionate and the mild) represent polarities of interest
within the Academy not immediately integrated and harmonious,
then Plato's direct interweaving of their concerns may have constituted an act of educational statesmanship, and the fulfillment
of a function within the Academy which he was never able to
achieve within the Athenian city-state—first forum of his political ambition.

The Platonic Writings

In the days of its founding the Academy must have had a specifically communal social structure, not secret like the Pythagorean
fellowship, but firm and "closed" nevertheless. Its appeal would
have consciously been to young men of noble houses and princely
future. It was an elite. Its ultimate purpose, at least in Plato's
mind, was surely the aristocratic reconstitution of the entire Greek
world, but for those who sought enlightenment within this *Gemeinschaft* of the mind, a more personal motivation was probably
paramount. As in the case of the Pythagorean communities, there
was a certain search for "salvation" within the Academy; but here
the agency of salvation is nothing so romantic as a sense of
identification with the cosmos or the unrestrained ecstasies of
religious feeling, but the more austere instrumentalities of mathematics and dialectic. The search for salvation within the Academy led toward the goals of intellectual comprehension and the
imposition of a sense of order. Plato was "an enthusiast of reason,"
and, like Anaxagoras in the previous generation, a believer in the
rulership of "mind" (*nous*). But he saw the growth of rationality
and the development of mentality as the outcome of a regimen of
intellectual (mathematical) discipline, and as a product of the
living interchange provided by the linguistic experience in the
community devoted to its exercise. This, on the most elementary
level, is the reason for his enduring espousal of dialectic.

The meaning of "dialectic" varies somewhat within the body of
the Platonic dialogues. It is presented as (1) a logic of discovery;
(2) an agent in the service of linguistic clarity; and (3) an instrument for the apprehension of ultimate reality. In the *Phaedrus*
and the *Sophist* it is defined as the dual process of collection and
division: "the bringing of a dispersed plurality under a single
form" and "the objective articulation of a concept whereby its
unity is broken up into its diverse component forms"—that is to
say, a simple logic of discrimination or, as the *Sophist* has it,

"dividing according to kinds." But these accounts are essentially logical and procedural. In the seventh book of the *Republic*, the *locus classicus*, a more elaborate and a more socially revealing account is presented. Dialectic "attempts through discourse of reason and apart from all perceptions of sense to find the way to the very essence of each thing, and does not stop until it apprehends by thought alone the intrinsic nature of the good" (532b). It is the systematic attempt to discover what things are. It is a method of inquiry that works from given propositions back to first principles. It is the art of viewing things in their interconnections. But with all its logical properties — its two-way movement of analysis and synthesis — its social and pedagogical form is a discipline in the asking and answering of questions.

The essence of "the dialectical method" (*he dialektike methodos*) as it is continually described, recommended, and exemplified in the dialogues, is that it applies to the structure of conversation, the procedure of social argument, and the art of conversing. From its first mention in the *Meno* (75d) to a last glancing reference in the *Laws* (965b) it never fails to elicit Plato's enthusiasm and approval. Useful in mathematics and linguistics as well as in psychology and rhetoric, its chief utility lies in its service to ethical knowledge and political conduct. Since Aristotle's separation of logic as an organon from metaphysics, physics, and the body of the sciences, since the Middle Ages when logic and dialectic were identified and treated as an instrument and a liberal art, method has been dissociated from content and activity, and it has therefore been possible to speak of "a philosophical method," abstracted from the *act* of philosophizing. But for Plato there is a sense in which dialectic is not a preparation for philosophy, but philosophizing itself. As Robinson pointed out in *Plato's Earlier Dialectic*, "the root figure in *methodos* is *odos*, the road or journey." An age which insists upon the technological distinction between means and ends will always be able to separate goals from instrumentalities, but for a more intuitive mind the journey and its quality are inseparable from its destination. Philosophizing for Plato is a speech act of reciprocal dimension; it implies a social duality, so that even when he deals with the moment of individual thought, he does so through an appropriation of the social model. Both the *Sophist* and the *Theaetetus* define the act of thinking or deliberation as "the dialogue which the individual soul holds with itself," and final judgment or decision as that moment when *the two voices* achieve unanimity.

Socr. And how do you accept my description of the process of thinking?
Theaet. How do you describe it?
Socr. As a discourse that the mind carries on with itself about any subject it is considering. You must take this explanation as coming from an ignoramus; but I have a notion that, when the mind is thinking, it is simply talking to itself, asking questions and answering them, and saying Yes or No. When it reaches a decision — which may come slowly or in a sudden rush — when doubt is over and the two voices affirm the same thing, then we call that its "judgment." So I should describe thinking as discourse, and judgment as a statement pronounced, not aloud to someone else, but silently to oneself.

If one asks why in Plato the supreme method and activity of philosophizing should consist in the social give and take of question and answer, no strictly logical answer can be given. To perceive the inherently oppositional, and therefore dramatic, element in the life of thought depends rather upon an original intuition than on an act of logical derivation. But in Plato's case the philosophic perception was assisted by the Greek sociological context. The classical Athenians were a loquacious people. Their *agora* was as much a forum for mere talk as a gallery of commercial transaction. They too, therefore, began with the acts of speech and from these derived the interior activities of mind. They regarded thinking as a social affair, and *thinking in common* as the root experience from which all other forms of thinking are derived. If we permitted ourselves a philosophical anachronism, we could imagine that they would have sympathized both with George Herbert Mead's doctrine of "the social genesis of the self" and with Wittgenstein's assertion of "the myth of pure privacy." And it is in this spirit that Plato's earlier and middle dialogues like the *Euthyphro* and the *Charmides,* the *Euthydemus* and the *Gorgias,* the *Protagoras* and the *Phaedrus* give such a striking picture — at once philosophical and social — of the most brilliant dialectician of the ancient world at work, and of the glint and sparkle of that social milieu within which his "conversations" are set.

Is it possible to think of the Academy without reference to those dialogues whose function is to explore in imagination the possibilities of the dialectical community? Or to doubt that the Academy itself was in part an attempt in some sense to create the dialectical community in a real social space? And if it is indeed true that Plato made no narrow metaphysical demands upon his associates in the later Academy, compelled no uniformity of philosophical interpretation, did not even himself lecture upon the theory of ideas, might this not too be due to his conviction (much like that of the later Wittgenstein) that procedure is more important than theory, the journey more revealing than the destination, and "dialectic" not a body of propositions to be learned but a mode of philosophizing inseparable from the qualities of the philosophic self? As mere doctrine, philosophy, like science, would have an independence and an objectivity which would cut it off from the demands of the intimate self; but as the very form of a mind thinking philosophically, as a mode of perception, as it were, it would (as in the case of Socrates) be expressive of personality in a fundamental way, and thus fulfill the Pythagorean demand that cognitive operations should mold character and determine style of life.

There are, of course, several difficulties in the way of this interpretation, and indeed of any theory which makes the dialectic central in the Platonic enterprise. One is the fact, remarked by all students of Plato, that the early and middle dialogues are the great exemplars of dialectical method, whereas in the later Plato, the method of question and answer either becomes purely artificial (as in the *Theaetetus, Sophist,* and *Statesman*) or is for all practical purposes abandoned in such dogmatic presentations of doctrine as the *Timaeus* and the *Laws.* Another is the intrinsic danger to which the dialectical method is subject. Since the time of Nietzsche's brilliant fragment *Homers Wettkampf,* cultural historians (beginning with Burckhardt) have come more and more to recognize the "agonal" character of Greek civilization; to see that the contest system, whether in poetic rivalry, athletic competition, dramatic contests, or warfare (the rivalry of heroes) is of its essence, and that this "thirst for preeminence" is itself an aristocratic characteristic. Any thrust of pure rationality, any attempt to achieve that consensus in which minds are coerced only by a universal and hence an "equal" reason, might be considered as an opposite counterweight, so that even the Platonic dialectic might be viewed as an unconscious attempt to rescue Greek thought from the tyranny of the contest system, at once its glory and its fate.

But a more Machiavellian mind might view the dialectic as itself a sublimation of the contest rather than its abandonment. Plato, who is obviously aware of the enormous energy inherent in conversational interchange, and of the threat to rationality in the competitive spirit, constantly tries to protect the dialectic against misuse. Dialectic is dangerous because it includes the method of *elenchus*, or refutation, and this can be used not philosophically but agonistically, not to uncover the truth but simply to win the argument. Platonic method requires a sharp distinction between the former, which is "dialectic," and the latter, which is mere "eristic." The *Euthydemus* is largely devoted to the unmasking of sophistry, which is not there taken to be the extreme relativism which is its definition in the *Theaetetus*, but rather that opportunistic temper of mind which will use any linguistic strategy to win the argument. The model of dialectic is the painstaking philosophic journey in search of the truth; that of eristic is the verbal duel to the death in the service of victory. And Plato's scorn and mistrust of the Sophists is based not merely upon their rootless claims as democratic educators, their emphasis upon the fee rather than upon the loving service of the true teacher, and their abject relativizing of all those moral and civic values which are anchored in the nature of man and thus eternal, but chiefly on their obsession with verbal victory, which he considers a criminal devaluation of the life of mind and a travesty upon the seriousness and responsibility of the true philosophical method of dialectic.

The importance of the dialectic in the total Platonic philosophy has particular relevance for the problem of the nature of the Academy, its procedures and teaching methods, and it raises with renewed urgency the question of the relationship between the lectures, discourses, dialogues, and conversations within the Academy to the written corpus of the Platonic dialogues as they have come down to us. For dialectic in the first instance is a species of oral discourse, and the Academy must originally have used all of the spontaneous and unrehearsed advantages of intense face-to-face interchange in creating and consolidating the dialectical community the Academy was intended to be. The written accounts of the Socratic dialectic comprising the early and middle dialogues must have been only a makeshift—a way of reaching a

wider audience to dramatize and portray a method of philosophizing through literature which in reality must be experienced in all
its oral immediacy. And here we find an explanation of that
somewhat puzzling and not completely consistent Platonic denigration of the philosophical efficacy of the written word. In the
Phaedrus (275c) Socrates is made to say: "Anyone who leaves
behind him a written manual, and likewise anyone who takes it
over from him on the supposition that such writing will provide
something reliable and permanent must be exceedingly simple-
minded." And he continues:

You know, Phaedrus, that's the strange thing about writing,
which makes it truly analogous to painting. The painter's products stand before us as though they were alive, but if you question them, they maintain a most majestic silence. It is the same
with written words; they seem to talk to you as though they
were intelligent, but if you ask them anything about what they
say, from a desire to be instructed, they go on telling you just
the same thing forever. And once a thing is put in writing,
the composition, whatever it may be, drifts all over the place,
getting into the hands not only of those who understand it, but
equally of those who have no business with it; it doesn't know
how to address the right people, and not address the wrong.
And when it is ill-treated and unfairly abused it always needs
its parent to come to its help, being unable to defend or help
itself.

The passage contains several interesting and characteristically
Platonic implications: the concept of "dead" (written) discourse
as an image or copy of "living speech"; an aristocratic bias lest the
work fall into ignorant or undeserving hands; perhaps even the
defensiveness of an explosive writer who wrote within a democratic
milieu, but in accents criticizing the heroes of democracy
(*Gorgias*), denigrating it on philosophic grounds (*Republic*), and
responding with an arrogant conservatism to all the freedoms it
espoused (*Laws*). But a moment later, in the contrast with another
"pastime"—one not indulged in literary gardens—Plato's chief
point becomes clear.

Far more excellent, I think is the serious treatment which em-
ploys the art of dialectic. The dialectician selects a soul of the
right type, and in it he plants and sows his words founded on
knowledge, words which can defend both themselves and him
who planted them, words which instead of remaining barren
contain a seed whence new words grow up in new characters,

whereby the seed is vouchsafed immortality, and its possessor the fullest measure of blessedness that man can attain unto.

The literary experience is both promiscuous and uncontrolled. It casts its bread upon an infinite and anonymous sea, and there can be no certainty of a proper reception and a fruitful outcome. But dialectic is personally directed and personally received. It involves not only a reference to mentality, but also to character. It thus has something in it of the dynamic of religious conversion, and its favored locale is neither the agora nor the wide forum of public discourse, but the intimate circle of the initiate, the quasi-Pythagorean fellowship—in short, the Academy.

The dispraise of the written word expressed in the *Phaedrus* is largely for the advancement of an oral dialectic, but the other basic references which express Plato's mistrust of the adequacy of language, and especially of the weakness inherent in the written word, occur in epistles 2 and 7. In the latter Plato denies that any of his works deal with ultimate metaphysical issues, since these do not admit of verbal expression, but "are brought to birth in the soul of a sudden, as light that is kindled by a leaping spark." Philosophical writing is not a blessing for men. The favored few discover for themselves with but little instruction; the rest, unable to understand, either scorn what they read or are filled with philosophical ambitions for which their limitations leave them unqualified. The words of epistle 2 are even clearer, but in the light of the dialogues, more puzzling.

Beware, however, lest these doctrines be ever divulged to uneducated people. For there are hardly any doctrines, I believe, which sound more absurd than these to the vulgar, or, on the other hand, more admirable and inspired to men of fine disposition. . . . So, bearing this in mind, have a care lest you should repent of what has now been divulged improperly. The greatest safeguard is to avoid writing and to learn by heart; for it is not possible that what is written down should not get divulged. For this reason, I myself have never yet written anything on these subjects, and no treatise by Plato exists or will exist, but those which now bear his name belong to a Socrates become young and fair. [314a-c]

It is extremely doubtful if this letter is by Plato, although it has been used as evidence to enforce the chasm between the real thought of Plato and the Socratic drama presented in the dialogues, and in support of the theory that the dialogues present

only a facade and the real Platonic philosophy is to be found in
these "unwritten doctrines" presented within the aristocratic privacy of the Academy. Neither claim seems to me supportable. In
the end Plato's dispraise of philosophical literature must be taken
simply as the superior faith in an oral dialectic and in the aristocratic mistrust of a philosophic message indiscriminately presented
to the many, not deliberately channeled to the few. After all,
another intellectual aristocrat, but of the modern world — T. S.
Eliot — has presented a similar doctrine of "the fit reader."

The riddle of the exact relationship of Plato's written works as
we know them to the Academy remains unsolved. Certain hypotheses are reasonable. Some works like the *Apology, Crito,
Phaedo*, and *Symposium* seem clearly meant for Athens. They are
full of literary charm and they consolidate the Socratic myth.
Others like the *Sophist, Timaeus,* and *Parmenides* contain technical doctrines; they are for the philosophically sophisticated.
Their use is either within the Academy or for a very restricted
circle outside. A few of the dialogues like the *Euthydemus* and the
Statesman seem to have a curiously double intention. The *Euthydemus*, on the one hand, is a public attack upon the Sophists, but
on the other hand it manages to present an extremely useful
catalog of sophistical fallacies — almost a prototype of Aristotle's
treatise of the same name — and it might well have been used as
such a manual in the Academy. And the *Statesman,* which in its
second half presents a political theory intermediate between the
Republic and the *Laws*, in its first half illustrates with tedious
exactitude the method of division for which the Academy was
famous. These are dialogues with a dual reference and a double
utility.

Plato's two book-length dialogues, the *Republic* and the *Laws*,
present difficulties of another kind. Although the latter indicates
just such a concern with the minutiae of exact legislative detail as
the constitution-constructing activities of the later Academy
would require, the former, as a synoptic philosophical work,
seems at once too popular in treatment and too early in time to be
a production for the use of the Academy. Yet both works would
have had certain disadvantages (perhaps even dangers) if published for the Athenian public. The aristocratic sympathies they
express and the conservative prejudices to which they appeal
would have made them unwelcome in the democratic city-state in
which the Academy was finally to exist, isolated and apart. There

is merit in Ryle's supposition in *Plato's Progress* that "Plato would have assembled his *Republic* and begun to rewrite his *Laws* for a very limited class of Greek individuals, namely for those who were at once cultured, comfortably off, conservative, leisured and studious." It seems reasonable to believe that the *Republic* was meant for some private circle of "conservative consumers," and that the *Laws* was intended for an audience which was both immune from democratic sympathies and, perhaps, no longer young. Ryle's thesis that there existed in Athens private social clubs of middle-aged or elderly and reliably conservative men (perhaps like the aged Cephalus himself) for whose eyes (or ears) alone these treatises were intended is possible, since Athenian political clubs seem to have been organized on a basis of equality in age and social standing. But both works are fairly elaborate to have been composed for so limited an audience, and little *within* either treatise suggests so drastic a restriction. More plausible, I think, is the supposition that the *Laws*, for all that it expressed the prejudices of a Plato grown old, was a useful codification for the Academy itself, and that the *Republic*, too radical perhaps for public presentation in Athens, was composed primarily for those more hospitably antidemocratic outposts of the Greek world.

Hierarchy and Permanence

Thus far we have examined the philosophy of Plato as the product of an aristocratic sensibility and temperament, and we have noted this predilection as it expressed itself in its most obvious and external directions: in a generally Greek drive toward excellence and preeminence, in a highly critical approach to the statesmen and the social conditions of Periclean and post-Periclean Athenian democracy, in the creation of a pervasive political theory critical of freedom, contemptuous and fearful of the many, and finding the proper rulership always in one or a very few, and, finally, in the foundation of the Academy — an educational institution dedicated to a general aristocratic restoration, an elite group recruited from "the rich, the well-born, and the able," an intimate coterie for whom the dialectic, itself a special technique for restricted, small-group, face-to-face education, is the approved and favored educational method.

These indications are conclusive, but they are external. For a philosophy which springs from and expresses a certain socially grounded and politically centered view of the world should also express in its inner nature the impulse which is its animating force. This, I think, the philosophy of Plato does. Plato's general insistence upon excellence and his unremitting distrust of the many receive support in his metaphysics from two principles which are aristocratic in the deepest and most essential sense: I would call them *the principle of hierarchy* and the *principle of permanence*.

Two major political passions dominate the course of Western history—the passion for freedom and the rage for order. The passion for freedom was the root impulse of the democratic revolutions which swept the eighteenth century; a rage for order was the root impulse of those aristocratic societies which dominated the West before this time. In one sense the French Revolution constitutes the great historical divide which exists not only in politics, but in the quieter areas of cultural life (like philosophy and literature) as well. Thus, whereas Shakespeare is essentially a dramatist of order, Schiller is in basic intention a dramatist of freedom. The democratic conception of freedom places great value upon "equality" and the possibility of a radical social alteration. For it, the structure of rulership is always contingent, and temporal change is the path to social good. But the aristocratic approach to the world insists upon the exact opposite. Adequately constituted and enduring rulership patterns are necessary and hierarchical. Value lies in conservation and in permanence. Time and historical transformation are the great metaphysical enemies of the aristocratic vision of the world.

That unified philosophy which is expressed in the Platonic dialogues is a reflection with infinite variations of the principle of hierarchy. The sociology comprehends a tripartite class division with the *archontes* at the apex, the *phylakes* (guardians) and *epikouroi* (auxilliaries) at the next remove, and the *demiourgoi* (laborers) at the lowest level. The division of labor is absolute, the separation of the classes complete. The rule of chaos and degeneration begins when the status lines are blurred, when the demarcations cease to be absolute and clear. The psychology comprehends a tripartite division in the individual soul, with rationality at the apex, passion at the next remove, and bodily appetite at the lowest level. Here too the divisions are absolute. As the just state is that in which the *archontes* rule, so the healthy soul is the one in which rationality is in control. The Platonic psychology, like the Platonic politics, expresses the principle of hierarchy. Its root metaphor is that of ruling or being ruled, dominating or being dominated, controlling or being controlled. The *Republic* is very explicit in this matter.

"But to produce health is to establish the elements in a body in the natural relation of dominating and being dominated by one another, while to cause disease is to bring it about that one rules or is ruled by the other contrary to nature." "Yes, that is so." "And is it not likewise the production of justice in the soul to establish its principles in the natural relation of controlling and being controlled by one another, while injustice is to cause the one to rule or be ruled by the other contrary to nature?" "Exactly so," he said. [444d]

The cosmology of the *Timaeus* is not as systematically articulated as are the sociology and psychology of the *Republic*, but it too expresses the principle of hierarchy and relates it to the principle of permanence. The universe also is a hierarchy, ruled or at least created, by God, the divine artificer, who, in imposing order upon the preexisting chaos, kept his gaze firmly fixed upon that which was uniform, eternal, and perfect. The created universe is itself generated, it has been created in time, but the pattern according to which it was created is eternal.

However let us return and inquire further concerning the Cosmos—after which of the Models did its Architect construct it? Was it after that which is self-identical and uniform, or after that which has come into existence? Now if so be that this Cosmos is beautiful and its Constructor good, it is plain that he fixed his gaze on the Eternal; but if otherwise (which is an impious supposition), his gaze was on that which has come into existence. But it is clear to everyone that his gaze was on the Eternal; for the Cosmos is the fairest of all that has come into existence, and He the best of all the Causes. So having in this wise come into existence, it has been constructed after the pattern of that which is apprehensible by reason and thought and is self-identical. [29a]

The *Republic* contains the most detailed exposition of the principle of hierarchy, and the *Timaeus* completes the presentation by a cosmic application which shows that the principle of permanence is its metaphysical correlate. Plato's metaphysics, like that of every essential idealism, links the notions of existence and of value, but the intermediate agent of this linkage is *the conservative notion of order*. Complete freedom is complete chaos, is complete disorder, is complete irrationality. And the good, the

eternal pattern of true being, is a paradigm of perfect rational
order. The *Timaeus* only makes explicit and gives cosmological
specificity to the central role of the theory of ideas in the Platonic
philosophy, for this entire metaphysical formulation is nothing
but an articulated expression of the principle of permanence.

Whether Plato was led to the theory of ideas through an examination of mathematical entities or devised it out of the need to fix
in universal form (and thus to save from ultimate relativization)
the individual instances of moral behavior is beside the point.
What is important is the centrality of the conception throughout
the Platonic philosophy. Cherniss, citing Friedländer, says it well:

> From among the earliest of the dialogues on through the last —
> and this means, then, to the very end of Plato's life — the doc-
> trine of ideas is the cornerstone of his thought. It is not dis-
> cussed at length in many; in some it is not even mentioned
> openly; but it is, to use the felicitous characterization of Profes-
> sor Friedländer, the center of gravity of all the Platonic writings.

It is the center of gravity of Platonism because the basic problem of an aristocratic vision of the world is the ultimate struggle
against temporality and against change. The theory of ideas is a
classic weapon in this eternal struggle. For it is the product of an
act of pure supposition — that behind the phenomenal world
which is temporal and in perpetual process lies a world of ideal
forms, a system of necessary relations, patterns fixed in the nature
of things which are eternal, not subject to the ravages of time;
unchanging, ungenerated, and indestructible. Here is the final
enthronement of the principle of permanence, which, by a brilliant twist of the metaphysical imagination (or by an act of blind
faith), has been given an extraterritorial and honored place for
which nothing in the shift and flow of ordinary human experience
has qualified it. And we are here far from a merely conceptualistic
account of the artifice by which the mind fixes the elements of
experience in logical constructs — pure *entia rationis*. The Platonic ideas are *real*, they are eternal *objects*, and they lie back of and
give the empirical world a significance which is not apparent in its
merely temporal structure.

It is now clear why, in Plato's opinion, the agents of an aristocratic restoration must undergo what is essentially a religious
conversion, and why they must in addition be naturally endowed
with what might well be called *the appetite for transcendence*. If

the higher education of the Guardian class outlined in the *Republic* is any clue to the course of study followed in the Academy, then it is clear that the entire program is based on the principle that education is at bottom nothing but the conversion of the soul from its blind immersion in temporal change to a contemplation of the patterns of permanence. This is the process by which philosophers are made, and it is why in the end the aristocratic vision of the world cannot be realized until philosophers are kings.

The beginning of book 6 of the *Republic* informs us that "the philosophers are those who are capable of apprehending that which is eternal and unchanging, while those who are incapable of this, but lose themselves and wander amid the multiplicities of multifarious things are not philosophers," and that it is the "trait of the philosophical nature, that it is ever enamored of the kind of knowledge which reveals to them something of that essence which is eternal, and is not wandering between the two poles of generation and decay." And the *Philebus* in final summation speaks of "the art of dialectic" as "the knowledge which has to do with being, reality, and eternal immutability" (58a). *Eternal immutability* is the dream of an aristocratic politics which analogizes the social order to fixity in the physical cosmos and which sees in the operations of generation and decay that fall from grace which has its counterpart in the ugliness of social revolution.

Conclusion

The philosophy of Plato may be generally interpreted in at least three different ways: (1) as a new quest for social power, (2) as a turning point in the evolution of Greek culture, or (3) as the symbol of a new social situation for philosophy in the ancient world.

As a new quest for social power, the perspective from which Platonism must be viewed is its claim to be the only authentic educational agency in the Greek world, since only it provided an education oriented toward the truth. From this point of view the attempt to satisfy social needs is underwritten by alternative social claims, and the education in values becomes a highly competitive occupation within the social fabric. The foundation of the Platonic Academy thus becomes the only aristocratic alternative to those conventional agents of Athenian democratic education: the poets, the rhetoricians, and the Sophists. Plato's continuous quarrel with

an education through poetry hinges on both ethical and metaphysical considerations. Its imaginative stories (as in Homer, for
example) are frequently immoral in their portrayal of the holders
of divine power, and their representations as pictorial images lie
three removes from the metaphysical truth. His strictures against
the rhetoricians (Gorgias, and through him certainly Isocrates)
are based upon the falseness of their claims to influence for the
better the democratic outcome of forensic and political debate.
They are too intent on popularity and success to be concerned
with virtue. And the attack upon the Sophists also castigates an
opportunism which cannot distinguish between dialectic and eristic, and which therefore continuously descends to verbal trickery
to conquer in every linguistic encounter. The battle against the
Sophists and the rhetoricians shows Plato intent upon possessing a
social power based upon a special claim of access to the truth, and
it likewise paints the portrait of a curiously rhetorical age, one in
which the spoken word defines the area of political power and
social influence.

   Eric Havelock, on the contrary, views the Platonic moment as
the turning point in the evolution of Greek culture in a twofold
sense, intimately related both to the attack upon the poets and to
the espousal of the special method of an abstract dialectic. In
Havelock's opinion the Platonic moment marks the transition
from a sensate to an ideational method which itself testifies to the
transformation of Greek culture from an "oral" to an essentially
"literate" civilization. If Homer represents one pole of Greek mentality and Plato another, then the essential naïveté and freshness
of the earlier stage is based upon an oral tradition in poetry in
which experience is rendered in concrete images, whereas the
philosophical sophistication of the latter depends precisely upon
an art of the written dialogue and upon a dialectical method
which seeks abstract essences and cognitive universals as it den-
igrates the image and its painterly particularity. From this point
of view, Plato's attacks upon poetry in books 2 and 10 of the
Republic are not afterthoughts or fortuitous insertions; they are
as important and as seriously meant as any doctrines to be found
in that great work, since for Plato the poetic experience as such
constituted a kind of psychic poison.

   Poetry as an educational experience poses at once a moral and
an intellectual danger. It is confusing to the consciousness of value,
and it robs men of insight into the truth. Despite the dramatic

flair and the brilliance of poetic imagination displayed in the Platonic dialogues, it is, paradoxically, just the dramatic experience and the imaginative act toward which Plato directs an unremitting hostility. For Platonism as *a revolution in favor of the abstract* (symbolized in metaphysics by the theory of ideas and in pedagogy by the dialectic, which is its educational correlative) poses the insistent demand that we think in terms of abstract classes rather than concrete individuals, and that the symbolic system we utilize should, like mathematics itself, stress a logic of relations which lie outside time rather than an organization of objects in all their temporal and qualitative immediacy. In short, even if the Academy was not an institution of pure research, Platonism is, as Whitehead insisted, the passport into the age of modern science. The evolution from Homer to Plato represents the passage "from the image-world of the epic to the abstract world of scientific description, and from the vocabulary and syntax of narrated events in time towards the syntax and vocabulary of equations and laws and formulas and topics which are outside time."

Havelock is certainly right that an important element in Platonism is to substitute a conceptual discourse for an imagistic one, and indeed also that the new definition he provides of the philosopher turns him into the member of a natural elite graced with a genius for the abstract. But his analysis is deficient and forgetful in two important respects. In the first place, if the Platonic dialogues are indeed "written" discourse, the living dialectic which they and Plato recommend is still an "oral" discipline and must have been so practiced in the Academy. Plato's profound mistrust of the written word fits poorly with a theory which sees him as a sharp break with the oral tradition. And second, Havelock's assumption seems to be that if poetry were to cease to be the chief vehicle of Greek education, what would become of the heroic and the aristocratic tradition and its values, "expressible as they were solely in poetry"? This is surely wrong. For it is just the "heroic" emphasis upon preeminence and excellence, the essence of the aristocratic tradition, which it is Plato's lifework to restore. He only saw, I think, that the survival of the Homeric poems in a democratic Periclean milieu meant the preservation of the decorative shell of the aristocratic tradition and not its moral kernel. His turn toward the abstract was precisely to establish a metaphysical validation for the aristocratic values where the poetic justification had obviously failed.

The philosophy of Plato can also be interpreted as symbolic of a new social situation of philosophy in the ancient world. With perhaps the exception of the Pythagoreans, all of Plato's predecessors (the Ionians, Parmenides, Anaxagoras, the Eleatics) were citizens of the Greek city-states, participating members of a local community. Only the Sophists are revolutionary in this respect. Rootless, restless, skeptical, they are forever "visiting intellectuals," and if Athens was temporarily hospitable to them, as to all new ideas—as are the cosmopolitan cities of Paris, Munich, or Vienna in our own time—there grew up nevertheless a sharp tension between them and the old landed aristocracy, particularly since the Sophists set themselves up as instructors of the young. The Sophists also ushered in a new age of "rational discourse." Hitherto the philosophers and the poets—semimythological and hieratic figures—had "proclaimed and asserted." The Sophists now attempted "to prove and persuade." An aristocratic culture does not need the guaranteeing instrumentalities of intellect; the self-evidence of hallowed tradition is proof enough.

Socrates set up his opposition to the Sophists not merely because they were "professionals" devoted to the fee, whereas he was a teacher out of love and inner necessity, but also because, whereas he stimulated a continuing community of truth-seekers, the Sophists were generally under short-term contract to impart a determinate and limited skill. But Socrates was in a paradoxically intermediate situation. Devoted to the excellences of mind and to the brilliant play of intellect, as were the Sophists, he was at the same time, like the aristocrats of tradition, *anchored* in his native community of Athens. The point is expressly made by Plato: except for the campaigns of military service he never left the *polis*. But in his double role as critical dialectician and Athenian patriot lie the seeds of Socrates' tragic destruction. Persecuted as a Sophist, he had not the Sophist's easy option for flight. (The *Crito* indicates the choice: death, or a rootless Sophist's life. The Athenian patriot chose death.) There is something in Socrates' situation two thousand years ago not unlike that of the poet Boris Pasternak in contemporary Russia. Both are critics of their native land to which they totally belong, and to both the life of exile is intolerable. Socrates' case was perhaps the more tragic, since with his love for, and inseparability from, his native land he had to die.

The Socratic lesson was not lost upon Plato, and one should not underestimate the step toward isolation from the *polis* which the founding of the Academy effects. It was Nietzsche, I think, who pointed out that after Plato, all the great philosophers of Greece were makers of schoools and founders of sects, separated from civic involvement. The Academy too was determinedly cosmopolitan rather than local. One did not have to be an Athenian to enter. Only nobility and authenticity of spirit were entrance requirements, and young aristocrats came to its door from the farthest reaches of the Hellenic world. This too set a new pattern for philosophizing and the philosophic life.

The ancient philosophers like Heraclitus and Parmenides had sought through metaphysical knowledge the healing purification of the social whole. At first Plato sought it too, but in the end his Academy came to spread a different message — that salvation is only for individuals, or for close-living groups of like-minded young men and friends. Socrates, like the ancients, had sought to instruct Athens as a whole, since he was essentially an Athenian patriot who honored the gods of Athens, and scorned the consolations of an individualistic metaphysics. But Plato separated himself spiritually from his native city, and it was his purpose to teach and to realize quite another social ideal within his academic community. Socrates, rooted in the daily realities of Athens, needed no codified metaphysics and no specific political doctrine. Plato, politically isolated and therefore less secure, was devoted to a metaphysics of the permanent and the eternal and, as if in opposition to the chaotic politics of everyday life, created the utopia of "the ideal city" — also timeless, eternal, untouched by the dirt and suffering of everyday reality.

The older philosophers of Greece protected and defended the homeland. After Plato philosophers were in exile and conspired against it. As a Socratic remnant and a born aristocrat, Plato was hostile to the Athenian democracy. But his disenchantment set a moving pattern for the future. He therefore was the boundary — the limiting figure — between the old organic role of philosophy in the age of Heracleitus and Parmenides and the new alienation which was to be reflected in the rise of the salvation sects and the coming atomization of the Hellenistic world.

Saint Thomas Aquinas. Detail of the painting *Christian Learning* by Andrea da Firenza in the Spanish Chapel of Santa Maria Novella, Florence.

3 MEDIEVAL PHILOSOPHY
The Age of the Saint
Aquinas

The Organic Society

With the possible exception of religious seminaries and the more extreme forms of socialist regimentation, philosophy in the modern world performs its functions theoretically exempt from religious determination and institutional pressure. Here too, modern individualism and the conception of civil liberty have had their effect upon the spiritual life. Philosophic problems are conceived as *personal* problems, the urge to philosophize is visualized as an individual "problematic situation" (as with Peirce and Dewey) or as a personal "torment" (as with Wittgenstein), and the ideas which are their outcome are considered to be the exclusive possession or private property of their discoverers, protected by copyright, first enunciation, and the right of eminent domain.

It is true that there is always a climate of opinion, a style of philosophizing dominant at a particular moment, even a seeming university monopoly of the rights of entry into the philosophic profession. But alternatives are possible, pluralism within the intellectual life is a ruling presupposition, and philosophic idiosyncrasy is at least permitted within a social situation chaotically open and unrestricted.

A return to the ambience of the medieval world is thus always slightly surprising and unreal. For to reconstruct a milieu of dialectical seriousness and hot disputation at the same time accompanied by institutional submission and the universal acknowledgment of the veracity of a single organic world view is to recognize institutional and religious claims which are at once massive, powerful, and unfamiliar. Thus in the twelfth century Saint Bernard, abbot of Clairvaux, not only criticized the abuses

English passages from the works of Saint Thomas follow the English Dominican Fathers for the *Summa theologica,* the Rickaby translation of the *Contra gentiles,* and the Mulligan translation of the *Disputed Questions on Truth.* The sermons appear in the Everyman edition edited by Father D'Arcy. For the translation of historical documents I am most indebted to Father Chenu's book *Toward Understanding St. Thomas* and to Vernon J. Bourke's *Aquinas' Search for Wisdom.* To Professor Bourke in particular I owe an enormous debt which I gratefully acknowledge. Other works used are listed in the Bibliography.

of the pontifical court and those monastery churches decorated
with useless luxury, but he dared to correct the teachings of the
most renowned professors of philosophy of the age—Abelard and
Gilbert de La Porrée—and to summon them to ecclesiastical
councils to rebuke their independence.

To our own age, dedicated to personal freedom of thought and
to the conception of philosophical ideas as private property, this
presumption of Saint Bernard is scandalous, but it is in perfect
accordance with the presuppositions of the age in which he lived.
Since the advent of Kierkegaard and Nietzsche and the flowering
of European existentialism, we have grown accustomed to finding
every philosophy branded with the benchmark of its maker, intensely personal in its style, idiom, and resolution of problems.
And this only reflects one consequence of the rise of a relativistic
theory of truth in philosophy, as the faith in an ultimately absolute truth to be slowly approximated has been surrendered to
science. But the twelfth and thirteenth centuries thought otherwise. Philosophic truth for them was a massive structure, built up
gradually over time, like a cathedral—the work being necessarily
cooperative and reflecting the continuity of the generations as
each contributor labored impersonally to add his increment of
knowledge to the common patrimony. In his commentary on
Aristotle's *Metaphysics* Saint Thomas wrote: "That which a single
man can bring, through his work and his genius, to the promotion
of truth is little in comparison with the total of knowledge. However, from all these elements, selected and co-ordinated and
brought together, there arises a marvelous thing, as is shown by
the various departments of learning, which by the work and
sagacity of many have come to a wonderful augmentation."

But if the assemblage of truths is a cooperative structure, a
common dwelling rather than a series of houses each with its own
architect and fence, then the selection and coordination and
bringing together is an act of some importance. Error, assym-
metry, or individualistic distortion cannot be tolerated if the
building of the edifice of truth is to continue firmly and the
product is to endure. And in the Middle Ages the authority of the
apostolic church provided the master plan for the acts of consolidation, coordination, and assemblage. This master plan outranks
the contribution of any single philosopher, theologian, or seer, so
that even in an age dominated by a respect for learned authority,
that authority is conceived as stemming from the institutionalized

church itself. No philosopher was more considerate of the procedures of documentation than was Saint Thomas, no medieval
professor was more assiduous than he in collecting and citing texts
which should relate his own work to tradition and the medieval
cultural context; yet he too perceived that the seat of all authority
lies ultimately with the Church. "The custom of the Church," he
said, "has the greatest authority and it is always to be emulated in
all matters. Now, since the very teaching of Catholic Doctors
receives its authority from the Church, one should rely on the
authority of the Church rather than on the authority of Augustine
or Jerome, or any Doctor." This from the philosopher who in the
first twelve questions of the *Summa theologica* refers to other
authors 160 times: 55 times to Aristotle, and 44 to Saint Augustine!

But the intellectual authority of the Church is itself only the
consequence of a congeries of social conditions, all contributing to
the formation and sovereignty of an organic Christian society. The
Catholic Church, for example, was intimately connected with the
feudal system, both through her bishops, who were at once lords
temporal and spiritual, and more particularly through the abbots
of her monasteries. Cluny and Citeaux, the two great branches of
the Benedictine stem, were founded by feudal lords, and their
institution was almost entirely the work of the baronial class. But
the monks of Cluny not only began a great work of restoration — of
religious zeal, monastic discipline, and popular faith — they also
effected far-reaching reforms in the federation of the monastic
system. Up to this time the Benedictine monasteries had been
independent, but Cluny organized these groups and placed them
under the head of its own centralized regime. From the twelfth century onward, all of Western Christianity was enmeshed in a great
network of monastic institutions of which Cluny was the soul and
inspiration. One mind and one polity permeated the entire system. In this process of federalization, as De Wulf said (in his
Philosophy and Civilization in the Middle Ages), "the abbey of
Cluny was successfully modelled after the feudal system; but it
then in turn proceeded to impregnate that same feudalism with
its own spirit. Thus, the feudal conception appears in the vow of
devotion which attached a monk to his monastery as a vassal to his
lord, and which he might not break without his superior's con-
sent; in the sovereignty of the abbot; in his visits as chief to his
subordinates; in the contributions of the affiliated monasteries to

the mother-house; and in the graded series of federated groups."
The influence was therefore reciprocal. First feudalism provided
the organizational model for medieval monasticism, but then in
turn Cluny and her offshoots Christianized feudalism.

Catholicism leaves its mark on the whole of medieval civilization. "Far from being an anachronism," De Wulf says, "this
remarkable fact of universal agreement in the West satisfies the
profound aspirations of the time. For, there was one system of
education for princes, lords and clerks; one sacred and learned
language, the Latin; one code of morals; one ritual; one hierarchy, the Church; one faith and one common western interest
against heathendom and against Islam; one community of the
saints; and also one system of feudal habits for the whole West."
Just, therefore, as there is a reciprocity between monasticism and
feudalism, so there is an unbreakable bond between the Christian
church and the dominant philosophy of the age. It is mediated by
the chief agency of higher education — the medieval university —
and by the ideal of the saint which is its quaint but unmistakable
dynamic force.

The bond between philosophy and the religious medium was
both ideological and, more formally, a matter of institutional
structure. There is a perfect harmony between Scholastic philosophy and medieval civilization, both because philosophy is for the
most part a preparation for theological studies and because the
teaching of the liberal arts, originally confined to the cathedral
schools, is seen as having essential ecclesiastical relevance. The
University of Paris, center and fountainhead of the Scholastic
philosophy, itself issued from the monastic schools of Notre Dame
and had only clerics among its professors; and these professors,
among them Albertus Magnus, Saint Thomas Aquinas, and Saint
Bonaventura, had the closest of personal relations not only with
the chancellor of Notre Dame, but with the papacy. It was at the
instigation of the higher church authorities that in 1248 Albertus
Magnus left the University of Paris to found a Dominican *studium
generale* at Cologne. Saint Bonaventura's leadership of the Franciscan order was on the direct recommendation of the pope. The
sermon "On the Body of the Lord" was preached at Orvieto by
Saint Thomas Aquinas on Thursday of Holy Week 1262 in the
presence of Urban IV and the college of Cardinals, and it was at

the bidding of the former that the already famous philosopher and theologian composed the liturgical offices for the Feast of Corpus Christi. In the thirteenth century, philosophical preeminence and the performance of ecclesiastical tasks were inseparably conjoined.

The great philosophical flowering of the thirteenth century was prepared for by the hundred years which came before. All over France philosophical life stirred and developed—in the many independent schools which grew up within the confines of the abbeys and cathedrals—Cluny and Citeaux, Bec and Aurillac, Tours and Laon, Chartres and Paris. Each school attempted to outrival the others in the compass of its library, the renown of its professors, and the drama of the dialectical contests in which they engaged. It was an age of feverish intellectual activity and brilliant teachers—Anselm of Laon, Theodoric of Chartres, Adelard of Bath, Hugo of Saint Victor, William of Champeaux, Gilbert de La Porrée, and above all the great Abelard—fiery, proud, intemperate, indescribably brilliant—who traveled endlessly, spreading his dialectical influence from Melun to Corbeil, from Corbeil to Saint Geneviève in Paris, and from Paris to his own private school at the Paraclete.

The life of Abelard illustrates at least three aspects of the intellectual situation in the twelfth century: the strong sense of interrelationship among its learned elements, the jealous supervision and control exercised by ecclesiastical authority, and finally the new cosmopolitanism which (in contrast to the localism of the French provinces) turned the city of Paris into the intellectual center of the medieval world. Born in 1079, Abelard began his studies with the distinguished logician Roscelinus, leaving only to attend the Paris lectures of William of Champeaux. Founding his own school at Melun in 1104, he returned once again to Paris to attend William's lectures on rhetoric, remaining only long enough to compel the latter (in the course of a painful dialectical encounter) to abandon his ultrarealist view of universals. Later he studied theology under Anselm of Laon, and John of Salisbury was one of his pupils at Mont Saint Geneviève in 1136. Thus, entering his dialectical career under the opposite influences of an extreme nominalist and an extreme realist, and falling under the influence of a great theologian, he in turn transmuted the dialectical legacy into the channels of humanism and the liberal arts, which were to gain great influence and recognition through his famous pupil John of Salisbury.

But throughout this brilliant academic career, Abelard's relations with ecclesiastical authority were never easy. His first theological work, *De unitate et trinitate divina* was condemned by the Council of Soissons in 1121. Condemned again twenty years later by the Council of Sens under pressure of Bernard of Clairvaux, on 21 July 1140 he was excommunicated by Innocent II. On his way to Rome to plead his cause in person, he rested at last with Peter the Venerable, Abbot of Cluny. He never went farther, and his last days were spent in Chalons-sur-Saône in reading, meditation, and prayer.

Of all the tokens of medievalism, none has so fired the imagination of subsequent generations as the life of Abelard. But it was also a source of fierce and awful interest to the imagination of his contemporaries. The acuity of his dialectical powers was legendary, and students from all over Europe flocked to his classroom to learn his secret and to witness the dramatic spectacle of his pitiless intellect at work. Not only John of Salisbury, but many others — from England, Italy, and Germany alike — were attracted by a reputation which dominated the intellectual life of the twelfth century, and from that time on Paris was the center of wandering scholars and the chief lure of scholarly promise for decades to come. Abelard lived two generations before the founding of the University of Paris, but Hastings Rashdall (in his great *The Universities of Europe in the Middle Ages*) associates him indissolubly with Paris and sees him as the spiritual father of the university movement of the future. "The stream of pilgrim scholars which set in towards Paris in the days of Abelard flowed continuously for at least a century and a half. From the days of Abelard Paris was as decidedly the center of European thought and culture as Athens in the days of Pericles, or Florence in the days of Lorenzo de Medici." Abelard, he holds, is the true founder of Scholastic theology — the man who inaugurated the intellectual movement out of which the universities sprang. The method of inquiry and of teaching of which he was the originator (the oppositional method illustrated in his *Sic et non* and the relentless dialectic with which he confronted William of Champeaux) was the method which finally prevailed in the medieval university system — fruit of his specific genius and of the cathedral school which provided the first environment for its rigorous exercise. "The University," says Rashdall, "was an outgrowth of the Cathedral School at Paris, the transference of educational activity from the monks to the secular clergy. In this sense we shall be right in finding the cradle of the University in the school of William of Champeaux, the first known master of the cathedral school. But it was the teaching of William's great pupil Abelard that first attracted students from all parts of Europe and laid the foundation of that unique prestige which the schools of Paris retained throughout the medieval period.".

The cosmopolitan influences which Abelard set in motion mark the transitional link between the twelfth and thirteenth centuries, and they are augmented by another factor which is crucial to understanding Scholasticism and the philosophy of Saint Thomas — the rise of the two new religious orders, the Dominicans and the Franciscans, and their incorporation into the structure of the University of Paris.

By this time the Benedictine monasteries — and with them Cluny and Citeaux — had begun to decline, largely through their very wealth and prosperity, which weakened their religious passion and the austerity of their life. The two new orders founded by Dominic and Saint Francis, the "mendicant" orders, were based on the principle of evangelical poverty. Their avowed purpose was to preach to the common people, and to participate more actively in the public and social life of the times. From the beginning they possessed two special characteristics. As teaching orders they fostered learning among their members, and they soon became the intellectual elite of the medieval world, seed ground for the philosophical and theological movements which were to dominate the thirteenth century. Second, whereas the Benedictines and the Carthusians had settled in the country and profoundly influenced the early feudalism which was itself essentially an institution of rural life, the Franciscans and Dominicans established themselves in the towns, thus illustrating once again that profound relationship between intellect and culture and city life which Simmel pointed out and which, as Rashdall intimated, characterized medieval Paris no less than ancient Athens and Renaissance Florence.

Established in Paris before 1220, the Franciscans and the Dom-

inicans created at this youthful university center separate estab-
lishments of advanced studies—*studia generalia*—for their own
members. But at the same time their intellectual preeminence
suggested their availability for chairs in the faculty of theology of
the university itself. Ten years later (by 1231) the Dominicans had
secured two of these professorships and the Franciscans one, and
the subsequent history of philosophy in the thirteenth century is
largely bound up with the creations of the men who occupied
these chairs: Alexander of Hales, Albert the Great, Saint Bonaventura, and Saint Thomas Aquinas.

The rise of the University of Paris as *the* medieval center of
learning, and the growth of the two mendicant orders which were
to supply it with professors, are only two of the causes which
cooperated to service philosophy in the thirteenth century. The
third is the new availability of philosophical texts, particularly
those of Aristotle, and of the vast commentaries upon them made
by the Arabs of Baghdad and Spain, as well as the large collection
of original Arabic and Jewish works in epistemology, metaphysics,
and ethics stemming from al-Farabi, ibn-Gabirol, Avicenna, and
Averroës. The work of translation begun almost two hundred
years before in the centers of Baghdad and Byzantium, Palermo
and Toledo, now reached the point of completion and dissemina-
tion in the West, so that Islam, Judaism, and Christianity now
formed practically one philosophical reservoir of a learned cosmopolitan culture, and the masters of Paris began to quote the
Islamic sources almost as lessons learned by heart. Albertus Magnus in his *De intellectu et intelligibili* appeals to Averroës almost
as frequently as to Aristotle, and in the pages of Saint Thomas
Aquinas's *Disputed Questions on Truth* one is almost as accustomed to meeting the name of Avicenna as that of Augustine!

Despite the incorporation of Jewish and Islamic elements into
the Western medieval heritage, its culture, like its social organization, remains profoundly Christian. Studying and teaching are
monopolized by one social class: the clergy. The University
of Paris is itself a Christian institution closely supervised by the
bishop of Paris, the chancellor of Notre Dame, and the Pope
himself. The international hierarchy of the church and the universal use of Latin as the learned language guarantee a natural
unity among the masters of the West and a common stock of

philosophic problems, only disseminated (but not lost) by the frequent migration of students and scholars which, indeed, facilitated the spread of a common philosophic task and a common theological vocabulary from Padua to Oxford and from Paris to Cologne. The twelfth century too had been preoccupied with a common set of philosophical problems: the relationship between faith and reason (and therefore between philosophy and theology); the metaphysical status of universals (bequeathed to the West by an Augustinian Platonism whose influence remained strong despite all nominalistic assaults); the more specifically theological issues of the proofs for God's existence, the precise nature of his infinitude, the relation between divine essence and existence; and, finally, those problems connected with divine predestination and human free will relevant to the attribution of man's moral responsibility. But these questions, the subject of intense individual concentration, had not yet been combined to form one comprehensive and integrated whole.

The new centralization of learning in Paris provided a mechanism of integration for the intellectual life comparable to that of the hierarchy of church organization centered under the papacy in Rome. For the first time the task of philosophic generalization and summary became a universal preoccupation of the learned class. The thirteenth century was doubtless no less rich in eccentric personalities than any other age, but the times possessed a great fund of common doctrine which constituted a binding tie between mentalities of extreme diversity. The ablest minds of the age — Alexander of Hales, William of Auvergne, Albert the Great, Bonaventura, Aquinas, and Duns Scotus — expressed the same devotion to a common task of organization and judgment, which united them like the wayward siblings of common parents; and the doctrines they shared — the axioms of medieval scholasticism — they themselves refer to as the *sententia communis*: "the reservoir of common belief."

The first of these axioms is a belief in generality itself — the faith, derived from Aristotle or at least in agreement with him, that it is possible in philosophy to come to an understanding of all things through their fundamental and universal reasons. As Saint Thomas put it in his *Commentary on Aristotle's Metaphysics*, "*Sapientia est scientia quae considerat primas et universales causas.*" The second axiom is an equal faith in the operations of the logical intellect to distinguish, divide, and deliver each substance, quality, and event into its proper place. The correlative of causal generality is *the principle of ordination.* To put order into knowledge is the basic Scholastic task, and to this principle all the masters of the thirteenth century would have given willing assent: "*Sapientis est ordinare.*"

Thus, as De Wulf has insisted, the one fundamental characteristic appearing throughout the philosophy and civilization of the thirteenth century is the tendency toward unity. And in this the Gothic cathedral, the *Divine Comedy,* the *Roman de la rose,* the great *Speculum quadruplex* of Vincent of Beauvais, and the *Summa theologica* of Saint Thomas Aquinas are as one. Strict classification, internal coherence, structural *zusammenhang* — these are the benchmarks of a civilization "athirst for order." And if a hierarchical arrangement of secular social structure, ecclesiastical power, artistic principles, and philosophic concerns rules the medieval consciousness, this is only because *peace* in the world is to be conceived essentially as a necessary intervention of an ordering *mind.* Augustine in *The City of God* had borne witness to the first: *Pax omnium rerum tranquillitas ordinis.* It was to be the greatness of Saint Thomas Aquinas to exemplify the last: *Intellectus solus est ordinare.*

The Philosopher as Saint

For contemporary philosophers like Wittgenstein or Quine or G. E. Moore, there is likely to be an unbridgeable chasm dividing their technical philosophical studies from their essential living practices and any implicit moral and spiritual principles which govern their lives. Philosophy today is primarily a matter of professional competence, and we no longer ask if the motive of its possessor is a deep spiritual commitment to the passionate search for some fleeting insight into the wisdom of life. The logical puzzles about dualism, or quantification, or the ontological argument, or transcendental predicates which engage our minds and the pages of our professional journals appear to have little or no relevance for how well men live, or for the moral quality of their daily acts. The divorce between technical concern and spiritual relevance seems to have become absolute.

In the thirteenth century and in the case of Thomas Aquinas, it was quite otherwise. We have here a life devoted to the pursuit and defense of a truth by which a man might live—a life itself permeated with, and motivated by, a deep spirituality. Of course he was a saint as well as a professor and so even if his spiritual passion is not always visible, shining through the formalism of his style and the rigorous logic of his argument, the meaning of his life as a whole is still clearly one of religious devotion and human love. His last years are not without their share of mystical ecstasies, and the sermons he delivered at Naples and the poetry he wrote for the Feast of Corpus Christi show an emotional sensitivity budding beneath the placid exterior of the dry-spoken, somewhat corpulent south-Italian dialectician. But only with the greatest rarity does the religious feeling find passionate outlet in the philos-sophic work itself: as in the margin of the rough draft of the *Summa contra gentiles* where various pious invocations (*ave, ave Maria*, etc.) are to be found. Saint Thomas's dedication to God and to the truth were parcels of a single motivation. But this is possible only when a whole cultural milieu and a dominant ideo-logical persuasion unite the truths of which a philosopher writes with the realities by which he lives.

The case of Aquinas, although it is outstanding, is not unique. Anselm and Bonaventura were also canonized. Peter Lombard, Albert the Great, and Duns Scotus were deeply religious monks. Grosseteste was bishop of Lincoln and a model of ecclesiastical administration. Perhaps only Peter Abelard and Ockham could with difficulty have been conceived of as saints. Abelard was too proud, arrogant, and perhaps worldly; Ockham was too nominal-istic, too negative, too critical of the theory of churchly power. Both were explosive and dangerous, yet both likewise were not without hidden reserves of spiritual power. Thus the entire twelfth and thirteenth centuries conceived of philosophical activity as the discovery and consolidation of spiritual truth—an activity which has a divine purpose and must therefore be guided by lives lived so as to grant it authentic moral authority. In this sense the medieval world was always grounded in a Platonic instinct which no novel Aristotelian science could supplant—it recognized a divinely pre-established harmony between the intellectual and the moral vir-tues. This harmony alone constitutes a preparation for the new spiritual vocation: that of the philosopher as saint. And this vocation is profoundly congruent with the spirit of the age.

The baronial side of the Middle Ages (certainly no less than Periclean Athens) had a secular, aristocratic bias; but what really

drove and possessed the minds of the medievals was the ideal of
the saint. This too has its sociological preconditions. The community of the saints represents no less a type of elitism than the
Platonic Academy, for the saint too is a spiritual aristocrat and
presupposes a hierarchically organized and spiritually directed
society with fixed class distinctions.

It may seem strange to analogize the class structure of feudal
society to the divinely created hierarchical structure of the cosmos,
but it is a universal medieval device. As God created all beings, so
all are subject to his providence, and as he is sovereign in the
kingdom of the universe, so the hierarchy and fixity he has instit-
uted depends upon him and tends toward him as its last end. The
angels, pure spirits, are arranged in degrees of perfection about
his throne, and man, in whom the spirit is united with matter,
dwells in a corporeal space below the circles of beatitude. The
saints represent the highest possibility open to beings tainted with
corporeality, and they are a kind of link between the angelic level
and common men. Like Christ himself, they demonstrate what
even man has it in him to become.

The saint, almost by definition, is a man torn between corporeality and spiritual compulsion, and this metaphysical ambiva-
lence has its worldly correlate in a certain tension between the
inner and the outer life. Anselm, deeply immersed in the metaphysical problem of finding a final and comprehensive proof for
the existence of God, was chosen abbot of the monastery of Bec.
He flung himself in tears at the feet of his brother monks and
besought them, though in vain, not to imperil his immortal soul
with this burden of worldly cares. It is probably true that all of the
saints — Saint Thomas with them — viewed the *vita contemplativa*
as the supreme ideal of life, and that they all remained loyal to the
inner utopia; but for the philosophers and theologians among
them, the conditions of life must have been particularly happy.
The life of adoration bears a certain intrinsic relationship to the
life of the mind, and meeting the epistemic challenge of intellectually reconciling faith and reason provides latent satisfaction for
lives balanced between the inward lure and outward responsibilities.

At the very threshold of the Middle Ages, Augustine, out of a
wide culture and a rich inner life, gives perhaps the final
statement of saintly piety, and the *Confessions* on the one hand

and *The City of God* on the other illustrate its two poles of inwardness and outwardness. It is not unlikely that all the saints were made unhappy by the clash between their vows of loyalty to the world-denying cloister and the demands the church made upon them. Their hearts were with their fellows in the cloisters; their consciences forced them to yield to the call of the church. But Augustine had added a reconciling postulate: that the church enters as a factor into every act of individual belief.

This prepares the way for the extraordinary situation of philosophy in the thirteenth century, where the founding of the preaching orders and the blossoming of the university out of the cathedral schools made education a center of the saintly life and, as an axiom of method, placed the determination of sacred doctrine within the sociological context of a public dialectic. It is no accident that the productivity of Saint Thomas, the greatest philosopher of the Middle Ages, is associated with the University of Paris, or that his life should be spent in obediently fulfilling the philosophical tasks set for him by his superiors in the church and in the Dominican order. If the sociological significance of Plato is that he is the great educator for an aristocratic restoration, that of Saint Thomas is that he is the angelic doctor of Christian enlightenment in its function of institutional support.

Philosophers occasionally quite unconsciously reveal the essence of their personalities and the spirit which animates their total enterprise. And this not always in their philosophical masterpieces or in their autobiographies or letters. Plato tells us more in a few scattered lines in the *Republic* than in all the dubious epistles; Kant reveals more in offhand statements in the *Lectures on Ethics* than in any of the three critiques; and Hume's essential outlook on life appears less in the reasoned argument of the *Treatise* than in the informal good humor of the *Dialogues concerning Natural Religion*. This, I think, holds for Saint Thomas also, and the key to his enduring spiritual endeavor is to be immediately recognized less in the dry dialectic of the great *Summa theologica, Contra gentiles,* and *Disputed Questions on Truth* than in the two sermons "For the Feast of Saint Martin of Tours" and "For the Feast of All Saints" which he preached in Italy late in the middle period of his life. For in these two sermons he laid bare the virtues of the saint, which with but little modification could have been applied to himself, and the saintly ideal of wisdom and union with

God through love and knowledge which was the animating intention of all of his writings, however serpentine, closely argued, and rationalistic.

Saint Martin, says Aquinas, attained to the heights of heaven by the will of God. This aid "lies ready to every one, and just as Saint Martin needed this divine aid in order to reach the pre-eminence of glory, so too, we stand in need of it to reach to glory." And he proceeds to expound the saintly life Scholastically and with a repetitiously and relentlessly trinitarian logic. In considering blessedness we must consider three things: its cause, its working out, and its end. And in the case of Saint Martin, who when ten years old became a catechumen against the will of his parents (Is there a hint here of the old story that the youthful Saint Thomas was abducted and isolated by his brothers to prevent him from becoming a Dominican monk?) God has provided three aids in his coming to blessedness: he has corrected him; he has schooled him; and finally he has taken him to himself. God's greatest gift lies in schooling, for it is not only a schooling which enlightens the mind, but one which equally warms the heart to receptivity. A man learns from the Father when the good inspiration comes; he fails to learn when he rejects the inspiration. For the learner (whether he be monk or professor) is he who bends his will to the divine inspiration.

There are three stages in God's schooling: the first is the enlightening of the intellect by faith; the second is the raising of the mind by hope; the third is the moving of the sentiments by love (*caritas*). True to the medieval presupposition, it is in the first that Saint Thomas finds the most excellent lesson, and there is indeed something infinitely touching in the sincere assertion of this, the greatest philosopher of the Christian Middle Ages, that "it is a greater thing that a man have a modicum of faith than that he should know everything that all the philosophers have discovered about the universe." The dichotomy is not, of course, meant to be exclusive, but the strategy is exemplary for philosophizing in the age of the saint. Rationality is a gift of God. Faith in God is a presupposition of enlightenment. What more fitting use of rationality than that it be dedicated to the divine service?

Aquinas completes his sermon by detailing the stages of Saint Martin's elevation through the sanctifying of his works, the wonder of his miracles, and the spreading of his renown upon earth, and he relates these to their three corresponding subjective conditions: the saint's sacramental regeneration, his rise in status, and his growth in merit. For in traversing a recognized series of stages on life's way (from the military state to the clerical, from the clerical to the religious, and from the religious to the pontifical) Saint Martin also acquired those virtues which were the hallmark of the saint in the Middle Ages and hence are a clue to Saint Thomas's own pantheon of values: first kindness, meekness, and obedience, and finally poverty, austerity of life, and humility.

In his sermon for the Feast of All Saints, Saint Thomas continues his dispraise of earthly things and his celebration of "the glory of the saints after which we strive." In true medieval fashion he sanctifies the current class division into *bellatores, laboratores, and oratores*—those who fight, those who work, those who pray. All our human activities, he says, are encompassed in three types. The actions of those who follow the active life constitute the search for power. Others, the "contemplatives," are runners, and, since they have nothing which holds them back, they run swiftly. Still others toil and labor, as, for instance, those prelates who perform the work of salvation among the people. The saints have succeeded in each of these three areas. They have obtained the crown like those who have striven well. They have also gained the prize like good runners and good workmen. And in this success they teach us the principle of valid striving:

The highest perfection of a thing is that it should be subject to that which perfects it. Matter is not perfect unless it be subjected to form, and the atmosphere is not beautiful save when it is transfigured by sunlight, and the soul is not perfect except it be subject to God. In this, then, consists our blessedness, that we be subject to God.

But between the lines we can discern the Thomistic preference for the "contemplatives." For if on principle all men are subject to God, it is the institutionalized clerical agents who direct and in the end effect this subjection. As he says in a significant triple association: it is "the *angels, prelates and pedagogues* who keep us in the way we ought to come to blessedness." This almost automatic linkage of the peculiarly blessed, the consecrated churchman, and the teaching professor, sounds bizarre in an unmoral and secular age, but it is almost a medieval commonplace, and it surely indicates a personal inclination of Saint Thomas himself—

one which was to receive its consummation in his canonization by
Pope John XXII at Avignon in 1323, and in the sobriquet by
which he was known even during his lifetime — the "Angelic
Doctor."

The "Life of Aquinas" which William of Tocco assembled
shortly before the canonization as a sort of codification of
materials which should serve as is justification (*Fontes Vitae S.
Thomae Aquinatis*, edited by Prümmer and Laurent, 1911-37)
itself falls into the characteristic pattern of the medieval legends of
the saints. Canonization in the primitive church was based upon
the belief that martyrs, having given their lives for Christ,
belonged to a special class of the elect. Later the qualifications
were extended to include special defenders of the faith, those of
unusually exemplary life, those excellent in Catholic doctrine, and
those bishops and missionaries of special apostolic zeal. Saint
Thomas's credentials are obviously of the first and third variety,
but in the long tradition of sainthood, efforts were also made to
emphasize the moral and spiritual rectitude of his life with such
increments of the miraculous as should provide tangible evidence
of God's own process of natural election. Each of these latter
William of Tocco provides in abundance.

Catherine of San Severina, niece of Aquinas, provided William
with a characteristic fable of "annunciation." It seems that a
mysterious hermit appeared before Thomas's mother during her
pregnancy and greeted her with the not unfamiliar words:

Rejoice, O Lady, for thou art with child and thou shalt bear a
son whom thou shalt name Thomas; and with thy husband
thou shalt plan to make him a monk in the monastery of Montecassino, where the body of blessed Benedict lies. Thou shalt
be in hopes of attaining the great revenues of this monastery,
through his advancement to the eminence of the prelacy. But
God will ordain otherwise, for he will be a brother in the Order
of Preachers, so renowned in science and of such sanctity of life
that, in his time it will be impossible to find his peer in the
world.

Other "saintly" stories William tells as well. How, after joining
the Dominican order as a novice at eighteen or nineteen against
the wishes of his family and leaving for Paris, Thomas is abducted
by his brothers near Acquapendente and returned home to
Roccasecca, where, held in detention by his family, he is visited by
a beautiful young girl whose sensual temptation he resists by the

mercy of God. How, as a young man studying under Albertus Magnus at Paris (sometime between 1245 and 1252) he "began to be wonderfully taciturn and silent, zealous in study and devout in prayer, inwardly collecting in memory what he was later to promulgate in teaching," so that his brother monks started to call him "the Dumb Ox" until that day when Thomas answered a question the master had put to him with such brilliance that "Master Albert was moved to speak in a prophetic mood: 'We call this man the Dumb Ox but he will eventually bellow so loudly in his teaching that he will resound throughout the whole world.' " There is indeed something of the miraculous concealed here. The Dominican genius was not fluent in verbal expression, and his handwriting was so notoriously illegible even in later life that his order constantly had to provide him with secretaries (his autograph manuscripts can be read only by skilled paleographers who have devoted their lives to this study). Yet he finally poured out his mature philosophical and theological wisdom in scores of folio volumes.

Although the "Life" of William of Tocco proceeds in the "saintly" tradition, there are other intrinsic sources which suggest that the imputation of saintliness is not without basis. There exists a letter of Saint Thomas, the *De modo studendi* (*Opuscula theologica*, edited by Verardo, 1954), generally accepted as genuine, which seems to sum up some of Aquinas's own scholarly experiences and the fruits of his own judgment concerning the Christian life of monastic learning. Presumably the answer to a young novice of the Dominican order who had written him for advice on how to pursue the search for knowledge, it tells us much of the moral presuppositions of Saint Thomas's own intellectual adventure.

Since you have asked me, my very dear John in Christ, how you should apply yourself in order to gain something from the treasure-house of knowledge, let this be the advice handed down to you by me on this subject.

Make up your mind to start on small streams rather than to plunge into the sea; for one should progress from easier matters to those that are more difficult. This is, then, my advice and instruction for you. I counsel you to be slow to speak and slow to take the speaker's stand. Embrace purity of mind; do not neglect prayer; cherish your cell most of the time, if you wish to be admitted to the vintage room of knowledge. Be friendly to all men;

do not be curious about the private activities of other people;
do not try to be overfamiliar with anyone, for too much familiarity
breeds contempt and provides an opportunity for neglecting one's
studies.

Do not get interested in any way in worldly talk or deeds.
Avoid idle talk on all matters; do not fail to imitate the example of holy and good men; do not be concerned about what
speaker you are listening to; instead, when something good is
said, commit it to memory. Be sure that you understand whatever you read. Make certain that you know the difficulties and
store up whatever you can in the treasure-house of the mind;
keep as busy as a person who seeks to fill a vessel.

Do not seek higher positions. Follow in the footsteps of Blessed
Dominic who brought forth and increased the buds, the flowers
and the fruits that were useful and wonderful in the vineyard of
the Lord of Hosts, as long as he lived.

If you follow these words of advice, you will be able to attain your
every desire.

The interweaving of intellectual method and moral precept is
notable, and it testifies to the medieval unification of knowledge
and purity of life in a single saintly idea. The Thomistic preference for the contemplative life and the conviction that dedication
to God and to the truth are aspects of but a single motivation
found confirmation in an Aristotelianism newly available for
authoritative use. In the first few pages of the *Summa contra
gentiles,* Aquinas makes this abundantly clear. Asking, in what
consists the function of a wise man? he argues thus:

Now the last end of each thing is that which is intended by
the first author or mover of that thing; and the first author
and mover of the universe is an intellect, as we shall prove
further on. Therefore the final cause of the universe must be
the good of the intellect: and this is truth. Thus truth must be
the last end of the whole universe, and the consideration of it
the chief occupation of wisdom.

It follows easily that the twofold function of the wise man
(philosopher) is to meditate on and publish the divine truth, and
to refute the error contrary to truth. This might be taken as a
capsule formulation of the very lifework of Saint Thomas himself,
and a moment later, adding his conviction that "of all human
pursuits, that of wisdom is the most perfect, the most sublime, the

most useful, and the most delightful," he specifically states the purpose of the *Summa contra gentiles* in these terms:

Wherefore, taking heart from God's loving kindness to assume the office of a wise man, although it surpasses our own powers, the purpose we have in view is, in our own weak way, to declare the truth which the Catholic faith professes, while weeding out contrary errors; for, in the words of Hilary, *I acknowledge that I owe my life's chief occupation to God, so that every word and every thought of mine may speak of Him.* [Italics added]

What the *Summa contra gentiles* treats cursorily and in preliminary fashion is to be found worked out in considerable detail in the later section of the *Summa theologica* (2.2.Q180), where Saint Thomas considers the nature of the contemplative life. Here, quoting Gregory to the effect that "the contemplative life is to cling with our whole mind to the love of God and of our neighbor," Aquinas asserts that the purely intellectual urge toward the contemplation of truth is tempered by that *amor Dei* which is its motive force and by the accompanying moral virtues which are, in a sense, its phenomenological precondition. Although the moral virtues do not in essence define the contemplative life, they do dispose one toward it by causing peace and cleanness of heart.

On the other hand, the moral virtues belong to the contemplative life as a predisposition. For the act of contemplation, wherein the contemplative life essentially consists, is hindered both by the impetuosity of the passions which withdraw the soul's intention from intelligible to sensible things, and by outward disturbances. Now the moral virtues curb the impetuosity of the passions, and quell the disturbance of outward occupations. Hence moral virtues belong to the contemplative life as a predisposition.

For Aristotle too (*Nicomachean Ethics,* 10) happiness in the highest sense is constituted by the contemplative life, and the philosopher — viewed as half scientist, half spiritual aristocrat — becomes the highest exemplar of virtue in the Greek city-state. But Saint Thomas transforms this essentially secular virtue to fit the requirements of the medieval ideal of the saint. Since sensuality more than any other cause confines the mind to the level of sensible things, it is the virtue of chastity which most of all makes a man apt for contemplation; and although contemplation, true to the Greek origins, is an essentially "cognitive" activity, yet a characteristic higher "vision" adheres to it as a kind of spiritual glow. Contemplation has, as the *Summa contra gentiles* has stated, the divine truth as its final purpose, but the achievement of this end is an act of grace furthered by the subjective rituals appropriate to the religious life. Thus, *prayer, reading,* and *meditation* are all ingredients in the contemplative life, and with these additions the life of the sage merges into that of the Christian saint. For Aristotle, contemplative men utilize the methods of scientific knowledge to discover the essential principles of the natural and social world. But Aquinas follows the Platoniz-ing tendencies of Augustine and Richard of Saint Victor to insist that contemplative men withdraw within themselves in order to explore spiritual things. Since contemplation takes as its object a consideration of the effects of God's activity, union with the divine is intrinsically hoped for as a consequence of the contemplative act. Thus in the Thomistic synthesis, scientific cognition and the urge toward mystical union are inseparably connected.

We have now finally come to the speculative rationale of that curious medieval conception of "the philosopher as saint"—one which the life of Aquinas exemplifies as his theory supports. For medieval thought, the fact that the contemplative life pertains to the intellect indicated the kinship of man with the angels. For their nature as disembodied intellects presents in its pure form the contemplative activity freed from the dislocations of material embodiment and thus able to acquire intelligible truth not through the agency of composite objects but directly through simple intuition. The human wisdom of contemplation can therefore function "angelically" only by analogy: the soul can provisionally withdraw into itself from externals, it can resist the material temptations of sensuality, and thus, freed from the errors of outward occupation, it can seek union with the things that are above it. It follows that this occupation is delightful—for each individual delights in those operations which define his nature and his habit; and since contemplation of the truth befits a man according to his nature as a rational being, it is the ultimate perfection of the contemplative life that "the divine truth be not only seen, but also loved."

In its logical essence the purpose of contemplation is to attain truth, but insofar as contemplation is regarded as *a way of life,* it requires anchoring in the medieval monastic and university setting. And here an interesting paradox emerges. Understood in its intrinsic nature as an act of withdrawal from the world and a retreat into the self, the contemplative act as rational activity also implies an effort toward the meeting of minds, the social con-frontation,of error, and a public propagation of the truth. Within an irrevocably institutional setting, the pedagogical enterprise becomes a center of the saintly life, and it becomes possible to render intelligible the content and the very literary style of a Saint Thomas Aquinas only through a careful examination of the institutional presuppositions of rational inquiry in the thirteenth century.

The Development of Scholastic Method

The transformation of the inwardness of the monastic and the saintly life into a situation where divine truth becomes the object of a public dialectic is accomplished through the agency of typical medieval institutions—through the new universities as ecclesiasti-cal foundations, through the cultural and teaching functions of the new mendicant orders, and thus, in general, through those pedagogical instrumentalities requisite for the training of a knowledgeable clergy and for the elaboration of those theses and principles which supply theological foundation for the active imperialism of the Christian church. For the fact of the matter is that from the time of Augustine, the institutional requirements of Catholicism and the incorporation of elements of Roman admin-istration and Greek philosophy develop together.

As the rights and duties of Christian bishops owe something to the anterior patterns of the Roman law, so the elaboration of Christian theology owes a great deal to the anterior patterns of Greek logic. But even Greek logic in its original sense as an organon is less a codification of principle than a reservoir of practice—of standards of active reasoning and argument. And what is of fundamental importance is that these standards of argument were themselves developed in the *schools* of Plato and Aristotle. Here, then, is an affinity of great interest, for the pedagogical experience is thus the central fact of medieval philosophy as it is of Greek, and the philosophical productions of the medieval saint (Aquinas), no less than those of the Greek aristocrat (Plato), are to be understood as the efforts of *school-men*—of practicing teachers.

The consequences this in turn had upon the form of ancient and medieval philosophical writings are not to be overlooked. In fact, they are critical for any consideration of "philosophy as literature." For oral practice is often at the foundation of literary composition in form and intent. As the active philosophizing of Socrates in the situational context of the Greek agora, and of Plato himself in the classrooms of the Academy, are the presupposition of the Platonic dialogues (both in origin of inspiration and in ultimate pedagogic use), so the classroom of the medieval university, the rationale of its instruction, and the public disputations with which this is allied are the presupposition of the philosophical writing in which Saint Thomas engaged and which he has contributed to our knowledge of the role of philosophizing in the age of the saint.

Philosophizing in the medieval world appears in a broad spectrum of literary forms: "dialogues" in the Platonic tradition as with Augustine, Erigena, and Anselm; "commentaries" upon a text, such as Boethius wrote upon the *Isagoge* of Porphyry and Duns Scotus on the *Sentences* of Peter Lombard; "glosses" such as Peter Abelard in turn wrote upon the commentary of Boethius; "lectures" which are to be found among the works of Saint Bonaventura and Duns Scotus; "opusculae," the detailed study of a particular problem, which both Albert the Great and Grosseteste composed; "disputed questions," such as those of Duns Scotus and Aquinas; "quodlibetal questions" composed by both Aquinas and William of Ockham; and finally the great "summas" of Alexander of Hales, Bonaventura, and Saint Thomas. In every case, an examination of the literary form reveals a profound connection between the mode of thought illustrated and the social environment and institutional setting within which it originated. In most of these instances, and particularly in that of Saint Thomas, university organization and medieval classroom method supply crucial clues. For Aquinas twice held a professorship at the University of Paris, and the bulk of his philosophical writings were the product of the busy life of one who almost continuously taught, expounded texts, wrote commentaries upon them, engaged in classroom and public disputes (and published their results), and finally, and with a special pedagogical purpose, wrote "summas"—as repositories and codifications of doctrine to serve as training manuals for a knowledgeable and militant clergy.

And yet Saint Thomas is only the culmination of a long historical process. The evolution of the Scholastic method (which, indeed, reached its full flowering in his great *Summa theologica*) is the product of two impulses, the combination of two theological interests. The first is the *authoritarian* effort to explicate the divine texts. The second is the *dialectical* effort to present, classify, oppose, and where possible to adjudicate the oppositions disclosed by a pluralistic approach to sacred doctrine.

As we have already seen, the historical beginnings are connected with the theological efforts of Anselm of Canterbury (whom Grabmann calls "the father of Scholasticism") and with the entrance of the more complete Aristotle into the literary culture of medieval Europe. But the institutional origins lie with the development of the cathedral schools in France and the founding of the University of Paris. For here literary productivity lies in intimate connection with pedagogical method. The earliest Scholastic literature is in large part a mere manuscript-fixing or consolidation of oral instruction as carried on in the schools of liberal arts or of theology, as is clearly attested by the prefatory remarks to Abelard's *Introduction to Theology*, to Hugh of Saint Victor's *Concerning the Sacraments of the Christian Faith*, and to the *Sentences* of Peter Lombard. Thus, around the middle of the twelfth century the living dialectical encounters—the "disputations" held within the schools of liberal arts and which provided the renown of William of Champeaux and the notoriety of Abelard—suggest the rudimentary examples of a form which is to serve both as a natural method of oral instruction and as a model for the dialectical examination of the sacred writings. And once the higher instruction was concentrated on the Ile de la Cité, the University of Paris received its charter, and, under the jurisdiction of the chancellor of Notre Dame, the *licentia docendi* (the formal permission to teach) was granted, then the habitual structure of teaching within the university became decisive for both the content and the quality of medieval philosophical writing.

Thus the higher pedagogical needs of a Christian society, the specific conditions of medieval university teaching, and the techniques of rational elaboration drawn from the models of Greek thought cooperate to produce the highly individual literary forms of the medieval philosophic tradition. The Platonic dialogues reflect the conditions of Greek civic humanism and private pedagogy—of the aristocratic circle around Socrates and the gilded youth whose search for wisdom and place prompted their entrance into the isolated community of the Platonic Academy. The treatises of Descartes ("discourse" or "meditation" as the case

may be) were, as we shall see, the product of a gentleman's
voluntary exile — of a reserve seeking privacy, and given intellectual and contemplative form by the quaint mathematical preoccupations of a certified member of the lesser French nobility.
But the writings of Saint Thomas share that peculiar medieval
machinery of thought: the careful divisions of subject-matter, the
eternal repetition of formulas of presentation, the constant semantic and formal distinctions, and even the flat impersonality of
a newly wrought technical philosophical style and language — the
hallmark of the Scholastic tradition. It is a dry, nonallegorical,
abstract method, replete with divisions, classifications, and formal
oppositions, which, because it was so admirably suited to intellectual economy and precision in argument, emerged from the closed
society of medieval masters and pupils in their narrow university
milieu. The Schoolmen (and Saint Thomas with them) were
professors, and the language of their philosophic communication
is one adapted to a highly selective audience engaged in mastering
an elaborate professional technique. Dialectic is a demanding art;
understanding a great book is a difficult achievement, and their
cooperation in the problematic (but finally dogmatic) exposition
of an "authentic" text in an attempt once and for all to "fix" the
content and interpretative significance of sacred doctrine was a
task reserved only for the devout, the supremely learned, and the
intellectually worthy. Saint Thomas was eminently qualified for
the task of reverential exposition and for passing critical judgment
upon the narrowly circumscribed body of canonical works in the
Christian tradition. He wrote commentaries, he produced quodlibetal and disputed questions, and he finally constructed two
remarkable summas. And each of these was the outcome of his
work as a teacher. But the forms he adopted were simply
appropriated from a century-old tradition of pedagogical usage
and Christian necessity. What, we may ask, was the nature of this
tradition?

When Martin Grabmann in his indispensible *Die Geschichte
der scholastischen Methode* derives the methods of higher university instruction, he does so from the two twelfth-century intellectual procedures of *lectio* and *disputatio* — the "reading" and the
"disputation." Already John of Salisbury, codifying the practice of
the cathedral schools, had spoken of the *lectio* as the clarification
of the text by the teacher (*explication de texte,* we now call it)
sentence by sentence and even word by word. And Hugh of Saint

Victor analyzed the method with a further semantic distinction. Such clarification, he said, implies three stages, or levels of attention: to the grammatical sense (*littera*), the immediately presented meaning (*sensus*), and the deeper underlying significance (*sententia*). Thus, in the middle of the twelfth century there already was an effort to rationalize the requirements of a bookish tradition with methods available from Quintilian and the Roman grammarians.

To this classroom interpretive effort is added the natural excitements of a verbal dialectic. Dialogue between teacher and pupil, the assertion of a meaning and its questioning by the student, and assertion and counterassertion, only prepare the way for the openly competitive interpretations of diverse teachers, displayed in the intellectual context of a public debate in which the apostolic word, the metaphysical consequences of the sacred doctrines, and hence even the ultimate destiny of the human soul are thought to be at stake. Here the life of the mind displays its own fiery passion in the dramatic excitements of intellectual antagonism and collision. Of these medieval disputations Grabmann writes:

These disputations exercised enormous attraction upon teacher and pupil alike. They provided a continuous coming together between the master and his scholars, they spurred the ambitions of the young, and stretched their intellectual capacities to the limit. In the disputation the personal capability of the student appeared most articulately and publically. The disputations also exhibited a certain dramatic interest. They were a kind of tournament, a contest or duel with the weapons of the mind. The alternating movement of these duels, the gradual development and complication of problems, the blow for blow presentation of suggestions and solutions, questions and answers, distinctions and negations, the various sophisms and entrapments in which one tried to entice the adversary—all these, and other moments too, were well calculated to keep the interest and expectation of both the participants in, and spectators of, such exercises of disputation at the highest tension and suspense.

These disputations, already institutionalized in the preuniversity cathedral schools, are reflected as literary expression in the actual writings of Abelard and Peter Lombard, where specific theological "questions" (*quaestio*) are raised, and all the available resources of Aristotelian logic are brought to bear upon their elucidation. And, since the same techniques of logical disputation are retained in literary form, much of the native drama and excitement of the living encounters is embodied in these compendia of dialectical oppositions in the writings of holy scripture and the church fathers. Abelard's famous *Sic et non*, which marshals the paradoxical oppositions of scriptural authority, and the even more influential *sententiae* of Peter Lombard only distill the practices of active disputation which Abelard had made notorious through the ruthless and arrogant displays of his intellectual genius and dialectical brilliance. These *sententiae*, or "books of sentences," reveal paradoxes, but their ultimate aim is to methodically introduce the whole domain of scriptural interpretation, and toward the end of the twelfth century they become more formalized and dogmatic—short, independent, and systematic exercises in "scriptural science": precursors of the true *summa* of the thirteenth century.

The chief presupposition of the kind of intellectual history we are employing to explain the philosophy of Saint Thomas Aquinas (and hence of medieval philosophy in general at its thirteenth-century culmination) is that the literary form of a philosophical masterpiece is not arbitrary and fortuitous, but is the natural bridge between its doctrinal content and the peculiar intellectual and social milieu in which it arose. Studying philosophic works by examining their literary form presupposes that a system of thought is not exactly neutral in expressive mode but utilizes formulas of language and structures of literary expression which, for all that they do mirror elements of personal originality, are finally historically anchored and institutionally grounded. By examining the clothing in which a mind is dressed one discovers not only the personal predilections of the wearer but the societal habits which help make up a general sartorial style. For Grabmann this presupposition is latent but is not expressed. It is the very great virtue of a similar effort on the part of Father Chenu (*Toward Understanding Saint Thomas*) that the presupposition is expressly stated and governs the whole strategy of his presentation.

His schema is not in contrast to Grabmann's—in fact, it depends heavily upon it—but it reduces to schematic simplicity a historical evolution of considerable density.

The "style" of the Scholastics in its development as well as in its modes of expression can be reduced, as if to its simple elements, to three procedures. These followed progressively one upon the other and typify, moreover, both their historical genesis and their progress in technique. First came the *lectio* (reading); from the reading was developed the *quaestio* (question);

from the question, the *disputatio* (disputation); and in *summas*, the "article," somewhat as the residue of the disputed question, became the literary component.

The reason for the primacy of the *lectio* has already been suggested. Christianity is a *revealed* religion. The word of God appears literally or metaphorically stated in "the Book." The interpretation of its contents, therefore, must be the clue to the meaning of life and the problems of its direction. Any Christian philosophy will depend heavily upon a concept of the supreme value of "the written word," and philosophical procedures will thus stem analogically from the necessities of theological con- struction. All wisdom is essentially a "commentary" upon the divine scripture, and it is consequently far from accidental that the entire medieval pedagogy was based on the "authoritative" reading of texts. The classroom of the cathedral school, and later of the university, was simply an exercise in "reading," where reading included not merely an immediate apprehension of the text but the act of "meditation" (*meditatio*)—that strictly per- sonal process of appropriation by which the deeper significance of textual content became accessible to the docile (teachable), but actively searching, understanding of the student. It is clear, therefore, that the concept of "reading" is somewhat ambigu- ous—more complex than it first appears. There is the magistral "reading" of the professor; the discipular "reading" of the pupil; even the devout "reading" done in private without the classroom interchange and dialectic. But what is crucial is that for the medieval world "to teach" means "to read" in the technical sense. The professor "read" his text; his performance was a "lecture," and he himself was expressly referred to as a *lector* or "reader"—a custom which persists at Oxford and Cambridge to this day.

It is an easy transition from the "reading" to the "question." Texts are inherently vague, certain words or expressions suddenly raise problems of meaning and intention, and with the clashing of two or more interpretations (sometimes given literary form in the opposition of divergent textual authorities), an ineradicable dialectical element enters into the pedagogical situation. Such dialectical issues not unnaturally spill over from the sequestered precincts of the individual classroom into the dramatic confront- ations of a public dialectic. Thus the "question" slowly detaches itself from the professorial textual exegesis or "reading" in which it originated, to emerge in the public debates of masters with students, or between individual masters who oppose one another; and these debates over sacred doctrine or ecclesiastical principle are formalized by explicit inclusion in the calendar of the medieval university. Thus the "disputation" is born.

These medieval disputations are of two types and issue in two forms of literary productivity: *disputed questions* and *quodlibetal questions*. The first grew out of a special oral exercise in which a bachelor in theology (or "graduate student") considered a question or problem set beforehand, stated various difficulties (numbered as "objections"), cited various authorities or reasons opposed to the objections, and then provided the best solution or answer to the original question of which he was capable. All this was done by the theology student himself, with the advice and direction of his teacher, who presided over the student's performance before a large audience of other students, masters, and distinguished visitors.

On disputation days, all other classes in the faculty of theology were suspended. After the first oral session, the presiding master held another in which, after stating the question, summarizing the arguments, and stating the objections, he provided his own "determination" of the issue (*determinatio*)—his own final answer to the question together with his replies to the objections. A written version of the master's summary, made by himself and published as a "disputed question" followed, and these publications constituted one of the most important parts of the literary output of philosophers and theologians in the thirteenth century. But most significant of all, the structure of this oral disputation, with its "*queritur*," its "*objectio*," and its final "*respondeo*," becomes the final form of each article of the great *summas* of the time, and as such remains permanently on display in the massive *Summa theologica* of Aquinas.

By the middle of the thirteenth century, as Father Chenu states, it had been established that the responsibility of every professor of theology (*magister*) included a threefold duty: *legere, disputare, praedicare*—"to read" (teach), "to dispute," and "to preach." And Father Mandonnet has described in some detail (and in a manner which recalls Grabmann's description of the twelfth-century cathedral school debates), the nature of the event that the disputation had come to be within the faculty of theology at the medieval university.

When a master disputed, all the morning lectures of the other masters and bachelors were dispensed with. Only the master who was to conduct the dispute gave a short lecture, in order to allow time for the audience to arrive. Then the dispute began: and it took up a more or less considerable part of the morning. All the bachelors of the faculty as well as the students of the master who was disputing had to be present at the exercise. The other masters and students, it would appear, were left free to do so; but there is small doubt that they too showed up, in numbers that depended on the reputation of the master and on the topic that was being discussed. The clergy of Paris, the prelates and other Church dignitaries who happened to be at the Capital at the time, were quite willing to attend these academic jousts that passionately absorbed the contemporary mind. A dispute was a tournament for the clergy.

The question to come under debate was fixed in advance by the master who was in charge of the disputation. Both the disputation and the day on which it was to be held were announced in the other schools of the faculty. The disputation was controlled by the master, but, strictly speaking, he was not the one who did the actual disputing. Rather, his bachelor assumed the task of replying, this starting his apprenticeship in exercises of this sort. The objections usually represented different currents of thought, and were first formulated by the masters present, then by the bachelors, and finally, if the situation warranted it, by the students. The bachelor gave response to the arguments proposed, and, if need be, got help from the master.

The objections put forth and solved in the course of the disputation without any pre-arranged order, presented in the end a doctrinal matter that stood in quite a state of disorder, resembling, however, much less debris scattered over a battlefield, than half-worked materials laid out acoss a construction job. That is why, in addition to this first session of doctrinal elaboration, a second one was held. It was called the "magisterial determination."

On the first day when the master who had conducted the disputation was able to lecture, he went over, in his own school, the material over which the disputation had been held a few days before. First, he coordinated in logical sequence the objections which had been opposed to his thesis and cast them in definite form. These were followed by a few arguments in favor of the doctrinal position which he was going to propose. He then passed on to a more or less extended exposé of his own doctrine on the question under debate. This exposition furnished the core and essence of his determination. He wound up by replying to each objection that had been stated against the doctrine of his thesis.

This second act following on the disputation was known as
the determination because the master gave an authoritative formulation of the doctrine that had to be held. To determine or
define a doctrine was the right or privilege of those who held
the title of master. A bachelor did not have the authority to
perform such an act. The acts of determination, set down in
writing by the master or an auditor, make up the writings that
we call the *Disputed Questions*.

A second type of disputation—that giving rise to the literary
form of *quodlibetal questions*—was so named from the phrase *de
quodlibet*, or "whatever you will," to characterize its indetermin-
acy. Twice each year, in the weeks just preceding Christmas and
Easter, masters in all the faculties of the medieval university, but
especially in the faculty of theology, were free to hold disputations in which they answered, or attempted to answer, the questions of all comers. Here there was no prearranged subject; the
members of the audience could raise any questions they liked,
from the highest issues of metaphysics to the smallest problems of
private life or personal ethics. The multiplicity of questions in a
single session might completely lack unity or coherence, and
probably could not be anticipated. Beginning early in the morning and continuing at length, the discussion could be pointed or
capricious, springing from genuine inquisitiveness and a deep
sense of philosophic responsibility or from malice and hostility,
in the hope that the presiding master would obviously contradict
himself, display his inadequacy, or compromise himself on some
cunning issue of sensitive church diplomacy or heresy. Anyone
willing to conduct a quodlibetal dispute therefore needed enormous coolness and presence of mind as well as an intellectual
capability almost universal in scope. For this type of extempor-
aneous exercise the mind and character of Saint Thomas were
ideal. As Professor Vernon J. Bourke says:

In the case of Saint Thomas we have a man who was eager to
play his full part in the academic life of the university, so he
seems to have engaged in more quodlibetal questions than his
contemporaries. Pierre Mandonnet was of the opinion, in fact,
that Aquinas had invented this type of exercise. However, this is
not so; both Franciscan and Dominican professors conducted
quodlibetal disputations as early as the 1230's.

In any case, the method of medieval Scholasticism which begins in the exposition of a sacred text in the classroom and ends

with the great literary productions that were the series of "disputed questions" and *summas*, is intimately related to the essential qualities of the medieval mind and to its psychological predisposition and sociological setting. Those "questions" which exercised both the professorial commentator in the presence of his students and the master disputing at Christmas or Easter against all comers are a fit measure of the inventiveness of the Scholastic age. For they place the contemplative occupation of the saint within the atmosphere of open competition and public striving. To examine "the word of God" as if it were ambiguous and problematic is to admit that for sacred truth to be efficacious it must filter through the imperfect medium of the human intelligence; and the existence of such social dimensions of the medieval theological venture seems an almost modern admission that "divine science" flourishes only in a milieu which brings to bear all the resources of shared intelligence in the hope that a commonly possessed rationality will flatten out all the threats of individual idiosyncracy and error. To convert a divine mystery into an intellectual problem was for the medievals no particular sign of churchly disrespect, no necessary compromising of the ultimate potency of the divine revelation. Reason searching out the indubitable grounds of faith was a pursuit respectable and respected, for it attested to man's exercise of a reason (*ratio*) which is itself the result of grace and the product of a divine gift.

Moreover, the close interweaving of the commentary, the dispute, and the *summa* in the university environment also reveals the intimate relationship within the medieval context of the institutional influences of church, society, and the law. The "commentary" of the solitary professor in his classroom is the product of a single voice, and the master lecturing to his students is not unlike the priestly sermon in the cathedral—an authoritative intelligence disseminating the will of God, mediating the divine scripture to the masses. But the "question," with its flavor of dubiety and antagonism, introduces a new dialectical element (the analogue of every instance of civil dispute), and its expressive mode is not a single voice, but *two* voices raised against one another in discord and shrill contrariety. It is inevitable, then, that the commentary as position stated, and the question as issue raised, should culminate in the "disputed question" and the *summa*, which introduce into the strife of dialectical opposites the adjudicating resources of the third voice. Here is the theological analogue of the civil law courts, the impartial consideration eventuating in the judicial decision. And it is as if the historical strategy of a completed Hegelian dialectic (which is, to be sure, not to be associated with the philosophy of Hegel himself) had supplied with the commentary a thesis, with the raw disputation an antithesis, and with the culminating *summa* a synthesis in which the inherent valences of the sacred doctrine are accorded a final equilibrium — that is to say, a peaceful resolution in which both doubt and strife are banished in an ultimate triumph of the rational mind.

The Saint as Dialectician

The conventionally accepted date of the birth of Saint Thomas Aquinas is 1225. It is probable that in his fifth year he was sent to the great Benedictine monastery at Montecassino, and that he remained there until the spring of 1239. At Montecassino it is likely that he read portions of the Latin fathers of the church: Ambrose and Augustine, Benedict and Jerome. It is possible that he became acquainted with the theology of Anselm of Canterbury and Hugo of Saint Victor. In the fall of 1239 he was sent to study in the faculty of liberal arts at the University of Naples, where he is believed to have remained until 1244. The University of Naples was at this time a great center of cosmopolitan learning, and during his five years there Saint Thomas would have learned the conventional foundations of liberal arts at this time: a working knowledge of the traditional Aristotelian logic, and perhaps some parts of the Aristotelian physics in addition; the Latin translations of Boethius, Porphyry's *Introduction* to the Categories, and the "New Logic": the *Prior* and *Posterior Analytics* as well as certain logical treatises of the twelfth century (Gilbert de La Porrée and perhaps Abelard's *De dialectica*) and selected Arabic logical works of al-Farabi and Avicenna. Two early logical productions of Saint Thomas himself found among his *opuscula* — a work *On Fallacies* and another *On Modal Propositions* — are thought to belong to these early years as a student of liberal arts at Naples. Here are the root experiences which served as foundation for Saint Thomas's later dialectical ability, although perhaps the most rewarding consequence of this early education was a more accurate knowledge of how to construe the text of Aristotle.

One year after completing his studies in liberal arts at Naples,

Saint Thomas arrived in Paris (1245), where he lived at the Dominican house in the Rue Saint Jacques and enrolled in the theological faculty at the university. Although there is some disagreement among Thomistic scholars in their account of these next few years, it now seems established that in 1248 he accompanied his teacher, Albert the Great, from Paris to Cologne, where the latter established a new *studium generale* for the German provinces. This means that from 1245 to 1248 Aquinas was engaged in theological studies under Albert at Paris, and that he returned from Cologne for advanced study at the University of Paris again in 1252, finally taking his degree as master in theology in 1256.

It is perhaps difficult for a modern man at this great historical distance to recapture the air of novelty and excitement, of a new world of intellectual possibility, which characterized the University of Paris in the first half of the thirteenth century. And Saint Thomas was particularly fortunate in that his master, Albert, was the very epitome of this new horizon opening out to the medieval mind. It was the age in which the Aristotelian studies of the non-Christian peoples were becoming available to make of the University of Paris a cosmopolitan synthesis of the most diverse strands of medieval culture. Albert read the new translations of the Arabic commentators on Aristotle: al-Kindi, al-Farabi, Avicenna, and finally Averroës. And he was fascinated equally by Grosseteste's translation of the *Nicomachean Ethics*, by the works of the mysterious Dionysius the Areopagite, and by the latest contributions to optics, biology, and the other areas of observational and experimental science. But of course the great event of the decade 1230–40 had been the arrival of "the new Aristotle," and Albert the Great was a real pioneer in utilizing the whole of the philosophy of Aristotle in the service of Christian theology.

Here is where Saint Thomas learned his most important lesson from his famous teacher. For temperamentally and philosophically the two minds were profoundly different. Encyclopedic, open to every new current of emergent medieval thinking, Albert the Great himself produced great compilations which were not only eclectic, but full of the kind of inconsistencies which are the inevitable price of extreme intellectual openness. His mature theology is a kind of advanced neo-Platonism which conceals difficulties which perhaps lead in the direction of Pantheism. From

Albert Saint Thomas surely derived his own open-minded interest in the Arabic and Hebrew commentaries and his ready reliance upon the whole of the Aristotelian corpus. But at the same
time his sympathy with the empirical and naturalistic emphasis
in Aristotle was too great to permit any wayward adventures with
Platonic emanationism. Both Albert the Great and Saint Thomas
shared the same cultural resources, but Albert was the "founder"
who uses them to write enormous encyclopedic treatises in the
effort to disseminate knowledge, whereas Saint Thomas became
the "classic," using these same resources to rethink the whole of
Christian philosophy and to enclose his conclusions within the
comprehensive boundaries of a consistent and cleanly articulated
speculative system.

Early in 1252 Aquinas was a bachelor in theology at the University of Paris, and for the next four years he lectured on the
Sentences of Peter Lombard in the Dominican house of studies
on the Rue Saint-Jacques. Some scholars now believe that during
this period Saint Thomas also engaged in academic disputations,
and that two sections now included in his *Quodlibetal Questions*
are actually "disputed questions" from these formative years. At
any rate, during this period both Saint Thomas and Saint Bonaventura taught theology in their respective orders in Paris without being accepted as full members of the university theological
faculty. For in this matter the secular professors at the university
were adamant. But the Pope, Alexander, was of another opinion, and in October 1256 he sent a peremptory message to the
recalcitrant administrative officers of the university, ordering
them:

> to receive, insofar as it is within their power, into the academic
> society and into the University of Paris, the Friars Preachers
> and Minors now stationed at Paris, and also their students; and
> in particular and by name, the Friars Thomas of Aquino, of
> the Order of Preachers, and Bonaventura, of the Order of
> Minors, as Doctors of Theology.

One year later both Aquinas and Bonaventura were granted
admission to the faculty of theology at Paris with full professorial
privileges in the university.

For the next few years (1256–59) Saint Thomas remained as a
teaching master of theology at the University of Paris (this period
is known as "the first Paris professorate"), living at the Dominican house of studies as master of their school for non-French

students, directing the education of young Dominican bachelors
in theology, one of two Dominican professors of theology teaching at the University of Paris at this time. Much of his work was
devoted to "reading" in theology, to the explication of various
books of sacred scripture from both the Old Testament and the
New Testament. In addition to a commentary on the sentences
of Peter Lombard (which may belong to the preceding two years)
and the *opuscula On Being and Essence,* his commentaries on
Isaiah and Matthew reflect his day-to-day teaching. But the most
important product of the first Paris professorate was the massive
set of over two hundred and fifty "questions" covering a host of
problems in metaphysics, theology, epistemology, cosmology,
and ethics, collected finally as the *Quaestiones disputatae de
veritate*—the *Disputed Questions on Truth.*

These "questions," treated at length in the dry, unadorned
Latin of the thirteenth century (which constituted a "Scholastic"
language—that is, a language originating in and suited to the
habits and customs of a medieval school of higher instruction),
reflect conclusively the sociological structure of the medieval university. The University of Paris in the middle of the thirteenth
century was a tight, insulated, linguistic community (to use the
image of Vossler and Wittgenstein) with highly individualistic
modes of expression reflecting both the quotidian and ritualistic
aspects of the learned life. Many of the questions treated here
must have originally been put to Saint Thomas in his classroom,
and of these the most significant and perplexing were then incor-
porated into the almost fortnightly ritual of the characteristic
public debate. The *Disputed Questions on Truth,* therefore, for
all their rigidly formalized presentation, reflect the dialectical
actualities of the pedagogical life of the Middle Ages.

In one of his most felicitous characterizations of the life and
character of Saint Thomas, Father Chenu remarks:

The reading of Saint Thomas' works confirms the testimony
concerning his temperament that, his contemporaries tell us,
was made up of great self-possession, mental and moral serenity, a somewhat heavy calmness in social contacts, and to crown
it all, a freedom of spirit embedded in contemplation. All his
life, from his first day to his last, Saint Thomas fought a relentless battle: either in the unfolding of the general undertaking
of his life, to constitute a science of theology with the help of
all the resources of Greek thought; or in the various episodes
connected with the entrance of Aristotle upon the scene ...

the development of theology . . . the evolution of institutions
(in particular, the new forms of religious life and of the apos-
tolate). All this battling cannot but have constantly made its
mark upon his work.

It is precisely this "agonistic" and dialectical character which
marks the disputative practices of the medieval university, and
despite the fact that William of Tocco, Aquinas's biographer,
declared of him that "brother Thomas refutes an opponent as
one would instruct a disciple," nevertheless I think the scars of
intellectual battle are to be discerned deeply embedded in the
Disputed Questions on Truth. And yet the formal organization
of the *Questions* is a demonstration of intense personal sincerity
in the impersonal search for truth, one in which the appeal to
authority, although it constantly appears, is used less to demonstrate a conclusion than to clarify a meaning, and where primary
dependence for the ultimate indication of demonstrative certainty rests simply upon the appeal to reason. Toward the end of his
life Saint Thomas was specifically asked in a quodlibetal question
whether a theological problem should be resolved by an appeal
to authority or to reason. In his reply (*Questiones quodlibetales*,
5.q.9.a) Aquinas beautifully illustrated the procedure he had
employed in his *Disputed Questions on Truth* almost fifteen
years before.

The purpose of the magistral disputation in the schools is not to
remove error but to instruct the listeners, so that they may be
brought to understand the truth which is looked to, as an end.
In this case, the argument should be based on reasons which
investigate the root of the truth, and which explain how the
statement is true. Otherwise, if a master determines a question
by means of bare authorities, the listener may become certain
that the point is so, but he will get no scientific knowledge or
understanding — and he will go away empty-handed.

The literary form of the "disputed question," already in use by
the time of Saint Thomas's first professorate at Paris, is one of
the greatest intellectual achievements of medieval Scholasticism,
and it is utilized not only by Saint Thomas, but by Saint Bonaventura and his famous disciple, Matthew of Aquasparta, as
well. But in the great collection of disputed questions on truth
which Aquinas produced at Paris between his thirty-first and his

thirty-fourth year, the dialectical format reaches its culmination.

In this literary form the element, the quantum, the building block of dialectical construction as it were, is the "article." And the article of a "disputed question" (almost identically with the article of a *summa*, which it resembles like a twin) consists in five essential parts or moments: (1) the posing of a philosophical or theological question or issue; (2) the marshaling of a series of "objections" or "difficulties" which suggest that the original question should be negatively answered; (3) a short section entitled "To the Contrary," presenting a brief scriptural or rational position contrary to the argument of the difficulties; (4) the magisterial determination, decision, or judgment, entitled *Respondeo* or "Reply"; and (5) a final section "Answer to Difficulties," in which for each of the objections or difficulties of (2) an answering, contrary, clarifying argument is presented in accordance with the position taken in (4), the "Reply." It is clear, then, that the "article" of the medieval disputed question contains two primary elements: a dialectical opposition of arguments in answer to a posited question, and a final judicial determination on which of these terms of the opposition is the "truth" — that is to say on which, to the medieval consciousness, most adequately recommended itself to the tradition of authoritative philosophical and scriptural writings and to the natural rationality of the human mind.

One example will illustrate the form. In the *Disputed Questions on Truth* section 2 treats the general topic of *God's Knowledge* in fifteen separate "articles" in each of which a basic theological question is asked. These questions are the following: 1. Is there knowledge in God? 2. Does God know or understand Himself? 3. Does God know things other than Himself? 4. Does God have proper and determinate knowledge of things? 5. Does God know singular things? 6. Does the human intellect know singulars? 7. Does God know the singular as now existing or not existing? 8. Does God know nonbeings, and things which are not, have not been, and will not be? 9. Does God know infinites? 10. Can God make infinites? 11. Is knowledge predicated of God and man purely equivocally? 12. Does God know singular future contingencies? 13. Does God's knowledge change? 14. Is God's knowledge the cause of things? 15. Does God have knowledge of evil things? Simply as illustration, I should like to present a somewhat abbreviated version of question 15.

Article 15

Does God have knowledge of evil things?

Difficulties:
It seems that he does not, for

1. All knowledge either causes the thing known, or is itself caused by it. But God's knowledge is not the cause of evil nor do evil things cause it. Therefore God does not know evil things.

2. As is said in Aristotle's *Metaphysics*, every being is related to truth as it is related to existence. But evil, as Augustine says, is not a being; therefore it is not something true, and, since nothing is known unless it is true, evil cannot be known by God.

3. Averroës says that an active intellect does not know a privation. But God's intellect is active in the highest possible degree, and thus knows no privation. And as Augustine says, "Evil is the privation of good." Therefore God does not know evil.

4. Whatever is known is known either through its likeness or through its contrary. Now evil is not like the divine essence, nor is evil its contrary, for evil cannot harm it and a thing is said to be evil because it is harmful. Therefore God does not know evil things.

5. That which cannot be learned cannot be known. But as Augustine says: "Evil cannot be learned through instruction, for only good things can be learned." Therefore evil cannot be known and so is not known by God.

6. Whoever knows grammar is grammatical. Therefore, whoever knows evil things is evil. But God is not evil. Hence, he does not know evil.

To the contrary:

1. No one avenges what he does not know. But God is the avenger of evil. Therefore, He *has* knowledge of evil things.

2. There is no good which God lacks. But the knowledge of evil things is good, for by it evils are avoided. Therefore, God *knows* evil things.

REPLY:
According to Aristotle one does not understand a thing unless he knows its distinction from other things. But the basis of dis-

tinction lies in affirmation and negation. Therefore, who knows an affirmation must know its negation. Accordingly, since God has proper knowledge of all His effects, he must know all the opposed negations and privations as well as the contraries found in things. Consequently, since evil is the privation of good, by knowing good, He knows every evil thing.

Answers to difficulties:
1. Evil is not known to God by its likeness, but through the likeness of its opposite. Consequently, it does not follow that God is the cause of evil things because He knows them. It follows, rather, that He is the cause of the good to which the evil is opposed.

2. As Aristotle says in the *Metaphysics*, even non-being is in some sense said to be. As a consequence, from the fact that evil is opposed to good, it has the character of the knowable and the true.

3. It was the opinion of Averroës that God does not know individual effects but only their nature as being. Since evil is not opposed to generic but to particular being, it follows from this that God would not know evil. But this is false from what has been already said. For from the fact that a thing is known, its privation is known and both thing and privation are known through the presence of a form in the intellect.

4. The opposition of one thing to another can be taken in two ways: in general and in particular. But in the second way evil is not opposed to God.

5. Insofar as evil is known, it is a good, for whatever can be learned is good, but only insofar as it can be known.

6. Grammar is known by possessing the art of grammar. But evil is not known by possessing it. Hence, no analogy can be drawn.

The Article is somewhat overextended, lacking (as we shall see) the elegance and economy of a corresponding article dealing with the same question in the *Summa theologica*. But the dry presentation of argument in a cultural ambience which takes Augustine, Aristotle, and Averroës for granted is characteristic, and through the formality of the literary structure one can neverthless glimpse the earnest professor, disputing with his theological colleagues in an effort to stabilize the divine attributes for a society moved and determined in every aspect by the major tenets of the Christian faith.

Saint Thomas did not remain at the University of Paris beyond 1259. Upon specific order of Pope Urban IV he returned from Paris to Italy—as a contemporary Bartholomew of Lucca, stated—for "well-determined reasons." It is not clear precisely what these reasons were, and there has been considerable speculation on the point. Some believe that Aquinas was removed because of continued friction with the secular masters at the university. Others think his services were especially required at the papal court. Still others note that it was desirable to transfer his chair at the university to another Dominican professor, especially since he had completed the usual three-year term. Whatever the reason, Saint Thomas at once set out for Italy, where he remained for almost ten years. It was not until 1268 that he received the news that his superiors had once again appointed him to teach theology at the University of Paris, although it was quite unusual for any Dominican in the thirteenth century to be appointed for a second time. Thus began Aquinas's second professorate at Paris, which was to last from the spring of 1269 to the spring of 1272.

This second term at Paris is notable in two respects. In the first place, it marked his famous polemic against Siger de Brabant and his colleagues in the faculty of liberal arts who had become converted to the Averroistic interpretation of Aristotle and who were the propounders of a new "Latin Averroism" which "threatened" the Christian world. To this matter I shall return subsequently. But the second, and more immediately relevant, concern is that Saint Thomas's great *Summa theologica* was written between 1266 and 1272, so that the larger part of its composition coincided with the second Paris professorate. It too is therefore a crucial part of his dialectical and disputative career.

However, despite similarities of form and content, it is a rather different type of endeavor from the *Disputed Questions on Truth* of the first Paris professorate. In the brief prologue to the *Summa theologica* Saint Thomas speaks of himself not as a philosopher pursuing an abstract idea but as a "doctor of catholic truth," whose chief concern is not primarily to reach those proficient in the sacred doctrine, but rather to teach elementary students. "We propose in this book," he says," to treat of whatever belongs to the Christian religion, in such a way as may tend to the instruction of beginners." And the combination of strict intellectual inquiry with pedagogical and institutional responsibility is exemplary of the role of metaphysics, epistemology, and ethics in the middle of the thirteenth century. Whereas the collections of disputed questions were treatises crystallizing the agonistic experiences of the masters, the *summa* is dedicated to the requirements of the pupil. Still, it would be misleading to believe either that there was something philosophically simple or elementary about it, or that it was completely independent of the dialectical experience represented in the disputed question. The *summa* is the architectonic summation of medieval learning—the ripest fruit of the conscientious teaching of the medieval university. The *summae* may have originated during the twelfth century as loosely organized, although elaborate assemblages of church dogma and scriptural materials, but the discipline of the medieval university environment contributed to the *summae* of the thirteenth century a synthetic and orderly character which gave authenticity to their pretensions of being the repositories of divine *science*.

Designed to expound concisely and economically a vast body of doctrine, to organize it definitively beyond the occasional and the piecemeal analysis (which the quodlibetal question perforce was and the disputed question often approached), and to perform this service with the aim of teaching elementary students, the *summa* became a type of philosophical treatise which combined a method of logical treatment with an almost unlimited range of subject matter. But its singularity lay in the fact that it could be the product of a quiet and contemplative creative effort.

Medieval philosophers, following Aristotle, habitually made a distinction in scholarly presentation between "the order of learning" and "the order of intrinsic intelligibility"—a difference in treatment required by the distinction between the competing claims of subject matter and of the teaching experience. The teaching method of the *lectio* was geared to the nature of the text being explicated; that of the "disputed question" to the accidental circumstances of public controversy. In neither case was there freedom of composition according to the inherent logic of the interior development of a system of ideas. But the writing of a *summa* implied just such an exercise of freedom—for it represented an effort of systemization freed from the situational demands of the occasional and the contingent. The Aristotelian inheritance which was part of the classical legacy placed the problem of organized knowledge—of "science"—at the center of medieval consciousness. The *summa* was par excellence the intellectual instrument for assimilating the Christian mysteries (the trinity, the incarnation, providence, creation, free will, original sin) to this rigid methodological demand.

But any distinction between the ad hoc immediacy of the disputed question and the more leisurely composition of the *summa* should not conceal the fact that their formal structure is identical. Both are composed of "articles," both raise identical theological and philosophical questions, both even contain identical or similar arguments. And if the *summa* is a more unified and comprehensive work, it too reveals the indubitable fact that the wisdom it contains has been won originally in the brutal arena of public disputation. The briefest comparison of Saint Thomas's *Disputed Questions on Truth* with his *Summa theologica* makes this abundantly clear. "Question 1: Truth" of the *Disputed Questions* reappears as "Question 16: Of Truth" of the *Summa*; "Question 3: Ideas" in eight articles of the *Disputed Questions* is reduced to three articles in "Question 15: Of Ideas" in the *Summa*; and "Question 2: God's Knowledge" in fifteen articles in the *Disputed Questions* has its exact analogue in "Question 14: Of God's Knowledge" in sixteen articles in the *Summa*. I append (again in somewhat abbreviated form) question 14, article 10 of the *Summa theologica*: "Whether God knows evil things?" as the precise counterpart of the similar article from the *Disputed Questions on Truth* given above.

Article 10

Whether God knows evil things?

Objection 1. It seems that God does not know evil things. For the Philosopher says that the intellect which is not in potentiality does not know privation. But as Augustine says: "evil is the privation of good." Therefore, as the intellect of God is never in potentiality, but is always in act, it seems that God does not know evil things.

Objection 2. Further, all knowledge is either the cause of the thing known, or is caused by it. But the knowledge of God is not the cause of evil, nor is it caused by evil. Therefore God does not know evil things.

Objection 3. Further, everything known is known either by its likeness or by its opposite. But whatever God knows, He knows through His essence. Now the divine essence neither is the likeness of evil, nor is evil contrary to it; for to the divine essence there is no contrary, as Augustine says. Therefore God does not know evil things.

Objection 4. Further, what is known through another and not through itself, is imperfectly known. But evil is not known by God through itself, otherwise evil would be in God; for the thing known must be in the knower. Therefore, if evil is known through another, namely, through good, it would be known by Him imperfectly; which cannot be, for the knowledge of God is not imperfect. Therefore God does not know evil things.

ON THE CONTRARY, it is written (Prov. xv. 11) "Hell and destruction are before the Lord."

I ANSWER THAT: Whoever knows a thing perfectly must know all that can be accidental to it. Now there are some good things to which corruption by evil may be accidental. Hence God would not know good things perfectly, unless He also knew evil things. Now a thing is knowable in the degree to which it is; hence, since it is the essence of evil that it is the privation of good, by the very fact that God knows good things, He knows evil things also; as by light is known darkness.

Reply Objection 1. The saying of the Philosopher must be understood as meaning that the intellect which is not in potentiality, does not know privation by privation existing in it. This is because simple and indivisible forms are in our intellect not actually, but only potentially. It is thus that simple things are known by separate substances. God therefore knows evil, not by privation existing in Himself, but by the opposite good.

Reply Objection 2. The knowledge of God is not the cause of evil; but is the cause of the good whereby the evil is known.

Reply Objection 3. Although evil is not opposed to the divine essence, which is not corruptible by evil, it is opposed to the effects of God, which He knows by His essence; and knowing them, He knows the opposite evils.

Reply Objection 4. To know a thing by something else only, belongs to imperfect knowledge, if that thing is of itself knowable; but evil is not of itself knowable, inasmuch as the very nature of evil means the privation of good; therefore evil can neither be defined nor known except by good.

Simple comparison of the two articles, written approximately
ten years apart, shows that the root problem and the metaphysical
presuppositions remain constant. The arguments of both are
grounded in the distinction between knowledge and its causes, the
Aristotelian theories of knowledge through likenesses to its object and of the difference between the actual and the potential
intellect, the Augustinian doctrine of privation. But whereas the
article from the *Disputed Questions on Truth* is more drawn out,
more rhetorical, more ready to score simple debater's points, that
from the *Summa theologica* is philosophically compact, homogeneous, and elegant. Both take Aristotle and Augustine as the
prime philosophical authorities, but in the *Summa theologica*
article Averroës, quoted extensively in the *Disputed Questions on
Truth,* has dropped out of the picture. Perhaps this represents the
cultural situation at the University of Paris during Aquinas's
second professorate, when the threat of Siger de Brabant made
Averroës less palatable to the orthodox Christian mentality. But
the chief impression remains: that the two articles are astonish-
ingly alike, and that the literary refinement of the *Summa theologica* would have been impossible without the actual dialectical
encounters upon which the *Disputed Questions on Truth* so clearly rests.

The Rationalization of Order

The concept of order, as we have seen from our consideration of
Plato, is essentially a conservative idea. And the passion for order,
expressed in the requirement of rulership patterns in society conceived of as both "hierarchical" and in some sense "natural" and
"necessary," always gives a philosophical system an inherently
preservative and ideological character. In Plato the concept of
aristocracy was explicitly adopted — through a sociological *principle of hierarchy* openly stated in the *Republic* and a metaphysical *principle of permanence* clearly adumbrated in the *Timaeus*.
Something quite similar is to be found in the Thomistic system,
despite the fact that its chief philosophic inspiration is more
Aristotelian than Platonic, for Platonic elements remain woven
into its texture, and where they appear their presence always
makes possible the derivation of principles undergirding a conservative approach to the world.

On the surface this is not completely clear. For if one argues (as
Paul Landsberg has in an interesting article "Zur Soziologie der
Erkenntnistheorie" in *Schmollers Jahrbuch*, 1931) that there is a

certain rough parallelism between extreme realism in interpreting the status of universals and social conservatism, on the one hand, and extreme nominalism and antiauthoritarian social attitudes, on the other, then the medieval situation places Saint Thomas in a middle position between the conservative Augustinian theology of Bonaventura, with its correlate of intense social conservatism, and the somewhat later extreme nominalism of William of Ockham, which was integrally connected with an attack upon the papal *plenitudo potestatis*, with the rights of subjects against rulers (expressed as sympathy with a dissenting minority against established opinion) and, specifically, with a plea for the limitation of sovereign papal authority in matters of faith. But the fact is that Aquinas is closer to Bonaventura than he is to Ockham, and if his own theological struggles during his second professorate at Paris were directed against both the reactionary Augustinianism of some extreme Franciscans and the radical Averroism of Siger (a position closely representing what Ernst Bloch has called that of *Avicenna und die Aristotelische Linke* — Avicenna and the Aristotelian Left) there is no evidence whatsoever that he questioned the constellation of churchly power represented by the social situation in the first half of the thirteenth century.

If Plato was a born aristocrat, Aquinas was that special medieval paradox, a saint of noble birth — a fact perhaps less paradoxical when one realizes the aristocratic bias of the medieval church as a whole. As early as the ninth century, the aristocratic character of the upper clergy is apparent. Louis the Pious was reprimanded for appointing the son of a serf as archbishop of Rheims. When Otto II elevated Gerbert of Aurillac, who was of lower-class parentage, to become Pope Sylvester, it produced an enormous outcry. And it was held against Suger, the famous abbot of Saint Denis (in whose abbey, as Panofsky has said, Early Gothic architecture was born) that he was of servile birth. The society of the church was as sharply divided as was lay society into an upper and a lower class; the hierarchy was in general closed against any but those of noble birth. From the nobility were chosen bishops and abbots, while the parish priests were usually recruited among lower-class villagers. Only in the late Middle Ages did this exclusiveness begin to break down.

But in the case of Saint Thomas the fact of noble blood is less important than the principles of ecclesiastical authority he represents, which are hardly more than the commonplaces of the times. The medieval church was enormously different from modern ichurches, whether Catholic or Protestant. It exercised everywhere not only spiritual dominion, but great political, administrative, economic, and social power. And its administrative structure in the thirteenth century was much like that of a modern state. Its ruler was the pope, its provincial governors were archbishops and bishops, it had its own law and courts of law, its own councils and synods, its own tax collectors and prisons. As an eminent medieval historian of the last generation (James Westfall Thompson) said:

The Roman Church in the Middle Ages was a governor, a landed proprietor, a rent collector, an imposer of taxes, a material producer, an employer of labor on an enormous scale, a merchantman, a tradesman, a banker and mortgage-broker, a custodian of morals, a maker of sumptuary laws, a schoolmaster, a compeller of conscience — all in one.

The union of spiritual authority and temporal power in the medieval church was inevitable. For no great historic institution can be effective unless it is strong not only in the doctrines it professes but also in the organization it needs. The function of the church was not to follow, but to lead, to guide, and to teach; to use for its society the heritage of culture and tradition it guarded. The organization of the church in Saint Thomas's time was fully feudalized, and its kinship with secular society, its reflection of its economic and social structure, was illustrated alike in its laws, its moral precepts, and the great systematic constructions of its philosophers.

Erwin Panofsky has been at some pains to show (*Gothic Architecture and Scholasticism*) how the early Romanesque architecture, ranging from Norman structuralism to the protoclassicism of Italy and Provence, has much in common with the ruthless rationalism of Abelard and Roscellinus and the early humanism of the school of Chartres, and also how the high Gothic system of the cathedrals of Chartres and Amiens achieved in the age of Saint Louis (1226–70), coincides with the great systematic constructions of Alexander of Hales, Albert the Great, William of Auvergne, Saint Bonaventura, and of course Saint Thomas. The *Summa theologiae* of Alexander of Hales, which, according to Roger Bacon, "weighed about as much as one horse can carry," was begun in 1231, the very year in which Pierre de Montereau began the new nave of Saint Denis. This analogy between medieval architecture and philosophy is neither fortuitous nor unique. It is simply one example of the morphological relationship that invariably binds together the expression forms of all branches of a culture. And it therefore suggests that the great *summae* of Aquinas may also be deeply expressive of the aristocratic and conservative presuppositions of the feudal order.

What sorts of evidence might we produce? There are several possibilities. Insofar as the Platonic *principle of permanence* is expressed in the eternity of the ideas or forms, this aspect of conservative value theory might be traced in the analogues it finds in the Thomistic system. And this, in turn, leads to the Thomistic stand on the problem of universals. For if Aquinas is no radical Augustinian, he is even further from the precincts of nominalism, and his moderate Aristotelianism yet contains Platonic overtones. If universals are *in re* in the sense of being imminent in natural objects, and *post rem* in that they are the products of abstractive knowledge, they are also *ante rem* in the mind of God as constituting his plan for the world. And this appeal to the being of God in turn leads to the use of the distinction between form and matter such that God's own perfection, his actuality, implies a devaluation of that potentiality which is the material principle. As Saint Thomas says in the *Summa theologica* (1.4.1.c): *Oportet quod primum materiale sit maxime in potentia et ita maxime imperfectum* ("Since matter as such is merely potential, the first material principle must be merely potential and therefore the most imperfect of all"). But the attribution of a certain independent existence to the universal, and the denial of the prime reality of matter (idealism) are not the chief considerations. They are only the points of criticism which would be leveled against Saint Thomas from the standpoint of a vulgar Marxism. Much more significant, I think, is the reintroduction of the Platonic *principle of hierarchy*, although here not so much in the political sense of the *Republic* as in a cosmological sense never worked out with complete fullness or consistency in any of Plato's most metaphysical dialogues. For it is in his cosmic gradations, his sense of hierarchy and degree in the entire universe, that Saint Thomas provides his purest rationalization of the principle of order — his clearest enthronement of the categories of social distinction of the feudal society in which he lived.

The Latin noun *ordo* means "order," "arrangement," "rank," or "degree," and the Latin verb *ordino*, from which it comes, has a range of meanings: "to arrange," "to set in order," "to regulate," "to ordain," and "to rule." When, therefore, in the dictum cited above Saint Thomas says: *Intellectus solus est ordinare,* this means both that the function of the intellect is customarily to arrange or set in order and, at the same time and by this very fact, to regulate and to rule. "Order" is then for the medieval mentality both a principle of logical disposition and a principle of power. In speaking here, therefore, of the Thomistic system as "the rationalization of order," I wish to preserve the full richness and ambiguity of the concept — to show that it is at once a method of intellectual organization and at the same time a mirror image of feudal gradations of rank.

With respect to the class organization of feudal society, the term "three orders" (*tres ordines*) appears as early as the second decade of the ninth century, and by the end of the century they are fully distinguished. Writing about the year 1000, the bishop of Laon, addressing Robert the Pious, king of France says:

Triplex ergo Dei domus est quae creditur una:
Nunc orant, alii pugnant aliique laborant.

(Triple, therefore, is the household of God which is thought to be one: Some pray, others fight, and others work.)

And Jacques de Vitry, of the generation just before Saint Thomas (he died in 1240), echoing the twelfth-century John of Salisbury (and ultimately the ancient metaphor of Saint Paul of the body and its members) said:

that the clergy were the eyes, for they saw and pointed out to men the road to safety; the nobles were the hands and arms, whose duty was to protect society, to enforce justice, and to war for defense of the realm; the common people (minores) were as the lower parts of the body, to sustain and bear the upper parts of the body politic.

Each of the two upper classes, clergy and nobility, had its own subordinate gradations of rank. Even more than the clerical hierarchy, the military made of itself a closed caste in which every member shared some quality of nobility. There was: (1) the king, (2) ecclesiastical princes as vassals of the crown, (3) the great dukes, (4) lay princes who were vassals of the church, (5) counts and barons who were vassals of greater lay noblemen, (6) free knights, and (7) *ministeriales,* or men of servile origin who through military power or distinction had risen out of serfdom into a status of semiknighthood. Back of Saint Thomas's great theological constructions lay the unarticulated but obvious presupposition of this principle of hierarchy, embedded in the social and economic structure of the times.

It was, I think, John of Saint Thomas who first called attention to "the golden circle of theology around which the divine *Summa* of Saint Thomas circulates to its completion"—the high argument of God as man's first cause and his last end; of the coming forth of all creatures from God as their source, and the ultimate return of these same creatures to God as their final resting place. Thus the content of the *Summa theologica* embodies the spiritual essence of Christianity in the literary form of a circular image. But precisely because the circle begins with the creative act, the material within the circle yields to a new and different image—that of the pyramidal or climactic ladder of being, hierarchically organized step by step, and with God himself as its transcendent apex.

The *Summa theologica* begins, therefore, with an extended consideration of God: his existence, goodness, unity, perfection, *eternity* and *immutability*—these last two characteristics once more reinstituting Plato's principle of permanence and guaranteeing that the source of value in the universe is forever fixed, beyond temporal decay and radical change. But the thrust of Thomistic Platonism goes further. For, a "Christian" philosophy is in its pristine content hardly different from theology; that is to say, its sole "object" is God. And as its first focus of attention must be an examination of his nature, its second must be an examination of his effects. The central position of the creation in Christian theology turns the mind to this second enterprise; a consideration of all creatures in their hierarchical ordering, their mode of issuance from their own divine first principle.

That God is the universal cause of all being is the premise from which the Christian philosopher begins, and it follows that all things proceed (as so many determinate effects from the infinite perfection of God) according to the determination of his intelligence and his will. But this raises the question of God's foreknowledge of his own creation in such a form as to admit only of an essentially Platonic solution. The Platonic "ideas" thus reappear in the mind of God also as exemplars or models. For there is not only one idea of the universe as a whole, but a plurality of ideas, each corresponding to a species of future natural existence which represents the divine intention, and it is the topography of the divine intention which constitutes the *order* of the universe. And here too "order" means at once a principle of divine "arrangement" and of divine "rulership" and "regulation."

I have spoken of "Platonic" ideas and a "Platonic" solution. But for Aquinas the Platonic legacy is, of course, mediated by the

Augustinian tradition. Early in the *Summa theologica* (1.Q15.2)
Saint Thomas quotes Augustine to indicate how the Platonic
forms, originated in a non-Christian context, are yet available for
a "creationist" perspective.

Ideas are certain principle forms, or permanent and immutable
types of things, they themselves not being formed. Thus they are
eternal, and existing always in the same manner, as being
contained in the divine intelligence. Whilst, however, they
themselves neither come into being nor decay, yet we say that
in accordance with them everything is formed that can arise
or decay, and all that actually does so.

Although it seems reasonable that there should be archetypal
"patterns" in the mind of God, it is not immediately clear why the
divine creation should have produced a creatural hierarchy; why,
in short, the principle of gradation of rank should be built into the
very nature of the universe. But Saint Thomas presents an argument for it which, although it might appear natural in the philos-
sophy of Whitehead (as the argument that plurality of effects
and even negative values are contrasts which produce massiveness
of feeling), is yet paradoxical in the metaphysics of an Aristotelian
only mildly touched by Platonic Augustinianism. Since a single
creature could never in itself mirror the divine perfection, it was
necessary for God (as his wish) to impart being to a plurality of
formally distinct species. And it is from this pluralism that we may
explain hierarchical arrangement, and the ordering of the universe in degrees, as mirroring an analogous perfection. As mixed
compounds are more perfect than elements, so plants are more
perfect than minerals, animals more perfect than plants, and men
more perfect than the other animals. Thus, the scale of forms,
"the great chain of being," as Lovejoy called it, is itself the highest
perfection of the universe, and its intrinsic rationality prompted
God to produce the observed distinction and inequality among
created beings. Here is a "rationalization of order" indeed!

The nub of the argument appears in the *Summa theologica*
(1.Q47.2), but perhaps is more complete in the *Summa contra
gentiles* (3.71); and it is worthy of note, not simply because of its
modern, Whiteheadean flavor, but also because of its almost
secular reference to the function of political rulership.

Perfect goodness could not be in creation if there were not
found an order of goodness among creatures, some being better
than others: or else all possible grades of goodness would not be
filled up; nor would any creature be like God in having pre-

eminence over another. Thus *a great beauty would be lost to creation in the removal of the order of distinct and dissimilar beings, one better than the other. A dead level of goodness would be a manifest derogation to the perfection of creation.* A higher grade of goodness consists in there being something which cannot fall away from goodness: a lower grade, in there being that which can fall away. The perfection of the universe requires both grades of goodness. But it is the care of a ruler to uphold perfection in the subjects of his government, not to make it less. Therefore it is no part of divine providence wholly to exclude from creation the capability of falling away from good. [Italics added]

Here is an argument from considerations of moral and aesthetic value which not only condones, but *demands* the unequal universe. And, transferred to the medieval social world, it would hold that the existence of the villein and the serf, the worker on the land whose lot is little better than that of a beast of burden, is indeed not a societal scandal, but an ingredient essential to the organic perfection of the social whole. Elitism thus becomes a distinct requirement of political and social life, and by analogy one might argue (although I do not believe that Saint Thomas ever actually did so) that "a dead level" of upper-class nobility would "be a manifest derogation to the perfection" of feudal social life. And yet the passage which immediately follows the one quoted above from the *Summa contra gentiles* comes very close to just such an argument. Saint Thomas says:

The best rule in any government is to provide for everything under government according to the mode of its nature: just administration consists in this. As then it would be contrary to any rational plan of human administration for the civil government to debar its subjects from acting *according to their offices and conditions of life,* except perhaps in an occasional hour of emergency, so it would be contrary to the plan of divine government not to allow creatures to act according to the mode of their several natures. [Italics added]

What is interesting about this passage is not simply the obvious analogy between divine and temporal rulership and the implied similarities between God's and man's administration of their respective domains; it is that the same type of argument for cosmological inequality is here implicitly applied to human inequality as well. Each rank of the civil hierarchy has its proper function, and it would be unreasonable for civil administrators to prevent any class "from acting according to their offices and conditions of life." It at once looks back to Plato's assertion in the *Republic* that one of the duties of the guardian class shall be to assure the functionalism of the social whole, to see that each class does its own proper work and does not interfere with the work of another, and looks forward to the Bradleyan ethics of "my station and its duties." For in each case there is the assumption of a valid class stratification, the presupposition of a social "organicism" not unlike that which underlies the construction of the feudal model of the social world.

That this comparison of the cosmological and the political realms is not accidental in the philosophy of Saint Thomas is shown by his similar use of the analogy (but with reverse intention) in the *De regno* — the treatise "On Kingship" which he addressed to the king of Cyprus. Here in the *Summa contra gentiles* he uses the political situation to illuminate the cosmological; there in the *De regno* he used the appeal to cosmology and divine rulership to illuminate the nature of the kingly office.

> Since things which are in accordance with art are an imitation of the things which are in accordance with nature, it seems best that we learn about the kingly office from the pattern of the regime of nature.
>
> In things of nature there is both a universal and a particular government. The former is God's government Whose rule embraces all things and Whose providence governs them all. The latter is found in man and it is much like the divine government. Hence man is called a *microcosmos*. Indeed there is a similitude between both governments in regard to their form; for just as the universe of corporeal creatures and all spiritual powers comes under the divine government, in like manner the members of the human body and all the powers of the soul are governed by reason. Thus, in a proportionate manner, reason is to man what God is to the world. Since, however, man is by nature a social animal living in a multitude, the analogy with the divine government is found in him not only in this way that one man governs himself by reason, but also in that the multitude of men is governed by the reason of one man. This is what first of all constitutes the office of a king. True, among certain animals that live socially there is a likeness to the king's rulership; so we say that there are kings among bees. Yet animals exercise rulership not through reason but through their natural instinct which is implanted in them by the Great Ruler, the Author of nature.
>
> Therefore let the king recognize that such is the office which he undertakes, namely, that he is to be in the kingdom what the soul is in the body, and what God is in the world.

It is perhaps not necessary to fill in the entire picture Aquinas paints of the hierarchically organized cosmos of God's creation. Just below God come the angels or pure spirits, for in them is realized the highest degree of created perfection. It is clear that Saint Thomas's metaphysical speculation about them draws heavily upon the neo-Platonic doctrine of emanation, and upon the prior speculations of Plotinus, Iamblicus, Proclus, and, above all, Pseudo-Dionysius. Like the latter, Aquinas divides the angelic realm into three hierarchies, each subdivided into three orders. These incorporeal beings, needed in the cosmology precisely to make the hierarchy of being continuous with the divine being and to clearly illustrate that the effects of divine power are naturally ordered in a continuous series of decreasing perfections, are therefore themselves ordered according to the differences in the several modes of intelligence which they display. At the first level are the seraphim, cherubim, and thrones, who know intelligible essences as they flow from the divine nature, and who burn with love of the divine goodness. The second hierarchy, the dominations, virtues, and powers, know intelligible being as subject to the most universal of created causes. And the final group, the principalities, archangels, and simple angels, know intelligibility as it appears to particular causes and beings. It is they, therefore, who are charged with the ordering of human affairs; they are the guardians of men and God's messengers on the most solemn and portentous embassies.

Below the angelic realm comes the whole complicated hierarchy of the corporeal world with the seven concentric planetary spheres, the fixed stars, earth, and the four elements, and that gradation of minerals, plants, animals, and human species with which earth is furnished. And it is just here, in the orders generally distinguished by physics or natural philosophy, that the originality of Saint Thomas is most limited, and that he follows Aristotle most closely. But for our purposes, all that is important is to gather the underlying principles of this great cosmological spiral: that man functions as the connecting link between the realm of the pure intelligences and the corporeal world; and that matter exists for the sake of form, lower forms for the sake of higher, and higher for their essential relationship to God.

We have seen that with Plato the principle of hierarchy receives a threefold philosophical exemplification: in the tripartite class division and the tripartite analysis of the human soul in the

Republic, and in the three elements of the cosmology presented in the *Timaeus*. And one cannot escape the conviction that with Saint Thomas also the hierarchical principle of an unequal society is built into the mental furniture of a typically medieval mind. Both the *Summa theologica* and the *Summa contra gentiles* are centrally concerned with cosmology, with the elaborate presentation of "the creatural hierarchy" with which the Middle Ages was obsessed. And the former contains elaborate formulations of the hierarchy of epistemic powers and of the levels of legal prescription (divine law, natural law, human law) as the *De regno* does of governmental functions and as the unfinished commentary on the *De trinitate* of Boethius does with the hierarchy of the content and the methods of the sciences. One illustration can perhaps stand for all. Toward the end of the *Summa theologica,* in the section on "The Contemplative Life," Saint Thomas presents (2.2.Q158.4) the epistemic correlate of the creatural hierarchy: the contemplative stages through which the mind rises from its lowest nature to its highest actualization, through the impingement of the lowest rung of the corporeal world to its last end, from the simplicites of empirical knowledge to the ultimate mysteries of faith.

These six denote the steps whereby we ascend by means of creatures to the contemplation of God. For the first step consists in the mere consideration of sensible objects; the second step consists in going forward from sensible to intelligible objects; the third step is to judge of sensible objects according to intelligible things; the fourth is the absolute consideration of the intelligible objects to which one has attained by means of sense-data; the fifth is the contemplation of those intelligible objects that are unattainable by way of sense-data, but which the reason is able to grasp; the sixth step is the consideration of such intelligible things as the reason can neither discover nor grasp, which pertain to the sublime contemplation of divine truth, wherein contemplation is ultimately perfected.

The rationalization of order which undergirds the Thomistic system like some dependable sociological substrate is a reflection of social preconceptions, received almost without thought from the daily experience of the medieval social system, and it finds its expression both in doctrinal content and in the repetitive *forms* of philosophical argument and style. The philosophy of Saint Thomas is built upon a classificatory system bursting with conceptual distinctions and gradations of rank. Like the great cathedrals with which it is contemporaneous, it is a monument to the medieval sense of the immutable *order of being.*

The Institutional Task

In the modern world a philosopher, although he may teach at a university to which he feels moderately attached and is a citizen of a nation to which he is loyal, is in general "a free spirit," staking out his areas of philosophic interest as he sees fit and doing his research and writing as his inclination points, without obligation to consider his philosophic activity in the light of organizational allegiance or institutional claims. In the medieval world, as we have seen, it was different. Members of the mendicant orders, Franciscans and Dominicans, mindful of their priestly calling, are the favored teachers at the University of Paris, which is itself almost an arm of the Christian Church. Men raised by and devoted to the ideas of the religious confraternities in which they live accept the pedagogical adventure as a duty within the frame-work of scriptural teaching and as an evangelical aim. Those pro-fessors who teach in the faculties of arts or theology are no longer monks living an isolated life of pious contemplation; they are clerics engaged in an active program of apostolic conquest. Their thinking is gospel-oriented; their philosophizing is in terms of a given Christian problematic; their students constitute for them a Christian challenge. The atmosphere of the learned world in the thirteenth century is one of dedicated earnestness, apostolic zeal, and pastoral enthusiasm. A philosophy arising in this milieu will be anchored and attached — a form of social expression reflecting the larger qualities of piety and churchly concern. Saint Thomas, the greatest philosopher of the Middle Ages, is no exception to this consideration. He is a Dominican and a pillar of the Christian Church. These are institutions to which, in the most passionate and literal sense, he *belongs.* The content and development of his life as a philosopher can therefore be understood only in terms of his devotion to *an institutional task.*

Sometime during his teens as an arts student at the University of Naples, Aquinas became acquainted with members of the Domin-ican order, and shortly afterward himself decided to become a Dominican friar. It is known that during these years Jordan of Saxony, master general of the Dominican order, visited and preached at Naples (as he did at the other great university centers of the medieval world: Paris, Oxford, Padua, and Bologna), and his vigor and personal impressiveness may have been one element in Saint Thomas's decision. Founded at the beginning of the thirteenth century and receiving papal approval in 1216, the Order of Preachers combined vows of poverty, chastity, and obedience with the ideal of scholarship and a special exercise of evangelical effort. In 1243 or 1244, at the age of eighteen or nineteen, Aquinas took the habit of a novice in the Order of Preachers at Naples. The monastery there was part of the Roman province, and Humbert de Romans was probably provincial at the time. It was soon decided to send the young Aquinas to Paris, and there, after the famous episode of the family kidnapping near Acquapendente, he finally arrived at the Dominican house of studies on the Rue Saint Jacques in 1245. He pursued his theological and philosophical studies with Albert first at Paris and then at Cologne, and his ordination as a priest probably took place in the cathedral of Cologne sometime between 1248 and 1252.

It was because John the Teuton, master of the order, directed Albert in 1252 to select a suitable Dominican student to go to Paris as a bachelor in theology, and because Albert named Saint Thomas, with the master general's approval, that beginning in the fall of 1252 Thomas completed his theological training at Paris. During this period he presented his lectures on the *Sentences* of Peter Lombard at the Dominican house of studies on the Rue Saint Jacques, where he remained for the next four years preparatory to his inaugural lecture as a master in theology in 1256. There then followed the first Paris professorate of 1256-59.

Sometime during the period of Saint Thomas's first Paris professorate or just after it (1256-63) Humbert de Romans, the new master general of the Dominican order, Thomas's superior, and the successor of John the Teuton, wrote his influential *Commentary on the Rule of Saint Augustine*. It is a work which in considerable measure indicates the degree to which problems of philosophical scholarship were seriously impinging upon the medieval church, and the very special place which philosophizing was assuming in this institutional setting. Considering here the value of philosophical knowledge, the usefulness of philosophical books and of their study, and the relevance of philosophy to the interests of the order, he noted six major utilities: (1) for the defense of the faith, (2) for the destruction of theological error, (3) for the understanding of the scriptures, (4) for the confirmation of the faith, (5) to sharpen the faculties on criticism, and (6) to bring honor upon the order. In this justification are mingled considerations of philosophic proof, local pride, intellectual education, and institutional support — considerations by which Saint Thomas himself was probably motivated, and of which he would undoubtedly have approved. For his own works, from the very early *Commentary on the Sentences of Peter Lombard* and the *De ente et essentia* to the very late third part of the *Summa theologica*, were precisely intended for the confirmation of the faith, for the destruction of theological errors, and to bring honor upon his church and to his order.

The institutional task which the philosophy of Saint Thomas was so largely devoted to accomplishing must be seen primarily as defined by two threats to the integrity of the Christian Church which came to a head in the middle of the thirteenth century. One was external and "spatial." It sprang from a recognition that at the precarious boundaries of the Holy Roman Empire — in Spain and North Africa and the Middle East — lay the power of Islam. This ideological as well as political power was mediated by the Jewish physicians and translators and therefore was a constant reminder that "Scholasticism" — the attempt to combine the resources of Greek philosophy and revealed doctrine — had three forms, not one, and that the theologies of Judaism and Islam competed with that of Christianity for the minds of those who shared the medieval world. In 1249, at the very time when Saint Thomas was at Cologne with Albert the Great, Saint Louis went to Egypt on the Sixth Crusade to destroy the Saracen power there, returning only in 1254 while Saint Thomas was completing his theological studies at Paris. And the Seventh Crusade of 1270, in which Saint Louis left from Aigues-Mortes upon the ill-fated expedition to Tunis from which he never returned, occurred during Saint Thomas's second professorate at Paris.

But at precisely the moment when the secular arm used naked power against the infidel, the church itself was mindful of its evangelical and missionary task. Sometime around 1256 or 1257 Saint Thomas received a request from Saint Raymond of Penafort, a Spanish Dominican and former master general of the order, to compose a treatise which would serve as a training manual for missionaries going to Islam with the hope of converting Mohammedans to Christianity. Peter Marsilio, a chronicler of the next century, is here our authority.

Furthermore, strongly desiring the conversion of unbelievers, Raymond asked an outstanding Doctor of Sacred Scripture, a Master in Theology, Brother Thomas of Aquino of the same Order, who among all the clerics of the world was considered in philosophy to be, next to Brother Albert the greatest, to compose a work against the errors of unbelievers by which both the cloud of darkness might be dispelled and the teaching of the true Sun might be made manifest to those who refuse to believe. The renowned Master accomplished what the humility of so great a father asked, and composed a work called the *Summa contra gentiles*, held to be without equal in the field.

This treatise, probably begun in Paris in 1257, was only completed seven years later (1264) in Orvieto, and its importance hinges on two facts. The first is that despite its traditional form, it is not primarily a consequence of university teaching. And the second is that, since it was intended for a universe of ideological conflict and addressed to those *errantes*—Jews, Moslems, even heretical Christians—rhetorical effectiveness required that the usual appeals to accepted scriptural authority be supplanted by a recourse to that "natural reason" which is the possession of all men "as men." Here then, already in the thirteenth century, and as a result of profound ideological discord, a cosmopolitan method reappears (it had also been a resource of Hellenistic Stoic rationalism) which seeks agreement across the irrational boundaries of dogmatic scriptural commitment and the strife of warring religious traditions.

The second great threat to the integrity of the Christian Church, in contrast to the first, might be called internal or temporal." It was simply the problem of assimilating the newly available philosophy of Aristotle in its entirety. And it had become a problem for two reasons: because of a new rigor in the requirements of ecclesiastical education illustrated in the reform of studies in the Dominican order, and because the complete works of Aristotle, newly fallen into Christian hands, were themselves a pagan product, and were already the subject of an influential literature of critical comment produced by "gentile" authorities—ibn-Gabirol, Avicenna, Maimonides, and Averroës. At the moment in which it became newly clear that every Dominican monk must be intellectually competent, came a subtle challenge to an intellectual tradition of Platonic assimilation already consolidated by Saint Augustine,

Scotus Erigena, and Saint Anselm. The immutable truths of the Christian faith were faced by a new philosophical cosmology of great rigor and persuasiveness. What intellectual stand should the church take upon the problematic issues of this encounter?

When in 1259 Saint Thomas, on the order of Urban IV, returned from Paris to Italy, his last assignment before taking up his new duties as *lector* in the Dominican monastery at Anagni was to participate in a conference of Dominican scholars at Valenciennes. Also present were a distinguished group of doctors of theology from the University of Paris, among them Albert the Great, Florent of Hesdin, and Peter of Tarentaise (later, in 1276, to become Pope Innocent V), and their purpose was to completely revise the regulations governing the course of studies in the Dominican order. As a consequence, intellectual standards were raised, all monastery residents were required to attend lectures in theology, and arrangements were made for the study of the liberal arts (and especially philosophy) to be intensified within the order.

Two years after taking up his post at Anagni, Saint Thomas was transferred to the Dominican monastery at Orvieto in the vicinity of the papal court, and for the next four or five years Orvieto became the center of a very special program of scholarly investigation and inquiry. Albert the Great was also transferred to Orvieto, as was the famous Dominican translator of scientific and philosophical Greek, William of Moerbecke. The situation has the air of constituting an extraordinary papal project to undertake a formal review of the total Aristotelian philosophy with the aim of determining to what extent it could be appropriated for Christian theology and teaching. It was thus at Orvieto that, at the request of Aquinas, William of Moerbecke began to revise and translate into Latin most of the philosophical writings of Aristotle, and that Aquinas himself, possibly upon papal order and certainly with papal approval and support, began between 1265 and 1268 the great series of commentaries on the *Physics* and the *Metaphysics*, the *De anima* and the *De interpretatione*, the *Nicomachean Ethics*, and the *Politics* of Aristotle.

There is little question that Saint Thomas made a long and thorough study of the philosophy of Aristotle, particularly the psychology and philosophy of nature, and that his own maturest work owes an enormous debt to Aristotle's metaphysical distinc-

tions between formal and material causes, substance and accident, actuality and potentiality. But it also remains true that the
great Aristotelian review of the years 1265-75 was to have extremely controversial consequences. Albert the Great had begun
the fight for the valid incorporation of Aristotle as a major resource of Christian theology, and in general Saint Thomas only
augmented more richly and deeply the efforts of his teacher. Yet
within the course of this Aristotelian triumph, a special and a very
serious problem had arisen. It is that, as Father Chenu has so well
put it: "Aristotle, the master of thought, concealed riches of an
equivocal nature."

It became apparent almost at once that in the course of its
history since Aristotle's own time, his philosophy had produced
disciples whose interpretations were at best dubious from the
standpoint of the orthodox Christian position; these were represented in the materialism of Alexander of Aphrodisias and the
almost mystic neo-Platonism of Avicenna. And now his most
brilliant and persuasive commentator, Averroës, was seducing
sober professors in the arts faculty at Paris by the seeming rationality of the doctrines of the eternity of the world and the unity of
the active intellect. It was thus that when Saint Thomas entered
into his second university professorate (1268-72) he found Paris a
hotbed of controversy and his own position caught in a crossfire
between two theological extremes: the conservative Augustinian
theology of Bonaventura and the Franciscans who argued that any
recourse to Aristotle was a departure from Platonic wisdom, and
the ultraradical Latin Averroists like Siger of Brabant, who
pushed the doctrine of the unity of the intellect to an extreme
which excluded individual personal immortality, and whose espousal of Aristotle's undoubted teaching of the eternity of the
world was fatally at odds with the basic tenet of Christian crea-
tionism. Between the fanatical Augustinians who felt that Saint
Thomas was ruining Catholic theology by his introduction of
Aristotelian novelties and the fanatical Averroists who felt that his
Aristotelianism was timid, lukewarm, and far short of the truth,
Aquinas at Paris was the target of a spectrum of hostilities which
challenged his interpretation of Aristotle, questioned his religious
orthodoxy, and even raised some question about his actual right to
teach.

The ultimate historical consequence is well known. Although
Saint Thomas wrote a famous treatise *On the Unity of the Intel-*

lect against the Averroists (*De unitate intellectus, contra Aver-roistas*) and another *On the Eternity of the World against Those Protesting* (*De aeternitate mundi contra murmurantes*), neverthe-less in 1270 Etienne Tempier, bishop of Paris, issued a list of thirteen condemned theses, all of which he forbade to be taught at the University of Paris on pain of excommunication. Saint Thom-as narrowly escaped. For although the condemnation was mainly directed against Siger and his philosophical associates, it is said that the list originally contained fifteen theses, two of which, held by Saint Thomas, were removed at the last minute. And seven years later (on 7 March 1277, three years after Saint Thomas's death) this same Etienne Tempier condemned 219 propositions — this time including some clearly held by Saint Thomas himself. It was only fifty years later, after Saint Thomas was canonized by Pope John XXII on 18 July 1323, that the condemnation of 1277 was quietly retracted.

Two things in all this are clear. One is that behind the phil-sophic movements that led to the condemnations of 1270 and 1277 lies the ancient opposition of the philosophies of Plato and Aris-totle which plays so crucial and so recurrent a role in the history of philosophizing in the West. The other is that the position of Saint Thomas in this controversy became important only because in his devotion to the institutional task, he had felt it his honest duty to make Aristotle available not as a pagan sage, but as a witness to Christian truth. That he suffered a curious historic fate in con-sequence, and a final apotheosis, testifies almost as much to institutional accident as to intrinsic merit. Henry Adams, no Roman Catholic, although a great defender of medieval culture, has indicated this perfectly.

The twenty-eight quarto volumes [of Saint Thomas' writings] must be closed books for us. None but Dominicans have a right to interpret them. No Franciscan — or even Jesuit — understands Saint Thomas exactly or explains him with authority. For sum-mer tourists to handle these intricate problems in a theological spirit would be altogether absurd; but, for us, these great theo-logians were also architects who undertook to build a Church Intellectual, corresponding bit by bit to the Church Adminis-trative, both expressing — and expressed by — the Church Archi-tectural. Alexander Hales, Albert the Great, Thomas Aquinas, Duns Scotus, and the rest, were artists; and if Saint Thomas happens to stand at their head as type, it is not because we choose him or understand him better than his rivals, but be-cause his Order chose him rather than his master Albert, to impose as authority on the Church; and because Pope John XXII canonized him on the ground that his decisions were miracles; and because the Council of Trent placed his *Summa* among the sacred books on their table; and because Innocent VI said that his doctrine alone was sure; and finally, because Leo XIII very lately made a point of declaring that, on the wings of Saint Thomas' genius, human reason has reached the most sublime height it can probably ever attain.

And yet his ultimate evaluation is appreciative and (although we should not today share the judgment on Descartes, Leibniz, and Hume) for the day in which he wrote (1904), perfectly just.

St. Thomas is still alive and overshadows as many schools as he ever did; at all events, as many as the Church maintains. He has outlived Descartes and Leibniz and a dozen other schools of philosophy more or less serious in their day. He has mostly out-lived Hume, Voltaire, and the militant sceptics. His method is typical and classic; his sentences, when interpreted by the Church, seem, even to an untrained mind, intelligible and con-sistent; his Church Intellectual remains practically unchanged, and like the Cathedral of Beauvais, erect, although the storms of six or seven centuries have prostrated over and over again, every other social or political or juristic shelter. Compared with it, all modern systems are complex and chaotic, crowded with self-contradictions, anomalies, impracticable functions and outworn inheritances; but beyond all their practical shortcomings is their fragmentary character. An economic civilization troubles itself about the universe much as a hive of honey-bees troubles about the ocean, only as a region to be avoided. The hive of Saint Thomas sheltered God and man, mind and matter, the universe and the atom, the one and the multiple, within the walls of an harmonious home.

It is this "harmonious home" of the Thomistic construction which is an appropriate symbol of the role of philosophy as ex-pressive of medieval culture—a perfect exemplification of the philosophic task in the age of the saint.

Descartes. Portrait attributed to Franz Hals in the Louvre.

4. Modern Philosophy
The Age of the Gentleman
Descartes

Outside the University

To move from the world of Saint Thomas to that of Descartes is like the experience of the *flâneur* in Paris who crosses the little footbridge, known as the Passerelle Saint Louis, which connects the Ile de la Cité and the Ile Saint Louis, and so leaves Notre Dame and the medieval remnants to its north for the noble town houses of the seventeenth century which line the Quai d'Orléans, the Quai de Bourbon, and the Quai d'Anjou.

Just to the north of Notre Dame is almost all that is left of the true medieval Paris, including the site on the Quai aux Fleurs where Abelard and Héloïse lived together, and the house around the corner on the rue Chanoinesse inhabited by her vengeful uncle, the Canon Fulbert of Notre Dame; and in these crowded precincts, as well as in the narrow, crooked streets across the river on the left bank, one senses the bustling activity of thirteenth century university life. But the Ile Saint Louis presents the quiet streets and the classic facades of the seventeenth century. In the portals of Notre Dame, decorated with the apostles and the saints, lies the spirit of Saint Thomas, just as in the exact proportions of the hôtels Lauzen and Lambert lies the heritage of Descartes. But before turning to Descartes himself, and the meaning of his philosophy as social expression, it is important to consider for a moment the special sociological character of his age and its philosophic implications.

Plato's aims for aristocratic reformation are inseparable from the foundation of the Academy — the first great school of higher learning in the West, and the residence of the medieval saint comes to be characteristically associated with the centering of

English passages from the works of Descartes generally follow E. S. Haldane and G. R. T. Ross, *The Philosophical Works of Descartes* (2 vols.), although they have usually been checked against the originals in the definitive Adam and Tannery, *Oeuvres de Descartes* (12 vols.), published in 1898-1910. Translations from the Letters are my own. Useful editions of Descartes are the Pléiade *Oeuvres et lettres*, edited by André Bridoux, and the Garnier *Oeuvres philosophiques* (2 vols.), edited by Ferdinand Alquié. The most important of the works used or cited are listed in the Bibliography.

165

Christian pedagogy in the medieval university with its texts, readings, learned authorities, "disputed questions," "quodlibetal questions," and its *summas*. But from the birth of Francis Bacon in 1561 to the death of David Hume in 1776—that is, for two hundred years—not one first-rate philosophic mind in Europe is permanently associated with a university. This fact is so singular as to merit our attention.

Sir Francis Bacon (1561–1626), Baron Verulam, Viscount Saint Albans, was lawyer, judge, and attendant upon the royal court. Thomas Hobbes (1588–1679) was the tutor and companion of young noblemen. René Descartes (1596–1650), son of a noble family, educated by Jesuits at the aristocratic school of La Flèche, traveled and studied, retiring to Holland to live out his life on inherited income. Gottfried Wilhelm von Leibniz (1646–1716), councillor and librarian in Hanover, courtier, diplomat, and scholar, became a privy councillor and baron of the Holy Roman Empire. John Locke (1632–1704), secretary and tutor to the Earl of Shaftesbury, held high public office and spent his last remaining years in the household of Sir Francis Masham. George Berkeley (1685–1753), well born, became the bishop of Cloyne. David Hume (1711–76), secretary to General Saint Claire and Lord Hartford, became under-secretary of state. Only Immanuel Kant (1724–1804), son of a humble saddler, studied and spent his entire life as professor at the University of Königsberg, thus ending one epoch and beginning another. From Bacon, indeed from Montaigne, to Hume is the reign of philosophy in "the age of the gentleman": with Kant begins the new reign of philosophy in "the age of the professional."

Separation from the university is perhaps only the most striking sociological characteristic of philosophy in the age of the gentleman, but there are others which equally well reinforce the concept of leisure and idleness, of *abstraction* from the busy world of politics, productivity, and active engagement that characterizes a philosophy which is primarily *epistemological* in its orientation and turns away both from the metaphysical horizon which controls human life and the moral concerns which reflect its problematic institutional activity to a more narrow concentration on the structure and the operations of *mind*.

Philosophers now, like Montaigne, were often of the lesser nobility (in France, of the *noblesse de robe*), or they were closely associated with the higher nobility to whom they dedicated their works: Locke's *Essay* to the Earl of Pembroke; Descartes's *Principles* to Princess Elizabeth of Bohemia; Hobbes's *De cive* to the Earl of Devonshire; Leibniz's *Monadology* to Prince Eugen of Savoy. They lived not only outside the universities, but independently: by pensions, gifts, or personal inherited income, or in the households of the nobility. Much of their lives was also spent outside their own country as rootless expatriates; Hobbes in Paris, Descartes in Holland, Locke in Montpellier. But, most interesting of all, they wrote neither for a cosmopolitan urban audience (as some of Plato's dialogues might be said to be directed to the Athenian literate intelligentsia), nor for the wide circle of scholars and clerics whose destiny was inseparable from the broad arm of the medieval Christian Church. Communication occurred within a loose, informal, but extremely narrow circle. To be sure, treatises were circulated; objections and comments were solicited; a considerable polemical literature was built up. But it was largely epistolary, at a distance, after the fact—almost, one might say, *private* in character.

In contrast, with the exception of Plato's works meant only for the Academy and Aristotle's esoteric writings, ancient and medieval thought had a certain *public* incidence. The Platonic dialogues repeat a battery of arguments which it is even possible that Plato, listening to Socrates or to some later-day sophists, heard in the marketplace, and the Thomistic *Summa* contains *in advance* "objections" and "answers to objections" which are a reflection of conventional university disputations which Saint Thomas had conducted, or in which he participated, or which he had a hundred times overheard. But it was necessary in the case of Descartes's solitary, almost, one could say, solipsistic *Meditations*, that his good friend, Father Mersenne, should circulate the work in manuscript among various theologians and men of philosophic bent, whose criticisms, indirectly forwarded to Descartes, are in turn "answered."

The whole performance, intensely interesting as it is, has the air of the loosely institutional, indeed the "provisional" atmosphere of seventeenth-century philosophical communication. And it is thus perhaps even possible to say that it is not the irritating inbredness of the argument that returns back upon itself, but rather the little society of Hobbes and Arnauld, of Huygens and Gassendi, of Mersenne and Clerselier, of Chanut and Balzac, which constitutes the true "Cartesian circle." The philosophers in the age

of the gentleman are not so much at the centers of civilization as at
its periphery—not like Plato in Athens or Saint Thomas at Paris
and the papal court, but rather in small villages, obscure town-
ships, or on country estates. And their work, for all its epistemological persuasiveness, has the quality of philosophy by men in
retreat.

For this entire period the case of Descartes is paradigmatic. His
family was one of the oldest and most respected in Touraine. He
was himself brought up in all the courtesies and conventions of
social intercourse in seventeenth-century France (the glancing arts
of dancing and fencing which he learned at La Flèche were to
stand him in good stead when he answered Gassendi's objections
to the *Meditations!*). In earlier days he affected the green velvet
dress and sword of a French nobleman, as for most of his later life
he took the title *gentilhomme de Poitou*. And his philosophy itself
is expressive of certain of the dilemmas faced by the philosopher in
an age in which inherited wealth and leisure are confronted by the
mounting challenge of industrial productivity and a rising bourgeoisie.

It is known that Descartes slept a great deal, remaining in bed
customarily until noon, and that he recommends idleness as necessary to the production of good mental work. Indeed, the famous
day in the stove-heated room in Germany where the Cartesian
philosophy originates "without cares or passions to trouble me,"
and "where I had complete leisure to occupy myself with my own
thoughts," suggests in more senses than one that Cartesianism is
indeed a "theory of the leisure class." Its generating perception,
Cogito, ergo sum, sets the ambience of philosophizing far away
from the marketplace and the necessities of the productive arts.
No Proust writing his great work at midnight in the silence of a
cork-lined room could be more inwardly turned, more isolated,
more secure.

This pattern had to some extent been set by Montaigne in the
generation before—nobility, leisure, meditation, inward-looking,
subjectivity—but if the *Cogito, ergo sum* seems an upper-class
proposition, its Cartesian use goes far beyond the subjectivity of
Montaigne. Montaigne did perhaps use "an experimental method"—that of following the subject himself and, as he said, "cease-
lessly listening to the changing voices which sound within me," but
Descartes, wishing something less random, less chancy, turned to
mathematics and the method implicit in its operations. Montaigne had little interest in the knowledge which the sciences of

nature furnish. Only things human and moral fascinated him, and in his opinion every kind of specialization falsified the moral picture. Montaigne's malice against the erudite expert and specialist is like Molière's, but he is really following Humanism and the Renaissance—that is, the ideal of the rounded, uniformly perfected personality as opposed to the new, purely technical needs for progressive specialization revealed by the rise of science. In Montaigne's day the upper classes had not yet discovered the duty, the technique, and the ethos of specialized scientific work. This Descartes knew, and it is his special sociological significance that, fully appreciating this need, he assimilated it to the demands of upper-class prestige. "Thanks be to God," he says in the *Discourse on Method*, "I did not find myself in a condition which obliged me to make a merchandise of science for the improvement of my fortune."

Descartes's first reflections by the heated stove in the little town in Germany colored the remainder of his life. The thinker, undisturbed by society, devoted all his attention to his own thoughts, and these thoughts are the foundation of all his subsequent speculations. But among these thoughts in the mind are the mathematical intuitions which proclaim its natural bent, and that preference for clear and distinct ideas which is its consequence is perhaps only a gentlemanly grace and decorum of the mind, as the dancing and the fencing work toward a grace and decorum of the body. Descartes's fascination with mathematics stems from its *order*, and his ultimate hope is that the train of its propositions should be imitated by all the sciences. For if he begins with subjectivity, hopefully, he does not end there.

The Cartesian movement from the self to God, and from God to the external world, is less a truly metaphysical speculation in the medieval sense than a hypothesis essential for the validation of all knowledge about the physical world. The *Discourse on Method* is not really "philosophy" in the speculative sense, but is an introduction to science; and even the *Meditations*, considered by most modern philosophers to be the heart of a Cartesian self-contained "metaphysics," was intended simply as the indispensible methodological propaedeutic leading up to a defense of mathematical physics. But the secret of Descartes's influence upon his contemporaries is that he brought a scientific philosophy well within the comprehension of an educated nobility. The *Principles of Philosophy* contains not only method and epistemology, but also general physics, chemistry, geology, and astronomy. And in his

dedicatory letter to his bluestocking friend and patroness, Princess
Elizabeth of Bohemia, Descartes, with enormous flattery but also
not without some truth, says: "In your case no diversions of the
Court nor that mode of education which ordinarily condemns
princesses to ignorance, have been capable of preventing your
study of all that is best in the arts and sciences. And the incomparable excellence of your intellect is evident in the fact that in a very
short time you have mastered the secrets of the sciences, and
obtained a perfect knowledge of them all."

The "secrets of the sciences" are the ultimate aim of Cartesianism, and in making them simply available to an upper-class
public, Descartes is at one level epitomizing the role of philosophy in the age of the gentleman and preparing that French
eighteenth-century upper-class public which is to read the difficult text of Newton's *Principia* with the same passionate enthusiasm it lavished on the dialogues of Fontenelle and the novels of
Marivaux and Lesage.

Whitehead, in a famous chapter of *Science and the Modern
World,* has called the seventeenth century "the century of genius."
But, as we have seen, it is a supreme paradox of this period that its
revolutionary theories of science and philosophy are almost completely dissociated from the universities. This is a fact which
Whitehead does not mention, although its causes are implicit in
his account of the history of ideas transmitted from the ancient
world and from medieval speculation. The three chief factors
which Whitehead chose for special attention were the rise of
mathematics, the instinctive belief in a detailed order of nature,
and what he termed "the unbridled rationalism of the thought of
the later Middle Ages." By this rationalism, he says,

> I mean the belief that the avenue to truth was predominantly
> through a metaphysical analysis of the nature of things, which
> would thereby determine how things acted and functioned. The
> historical revolt was the definite abandonment of this method in
> favor of the study of the empirical facts of antecedents and
> consequences.

But this very rationalism, which in the last chapter we found enshrined in the philosophy of Saint Thomas Aquinas, that profound belief that "the avenue to truth was predominantly through
a metaphysical analysis of the nature of things," although it has
its own theological account of a detailed order of nature subord-
inated to the inferred decrees of a divine plan, is yet far indeed

from the spirit of a rigorously developed mathematics, the appeal to physical experiment, and the inductive method of reasoning.

Perhaps if the Dominican order had chosen Albert the Great rather than Aquinas as its spiritual representative, something of Albert's openness to the natural sciences might have survived the medieval period. And if the Franciscans had chosen Roger Bacon rather than Saint Bonaventura as the favored vehicle of their Augustinian message, then that very enthusiasm for experimental science which set Bacon so clearly apart from his contemporaries might have carried the universities into the modern period without severe loss of continuity. For much of Roger Bacon's work was undertaken for the sake of a profound reform of philosophical learning — an attitude and intention that reminds one of the similar attitude and intention of his namesake Francis Bacon and of René Descartes in the seventeenth century. And it is interesting that whereas for Roger Bacon science is a valuable, if neglected instrument by which to further the Augustinian ideal of a knowledge of God through a knowledge of his creation, Descartes, not too strangely, inverts this procedure and turns the tables by making God a valuable (if neglected) instrument for the validation of natural science.

The very triumph of the brand of rationalism exemplified in the philosophy of Saint Thomas therefore meant that it was profoundly necessary for the great thinkers of the early modern period to consciously break with the tradition of institutionalized learning. For science and for philosophy the seventeenth century was indeed "the century of genius." But for the universities of western Europe it was a century of decadence and decay. And it is little wonder that the great men of the century — Hobbes and Locke, Leibniz and Bayle — spoke of the university professors and their work with indifference or contempt.

The basic factor, of course, is that the ecclesiastical influence in the universities was powerful and repressive. It had always been powerful, but in the thirteenth century that power had been tempered by considerable uncertainty and by the competition of diverse strands within medieval thought. But three hundred years had erased competition and solidified dogma. The universities of the seventeenth century not only persisted in holding lectures in Latin long after the establishment of the vernaculars had made this anachronistic, but with the same dogmatic conservatism continued to transmit a narrow body of knowledge, as Sir George

Clark said, "by the requirements of a rigid orthodoxy, and by the belief that authority in the past had established the main principles of what was useful and true." The universities were ruled by a decadent Aristotelianism — decadent not because it drew upon the past, but because it drew automatically and uncritically, as upon an established intellectual convention which had become a conditioned reflex. Even the great intellectual revolutions of the fifteenth and sixteenth centuries, the rise of a Christian humanism and of a new observational and anti-Aristotelian physics, anti-Scholastic as they surely were, had made little headway in ousting it from the curriculum of the universities. Thus institutions, fitted by organization and tradition to become seedbeds of new knowledge and exciting intellectual confrontation, had become repositories of an old-fashioned intellectual conservatism.

The decadence of the seventeenth century is directly traceable to the power of the Inquisition. Books were subject to rigorous censorship, lectures were supervised, and professors who succumbed to the lure of the slightest novelty were immediately threatened with the displeasure of the church. In Descartes's own time the Sorbonne had become impotent and quiescent under the threats of fanaticism and oppression, and although he made a show of seeking its approbation and submitting his new ideas to the approval of the theologians, this was more a prudently conventional gesture than a deep-seated wish. What he really cared for was the approval of men of distinction outside the university — of Hobbes and Gassendi, Huygens and Balzac, Arnauld and Pascal.

It is true that Descartes distributed about two hundred copies of the *Discours de la méthode*, including one copy to Louis XIII and one to Cardinal Richelieu, and that he was anxious to know how his old teachers, the Jesuits of La Flèche, would react to his metaphysical ideas. He was even at some pains to prove to Father Fournet that his views are in accordance with the basic tenets of the Roman Catholic church, and he was naturally pleased when Father Vatier approved of his proofs of the existence of God; but the fact is that publication of the *Discourse* plunged him into a sea of violent controversy from which he learned the lesson of a prudent caution. Writing in November 1639 to Mersenne on the subject of the *Meditations* upon which he was currently working, Descartes said: "My design is to print only twenty or thirty copies and to send them to twenty or thirty of the most learned theologians whom I may know, in order to have their criticisms on it and to learn from them what it were well to change, correct, or add to it, before publishing it." And indeed, when the first edition of the *Meditations* was published in Latin at Paris in 1641, *cum privilegio et approbatione doctorum* (the royal "privilege" had indeed been secured, but the "approbation" was most vague and indefinite), it was preceded by a letter addressed "To the Most Wise and Illustrious: the Dean and the Doctors of the Sacred Faculty of Theology at Paris," in which Descartes humbly asked for criticism and correction ("for being conscious not only of my infirmity, but also of my ignorance, I should not dare to state that it was free from errors").

The treatise seems to have been neither bitterly attacked nor gratefully accepted by those addressed, and perhaps this was just as well; for when some years later a few professors at the university became mildly infected with Cartesianism, the government at once sent the archbishop of Paris to warn them to abandon these novel and dangerous ideas. Even as early as 1624 the first president of the Paris Parliament forbade a debate on the theses of three opponents of Aristotelianism, after it had been publicly announced and an audience of over a thousand had assembled to hear it. But in general, the universities were willing accomplices of the power of ecclesiastical repression. There was not a single important philosophical or scientific treatise of the age which was not condemned by the Sorbonne and refused the license of its printers!

It is true that after the Reformation had weakened and divided the church, universities became more and more organs of the state. Governments began to take over the direction of an education previously vested entirely in ecclesiastical authority. But if the intervention of the state was the first conspicuous educational consequence of the Reformation, its effect upon freedom and intellectual quality was not immediately apparent in the seventeenth century. The humanistic impulse had indeed founded a few new universities, mostly in Germany. The University of Strasbourg was founded in 1621, a new Protestant foundation was established in Königsberg about the same time, and in 1607 the University of Giessen was set up by the Lutherans because Marburg had fallen into the hands of the Calvinists. But the religious changes of the Reformation and Counter-Reformation did little to further freedom and peace. At Oxford and Cambridge there were successive purges of Catholics, Protestants, Puritans, and Anglicans; Paris wasted years in barren theological controversy; and in

Germany the Thirty Years War was to ruin the universities as it ruined everything else.

In the early seventeenth century liberty of teaching and the curricular excellence which is its usual accompaniment were surely greatest in the Dutch universities which had been created as a direct consequence of the successful political revolt: Leyden immediately after its siege, Groningen in 1614, amd Utrecht in 1634. Under municipal rather than ecclesiastical authority, and with the diversity of the Dutch provinces giving considerable support to the distinct individuality of each, the emergence of the universities of Holland is one of the brighter spots in the intellectual history of the seventeenth century. And it is probably because of their proximity, as well as the ideal of toleration embodied in the nation and its government, that at thirty-two Descartes took up permanent residence in Holland. He lived there for the last twenty years of his life, leaving only for occasional trips to Italy and France, and finally died in 1650 during his visit to Queen Christina of Sweden in Stockholm.

But the Dutch universities were a notable exception to a miserable rule, and with the generally low estate of the intellectual life of higher education, it is little wonder that philosophy and science had detached themselves from the universities and that the courts of princes and the homes of noblemen provided housing, society, and livelihood for a Hobbes, a Leibniz, and a Locke. Newly founded scientific and "philosophical" associations like the Royal Society and Richelieu's French *Académie des sciences* mark the brilliant alliance between the philosopher and man of science and the courtly nobleman, and the rise of the private tutor signifies the justified mistrust of organized education in a "gentlemanly" age. Only toward the very end of the century—marked by the foundation of the University of Halle in 1693—was a new direction apparent. Here for the very first time a professor lectured in his native German. Here appeared the unique beginnings of that *libertas docendi* which was to usher in the Enlightenment, restore philosophy to the universities, make possible Immanual Kant in Königsberg, and transport philosophy from the age of the gentleman into the age of the professional.

The Philosopher as Gentleman

There is little question that the general cultural characteristics of the age also influenced the institutions of higher learning. The ideal of an aristocratic society, with its continuing need for the liberal education of the gentleman, had considerable influence upon the lower schools — indeed upon the very school of La Flèche (founded by Henry IV for the sons of noblemen) to which Descartes was sent at the age of ten and where he spent the next eight years — but the frozen curriculum of the universities made little adjustment. In fact, as often happens, the cultural ideal had more effect upon externals than upon fundamentals. The ideal did serve to alter the dress and manners of students and professors, if not the intellectual content of the course of studies which should have been their common concern. Preserved Smith, a distinguished cultural historian of the last generation, expressed it with some wit. "Both teachers and pupils at sixteenth century universities had dressed and looked like clergymen even when they were not. Both professors and students at the seventeenth century universities disguised themselves as gentlemen even when they were not." "Disguised" is the proper word, for if the great scientific and philosophic minds of the seventeenth century scorned and avoided the universities, it was only partly because of their backwardness and illiberality. It was also because the very nobility of the gentlemanly ideal suggested qualities which were in opposition to a narrowly pedantic and a "quasi-professional" approach to the world.

The "age of the gentleman" in Western European culture cannot be precisely fixed, but roughly it runs from the lifetime of Baldasarre Castiglione (1478–1529) whose *Book of the Courtier* first defined the ideal etiquette of gentlemanly existence, to that of Philip Dormer Stanhope, Lord Chesterfield (1694–1773), whose *Letters to His Son* crystallizes the last behavior patterns of a soon extinct way of life. This is almost exactly the time span bounded by the lifetime of Montaigne and that of Kant.

For our purposes Montaigne is the key figure. Not simply because, as Léon Brunschvicg has shown (*Descartes et Pascal, Lecteurs de Montaigne*), Descartes and Pascal were his devoted readers, and not even because, as Richard Popkin has indicated (*The History of Scepticism: From Erasmus to Descartes*), between his skepticism and Descartes's there is an important continuity, but rather because his *Essays* display what is undeniably a philosophical mind at work, meditating upon the human theme and the human condition — with that leisurely pace and rurally isolated concentration which bespeaks the wealthy, landed nobleman. Like that of Epicurus or Seneca, his ultimate concern is with how a man ought to live ("le grand et glorieux chef d'oeuvre de l'homme, c'est vivre à propos"). But although he quotes them both, he nonetheless has impatience and dislike for all the formal systems of moral philosophy; for they are abstract, and they tend to disguise the immediacies of life in logical constructions and pedantic terminology. Behind this perfectly reasonable line of criticism lies something else; the prejudice of the bred-in-the-bone nobleman and the presuppositions of sixteenth- and seventeenth-century French class structure, which are no less strong for being rationally disguised. Montaigne's malice against the erudite expert and against philosophic "specialization" is on the surface "humane," but the very success of his *Essays* also testifies to the late Renaissance flowering of a greatly augmented class of intellectual consumers — largely noblemen — whose claims to participate in cultural life required an ambience for knowledge distinctly removed from the Scholastic and the erudite specialist.

In the age of Saint Thomas "the educated" and the clergy are identical, and the functional class term *oratores* indicates this fact by meaning simultaneously "those who pray" and "those who think." But that the Renaissance ideal of the courtier and the gentleman was so clearly professed by those of the wealthiest and most aristocratic circles means that from the sixteenth century onward, the class of "the educated" assumes a new significance, intimately connected with learning, the classicizing ideals of hummanism, and the concept of intellectual culture as a kind of personal adornment, but also with generalized good breeding, amiability in social intercourse, and a sense of appropriate conduct — in short, with "decorum." And this general assimilation of right social conduct to learning and the intellectual life carried with it, as the other side of the coin, a contempt for that professional specialization which rendered any man too narrowly commited to a profession, too exclusively absorbed in his specialized knowledge, boorish, plebian, and, indeed, *comic*. This attitude (of which clear traces are to be found in Montaigne) reached full development in the French seventeenth century, and comes to classic expression in the portrayal of doctors, lawyers, and successful businessmen in the theater of Molière. One imagines with horror what Molière would have done with the examples of Kant or Carnap, of Wittgenstein or G. E. Moore. And for all practical purposes, Molière and Descartes were contemporaries!

It is therefore interesting to speculate about the similarities in the intellectual situations of Descartes and Montaigne—and also of the differences which separate two minds radically opposed, although subject to the same social presuppositions. Both belonged to the French nobility—to the *noblesse de robe*—although Montaigne's family was more aristocratic, more natively allied with the powerful, more feudally attached to land, landed possessions, and specific *place*. And the testimony to this difference is that, although Montaigne traveled to Italy and was deeply attached to Paris, his roots were always in Guyenne—in Bordeaux and his beloved Château de Montaigne, which was not overly far from it. Descartes, on the other hand, stemmed from Touraine, and lived upon the interest of a landed patrimony; but although his letters reveal some fondness for the local soil of his birth, like Erasmus he was a restless traveler and an exile, constantly changing his dwelling through whim and the promptings of a secretive nature, but paradoxically seeking out for his adopted home that very country from which Erasmus had fled something over a hundred years before.

Upon a first reading of the *Essays* and, say, the *Discourse on Method*, the style and even the mode of perception of Montaigne and Descartes seem much alike. A meditative frame of mind and the typical subjectivity of the French *moraliste* is common to them both. But with extended attention the differences grow greater and finally become immense. For Montaigne the subjectivity is real: the *Essays* are a self-portrait, and their perpetual quest is to use philosophy *practically*—to uncover those maxims embedded in experience which should serve as authentic "guides for living." But in Descartes there is a radical split between "knowing" and "acting," between science and life, and the metaphysical and epistemological isolation of his thinking (appropriate, indeed, to the essential purity of an abstract *res cogitans*) is far removed from the existential involvement, and even the occasional humanistic vulgarity, of Montaigne. Thus what initially seems a subjective method in Descartes is finally seen as the device to service an objective ambition. For if Montaigne's final aim is to delineate a specific person, Descartes's is to constitute a universal science. Montaigne's ultimate subject is *l'homme*; Descartes's is *le monde*. And this difference of objective finally reveals a sharp difference in attitude, even toward those elements which at first make them seem so much alike—their skeptical doubts and their plain use of the idiomatic resources of the French language.

There is, of course, skepticism in Montaigne — the surfacing of a Pyrrhonistic doubt even within the texture of a fideistic framework — but its function is irenic; to bring comfort and relief; to avoid in the mind the conflicts of dogma and fanaticism which racked a bloody century of fratricidal religious strife; to mitigate the discomforts of life in an age of rampant religious ideology. There is skepticism in Descartes also, but the method of universal doubt is merely assumed as a device to establish the bedrock certainty of what in knowledge can be universally guaranteed, and therefore, to firmly ground a "scientific" ideology. And they differ with respect to linguistic bias also: Montaigne is a philosopher who mistrusts a technical and impersonal language but who utilizes to the full the racy, flavorful, intense language of the Bordeaux streets, whereas Descartes's classic purity preserves the precise, scientific ideals of the Académie française, in a prose which is limpid, lucid, and cool — a perfect medium for "clear and distinct ideas." Montaigne frankly advocated the acceptance of "ordinary language." "I do not," he says parenthetically in the essay "On Some Verses of Virgil," "avoid any of the phrases that are used in the streets of France; those who would combat usage with grammar make fools of themselves." But Descartes, who wrote a serious treatise *Rules for the Direction of the Mind,* and who was devoted to the method of mathematics, confesses in his second *Meditation* that "words however impede me, and I am almost deceived by the terms of ordinary language" ("les paroles toutefois m'arrêtent, et je suis presque trompé par les termes du language ordinaire").

Yet in certain respects the style of Descartes is in no way inferior to that of Montaigne, and for a "scientific" philosopher it is indeed remarkable. Bertrand Russell in his *History of Western Philosophy* has only admirably stated what we all know.

There is a freshness about his work that is not to be found in any eminent previous philosopher since Plato. All the intermediate philosophers were teachers, with the professional superiority belonging to that avocation. Descartes writes, not as a teacher, but as a discoverer and explorer, anxious to communicate what he has found. His style is easy and unpedantic, addressed to intelligent men of the world rather than to pupils. It is, moreover, an extraordinarily excellent style. It is very fortunate for modern philosophy that the pioneer had such admirable literary sense. His successors, both on the Continent and in England, until Kant, retain his unprofessional character, and several of them retain something of his stylistic merit.

The crucial difference between Montaigne and Descartes is clear. Montaigne is a moralist; Descartes is a mathematician, an experimentalist, and a man of science. So that even where their subject matter overlaps, Descartes either pursues the method appropriate to his scientific commitment or plays the simple role of moral sage with insights hardly elevated above the conventional and polite Stoicism of the age. In his treatise *The Passions of the Soul,* Descartes turns to a theme which was Montaigne's constant preoccupation, but he attempts, characteristically, to explain the passions not through their moral relevance, but by their physiological grounding (something that Freud always hoped for, but never accomplished) in the primitive biological and medical science of the seventeenth century. And where Descartes shows himself most allied to the French moral tradition, in his sagacious letters to Princess Elizabeth of Bohemia (as, for example, in those written from Egmond in the fall of 1645 expounding Seneca, or in that of September 1646 presenting his reaction to a reading of Machiavelli's *The Prince*) his prescriptions run little deeper than a quiet underwriting of a Stoical acceptance of the arrows of misfortune and a gentlemanly preference for honorable behavior and keeping one's word.

And yet there are striking similarities between Descartes's and Montaigne's insights and their perceptive modes. In the essay "Of Three Kinds of Association" Montaigne stated:

Meditation is a powerful and full study for anyone who knows how to examine and exercise himself vigorously: I would rather fashion my mind than furnish it. There is no occupation that is either weaker or stronger, according to the mind involved, than entertaining one's own thoughts. The greatest minds make it their profession, *to whom living is thinking (quibus vivere est cogitare* — Cicero.)

It is all here in this brief passage. For Descartes too, to express himself in "meditations" is a powerful philosophic device. He likewise (and in fact much more frankly and rigorously than Montaigne) preferred to "fashion" his mind rather than "furnish" it — to guide it methodically by reason rather than to bookishly fill it with the classical wisdom of the past. Montaigne's mind, as revealed in the *Essays*, is one both fashioned *and* furnished — since one of their chief characteristics is that they are studded with quotations from the Greek and Latin classics; from Plutarch and Tacitus, Lucretius and Horace, Virgil and Catullus. But in the *Discourse on Method* Descartes expressly disclaims "the study of

letters" and turns "to the great book of the world," saying that
"the sciences found in books . . . composed as they are of the
gradually accumulated opinions of many different individuals —
do not approach so near to the truth as the simple reasoning which
a man of common sense can quite naturally carry out respecting
the things which come immediately before him." Throughout the
entire body of his written treatises, one is hard put to find a single
reference to Plato or Aquinas, to Aristotle or Augustine! But
above all, in that last phrase from Cicero, who can resist the
temptation to infer that Descartes has been reading Montaigne,
and that the *cogito, ergo sum* is but a modified transcription of
the *quibus vivere est cogitare* — the unconscious reconstruction
that shall found a new world of philosophizing upon a faint breeze
blowing through from the classical past?

I have included this brief comparison of Descartes and Montaigne to show that, different as they undoubtedly are, their sociological similarities are decisive for philosophizing in the early
modern period. Neither wrote for pupils, but for "intelligent men
of the world." Neither were conscious pedagogues, but rather
"discoverers" and "explorers" communicating their self-
knowledge, or knowledge of the external world, as the case may
be, to a mature, upper-class audience. Both, in the details of their
lives and in their devotion to their vocation, illustrate the pursuit
of philosophic knowledge in the age of the gentleman.

In the preface to the first complete (and still authoritative)
biography of Descartes (*La vie de Monsieur DesCartes*, 1691),
Adrien Baillet gives a brief statement of his method and of his
attitude toward his subject. Men, says Baillet, have both an interior and a public life, and to explicate the latter for Descartes it
would be necessary to relate him narrowly both to the general
history of science of his time and to the course of public affairs to
which he was allied even in his solitude. But he also proclaimed
himself interested in an attempt to discover the inner man (*à
découvrir l'intérieur de M. DesCartes*) as a "hidden treasure" (*un
trésor caché*). In fact he suggested that in the life of a philosopher
removed from the great world one should not expect to find
diverting variety and astonishing events, but rather the solid evidences of wisdom and virtue in their natural state. "The life of
a philosopher," he said, "consists less in actions and public ex-
ploits than in sentiments and thoughts, but because 'the philosopher' is inseparably attached to a man, it is of primary concern

to note how 'the philosophy' controls his human responses even in the most ordinary and private action." With this humanistic — or moralistic — bias (quite gone out of fashion in our present age of professionalism and specialization, where a man is so clearly separated from his technical skill) it is not surprising that Baillet found Descartes an admirable example of the moral ideal of the classical age in which he lived, and that he cited with approval how Descartes had always taken enormous care to avoid extremes — all that is *outré et excessif* in the conduct of life — and thus found him almost always near to that *juste milieu* which is our proper place in the domain of human behavior. But my concern is less moral than sociological, and I wish rather to briefly consider his life, less for what it reveals about his character than for what it tells about the social class to which he belonged — less, that is, for the relation between his theoretical principles and his conduct, than for the unconscious social and class presuppositions which generally conditioned the philosophic enterprise in the seventeenth century.

Descartes was born on 31 March 1596 at La Haye in Touraine into one of the oldest and most respected families of the region. His grandfather was a gentleman in easy circumstances who had retired early from the army to lead the life of a country gentleman. His father, more professionally oriented, became in 1586 councillor of the parliament of Brittany, and three years later married Jeanne Brochard, daughter of the Lieutenant-general of Poitiers. It sounds a little like the background of Montaigne, although not quite so highly placed, wealthy, and ambitious.

But Montaigne and Descartes are still essentially of the same social class. It is an age of sharp distinction between the *noblesse* (including the *noblesse de robe*), on the one hand, and those who engage in trade and commerce on the other, and in this sharp divide, Descartes's connections are altogether with the former. Brought up as a gentleman in all the courtesies and conventions of social intercourse, he was early sent to the Jesuit college of La Flèche, recently founded by Henry IV for the special education of the young nobility. Situated in a royal palace, the Château Neuf, the school included fifteen hundred pupils in Descartes's time, of whom something over a third are said to have been of the *première noblesse*. Descartes entered in 1606 at the age of ten and remained for eight years, studying in that time Greek, Latin, history, the liberal arts, science, mathematics, and philosophy, as well as the social arts of music, dancing, and fencing. Despite his later distaste for the classics and the humanities (a sentiment clearly detailed in the *Discourse on Method*), his introduction to science and mathematics at La Flèche was decisive for his entire career, and the Thomistic metaphysics and Augustinian theology which was the permeating climate of any Jesuit foundation in the early seventeenth century served as a subtle backdrop for his later thought and influenced his mature metaphysics in ways never specifically acknowledged, although they are obvious to any reader of the *Meditations* familiar with the strands of medieval thought (and detailed persuasively and exhaustively by Etienne Gilson in his *Etudes sur le rôle de la pensée médiévale dans la formation du système cartésien*).

Descartes is one of the most astonishing examples of the Middle Ages turning into the Renaissance: a man drawn to all the newest elements of experimental science and mathematical physics, and yet insisting upon a metaphysical foundation for them in con-siderable degree determined by medieval philosophical presup-positions. La Flèche was the first stimulus and the moving agency in this confrontation.

The years immediately following his graduation from La Flèche were spent in a manner befitting one who clearly qualified as a *gentilhomme breton*. Baillet says that he passed the time for the next four years at Rennes, where he practiced fencing, rode horseback, and engaged in "other exercises fitting his station"; at the University of Poitiers where, like Montaigne at Toulouse, he received a degree in law; and finally at Paris, where he gambled and lived the life of a young man of the world. To these early years belong his first gentlemanly writings — the *Compendium Musicae,* probably written before he was twenty-two, and the now lost *Art de l'escrime*, an opuscula on fencing, which was possibly his first literary effort.

In 1618, at twenty-two, just after the Thirty Years War broke out in central Europe, Descartes enlisted as an unpaid volunteer in the army of the Dutch Prince Maurice of Nassau (which was a kind of war school for the younger nobility of that period), fur-nishing his own equipage and following leisurely in the footsteps of the advancing army so as to continue his studies in music and mathematics. The following year he transferred to the army of the Catholic duke of Bavaria, and the next winter, on 19 November 1619, occurred that famous day spent by the warm stove in the little town close to Ulm, so brilliantly described in the *Discourse on Method*, when the great intellectual conversion took place, and he received the intimations of a method which should permit the total reform of human learning and its inclusion under a single wonderful science or *mathesis universalis*. No doubt these crises of the intellectual life are the product of cumulative study and continuous meditation, but with a magnificent dramatic flair Descartes presents the moment as the flash which determined his entire future; as the moment of the revelation of his philosophic and scientific vocation.

If so, it was not immediately apparent in the details of his outward life. For turning, as he said, from the confinement of the study to "the great book of the world," he spent the next ten years in various ways. From 1620-1625 he traveled with his valet through central Europe, Scandinavia, to the low countries, and to Italy, pursuing his studies quietly and "discoursing with learned and noble gentlemen." In 1622 or 1623 he returned to France, to Rennes, where he received from his father his share of his mother's inheritance. He sold his property of Le Perron and other lands in Poitou to provide for himself a more convenient permanent income, but, cognizant of the gentlemanly significance of landed property, he retained long into his permanent residence in Holland the title of "Seigneur du Perron." Then he journeyed to Italy by way of Innsbruck, was at Venice and Loretto, attended the jubilee in Rome in 1625, and returned by way of Florence where Galileo was living, although Descartes did not see him there. The next two years he spent at Paris, living the life of a gentleman of leisure: gambling, going much into good society, even, it is said, engaging in a duel over an affair of honor. Such fragmentary writings as survive from the time show him interested in mathematics and mechanics, but without the concentration and fixity of purpose displayed in his writings after 1628. His friends were now largely bons vivants like Balzac or cosmopolitan churchmen like the oratorians Gibieuf, de Condrieu, and the general of that order, the Cardinal de Bérulle, before whom, on one famous occasion in 1627, he participated vividly and brilliantly in a critique of the lecture of the papal nuncio, on the basis of which the cardinal seriously urged him to forsake his aimless life and devote himself to a reform of current philosophy. Was this perhaps the second turning point which caused Descartes to begin serious work on his *Rules for the Direction of the Mind* of 1628 (the explicit exposition of the insight of his first conversion of 1619) and to take up permanent residence in Holland, living quietly in a jealously enforced seclusion to permit the progress of a richly diversified philosophic and scientific work?

In the autumn of 1628 Descartes left for Holland where he intended to take up residence, and where in fact he remained for the next twenty years. In April 1629 at Franeker he inscribed at the university as a "French student of philosophy." But by autumn he was living at Amsterdam, where he became friends with local scientists and scientifically minded instrument-makers and began to dissect animals in his studies of anatomy and physiology. But by the summer of 1630 he had already transferred to Leyden where he inscribed at the university as a mathematician, consorted with the most learned professors in the sciences, and undertook experiments in the refraction of light.

These first two years in Holland are only a representative sample of the characteristic restlessness of the entire twenty. During his years in Holland Descartes lived in thirteen different houses in Franeker, Amsterdam, Leyden, Utrecht, Endegeest, Deventer, Egmond, and at The Hague, largely in the country and suburbs, where he hoped to be free of city distractions and casual acquaintances, engaging his passion for solitude, guarding his privacy, and keeping his address carefully hidden from all but his dearest friends. Thus he secured the uninterrupted leisure for experiment and mathematical creation, for philosophical meditation, and for internal peace of mind, unencumbered by the age's turbulence in politics and religion. Thus, congruent with the temper of the age, most of his philosophical intercourse was conducted by letter. His scientific and philosophic treatises, although published, were privately circulated rather than widely disseminated; yet, through the offices of his great friend in Paris, the Franciscan Marin Mersenne (who served at once as his literary agent and international post office), he was kept informed of all the recent scientific discoveries on the continent of Europe, and himself participated fully in the restricted seventeenth-century fellowship of scientifically and philosophically learned men.

It was a life well suited to Descartes's prudent, cautious, and secretive nature, but it is expressive too of a gentlemanly isolation and a noble reserve. In a letter of 5 May 1631, Descartes writes from Amsterdam to his friend Balzac in Paris expressing his enthusiasm for his latest city of residence:

And thus in this large city where I now am, since I seem to be practically the only one here who is not a merchant or in trade; all are so bound up in their profitable business transactions that I could remain here my entire life without being noticed by anyone. Each day I go walking among the bustling crowds with as much freedom and tranquillity as you find in your country lanes, and I do not regard the men who pass before my eyes any differently than the trees that grow in your forests or the animals who graze there. Nor does the noise of their bustling life impinge more upon my meditations than the gentle murmur of some country brook. . . . What other place could one prefer in the entire world, where all the necessities of life and all the curiosities which one could desire are as available as here? What other country gives one a liberty so complete, where one can sleep with more security, where there are better police to protect, where poisonings, treasons, libels, are less known, and where, indeed, so much of the innocence and simplicity of our ancestors still remains?

The emphasis upon peace and security is obvious, but the image of the man of leisure, walking unnoticed and slightly scornful among the active Dutch merchants and tradesmen intent upon their profit, is worthy of a canvas by de Hooch or Vermeer, and reflects in tranquil and unconscious commentary the gentlemanly presupposition in the age of the rapidly rising commercial bourgeoisie. A large share of human activity is social, but the insights of philosophy (as we know from Montaigne and Descartes) have their origins in the purest privacy.

Descartes's sheltered life, despite his frequent changes of place, was infinitely suited to his varied philosophic and scientific intentions. By 1633 he had prepared for publication his *Le monde ou traité de la lumière*; but when in November he heard that Galileo had been condemned by the Inquisition the previous June, he hastily retreated from his publication plans, although he nevertheless continued his philosophical reflections and physical experiments. In Amsterdam he produced in 1634 the *Dioptrics* and in 1635 the treatise on *Meteors*, all the while projecting the outlines of his new universal science. In 1636 he transferred to Leyden, reading parts of his treatise to Huygens and frequenting the anatomy rooms of the university. In 1637 he sent the whole of the *Discourse on Method* to Mersenne. But in 1639-40 he again moved, this time to Santpoort, where he became friendly with Regius, professor at the University of Utrecht (who became his disciple), and wrote his chief work in metaphysics, the *Meditations*. The publication of the *Discourse on Method* in 1637 and the

Meditations in 1641 initiated Descartes's international philosophic reputation—a reputation originating in the scholarly circles of his correspondents, but spreading also to the society of noble gentlemen and to the outposts of the highest royalty. It was not by accident that Mersenne presented copies of the *Discourse* to King Louis XIII and to Cardinal Richelieu, and that between 1638 and 1641 at The Hague Descartes became intimate with certain gentlemen of the courts of the prince of Orange and the ex-king of Poland. His material condition becoming ever better, he transferred to a country house at Endegeest, just outside Leyden, where he lived, if not in luxury, at least in extreme comfort. We are indebted to a certain M. de Sorbière for an account of Descartes in 1642—how he lived in a small château near Leyden with a sufficient staff of servants, all well-chosen and comely people. There was a pleasant garden, and an orchard surrounded by pastures, and all this was within one day (by canal) of Utrecht, Delft, Rotterdam, Haarlem, and Amsterdam, and even closer to The Hague. The Hague was one of the finest towns in Europe and the residence of three courts: that of the prince of Orange, the States-General, and the exiled queen of Bohemia, into whose fashionable world the philosopher seems to have come to pay court to her and to her youthful daughters, the oldest of whom, Princess Elizabeth, had a fancy for Descartes's conversation.

Nor are these courtly liaisons unconnected with the receptivity to his works. The *Principles of Philosophy* of 1644 was, as we have seen, dedicated to the princess Elizabeth Palatinate in terms which show Descartes more the courtier and the gallant gentleman than the aloof and arrogant philosopher to which we have been accustomed. The youthful duc de Luynes somewhat later translated the *Meditations* (written in Latin) into French, which so pleased Descartes that he asked that it be published. And the late work, *The Passions of the Soul* written in French during the winter of 1645–46, was sent to Princess Elizabeth in April 1646 for her criticism and approval, and finally to Queen Christina of Sweden, with whom, through Chanut, Descartes's friend and the French ambassador to Sweden, Descartes had carried on a correspondence on moral and psychological subjects since 1647. The work was placed in the hands of Clerselier or the Abbé Picot in Paris in August 1649, and was published by Elzevir in Amsterdam in November of the same year. This work reflects as much the responses of a philosopher placed somewhat unwillingly in the role of moral sage by intelligent, if importunate, women of royal blood

as the conclusions of a scientist who by nature and disposition saw
the problems of the emotions and the moral virtues more in terms
of physiological psychology than in purely ethical categories.

In his later years Descartes made three separate visits to France:
in 1644, in 1647, and in 1648. On the first Descartes met the
well-placed Cherselier, who subsequently trnslated the "Objections" and "Replies to Objections" of the *Meditations* into French,
and also his brother-in-law, Pierre Chanut, who later became
French ambassador to Sweden and the agent for introducing
Descartes's work to Queen Christina. The second visit was oc-
casioned by Descartes's nomination by the youthful Louis XIV (on
the advice of Cardinal Mazarin) to a royal pension of 3,000 livres.
Descartes already had important friends at the French court, but
this trip is notable because while he was in Paris, Descartes had
two important conversations (on 23 and 24 September) with the
young Blaise Pascal and was entertained by the Englishman William Cavendish, Marquis of Newcastle, at a dinner of reconcilia-
tion attended by both Hobbes and Gassendi, philosophical
adversaries of Descartes who had written, respectively, the third
and fifth sets of objections to the *Meditations*. But the political
upheaval of the Fronde was agitating Paris, and Descartes returned rather suddenly to Holland, remarking of his trip that it was as
if, being invited for dinner, he arrived to find the kitchen in
disorder and the cooking pots overturned on the stove! His third
trip ended even more precipitously. Paris was again in political
uproar, and Descartes found the security of Egmond infinitely
greater than the turbulent precincts of the Place royale and the
Rue Saint Honoré He returned from France for the last time, as
his acquaintance Brasset said: "like a prudent seaman to a quiet
port."

As one reads carefully the considerable body of Descartes's
correspondence in the last ten years of his life—from, say, the
letter of mid-January 1641 which he sent from Leyden to M.
Alphonse Pollot, *gentilhomme de la chambre* of the prince of
Orange, to the last letter he wrote, on 15 January 1650 just before
his death in Stockholm, to M. le Vicomte de Brégy, French ambassador to Poland, with its somewhat pathetic comments upon
his physical and mental discomforts in the frigid north ("It seems
to me that men's thoughts freeze here during the winter just like
water"; and "But I am not here really in my proper element, for I
only desire tranquillity and repose—gifts which the most powerful monarchs of the earth cannot give to those who do not know

how to take them for themselves")—one is struck with the volume
of those addressed to noble gentlemen and royal personages, and
with how consistently they exhibit Descartes in the role of "philosopher in waiting" to noble ladies, and "courtier extraordinary"
to those who frequent the corridors of power and the antecham-
bers of princes.

As early as 6 October 1642 Descartes had written glowingly to
M. Pollot about the Princess Elizabeth. "I have already formerly
known by hearsay," he says,

> so many marvellous things about the fine mind of Madame, the
> Princess of Bohemia, that I am less astonished to learn that she
> pores over metaphysical treatises, than when I consider that,
> having read mine, she attests that she does not disapprove of
> them, and I must say that I consider the quality of her judgment
> more favorably than that of Messieurs the Doctors (of theology)
> who take as their criterion of truth the opinions of Aristotle rather
> than the evidence of our reason.

It is not only the general preference for royal persons of philosophic discernment over the narrow pedantry of the schools, but a
personal tribute to a quite remarkable young woman. Elizabeth of
Bohemia, princess Palatine and daughter of the elector Frederick
V, who lost his throne by the battle of Prague in 1620 (when she
was two years old), was now living in exile with her mother and
sisters at The Hague. After reading Descartes's *Meditations* in the
year of his letter to Pollot, upon her invitation he visited her
several times at The Hague. And from the following year, when he
removed to Egmond, began their correspondence, chiefly upon
moral subjects, which was to last from 16 May 1643 to the end of
1649. This correspondence reveals much about the class presuppositions of intellectual communication in the seventeenth century. She was intellectually curious and extremely intelligent. He
was grateful to be approached by a woman of so much distinction.
As the friendship advanced, mindful of her spiritual self-isolation
and her family problems (epitomized by the catastrophe of June
1646, when her brother Philip murdered a French nobleman, and
that of January 1649 when her uncle, Charles I of England, died
on the scaffold) Descartes gave the Princess Elizabeth good and
remarkably candid advice about her personal health and happiness at the same time as he provided her with moral maxims
congruent with the Stoical fashion of the times. In return he
expected some sympathetic understanding of the tenets of his

metaphysics, and perhaps even some gesture of protection against the local persecutions he fancied, and which in 1641 and 1643 were very real, as he was accused of atheism by Voetius, minister and rector of the University of Utrecht, and threatened by the council of that city with arrest and the confiscation of his books. Yet surely it was for far more than self-interest that Descartes was willing to welcome Princess Elizabeth, and later Queen Christina (and other gifted women) as companions in a common methodical search for truth. And it was in this way that Cartesianism set the fashion for that sympathetic contact with the highest type of noble and educated ladies which was to flower in the salon of the Marquise de Rambouillet, and to receive its comic parody in Molière's *Les précieuses ridicules* only nine years after Descartes's death.

From 1646 on, Descartes had another highly placed correspondent—Hector-Pierre Chanut, brother-in-law of Clerselier, whom he had met two years earlier on his visit to Paris and who was now French ambassador to the court of Queen Christina of Sweden in Stockholm. She too, although quite young, was a remarkably cultivated woman, and Chanut, knowing her desire to attract artists and learned men to her court, had acquainted her with Descartes's fame and introduced her to his works. He recommended to her the French translation of the *Meditations*, and she in turn through Chanut sent Descartes (as to a world-renowned sage) certain questions about the nature of love and the role of "the natural light" in our knowledge of God. These questions and their answers led, as had similar ones from Princess Elizabeth, to a final question about "the ultimate good for man"; and despite an initial show of reluctance Descartes retailed to her the same sort of observations concerning ethics and the passions of the soul as he had sent to Elizabeth. On 20 November 1647 he wrote to Chanut:

It is true that my custom is to refuse to write my thoughts about morals, and that for two reasons: first because there is no subject upon which the malicious can find a better pretext for their slanders, and second because I think it is only for sovereigns or for those authorized by them to intervene in ordering the customs of others. But these two reasons cease on the occasion which you have: the honor of writing me in behalf of the incomparable Queen whom you serve, that it pleases her that I should write her my opinion concerning the Summum Bonum.

In the end (and fatally) Chanut succeeded far better than he knew. Queen Christina invited Descartes to her court, and finally even sent an admiral of the Swedish navy to seek him out. At first he refused, and it would have been better if he had finally done so, but the honor was too great to give up. Hesitating, and of two minds until the very last, on 31 March 1649 Descartes finally wrote to Chanut in the best courtly and gentlemanly tradition:

I hold it a signal favor to learn from the Queen of Sweden that it pleases her that I should have the honor to make my reverences to her in person. And so great is my veneration for the exalted and rare qualities of this princess, that her least wishes are for me absolute commands. This is why I do not make this voyage a matter of deliberation. I am resolved only to obey.

In September Descartes left for Stockholm. But despite his welcome by the queen, Descartes was not happy in the north. He lived comfortably enough in the house of the French ambassador, made a few physical experiments, and devoted himself to the service of the queen, breaking his lifelong habit of late rising to instruct her in philosophy at five in the morning and even writing a ballet for performance upon one court occasion. But the duties of the active courtier were not compatible with the life-style of the philosophic and scientific recluse, developed over many years of tranquillity in the towns and villages of the Dutch countryside. The rigorous climate also took its toll of the aging man. Toward the end of January, the ambassador suffered a severe pulmonary illness, and he had hardly risen from his bed when Descartes was stricken with the same malady. Pneumonia killed him within ten days. He died quietly on 11 February 1650, less than two months away from his fifty-fourth birthday.

In important respects, I think, the life of Descartes is illustrative of the gentlemanly ideal of the French sixteenth and seventeenth century—something between the situation of the vigorous, but uncultivated, feudal nobility and the decorative, somewhat effeminate, but undistinguished courtiers of Louis XIV and Louis XV. In Descartes's time the *gentilhomme* was always a man of good family, with social position, general culture, and some fineness of feeling. And if he was a person of some distinction without precise heraldic definition of rank, his lack of exact placement within the social hierarchy was compensated for by the new association of nobility and learning. At a time in which a decaying Scholasticism discouraged novelty and the church exercised a strong repressive influence, the learned ideal moved in the direction of private rather than public scholarship, amateur rather than professional competence, and gentlemanly rather than middle-class learning. In the age of the gentleman (to paraphrase what Max Weber later said about the politicians) philosophers did not live *by* philosophy, but *for* it.

As we have seen, in more youthful days Descartes wore the green velvet dress and sword of a French nobleman. As we have also seen, he slept a great deal, and recommended idleness as a necessity for good mental work. Actually, to keep up the appearance of a gentlemanly amateur, he may have pretended to work less than in fact he did. Throughout, he lives the life of a conservative French gentleman, determined to philosophize *apart* from the divisions of religion and the conflicts of politics. And like Montaigne before him he maintained great outward reverence for the ceremonies of religion, a conservative loyalty and obedience to royal persons, and an infinite respect for court favors. None of this inhibited a profound conviction of his own originality and intellectual infallibility, reflected in a correspondence as sharply polemical with his peers as it is bland and respectful to royalty and his social superiors. The philosophy does not lose in either boldness or brilliance because it is embedded in the matrix of seventeenth-century upper-class social life.

The Development of Method

Like any classic in the history of philosophy, Descartes has been the subject of extreme diversity of interpretation. For Gouhier and Laporte he is the mystic, religious irrationalist. For Milhaud, Alain, Liard, and Brunschvicg he is the classic, modern founder of an autonomous reason. For Koyré he is close to Pascal. For Angrand he is a strict materialist. For Sartre he is an existentialist in his doctrine of human freedom. For Alquié he is a precursor of Marxism. For one Marxist, Henri Lefebvre, his *Discourse on Method* is a manifesto of the ascendant liberal bourgeois class, as two hundred years later Marx produced one for the European industrial proletariat; for another, Maurice Thorez, he is the prophet of the French Revolution. Speaking at the Sorbonne on 2 May 1946 in a ceremony celebrating the 350th anniversary of Descartes's birth, Thorez said: "What revolutionary force is there in Descartes' appeal to the omnipotence of reason! Descartes proclaims the liberty of the spirit, the equality of minds, the solidarity between them which is the basis of fraternity. Liberty, equality, fraternity are the basic principles of the great French Revolution, and one meets them for the first time in Descartes."

But for all the excesses of Marxist rhetoric and of irrationalist special pleading, there *is* a problem of Descartes's interpretation in the history of philosophy which indicates less a bias in the interpreters than an ambiguity in their subject, and it is a problem of interpretation which opposes the claims of tradition to those of modernity. For Kuno Fischer, whose famous monograph of 1852, *Descartes' Leben, Werke und Lehre*, formed the first volume of his *Geschichte der neueren Philosophie*, Descartes was the great pioneer, the father of modern philosophy, whose subjectivist innovations were the foundation of the idealist tradition and the cornerstone of modern thought. But for Etienne Gilson, writing more than sixty years later (*Index scholastico-cartésien*, 1913; *La liberté chez Descartes et la théologie*, 1913; *Etudes sur le rôle de la pensée médiévale dans la formation du système cartésien*, 1921), Descartes was a theologian and a medievalist whose manifest purpose was to adapt traditional theology to the requirements of the new physics with a minimum of deformation. One sees Descartes as the father of the moderns; the other sees him as the grandson of the medievals, and if, as I think, their opposition is only superficial, it is because there are no epochal breaks in the history of philosophy, no dramatic discontinuities between past and future which vitiate the temporal complexities of any philosophic present.

The fact is that Descartes is a fascinating figure in the history of philosophy precisely because he symbolizes the intersection of the medieval and the Renaissance worlds. Although he is a scornful critic of the purveyors of a decadent Aristotelianism, his metaphysics is yet clearly indebted to the insight of a Thomism which forms the presupposition of the age and an Augustinian theology from which he derives his doctrine of freedom and the theory of innate ideas. At the same time he is an acute prophet of the technology of the modern world whose faith in abstract scientific method and the rationalism of clear and distinct ideas points ultimately toward the development of a science useful for the conduct of life, the conservation of health, and the invention of the technical arts. And, to cap it all, he is a methodical skeptic, sensitive to the Pyrrhonian message, which he uses to establish the unshakable foundation of a strict scientific certainty. These paradoxes arise from the elaborate heterogeneity of the times.

The Cartesian philosophy derives its originality from its responsiveness to the diverse intellectual elements of the seventeenth century and from the way it fuses them into a vivid, if not always completely consistent, pattern. Its ingredients are (1) the Scholastic tradition derived in Descartes's case from the Thomism of La Flèche and the Augustinianism of the Oratory; (2) the first fruits of Renaissance mathematics and natural science, represented by Cardan, Clavius, and Galileo; and (3) the ideas of skepticism and atomistic mechanism (the accidental discovery of ancient texts of Lucretius and Sextus Empiricus), transmitted through the respective agencies of Montaigne and of Galileo and Gassendi. Descartes's philosophy is a fusion of these elements, derived from the reading of Montaigne, the schooling of La Flèche and a precocious passion for the new mathematics of Clavius and Cardan.

Perhaps this fusion, this breadth of philosophic concern and scientific reference, is most clearly indicated in the *Discourse on Method* of 1637. Philosophers who deal with Descartes have traditionally concentrated their attention upon the *Meditations* of 1641, and it is true that this work exhibits Descartes the metaphysician at his purest; but at the same time this preference for the *Meditations* over the *Discourse* has introduced a certain distortion into Cartesian studies. For it is the fusion of scientific aims and philosophic means that makes Descartes a unique figure in the history of seventeenth century thought: his primary passion for completely certain knowledge of nature, where metaphysics is less valued for itself than as the firm foundation upon which any reliable knowledge of the physical world must be based. In fact, the "Cartesian revolution" in philosophy as a denial of Aristotle may be seen as an attempt to substitute a physics based upon metaphysics for a metaphysics based upon physics — an effort, as Descartes himself stated, "demonstrire les principes de la Physique par la Métaphysique."

By "fixing" on the *Meditations* as embodying the essence of Cartesianism, the history of thought has concealed the real direction of the modern mind, for the crucial problem here is not the creation of an independent metaphysics, but the exploration of the relationship between metaphysics and science. Modern positivism has done its best to conceal this crucial link, and the contemporary dream of a "logic without ontology" and of a "scientific method without metaphysical presuppositions" has abandoned the Cartesian framework. But the philosophy of Descartes is "scientific" in a different sense. It insists that both induction and deduction presuppose metaphysics, and it rests, therefore, upon

an antecedent rationalism. The *Discourse on Method* is not merely "philosophy," but "an introduction to science," and for the
seventeenth century in general—for Bacon and Descartes alike—
the aim of science is ultimately pragmatic; it envisages the control
of nature for the betterment of human life.

In the "Author's Letter to the Translator" which he wrote in
1647 as a preface to the French edition of the *Principles of
Philosophy* (originally published in Latin in 1644), Descartes provides both a concise account of his ordered presentation of method, metaphysics, and the philosophy of nature, and at the same
time the metaphor which represents his view of the divisions of
philosophy. Describing the sources from which comes all of the
knowledge we now possess as (1) immediately clear ideas, (2) the
experience of the senses, (3) conversations with other men, (4)
books, he adds a fifth: the special efforts of the philosophers to
seek out "first causes" and "true principles." And here, mentioning Socrates, Plato, and Aristotle (in one of those extremely scarce
references to the history of philosophy in his works) he assails the
philosophy of Scholasticism—"those who aspired to be philosophers by blindly following Aristotle, so that frequently they have
corrupted the sense of his writings"—and its epigones, those minds
so imbued with the teaching of the schools that they are "incapable of attaining to a knowledge of true Principles." And from this
follows Descartes's characteristically antitraditional bias: that
those who have by formal instruction learned least about philosophy are probably the most capable of apprehending the truth.
For in his view, to philosophize requires only two things: that one's
first principles should be entirely "clear and distinct," and that
from them one must rigorously deduce all other conclusions.

The basic moral is that philosophic instruction ought to be
"self-instruction," and in his presentation of the ideal order of
self-instruction Descartes suggests *methodology* ("the logic that
teaches us how best to direct our reason in order to discover those
truths of which we are ignorant"), *mathematics*, on whose problems we might well begin the practice of our methodology, *metaphysics*, the first part of true philosophy, to which, after we have
acquired a certain skill in answering questions and solving problems, we turn for the basic principles of knowledge (the nature of
God, the attributes of mind, the reservoir of clear and distinct
ideas), and finally, *Physics*, the second section of true philosophy,
"where, after having discovered the true principles of material

things, we turn to examine how the whole universe is composed, the nature of the earth, planetary bodies, the physical elements, and the structure of plants, animals, and men, so that we may finally discover the other applied sciences which are useful to man." The Cartesian panorama of the realm of human knowledge is impressive, and it is perhaps more Aristotelian than Descartes would have liked to believe. For, beginning with an organon of intellectual achievement (methodology), it passes by way of the theoretical sciences (mathematics, metaphysics, physics) to the practical sciences, the ultimate stage of application.

Descartes's conception is Aristotelian in another sense also. For the methodology, lying somehow outside of and anterior to the derivation of substantive principles and conclusions, is not itself strictly philosophy, but the foundation upon which philosophizing, in both its theoretical and its practical branches, must be based. Thus he presents his own philosophical variation of the ancient image of "the tree of knowledge":

Philosophy as a whole is like a tree whose roots are metaphysics, whose trunk is physics, and whose branches, which issue from this trunk, are all the other sciences. These reduce themselves to three principal ones, namely, medicine, mechanics, and morals—I mean the highest and most perfect moral science which, presupposing a complete knowledge of the other sciences, is the last degree of wisdom.

The metaphor is vivid, since it demonstrates that in the order of intelligibility metaphysics is the ultimate source of nourishment for even the applied sciences with which the modern world is so compulsively preoccupied; but if taken literally it falsifies the order of growth of Descartes's own philosophical system. For even that order of philosophic self-instruction he proposes (the passage from methodology to mathematics, from mathematics to metaphysics, and from metaphysics to physics) is not to be found in the progression of his own philosophic writings, although in the preface to the *Principles* he makes out the best possible case for this development. Here he speaks of the *Discourse on Method* of 1637 as his methodology, followed by the *Dioptrics, Meteors,* and *Geometry* as exercises in its use; of the *Meditations* of 1641 as a return to fundamentals required by the fragmentary character of the *Discourse*; and of the *Principles of Philosophy* of 1644 as a summary work recapitulating the metaphysical essentials in order to pass on to the mature physics. But this account attributes to the crucially important *Discourse on Method* a single-mindedness which it does not in truth possess.

The fact is that this first really important published work of Descartes is much less a mere methodological introduction than a summary overview of the entire Cartesian spectrum of knowledge and concern. It contains metaphysical principles and presuppositions, rules of method valid for knowledge universally, a description of the physical problems Descartes has investigated, and his theory of science and physical research, all embedded in a quasi-personal format which makes this essay one of the great works of intellectual autobiography of the seventeenth century. The *Discourse* is therefore both a history and a commentary describing "how Descartes became a Cartesian." It is as much a retrospective summing up of a life's philosophic and scientific achievement as a prospectus announcing or laying down a scientific program, and, to borrow Leon Roth's striking comment, "although being Descartes's first published work, it is, in effect, his last."

To understand this it is only necessary to piece together the facts from Descartes's correspondence: that as early as 1628 he had formulated the chief tenets of his metaphysics, and that by 1633 he had produced the chief conclusions of his mathematics and physical science, which were kept from immediate publication only by the condemnation of Galileo and were finally published as the *Principles* a decade later. This recognition, clearly, I think, substantiated by the facts, gives Roth's thesis its cogency and suggests how we ought to approach the complicated richness of the *Discourse on Method*.

Because the *Discourse* was published in 1637 and the *Meditations* in 1641, we think of the *Meditations* as posterior to the *Discourse* in the same way as the *Principles*, published in 1644, is posterior to the *Meditations*. But the *Discourse* itself tells another story. The true date of the *Meditations* is 1628-9, the true date of the *Principles* 1629-33. It follows that the *Discourse* written in 1636 is far from being a preliminary manifesto. . . . It is the retrospect of a Descartes who has been through the stages of the *Meditations* and *Principles*, and now looks back on them. He is not sketching a program, but summing up results.

But the *Discourse* is crucially significant for another reason also. Written in 1636 and published anonymously by Jan Maire of Leyden in 1637, it marked a turning point in European thought, anticipated perhaps only by Montaigne in the century before.

Addressed not the the scholar or pedant, but to the ordinary cultured reader, it constituted a narrative of the highest personal interest. It was as if philosophy had been brought down to earth (or at least to the level of the gentlemanly learner) and was no longer the game of professionals and academics, as in the age of Aquinas, but a pastime honored by fashionable clerics, noblemen of cultured instinct, and ladies of the court. With the *Discourse on Method,* the only one of his major works written in an elegantly straightforward French rather than a scholarly Latin, Descartes purposely restored philosophy to the tribunal of the unaided individual reason rather than the bookish tradition of the Roman Catholic church in which he had himself been educated at La Flèche. And if, he said,

I write in French which is the language of my country, rather than in Latin which is that of my teachers, that is because I hope that those who avail themselves only of their natural reason in its purity may be better judges of my opinions than those who believe only in the writings of the ancients; and as to those who unite good sense with study, whom alone I crave for my judges, they will not, I feel sure, be so partial to Latin as to refuse to follow my reasoning because I expound it in a vulgar tongue.

The *Discours de la méthode pour bien conduire sa raison et chercher la verité dans les sciences* begins with a typically French appeal to "le bons sens"—good sense—which is equated with "Reason," "the power of forming a good judgment," and the capability "of distinguishing the true from the false." This *vis cognoscens,* or power of knowing, is seen by Descartes not merely as a "natural light," an intellectual vision or a native power of discrimination, but as a faculty, fundamental to philosophy and to the sciences, which yields results only through a concentrated and disciplined cultivation—through its subjection to a *method.* Here Descartes shows himself at once as a participant in an ancient philosophic tradition and a specific Renaissance hope.

From the time of Plato and Aristotle onward, philosophy has continually wagered its adequacy upon the discovery of a proper method (dialectical, demonstrative, mathematical, inductive, pragmatic, positivistic, or phenomenological, as the case may be). It has maintained a faith that the attainment of all substantive results in philosophy must await the discovery of the appropriate "mode of philosophizing" and has concluded that from the rational establishment of this method, reliable philosophic knowledge

will automatically flow. Sometimes philosophic method has been
sharply distinguished from scientific; more often (at least before
the eighteenth century) they were conceived of as the same. And
the Renaissance, intoxicated by the dream of novel scientific
discovery, was especially vulnerable to these methodological hopes.
Bacon, Descartes, and Leibniz all share the unbounded confidence that a commitment to the proper method will result in the
maximum development of science, and Descartes was particularly
under this spell, since he imperialistically advocated *a single
method* for every justifiable result. The Scholastic tradition following Aristotle had distinguished various kinds of knowledge
based upon an essential diversity of knowable objects, whereas
Descartes specifically rejected this pluralism for a singleness of
knowledge and of certainty, based upon the unity of the method
of obtaining it. Although he distinguished between mathematics
and metaphysics, and between metaphysics and physics, science
and philosophy were *one* precisely because they are determined by
a single law of evidence. The problem of method in Cartesianism
is therefore identical with the problem of the nature and the limits
of human knowledge. Method, indeed, for Descartes, is simply the
mind itself properly at work.

 · But what is unique about the *Discourse* is the way the logic of
method is illuminated by the narration of a very personal path of
discovery; and the work is striking for its curious discrepancy
between form and content and its ingratiating use of intellectual
autobiography as the vehicle for presenting the rigorous structure
of rational thought. Not since Plato in the *Theaetetus* had used
the rambling dialectic of comfortable conversation to expound the
nature of knowledge had the literary resources of a personal style
been available for so fundamental an exercise in technical presentation. "But in this Discourse," says Descartes,

> I shall be very happy to show the paths I have followed, and to set
> forth my life as in a picture, so that everyone may judge of it for
> himself; and thus in learning from the common talk what are the
> opinions which are held of it, a new means of obtaining self-
> instruction will be reached, which I shall add to those which I
> have been in the habit of using. . . . Thus my design is not here
> to teach the Method which everyone should follow in order to
> promote the good conduct of his Reason, but only to show in what
> manner I have endeavored to conduct my own. . . . Regarding
> this Treatise simply as a history, or, if you prefer it, as a fable. . . .

I hope that it will be of use to some . . . and that all will thank me for my frankness.

The Cartesian modesty is, perhaps, a little disingenuous. For to regard the *Discourse* simply as a history is not to take that history *merely* personally. And if it is a "fable," then it is meant not as a fable which concerns a gentlemanly philosopher of the seventeenth century, but rather as a fable of the destiny of human reason itself (as twenty years earlier in *Don Quixote* Cervantes had presented a fable of the destiny of human folly and illusion). And this will become even clearer when we arrive at the famous *Cogito, ergo sum* — "I think, therefore I am," which is the rock-bottom Cartesian refutation of skepticism and the fulcrum of Cartesian science, presented in the fourth section of the *Discourse*.

The fact is that the "I" of the *Discourse* is at once Descartes and univeral man, and as the treatise slowly proceeds, it becomes progressively clear that "the history of his mind" is only introductory to the presentation of "his system of thought." The intellectual history of Descartes the man is imperceptibly transformed into the impersonal ground of all consciousness, so that the "I" that relates the education at La Flèche and the illumination by the heated stove in Germany is not the "I" that so boldly declares: *Cogito, ergo sum.* The "I" that narrates is not wholly the same as the "I" that affirms, since the first details a unique story as the second affirms a universal and necessary truth. The specific Cartesian search for truth is interesting both in itself and for what it discloses about all thinking at its end, but the subtle modulation by which this transition is accomplished should not blind us to the transition itself. The temporal world of lived human experience with which we start becomes the atemporal universe of a logical postulation, and we are confronted with philosophic magic — the transformation of personal thinking into the abstract ego, the "thing which thinks," the *res cogitans* or *chose qui pense*, which is a negation of historicity and concrete selfhood. Thus in Descartes's *Discourse on Method* (as happens later in "the transcendental unity of apperception" in Kant's *Critique of Pure Reason*), the *real process* of thinking disappears, along with its historical grounding and dialectical movement, and we are left with a consciousness *überhaupt*, impersonal and static, cut off from historicity, past time, and memory, a pure mental act and center constituting the scientific observer, as clear and transparent a medium as a reflecting pool or the lens of a microscope. It is precisely this distinction which separates the story of the questing philosopher from his achievement of an impersonal scientific method. The *Discourse on Method* is unique as the register of this existential but productive duality.

The story itself is of the greatest interest, although it carries a curiously antihumanistic message. Descartes severely criticizes the education in humane letters he had received at La Flèche, since its very breadth and comprehensiveness showed him the futility and intellectual bankruptcy of the scholarly resources of the age for one turned toward science and questing for certainty. He learned languages, history, and poetry, mathematics, morals, and theology, and at first his response to the wisdom of the past is a perfect mirror of Montaigne's:

I was aware that the reading of all good books is indeed like a conversation with the noblest men of past centuries who were the authors of them, nay a carefully studied conversation, in which they reveal to us none but the best of their thoughts. . . . For to converse with those of other centuries is almost the same thing as to travel. It is good to know something of the customs of different peoples in order to judge more sanely of our own, and not to think that everything of a fashion not ours is absurd and contrary to reason, as do those who have seen nothing.

But the moment is short-lived. When, says Descartes, one spends too much time in traveling in other countries, one becomes a stranger to one's own. Such travel convinces one of the great variety of opinions and the relativity of them all. It therefore inclines one to skepticism, as it turns one away from the deepest resources of the self. "For it seemed to me," said Descartes, "that I might meet with much more truth in the reasonings that each man makes on the matters that specially concern him, and the issue of which would very soon punish him if he made a wrong judgment, than in the case of those made by a man of letters in his study." It is from this line of reasoning that Descartes resolves to turn from the reservoir of accumulated wisdom and make himself the object of his study.

The second section of the *Discourse* opens with the famous episode of the stove-heated room, where as a young man of twenty-three, returning from the coronation of the Emperor to rejoin the army, he passed the day in idleness, given over to rumination and the examination of his past education. And it was here that, returning again to the folly of historical learning and the inadequacy of "mere opinion," he resolved upon the device of methodical doubt — of stripping himself of all opinions and beliefs formerly held in order to arrive at a method adequate for achieving certain and reliable knowledge. This method is suggested by, though not strictly derived from, his studies in mathematics. Scholastic logic as the art of the syllogism he had abandoned as irrelevant to a technique of real discovery, but from the geometrical analysis of the ancients and the algebra of the moderns there was indeed something to be indirectly learned. "Obscure" and "confused" as they undoubtedly were, their logical development suggested the method which he here briefly details, and which can be summarized as a principle of *certainty*, of *division*, of *simplicity*, and of *completeness*; or, stated as *rules of method*, (1) to accept nothing that was not so clearly and distinctly presented as to resist doubt, (2) to divide every difficulty into its least component parts, (3) to follow the order of reflection of going from the simple to the complex, and (4) to enumerate completely and omit nothing.

These rules, suggested by the order and structure of geometrical chains of reasoning, and ultimately nourished by the conviction that "of all those who have hitherto sought for truth in the sciences, it has been the mathematicians alone who have been able to make demonstrations — that is to say, to produce reasons which are evident and certain," were the foundation of Descartes's own highly original work in analytic or coordinate geometry. Using this method to put together the best from geometrical analysis and algebra, his success in solving mathematical problems and creating a new mathematical science convinced him that these rules which give certainty to the principles of arithmetic can be generalized so as to solve the difficulties *of any science whatsoever*. The development here is from a specific mathematical success to the creation of a universal scientific method.

In the first and second sections of the *Discourse*, Descartes has announced his program of universal doubt and propounded a "revolutionary" method for achieving certainty in the sciences. Now in the third it is as if, appalled by his theoretical temerity, he prudently counters it with a principle of moral conservatism as he turns to the elaboration of his "provisional" or "interim" code of ethics. It is in itself of little importance for the Cartesian philosophy, but it is indicative of the essentially conservative nature of the man. For just as the Cartesian dualism between mind and body is to constitute a philosophic problem for a hundred years, so the Cartesian split between a bold adventure in intellectual method on the one hand and a prudent, even reactionary approach to the perplexities of social action and moral behavior on the other is to remain an unsolved paradox even for the modern world.

Thus, instead of pointing to Descartes as a prophet of the ideals of the French Revolution, as we have noted, the communist Maurice Thorez would have been better advised to note here in the *Discourse on Method* the extreme gentlemanly distaste for novelty and social disruption which makes Descartes and Montaigne so similar in their social philosophies — so *antirevolutionary* in spirit. By the second section of the *Discourse* Descartes already had argued against the social consequences of unrestrained rationalism in its destructive tendencies, and in fact had specifically denied that the *Discourse* had this in mind:

I argued to myself that there was no plausibility in the claim of any private individual to reform a state by altering everything, and by overturning it throughout, in order to set it right again. . . . In the case of great bodies it is too difficult a task to raise them again when they are once thrown down, or even to keep them in their places when once thoroughly shaken; and their fall cannot be otherwise than very violent. Then as to any imperfections that they may possess . . . custom has doubtless greatly mitigated them. . . . And finally the imperfections are almost always more supportable than would be the process of removing them. . . . This is the reason why I cannot in any way approve of those turbulent and unrestful spirits who, being called neither by birth nor fortune to the management of public affairs, never fail to have always in their minds some new reforms. And if I thought that in this treatise there was contained the smallest justification for this folly, I should be very sorry to allow it to be published. My design has never extended beyond trying to reform my own opinion and to build on a foundation which is entirely my own.

Descartes's provisional ethics expresses a similar concern and follows a similar strategy. Since, as he says, it is imprudent to pull down and rebuild the house in which we live without having found other temporary lodging, the assumption of complete skeptical doubt must be practically supported by "a code of morals for the time being" (*une morale par provision*). And for this he suggests four related maxims. The first might be entitled *the maxim of orthodoxy, moderation, and conformity* or, as he said, "to obey the laws and customs of my country, adhering constantly to the religion in which by God's grace I had been instructed since my childhood, and in all other things directing my conduct by opinions the most moderate in nature, and the farthest removed from excess." The second was *a maxim of resolution and consistency:* "to be as firm and resolute in my actions as I could be, and not to follow less faithfully opinions the most dubious, when my mind was once made up regarding them."

The third was *a maxim of Stoicism, self-discipline, and resignation*: "to try always to conquer myself rather than fortune, to alter my desires rather than change the order of the world, and generally to accustom myself to believe that there is nothing entirely within our power but our own thoughts," and it follows in essence the fashionable Stoicism of the age. That this Stoicism is not the product of low birth and need but, quite the contrary, of material comfort and aristocratic outlook is too often forgotten. Stoicism is essentially the moral philosophy of the affluent. The Roman Stoicism of Cato and Seneca presupposes a comfortable private income, as does the Stoicism which Montaigne propounds in "Judging of the Death of Others" and "That the Taste of Good and Evil Depends in Large Part on the Opinion We Have of Them." And when, as we have seen, Descartes later expounds Seneca and counsels self-discipline and resignation to both his royal patronesses, Princess Elizabeth of Bohemia and Queen Christina of Sweden, this is neither an affront to the royal nature nor an incongruous ethical suggestion, but a fashionable moral convention of an essentially aristocratic age.

Descartes's last maxim was *the maxim of rationality*: "And last of all, to conclude this moral code, I felt it incumbent on me to make a review of the various occupations of men in this life in order to try and choose out the best; and without wishing to say anything of the employment of others I thought that I could not do better than continue in the one in which I found myself engaged, that is to say, in occupying my whole life in cultivating my Reason, and in advancing myself as much as possible in the knowledge of the truth in accordance with the method which I had prescribed myself." This last maxim returns us again to the methodological quest from which this moral interlude has temporarily withdrawn us, and it shows that Kant's later distinction between the theoretical and the practical reason has been prepared in the seventeenth-century intuition which separates the constructions of natural science from man's basic institutional and moral behavior.

The fourth section of the *Discourse* outlines Descartes's metaphysics, and it sets forth in the briefest compass all of those classic Cartesian doctrines which four years later the *Meditations* spelled out in requisite philosophic detail. In both the essential strategy remains the same: from absolute doubt to the indubitable evidence of personal self-consciousness; from the certainty of the self to the general principle that the things we clearly and distinctly perceive are true; from the clarity and distinctness of God as idea to the indubitable existence of God as a perfect being; and, finally, from the perfect existence and agency of God to the external world and our knowledge of it, which depends upon God's veracity and his creative power. In this way the resources of doubt are made the ground of the purest certainty, and the existence of God becomes a proposition essential to the existence of the natural world which is the subject of the propositions of natural science. The natural progression of metaphysical thought is from *self* to *God* to *the external world*, and the function of philosophy for Descartes is not primarily to establish the autonomy of metaphysics, but to lay those theoretical foundations which lead up to a defense of mathematical physics. It is this important fact which exclusive attention to the *Meditations* obscures, and the *Discourse* (by fixing metaphysical concern within the context of a total philosophy of science) makes plain.

It has been clear from the beginning that the Cartesian assumption of universal doubt — the rejection of everything for which one could imagine the least ground of doubt, and therefore of all the reasons formerly accepted as demonstrations — was not undertaken to maintain a polite and permanent skepticism, but to arrive at last at the absolute bedrock of certainty. Yet the indubitability of the self as a cognitive center which is its outcome carries with it an enormous degree of abstraction and a dualism of mind and body, as extreme as anything to be found in the most exaggerated Platonism. "I noticed," says Descartes,

> that whilst I thus wished to think all things false, it was absolutely essential that the "I" who thought this should be somewhat, and remarking that this truth "*I think, therefore I am*" was so certain and so assured that all the most extravagant suppositions brought forward by the skeptics were incapable of shaking it, I came to the conclusion that I could receive it without scruple as the first principle of the Philosophy for which I was seeking. And then, examining attentively that which I was, I saw that I could conceive that

I had no body, and that there was no world nor place where I might be; but yet that I could not for all that conceive that I was not. . . . From that I knew that I was a substance the whole essence or nature of which is to think, and that for its existence there is no need of any place, nor does it depend on any material thing; so that the 'me,' that is to say, the soul by which I am what I am, is entirely distinct from body, and is even more easy to know than is the latter; and even if body were not, the soul would not cease to be what it is.

But the second stage of the argument is equally improbable, for it requires an appeal to the ontological argument for the existence of God—one of the cornerstones of the Augustinian tradition, yet one of the most logically suspect of the theses of medieval theology. Since it is obviously a greater perfection in a self to know rather than to merely doubt, it is clear that human existence is imperfect. But the mind, says Descartes, has implanted within it the idea of a being more perfect than its own. And, unlike the figures of geometers, whose triangles and polygons exist in the mind together with a knowledge of their properties, but without the slightest persuasion that they have an existence outside the realm of mere conception, the idea of God carries with it a clear and distinct notion of his existence, since the very concept of a perfect being implies existence in the same manner in which the concept that its three angles equal two right angles is implied in the very notion of a triangle. Descartes might doubt the authenticity of the ideas of objects in the external world as following from a weakness of his own cognitive nature,

but this could not apply to the idea of a Being more perfect than my own, for to hold it from nought would be manifestly impossible; and because it is no less contradictory to say of the more perfect that it is what results from and depends on the less perfect, than to say that there is something which proceeds from nothing, it was equally impossible that I should hold it from myself. In this way it could but follow that it had been placed in me by a Nature which was really more perfect than mine could be, and which even had within itself all the perfections of which I could form any idea—that is to say, to put it in a word, which was God. To which I added that since I knew some perfections which I did not possess, I was not the only being in existence; but that there was necessarily some other more perfect Being on which I depended, or from which I acquired all that I had.

The establishment of the existence of God now serves as an epistemic guarantee; for if we are disposed to hold that all the things
that we conceive clearly and distinctly are true, this is ultimately
certain only because God exists, because he is a perfect being, and
because all that is clear and distinct in our consciousness issues
from him. Unless we had the assurance that all our convictions of
reality and truth proceeded from a perfect and infinite being,
however clear and distinct were our ideas, we could never be
completely sure that they possessed the perfection of being true.
From all this follows the ultimate certainty of the propositions of
mathematics, and the contingent certainty of all propositions
concerning the external world.

It is indeed ironic that in the Cartesian system, while the
authority of natural science derives ultimately from the establishment of two basic propositions of metaphysics, these propositions
themselves are the most questionable and the most vulnerable to
external philosophical criticism. In the "Preface to the Reader"
which Descartes placed at the head of the *Meditations*, published
four years later, he refers back to the *Discourse* of 1637 of which
he had freely solicited criticism, and to the two chief criticisms
which he had in fact received. These were (1) that from the fact
that the human mind, reflecting on itself, does not perceive itself
to be other than a thing which thinks *it does not follow* that its
nature or its essence *does* indeed consist only in thinking; and (2)
that from the fact that I have in myself *the idea* of something more
perfect than I am, *it does not follow* that this idea *is* more perfect
than I am, and even less that what is represented by this idea
exists. The *Cogito* and the *ontological proof* are the ultimate
foundations of Descartes's philsophy of science, as they are the
cornerstone of his metaphysics, but they are just those elements
which subsequent philosophers have been most reluctant to certify
as acceptable components of the Cartesian system.

In a course of lectures given at Cambridge in 1933–34, G. E.
Moore dealt briefly with "philosophical methods," and about
Descartes he had this to say: "A method has been used by Descartes, in which one of the premises is the existence and veracity of
God. I do not think this is successful; because I don't think there is
any good reason for thinking that God exists. But I suppose this
sort of argument *ought* to be investigated." As usual, Moore is
more candid and outspoken than most, but he touches upon a
crucial point. Analytic philosophers and even philosophers of
science have spent much time of late in a new rebirth of Cartesian

studies. In most cases too, they would not care to take seriously the Cartesian emphasis upon the existence of God. Yet there can be little doubt that, hostage to his age, Descartes was completely sincere in putting it forward, and that in him we have the paradoxical spectacle of one of the founders of modern mathematical and experimental science who believed that science itself was only epistemically secure when it rested upon the guarantee of the divine perfection and grace.

The fifth section of the *Discourse* (except for a long digression on the circulation of the blood which will be of interest when we turn to Descartes's theory of scientific experiment and observation) draws the conclusions for science of the metaphysical principles just presented. Since we can now consider ourselves warranted in accepting nothing as true which does not appear to be even more clear and certain than the demonstrations formerly presented by the geometers, we may pass to those laws "which God has so established in Nature, and of which He has imprinted such ideas on our minds, that, after having reflected sufficiently upon the matter, we cannot doubt their being accurately observed in all that exists or is done in the world." It is precisely these laws which Descartes claims to have established with respect to natural objects, light, the planets and astronomical bodies, and man himself, in the unpublished treatise *Le monde,* withdrawn in 1633. For the enterprise of constructing a complete cosmology rests upon a prior recognition of those laws of nature, or "eternal truths" created by God (and in some sense even binding upon him) such that, as Leibniz also later observed, "even if God had created other worlds, He could not have created any in which these laws would fail to be observed."

The elaboration of these laws is accomplished by recognizing a certain hypothetical character in the demonstration. Although it is a dogma of the theologians that the action by which God preserves and supports the world is the same as that by which he at first created it, this supposition is not requisite for physical science. For although theology attests the *that* of God's creation, science elaborates its *how*, and it is only necessary for the scientific cosmologist (which Descartes asserts himself to be) to assume God's activity—that he has merely "lent his concurrence to Nature," leaving her to act in accordance with the laws which he has established—and to turn to those laws themselves as the subject of his science. What we then learn is that the laws of nature are identical with the laws of mechanics, and that to universalize

them is finally even to apply to the human body the same principles which explain the motions of inanimate matter. "From this
aspect," says Descartes, "the body is regarded as a machine which,
having been made by the hands of God, is incomparably better
arranged, and possesses in itself movements which are much more
admirable, than any of those which can be invented by man."
And it thus becomes possible to assimilate all biological activity, as
well as the psychologically inspired human movements, as special
cases of the operation of general mechanics. It is this aspect of the
Cartesian philosophy of nature which, although it also found a
certain sympathetic echo in the cosmology of Isaac Newton, was to
spark the rise of mechanistic materialism in such men as Diderot,
Buffon, La Mettrie, Holbach, and Maupertuis in the French
eighteenth century.

The sixth and final section of the *Discourse*, like the preceding,
also contains much material which elucidates Descartes's philosophy of science and experiment and his attitude toward them. It
demonstrates for a later age, which prefers to separate its scientists
and its philosophers, that the seventeenth century made no such
distinction. And in Descartes's case it indicates once again that the
complicated metaphysical web he wove was not kept sealed off
from the concerns of the active experimental scientist as irrelevant
and intrinsically inappropriate speculation, but was conceived
rather as comprising introductory philosophical exercises which
permitted the scientific mind to proceed more confidently with its
concrete and experimental task.

It is true that in this concluding section of the *Discourse* Descartes includes many loosely connected attitudes and arguments —
for example, an explanation of how the persecution of Galileo
caused him to abandon publication of *Le monde*; his view of
science as ultimately practical and applied, and of the difficulties
which beset it both as an individual and as a collective enterprise;
the hazards of public philosophical debate; evidences of his own
personal egoism and difficulties in controversy ("Although I have
often explained some of my opinions to persons of very good
intelligence, who, while I talked to them appeared to understand
them very clearly, yet when they recounted them I remarked that
they had almost always altered them in such a manner that I could
no longer acknowledge them as mine"; and "Hardly ever have I
encountered any censor of my opinions who did not appear to me
to be either less rigorous or less judicial than myself"); and finally,
one of the most bitter attacks upon the obscurity and blindness of

the philosophy of the Schools to be found in the whole body of his writings.

I shall turn later to his more detailed views of science, and the clear evidences here of the attitudes of Descartes the experimenter; so the only thing to further note is the concluding pages of the *Discourse*, which frankly tell us its purpose and exhibit its introductory task in presenting the optical, astronomical, and geometrical treatises which follow it in the original edition. The function of the whole, *Discourse* and scientific treatises alike, says Descartes, is to constitute "a pretty clear manifestation of what I can do and what I cannot do in the sciences." And he invites all those who have objections to what he has presented "to take the trouble of sending them to my publishers, so that, being made aware of them, I may try at the same time to subjoin my reply." He does not apologize for his opinions, for he thinks them eminently simple and conformable to common sense. "I have adopted them," he says, "not because they have been held by others, nor because they have not been so held, but only because Reason has persuaded me of their truth." His last words concern the future use he will make of his life: "I have resolved not to employ the time which remains to me in life in any other matter than in endeavoring to acquire some knowledge of nature, which shall be of such a kind that it will enable us to arrive at rules for Medicine more assured than those which have as yet been attained." And he adds the declaration which expresses his own basic values: "I shall always hold myself to be more indebted to those by whose favor I may enjoy my leisure without hindrance, than I shall be to any who may offer me the most honorable position in all the world."

The Gentleman as Metaphysician

To turn from the *Discourse on Method* of 1637 to the *Meditations* of 1641 is to pass into another intellectual climate. A certain informality of speech still remains, but the metaphysical content is concentrated, and the element of rambling intellectual autobiography which makes the *Discourse* so personally interesting, and so descriptive of the entire Cartesian philosophic-scientific enterprise, has now contracted to a focus of metaphysical concern. And this is only the first stage in that curious stylistic transformation in Descartes's major works as we see the autobiographical element recede before the scientific necessity. The autobiographical informality of the *Discourse* turns into the systematic informality of the *Meditations* as the stylistic informality of the latter turns into the serial formalization of the *Principles of Philosophy*. And it is as if we are on that gradually steeper and more difficult road which leads from Montaigne's *Essays* to the *Ethics* of Spinoza.

But the most striking thing about the *Meditations* is not its relationship to Descartes's other works, but the extraordinary congruence between its form and intention and its philosophic content. The essential preoccupation of the *Meditations* is what Anthony Kenny calls "Cartesian privacy"—that making epistemology the center of philosophical inquiry which created a new philosophy of mind. Kenny is surely correct, although his insight is hardly new. For whether we call it "Cartesian privacy" with Kenny or "the subjectivist principle" with Whitehead, it cannot be doubted that Descartes has turned the more objective interests of the ancient and medieval periods from the external world of "things" to the internal world of "ideas," "impressions," "sense-data," and "perceptions"; from the description and analysis of "public objects" to the description and analysis of "private subjects"; and from the conditions of physical existence to the conditions of mental consciousness.

All this is not completely accidental. If one can consider Cartesianism as a function of the tasks imposed upon the gentlemanly scholar by his epoch, then the task of epistemological reflection becomes possible only upon the condition of idleness, tranquillity, and economic independence. The very title *Meditation* is worthy of attention. A hundred years later Ignatius Loyola in his *Spiritual Exercises* (1521) had used "contemplation" and "meditation" as equivalent, and something of this aura of isolation, tranquillity, and religious privacy enters into the Cartesian effort. This is clearly recognized by Descartes himself. His insistence at the end of the *Discourse* that he prefers the enjoyment of his leisure without hindrance to the most honorable position in the world is no empty assertion, and toward the beginning of the first Meditation he clearly sets the stage for the leisurely meditative (metaphysical) enterprise.

Today, then, since very opportunely for the plan I have in view
I have delivered my mind from every care (and I am, happily,
agitated by no passions) and since I have procured for myself an
assured leisure in a peaceable retirement, I shall at last seriously
and freely address myself to the general upheaval of all my former
opinions.

Descartes's metaphysics, as he so clearly sees himself, is the natural product of a precious ingredient of the past which today is in danger of rapid extinction — *privacy* — that marvelous compound of withdrawal, self-reliance, quiet, solitude, contemplation, and concentration which seems the exclusive possession of a bygone age. Descartes's world was backward, pretechnological, from our point of view almost primitive, but still a world of nobility and leisure in which nature was a "presence" and not a mere instrumentality, and men could be individuals quietly pondering the nature of mind. Of this world Herbert Marcuse could say:

With its code of forms and manners, with the style and vocabulary of its literature and philosophy, this past culture expressed the rhythm and content of a universe in which valleys and forests, villages and inns, nobles and villains, salons and courts were a part of the experienced reality. In the verse and prose of this pretechnological culture is the rhythm of those who wander or ride in carriages, who have the time and the pleasure to think, contemplate, feel and narrate.

Thus Descartes's is a philosophy of privacy in a double sense. It is a philosophy which originates in tranquillity and independence, and one which culminates in the centrality of the tranquilly thinking human subject — the *res cogitans* But it shares another quality with the class structure of the seventeenth century; its rationalism has a highly aristocratic flavor. To be sure, the *Discourse on Method* begins on what looks like a democratic note — "Good sense is of all things in the world the most equally distributed" — and this hypothesis is further supported a moment later by the view that "the power of forming a good judgment and of distinguishing the true from the false, which is properly speaking what is called Good sense or Reason, is by nature equal in all men." But the evidence is deceptive. It may hold as a maxim of common acceptance, but it is inapplicable to the talent for metaphysical speculation. Here Descartes's aristocratic bias with respect to philosophizing is as pronounced as anything to be found in the *Republic* of Plato. For him also the boundary line between the vulgar and the choice spirits is absolute. "A man," he says toward the end of the second Meditation, "who makes it his aim to raise his knowledge above the common should be ashamed to derive the occasion for doubting from the forms of speech invented by the vulgar"; and in the "Preface to the Reader" of the *Meditations*, the presupposition of intellectual aristocracy is clear:

Now that I have once for all recognized and acknowledged the
opinions of men, I at once begin to treat of God and the human
soul, and at the same time to treat of the whole of the First
Philosophy, without however expecting any praise from the vulgar
and without the hope that my book will have many readers. On
the contrary, I should never advise anyone to read it excepting
those who desire to meditate seriously with me, and who can
detach their minds from affairs of sense, and deliver themselves
entirely from every sort of prejudice. I know too well that such
men exist in a very small number.

The truth of the matter is that our modern democratic as-
sumptions, combined with the omnipresence of the mass media,
predispose us to a quite different view of learned communication
in the past than in fact prevailed. Descartes's reluctance to publish
was not simply the fear of meeting Galileo's fate. It was also in
large part the conviction registered above that the number of
those capable of serious metaphysical reflection was indeed small.
That this conviction was shared is attested by the conditions of
learned communication in the seventeenth century to which I
have already called attention. Today we believe that every man is
a potential philosopher. But as Leo Strauss has insisted, "The
attitude of an earlier type of writer was fundamentally different."

They believed that the gulf separating "the wise" and "the vulgar"
was a basic fact of human nature which could not be influenced
by any progress of popular education: philosophy or science was
essentially a privilege of "the few." They were convinced that philosophy as such was suspect to, and hated by, the majority of men.
Even if they had had nothing to fear from any particular political
quarter, those who started from that assumption would have been
driven to the conclusion that public communication of the philosophic or scientific truth was impossible or undesirable.

It may seem that Descartes's publication of the *Discourse* in the
more available French bespeaks a contrary ambition, but I do not
believe that this was so. For in the same passage in which he
addresses "those who avail themselves only of their natural reason
in its purity," the context makes clear the restricted nature of the
appeal. It is "to those who unite good sense with study whom alone
I crave for my judges " he says, and this is clearly the limited
audience of the Cartesian circle around Mersenne and the elite
body of the scholarly nobility.

In his reply to the second set of Objections to his *Meditations*
(contributed by "several theologians," but probably written at

least in part by Father Mersenne himself), Descartes makes perfectly clear the philosophical method he had adopted in writing
them. In response to the suggestion that he might better have
propounded his arguments in geometrical fashion (since his skill
as a mathematician was well known, and this mode would have
exhibited his reasoning at a glance) Descartes sets great store by
presenting arguments in the order of their intelligibility—"in
putting forward those things first that should be known without
the aid of what comes subsequently, and arranging all other
matters so that their proof depends solely on what precedes them.
I certainly tried to follow this order as accurately as possible in my
Meditations." This is the *analytic* or a priori method, which shows
the true way by which a thing was methodologically discovered
and derived, as it were, going from effect to cause. This requires
only great application and attentiveness in the reader, since,
putting himself sympathetically in the place of the author, he
follows the argument and understands it, making it "as much his
own as if he had himself discovered it." It is for this reason that
Descartes so continually begs from his reader not only an intense
and single-minded application to his text, but also an effort
specifically to comprehend "l'ordre et la liaison de mes raisons"—
the order and connection of my reasonings.

Synthesis, or the a posteriori method, on the other hand, em-
ploys an opposite procedure—that of going from causes to effects.
It is the geometric method of the ancients, which does indeed
clearly demonstrate its conclusions through a long series of definitions, postulates, axioms, theorems, and problems; yet as a
method it is not as pedagogically satisfactory as analysis; it does
not so well content the eager learner, for it is further removed
from the method of discovery. This not only is an implicit criticism of, for example, the method rather artifically adopted by
Spinoza in his *Ethics*, but explains why Descartes's own *Principles
of Philosophy*, which also uses it, was produced so late in his
philosophical development. For it has been prepared for by both
the *Discourse* and the *Meditations*, which, in their autobiographical and informal style, have done so much to explicate the
Cartesian "route of discovery." "I have," says Descartes, "used in
my Meditations only analysis, which is the best and truest method
of teaching"; and his rationale for this is very persuasive. In
geometric proof, the basic axioms or primary notions harmonize
with our sense experience, and are readily granted by all, whereas

in metaphysics nothing causes more trouble than the attempt to makes its first principles and primary notions clear and distinct. They often seem to be contradicted by the most commonplace (but uncriticized) experience of our senses, and therefore the first exercise in metaphysical method is *to systematically withdraw the mind from its preoccupation with the senses and from matters corporeal.* It is as if once again we are in the presence of Plato and his insistence that the philosophic nature is the one capable of turning from the world of change to eternal things.

In detail the Cartesian metaphysics is subtle, but broadly and in outline it presents in sequential order a few primary concepts by which, beginning with universal doubt, we pass finally to the givenness of the corporeal world. It is a strategy which, as we have seen, permits Descartes to begin with the fashionable skepticism of the period and to arrive at last at the presented field of inquiry which constitutes the subject matter of physical science. And it shows a certain analogy with the enterprise of Kant's first Critique, although in reverse. Kant's question was, essentially, How is the flourishing subject of Newtonian mechanics epistemologically possible? And his answer was, Because the mind is so constituted as to fit the data of sense into its ordering categorial modes. In one sense this is a passive response, since it envisages the mind as an instrument with fixed capacities, whose functioning produces valid physical knowledge. Descartes's question is also, How is valid (certain) knowledge of the physical world possible? But his problem is that of *constituting* such a science rather than simply accounting for it as a going concern. And this constitution involves the actual metaphysical *process* of traversing the ground which *any mind* must traverse (or so Descartes thought) if it is to banish the torment of skepticism and arrive at the firm and reassuring ground of scientific certainty. Bonaventura in the Middle Ages had explored the *Itinerarium mentis in Deum* — the journey of the mind toward God. Descartes in the seventeenth century proposes a similar journey of the mind toward the constitution of a physical science, where God is not the journey's end but only one of the stations visited along the way.

The identical structure of Descartes's metaphysics is endlessly repeated — in the *Discourse*, in the *Principles*, and in the *Meditations* — so that it is unnecessary to present the details of the latter here. And, fortunately, in the preface to the *Principles*, Descartes has himself summed up in capsule form the outline of the metaphysical journey he prescribes:

Thus in considering that he who would doubt all things cannot yet doubt that he exists while he doubts, and that what reasons so in being unable to doubt of itself and yet doubting all else, is not what we call our body but what we call our soul or thought, I have taken the being or existence of this thought as the first principle from which I have very clearly deduced the following: viz. that there is a God who is the author of all that is in the world, or who, being the source of all truth, has not created in us an understanding liable to be deceived in the judgments that it forms on matters of which it has a very clear and distinct perception. These comprise the whole of the principles of which I make use respecting immaterial or metaphysical things, from which I very clearly deduce those of corporeal or physical things, to wit, that there are bodies extended in length, breadth and depth, which have diverse figures and move in diverse ways. These, in sum, are all the principles from which I deduce the truth of other things.

Descartes's first principle is the existence of consciousness and his last metaphysical act is the establishment or deduction of physical bodies in motion; and the coexistence of these two provides that unresolved dualism which is both the failure and the most characteristic feature of his system. It is a system haunted by the contrast between *res cogitans* and *res extensa*, between the "immaterial or metaphysical things" which people his metaphysics, and the "corporeal or physical things" which inhabit his science. And these difficulties, metaphysical and physical, coalesce in the problem of the human self, which, although it is essentially a "thing that thinks," is yet experienced as attached to a body so that we must perceive that it is a composite of mind and body. Yet the consistent interaction between these two has remained one of the unresolved riddles of the Cartesian system.

The whole of the sixth Meditation is an attempt to set forth this dualism and to canvass its difficulties. We are assured of the existence of material things by the faculty of sensory imagination; yet this power of imagination (since it differs from the power of understanding which is of the essence of the mind) is no "necessary" element in man's nature. As mind can exist without body, so intellectual understanding can exist without imagination — the former, in fact, as the agent of both self-knowledge and mathematical knowledge, can provide reliable epistemic contents (clear and distinct ideas) and therefore "certainty" in a fashion that can never be guaranteed by the latter (which is only capable of "probability"). Another interesting consequence also follows. Although the understanding alone is capable of producing certain theoretical knowledge, the perceptions of sense, "having been placed

within me by nature merely for the purpose of signifying to my
mind what things are beneficial or hurtful to the composite whole
of which it forms a part," become the practical guides to bodily
action at the very moment in which they are deprived of epistemic
certainty. As we might have learned from the *Discourse* and its
separation of the search for theoretical certainty from the conventional and conservative acceptance of a provisional moral code
to govern interim practical behavior, Descartes's separation of the
mind and the body likewise entails a profound separation of the
theoretical and the practical — of the values of knowledge and the
values of action. And this too is capable of sociological interpretation along the lines which (in *The Quest for Certainty*) have constituted Dewey's critique of Plato.

It is nothing so crude as the distinction between the laboring
classes and the classes of lordly leisure, although it bears some
relationship to it. There is an age-old association of thinking and
knowing with immaterial and spiritual and "metaphysical" principles, and of all practical activity in the arts and crafts with
"things" and with "brute matter." But a latent contempt for
matter and the corporeal and the glorification of spirituality and
mind are far from self-explanatory. And it is especially paradoxical for Descartes, who separates thinking and knowing from
intimate connection with physical objects, while, as we shall see,
at the same time pressing for the whole-hearted adoption of
experimental method in the natural sciences. It is true that
Descartes, like Plato, is a mathematician, and that this leads to a
quest for epistemic certainty based on the idealization of a mathematical and intrinsically deductive model. Descartes's exaltation
of pure mind above the contingency of the corporeal is undeniably
connected with "the quest for a certainty which shall be absolute
and unshakable," but the quiet achievement of the mathematician is at the same time materially dependent upon that upper-
class independence and privacy of which I have previously spoken.
Just three years after the publication of the *Meditations* Descartes,
addressing the city of Utrecht to obtain justice and protection
against Voetius's virulent charges against him, put at the head of
his letter: "Reply of the Gentleman René Descartes, Lord of
Perron," and the self-esteem so registered is not totally irrelevant
to a metaphysical doctrine which holds that the quest for complete
certainty can be fulfilled in pure knowing alone. With those, like
Descartes, to whom the process of pure thinking is overwhelmingly
congenial, and who have the leisure and the aptitude — indeed the

genius—to pursue their preference, the satisfactions attending knowledge are unalloyed—untangled in the risks of overt action and the perplexities of decisive moral choice. In such a favorable and permissive setting, it is not difficult to understand how thought can be alleged to be a purely "inner" activity, intrinsic to a "mind" complete and sufficient unto itself.

But there is also something more, and it springs from the paradox to which we have previously called attention: that the pioneer in mathematical physics and experimental science is also profoundly influenced by the residues of medieval thought. Anselm's ontological argument, the Thomistic principle of hierarchy, the Augustinian *lumen naturale* and theory of the will, all appear at one time or another in the writings of Descartes, and, although it would be a complete distortion to say that he valued medieval theology for its own sake, or even that the metaphysics he propounded (including the existence of God and an immortal soul) was meant to be independent of a justification of natural knowledge, nevertheless his dependence upon medieval foundations is not irrelevant, and he claimed an orthodoxy in religious belief which was taken in good faith by many, if not all, of his contemporaries.

The founding, then, of a physical science upon a spiritual metaphysics is dualistic and problematic, but it does enable one to have it both ways—to look back conservatively to a religious age, and to look forward hopefully to a millenium of applied technological science. In this respect Descartes is exemplary of the great problems of modern—that is to say, of seventeenth- and eighteenth-century—philosophy, and of the general class of intellectuals of this period, torn between the claims of past and future. Dewey has stated it precisely:

Since science has made the trouble, the cure ought to be found in an examination of the nature of knowledge, of the conditions which make science possible. If the conditions of the possibility of knowledge can be shown to be of an ideal and rational character, then, so it has been thought, the loss of an idealistic cosmology in physics can be readily borne. The physical world can be surrendered to matter and mechanism, since we are assured that matter and mechanism have their foundation in immaterial mind. Such has been the characteristic course of modern spiritualistic philosophies since the time of Kant; indeed, since that of Descartes, who first felt the poignancy of the problem involved in reconciling the conclusions of science with traditional religious and moral beliefs.

It would certainly go too far to say that Descartes was consciously aware of the problem of "reconciling the conclusions of science
with traditional religious and moral beliefs." This is the way the
history of philosophy looks back upon an age to understand it
better than it understood itself. But the presuppositions of "an age
of faith" were Descartes's presuppositions also, and his constructive efforts to found the science of the natural world, which was
probably his deepest philosophical commitment, are never independent of those medieval elements which are so insidious just
because the mind of the time cannot perceive any horizon other
than that bounded by their principles of transcendence. And that
is why Descartes is so emblematic of the whole social dilemma and
climate of opinion of the seventeenth century.

It is always important to distinguish between "a philosophy,"
which is the work of one individual, expressing his experience and
his thought, and "a conception of the world" (Dilthey called it a
Weltanschauung or a *Weltbild*; Lucien Goldmann, following
him, a *vision du monde*), which is more the work of an epoch, a
civilization, or a period in history. Descartes produced a philosophy which is at the same time a conception of the world,
because the dualisms which haunt his thought are little more than
the dilemmas of his age. And this is why it has been so tempting —
particularly to his French Marxist interpreters — to see his dialectical contradictions as simple images of his social world. If Descartes is at once an idealist and a materialist (an idealist in
metaphysics, a mechanistic materialist in science), this is but a
mark of his genius and a sign of his time. For dualism is always a
compromise, an accommodation, and a dilemma. And the Cartesian dualism too is a compromise within the realm of mind
perfectly expressing the dilemma of the epoch. The seventeenth
century lies between a dying feudalism and a rising bourgeoisie,
between faith and science, theology and rational criticism, and
this is perfectly expressed through that curious mixture in Descartes himself of prudence and audacity, timidity and assertive-
ness, impertinence and discretion, which are to be found so conspicuously in his response to the institutions of his time, in the
letters he addresses to his contemporaries, and in the prefaces and
prefatory materials of his major published works.

Descartes's *modus vivendi* was meant to be profoundly critical,
and yet acceptable to powerful officials, to the established order,
and to the major intellects of his time; that is to say, to savants

and to free-thinkers as well as to priests, professors, and princesses. There is a sense then in which the *Discourse on Method* announces modern civilization: it is secular, individualistic, technological, and rationalistic all at once; but it is also medieval, conservative, metaphysical, and aristocratic in tone. It lies between two worlds, as Dewey noted, and like the *Meditations* is the expression of a series of dichotomies which are to become even more pronounced, exaggerated, and scandalous in Kant.

The Ennoblement of Science

A few weeks after the death of the famous and immensely rich Cardinal Richelieu in December 1642, Descartes wrote from Endegeest a somewhat ironic and gossipy letter to his good friend Mersenne in Paris, in which he said:

Monsieur le Cardinal should have left us two or three of his millions so that we could make all the experiments necessary to discover the specific natures of individual bodies, and I have no doubt that we could have come to important conclusions of even greater value to the public than all the victories attainable by making war.

As a statement asserting the superiority of scientific research over warfare, it seems very humane, very modern. Only the personal interest in physical experiment appears a little incongruous in one whose subsequent reputation rests upon his construction of a deductive metaphysics and the discovery of analytic geometry. And yet this interest is typical and recurring. Descartes's correspondence is full of references to the experiments in pressure and temperature, perspective and anatomy he is conducting, and treatises like the *Optics* and the *Meteorology* relate the experiments in detail. And his early educational experience at La Flèche seems to have soured him upon the humanistic learning to be obtained from books and to suggest instead the resources of the mind itself, as in mathematical invention, or of nature, as in physical observation. Descartes's metaphor of "turning to the great book of the world" is endlessly cited, for it makes a kind of symbolic sense, and although when he permanently removed to Holland he is said to have taken with him only the holy scriptures and a complete edition of Saint Thomas's *Summa theologica*, evidence that he read either cannot be specifically cited from his writings. Much more plausible is the story that sometime later, while he was living in the vicinity of Utrecht or Leyden, a visitor asked to see his library, whereupon, leading him to a vestibule where there was hanging a half-dissected calf, Descartes said: "This is my library!"

The preface to the *Principles*, written when Descartes was approaching fifty, is indeed one of the most interesting documents among his works; for it, even more precisely than the *Discourse*, provides a later and a more specific view of his relationship to the philosophical tradition, the order and rationale of his works, and his central passion for scientific discovery. The *Principles*, as he says, is a kind of substitute for *Le monde*, the suppressed scientific treatise of a decade before. It is the progress report on his scientific system, but, even so, only a beginning. It is the one work in which he thought that he had "commenced to expound the whole of philosophy in its order." Yet he justly recognizes that the attempt is still fragmentary and incomplete, and his wistfulness in this respect, as he views the probable future of his scientific accomplishment, is very modern in its recognition of the material conditions of scientific research and at the same time very Cartesian in its stubborn individualism:

> But in order to carry this plan to a conclusion, I should afterwards in the same way explain in further detail the nature of each of the other bodies which are on the earth, i.e. minerals, plants, animals, and above all man; then finally treat exactly of medicine, morals, and mechanics. All this I should have to do in order to give to mankind a body of philosophy which is complete; and I do not feel myself to be so old, I do not so much despair of my strength, I do not find myself so far removed from a knowledge of what remains, that I should not venture to endeavor to achieve this design, were I possessed of the means of making all the experiments necessary to me in order to support and justify my reasoning. But seeing that for this end great expense is requisite to which the resources of an individual like myself could not attain were he not given assistance by the public, and not seeing that I can expect that aid, I conceive it to be henceforward my duty to content myself with studying for my own private instruction, trusting that posterity will pardon me if I fail henceforward to work for its good.

The irony is unmistakable and yet it is also seriously meant, but I have quoted the passage chiefly for the light which it throws on Descartes's concept of physical experiment. It reveals that for him this is less a means of scientific *discovery*, than a "support" and "justification" of *reasoning* independently pursued. This scientific rationalism has already been put forward to some extent in the

Discourse, both as to the role of scientific experiment and as to the nature of scientific theory. When in the fifth section of the *Discourse* he wishes to concretely illustrate his scientific mechanism — his belief that the laws of mechanics are identical with the laws of nature — he begins the long digression on the circulation of the blood (a theory admittedly derived from Harvey) with an appeal to anatomical observation.

But in order to show how I there treated of this matter, I wish here to set forth the explanation of the movement of heart and arteries which, being the first and most general movement that is observed in animals, will give us the means of easily judging as to what we ought to think about all the rest. And so that there may be less difficulty in understanding what I shall say on this matter, I should like that those not versed in anatomy should take the trouble, before reading this, of having cut up before their eyes the heart of some large animal which has lungs (for it is in all respects sufficiently similar to the heart of a man), and cause that there be demonstrated to them the two chambers or cavities which are within it.

The use of dissection here is not experimental in the strict sense. It is observation for the use of persuasive demonstration. And in the concluding section of the *Discourse* too, Descartes makes clear that, quite in line with the hypothetico-deductive method which has achieved such triumphs in contemporary science, his general appeal to experiment is a relatively late stage in the process of scientific research. "I remarked also respecting experiments, that they become so much the more necessary the more one is advanced in knowledge, for to begin with, it is better to make use simply of those which present themselves spontaneously to our senses, and of which we could not be ignorant provided that we reflected ever so little." The reason for this lies in Descartes's proposal of a scientific method which, utilizing his customary rule of order, proceeds in the movement of intelligibility from the most general to the more particular. "I have first tried to discover generally the principles or first causes of everything that is or that can be in the world. . . . After that I considered which were the primary and most ordinary effects which might be deduced from these causes. . . . Then, I wished to descend to those which were more particular."

And yet in all of this Descartes adheres to his impregnable rationalism: not only does generality precede particularity, but also we must observe that in science the senses have originated nothing that could not have been deduced by our reason. This envisages a scientific method which begins with general principles, then produces alternative particular hypotheses, and finally uses experiment to choose between them. The following quotation from the *Discourse* is a crucial text, for in relatively short compass we are provided, I think, with the complete Cartesian philosophy of method for the domain of physical science:

> In subsequently passing over in my mind all the objects which have ever been presented to my senses, I can truly venture to say that I have not there observed anything which I could not easily explain by the principles which I had discovered. But I must also confess that the power of nature is so ample and so vast, and these principles are so simple and general, that I hardly observed any particular effect as to which I could not at once recognize that it might be deduced from the principles in many different ways; and my greatest difficulty is usually to discover in which of these ways the effect does depend upon them. As to that, I do not know any other plan but again to try to find experiments of such a nature that their result is not the same if it has to be explained by one of the methods, as it would be if explained by the other. For the rest, I have now reached a position in which I discern, as it seems to me, sufficiently clearly what course must be adopted in order to make the majority of the experiments which may conduce to carry out this end. But I also perceive that they are of such a nature, and of so great a number, that neither my hands nor my income, though the latter were a thousand times larger than it is, could suffice for the whole; so that just in proportion as hence-forth I shall have the power of carrying out more of them or less, shall I make more or less progress in arriving at a knowledge of nature.

It is interesting that at this late stage of his scientific career, physical experiment looms largest in the effort to validate competing intermediate hypotheses about the natural world. Descartes had begun with an interest in a universal method, and with a commitment to pure mathematics which only slowly yields to a passion for application. His *Rules for the Direction of the Mind*, found only after his death but thought to stem from around 1628, rejects the concept of a plurality of sciences divided by *differences* in the *objects* which they study in favor of a unity of all science dependent upon the *unity* of its *method*. And it is this belief in the interconnectedness of the sciences as knowledge, reflecting an ultimate interconnectedness of the cosmos they describe, which underlies his never-wavering conviction that rationality and generality are one — the usual axiom of all Platonizing mathematicians.

Because he held that "of all the sciences known as yet, arithmetic and geometry alone are free from any taint of falsity or uncertainty," and that deduction, the operation upon which they rest, "cannot be erroneous when performed by an understanding that is in the least degree rational," Descartes was convinced of the enormous fruitfulness of a series of rules of method which, by expressing the primary rudiments of human reason, might constitute a powerful instrument for eliciting certain results in any scientific enquiry whatsoever.

It is true that he begins with the medieval tradition of the quadrivium — arithmetic, geometry, astronomy, and music — all mathematical in the ancient Pythagorean sense, and that he adds to them the Renaissance accretions of optics and mechanics to form one "mathematics" which investigates not only "quantity," but even more fruitfully "measurement" and "order." And it follows that methodologically the "objects" of this science, whether numbers, figures, stars, sounds, light rays, or corporeal motions, are as such unimportant. From this arises his dream of a *mathesis universalis.*

I saw consequently that there must be some general science to explain that element as a whole which gives rise to problems about order and measurement, restricted as these are to no special subject matter. This, I perceived, was called "Universal Mathematics," not a far fetched designation, but one of long standing which has passed into current use, because in this science is contained everything on account of which the others are called parts of Mathematics. We can see how much it excels in utility and simplicity the sciences subordinate to it, by the fact that it can deal with all the objects of which they have cognizance and many more besides.

As the Cartesian metaphysics proposes an ultimate dualism between mind and body, paralleled in epistemology by the dualism of the faculties of understanding and imagination, so the Cartesian science is haunted by the dualism between the mathematical components of science supplied by the mind alone and those corporeal or extended objects to whose movements these components must be applied. Descartes's first recognition came in pure mathematics, and the transition to physics represented almost a conscious decision. "I have resolved to quit abstract geometry, that is, the seeking after questions which only involve the mind," he wrote to Desargues in 1634, "so as to give myself leisure to cultivate another sort of geometry which proposes to explain the phenomena of nature." And that the basic natural science is mathematical physics is thereafter the cornerstone of his philosophy of science. Quantification and demonstration are for him the very defining properties of science. It is precisely this unwavering conviction which is to be found much later at the conclusion of part 2 of the *Principles of Philosophy*:

I do not accept any principles in physics which are not also accepted in mathematics, so as to be able to prove by demonstration all that I have deduced, and these principles suffice as far as the phenomena of nature can be explained by their means. For I add here frankly that I do not know any other quality of corporeal things than those which can be divided, delimited, and moved, that is, than those which geometers call quantity, and which they take for the object of their demonstrations, and I can only consider in this matter divisions, figures, and motions . . . and I do not wish to accept anything as true which is not deduced from these with so much evidence that I think it can take the place of a mathematical demonstration. I think therefore that no principles in physics other than those which are here expounded are necessary or permissible.

It is this Descartes, the passionate advocate of a mathematical physics, who is best remembered, and it is the Descartes of the letter about Cardinal Richelieu and the story of the half-dissected calf—the relentless experimentalist—who is today largely forgotten. But this difference was not so clearly perceived by his contemporaries. Little of Descartes's substantive science has remained to this day. He is, to be sure, honored as the discoverer of analytic geometry, but most of his physical theory (including his theory of vortices) was displaced by Newtonian mechanics, and his work in magnetism and refraction is considered only ancillary to the later and better work of other men. Even his proud studies in anatomy and animal physiology, based upon his dissections and experiments, are today considered primitive and unsystematic.

But to the seventeenth century Descartes was profoundly influential—almost the new forces of natural science personified—and his theory of vortices was discussed by learned high-born ladies as his experiments were imitated by dukes and princes. In fact it can almost be said that Descartes single-handedly is responsible for the *ennoblement* of science—the inclusion of scientific concern in upper-class experience, unknown in the time of Montaigne—and for bringing physics and physiology to join ancient languages, philosophy, and *belles lettres* into the humanistic pantheon. By 1667—less than twenty years after Descartes's death—Spratt could say that the love of natural science "was so strongly aroused that there seemed to be nothing more in vogue throughout Europe." Science had become fashionable, and among its amateurs were many of the highest station. In France the duke of Orleans, the brother of Louis XIV, made physical experiments, Prince Rupert, nephew of Charles I of England, dabbled in natural philosophy, and his cousin Charles II diverted himself in a chemical laboratory. Jan De Witt, pensionary of Holland and the friend of Spinoza, not only patronized science, but made mechanical inventions and wrote ably on statistics. Grand Duke Ferdinand of Tuscany and his brother Leopold were fond of experimenting. And of course Descartes's own eccentric but intelligent patron, Christina of Sweden, corresponded avidly with physicists and mathematicians.

But perhaps the most striking evidence comes from that man of common sense and considerable scientific skepticism, John Locke. Writing in 1690 in his celebrated treatise *On Education*, Locke addressed himself to natural science and its place in the education of a gentleman.

To return to the study of natural philosophy: though the world be full of systems of it, yet I cannot say I know any one which can be taught a young man as a science wherein he may be sure to find truth and certainty, which is what all sciences give an expectation of. I do not hence conclude that none of them are to be read; it is necessary for a gentleman in this learned age to look into some of them to fit himself for conversation: but whether that of Des Cartes be put into his hands, as that which is most in fashion, or it be thought fit to give him a short view of that and several others also; I think the systems of natural philosophy that have obtained in this part of the world are to be read more to know the hypotheses, and to understand the terms and ways of talking of the several sects, than with hopes to gain thereby a comprehensive, scientific, and satisfactory knowledge of the works of nature.

It is ironic that Descartes's own "hopes to gain a comprehensive, scientific, and satisfactory knowledge of the works of nature" have come to this: that although his system is that which is now "most in fashion," its borrowed function is less that of "finding truth and certainty" than what "is necessary for a gentleman in this learned age . . . to fit himself for conversation." The utilities of ideas, and of scientific and philosophic ideas especially, are a function of the necessities of the age in which they originate, even an unconscious expression of social forces undreamed of by their authors. The medieval base of the Cartesian metaphysics, and the prophetically practical orientation of the Cartesian science, cannot condone or prevent the uses to which they were put in the transitional epoch in which he lived.

The Spirit of the Age

The philosophy of Plato can be seen as the expression of the vigorous effort toward an aristocratic restoration in an Athens sinking into "degenerate" democracy, and the philosophy of Saint Thomas, mirroring many of the characteristics of an "organic" medieval society, can be considered a rationalization of social order and the defense of the profoundly influential institution of the Roman church. The philosophy of Descartes is capable of no such obvious anchorage in sociological fact. And yet it too expresses the dilemmas of a society transitional between feudal hierarchy and the democratic revolutions of the modern world. Essentially an upper-class, or "gentlemanly" phenomenon, both in its inspiration and in its influence, Cartesianism nevertheless looks forward to an age in which science, with all its details of application and technological elaboration, has become the master of life. Implicit in the intellectual products of Descartes's isolated and sheltered existence is the relentless publicity of the machine age.

Of any philosopher, the historian of ideas naturally asks: What was the structure of the society in which he lived? And within that society, what was the function of his works? But for Descartes, his self-imposed exile in Holland and his absence from the throbbing Parisian center of French seventeenth-century society raises problems more of "action at a distance" than of the kind of immediate engagement of Plato in Athens and Saint Thomas in medieval Paris or at the papal court at Orvieto. Yet two things about the social implications of Cartesianism seem clear: first, the degree to which both its genesis and its influence are related to small elitist groups and, second, the astonishing harmony between its implicit message and the overall quality of the seventeenth-century classical spirit in France. As Plato stands for the spirit of all Greek philosophy, and Saint Thomas for that of medieval, so Descartes both represents philosophy in the modern period and symbolizes the cultural meaning of the French seventeenth century.

Cartesianism, as we have seen, develops within the elitist circle of true seventeenth-century intellectuals and flourishes within the elitist circles of noble and high-born amateurs. Groups of disciples formed in Paris around Marin Mersenne, whose role as dependable friend, correspondent, and general clearinghouse for the master's ideas was crucial. And Mersenne, who organized meetings and informal conferences for bringing together philosophers, mathematicians, and physicists — Hobbes, Arnauld, Fermat, Gassendi, Roberval, Pascal, and Descartes — probably contributed more than any other single Frenchman to making Paris the intellectual center of the learned world in the middle of the seventeenth-century.

These informal conferences also have their literary analogue. In 1629, about the time when Descartes was completing his *Rules for the Direction of the Mind* and was permanently transferring to Holland, a number of high-born gentlemen were in the habit of gathering at the home of Conrart in Paris for informal discussions of language and literature — whereupon Cardinal Richelieu proposed that they form themselves into an academy under his protection. Somewhat reluctantly they did so, and in 1635 the Académie française received its formal authorization from the king. This foundation, too, was the epitome of high society — an exclusive intellectual club, the last refuge of elevated conversation and an organization for the conservation of language and literature with an authority (like the philosophy of Descartes himself) rooted at once in "tradition" and in "reason." And from these two sources, the intellectual circle about Mersenne and Richelieu's literary coterie, grew the inspiration for those later scientific societies — the Royal Society in England and the *Académie des sciences* in France — whose researches, publications, and discussions were so susceptible to Cartesian influence and which were to transport science and philosophy from their temporary flight from the sterile Scholasticism of the universities back to a budding seriousness and professionalism in the German universities of the late eighteenth century.

But even more striking is the way classical French literature, and even the very presuppositions underlying French civilization during this period, can be understood as an aesthetic and social expression of Cartesian doctrine. From the accession of Henry IV to the death of Mazarin, the constant craving of French politics is for a rational *order*, and this in turn had had its obvious effects upon both literature and society. The monarchical spirit and the classical literary stance are both fruits of the same political compromise. And particularly against the impatient presumption, the generous but turbulent indiscipline of the literature of the sixteenth-century (Rabelais, and even to some extent Montaigne), there arose at the beginning of the seventeenth century a solemn reaction of which the *Discourse on Method* is a majestic, if unconscious, embodiment. In its fourth part Descartes had said: "Je pouvais prendre pour règle générale que les choses que nous concevons fort clairement et fort distinctement sont toutes vraies." And of the rules of method which he had already presented in the second part, the first and third ("De ne comprendre rien de plus en mes judgments que ce qui se présenterait si clairement et si distinctement à mon esprit qu je n'eusse aucune occasion de le mettre en doute" and "De conduire par ordre mes pensées, en commençant par les objets les plus simples et les plus aisés à connaître") had already anticipated the classical age. *Clarté* and *ordre* — "clarity" and "order" — these are also the guiding principles which animate the theater of Racine, the architecture of Mansart, the literary theory of Boileau, the landscapes of Poussin, and the economic administration of Colbert!

Generally, when one thinks of the metaphysics of Descartes, substantive considerations primarily come to mind: universal doubt, the *cogito*, the ontological argument, and the sharp dualism of mind and body. But when one simply considers the titles of many of Descartes's works (*Rules for the Direction of the Mind, Discourse on Method, Principles of Philosophy*), one is impressed with the ubiquity of *formal* considerations and with the overwhelming importance of "rules," "principles," and "method." What is striking about the mental habits of Descartes's time is the almost universal taste for analysis — to divide up the task, to limit its object, to isolate according to categories, to make absolute the separation of types (for instance, in literature), and to erect this separation into a supreme law for the discovery of truth and for the success of the artistic enterprise.

The aesthetic ideal of the seventeenth century accorded exactly with the principles of Cartesian logic, and the rules given for its realization were the same rules of method, transferred from the realm of the true into that of the beautiful. But whereas in the Cartesian metaphysics the emphasis is upon "clear and distinct ideas," in literature the emphasis has shifted from "ideas" to "words"—from the logical purity and cleanliness of the mind to purity and cleanliness in the use of the French language. Malherbe (who was in fact of the preceding generation and who died in 1628) insisted upon reason, logic, clarity, simplicity, and purity of style. Guez de Balzac (whose life almost exactly coincides with that of Descartes) devoted his efforts to saving prose from disorder, whimsey, and discursiveness and to making it an instrument of the greatest precision. And Vaugelas (1585-1650), author of the very influential *Remarques sur la langue française*, insisted that each word must have a single and exact meaning. These three set up as the norms of language reason, clarity, and the exactitude of speech of the cultivated French gentleman.

It is not difficult to discover in this logical demand a definite class bias. For although we have today come to feel that logic, like science itself, is a sociologically neutral instrument, in the seventeenth century it had a class incidence and a special aristocratic meaning. It is not simply that Descartes himself (as we have seen) lived the life of a gentleman, and that his science became the plaything of dukes and princes. It is also (somewhat as the employment of a principle of metaphysical hierarchy in Saint Thomas mirrors a hierarchical and unequal feudal order) that the passion for strict delimitation and the application of fixed categories to language and to definition reflects a fixity of political frontiers and of social classes. The court and the town, the language of the salons and that of the public markets, the elevation of poetry and the proletariat of prose, the gentleman and the man in trade, the special metaphysical talent against the understanding of the vulgar—these all attest that the habit of logical distinction is nourished within the atmosphere of the social a priori.

It is not necessary to describe in detail how the aristocracy of logical demand is reinforced by an elevation of dramatic content. The classic genre introduced a second aristocracy into art: it has only taken the *noble* and the *essential*. In this the great dramas of Corneille and Racine are as one: they have appropriated *man* but not nature, from society *the great* but not the-petty, from the human individual *mind* but not body, and from the mind its *essence* but not its peripheral phenomena. This too is the strategy of Descartes. Even the Cartesian superiority of thinking over extended substance is reflected in the classical seventeenth-century drama as *the rejection of action*. Phèdre and Bérénice, Iphigénie and Andromaque analyze and reflect; they do not move with dispatch and violent gesture. All the crucial action is within the minds of the characters, and neither nature nor history figures as causal agency or determining influence. It is like a Cartesian "Meditation" where the *cogito* reigns supreme and all movement is reflective and interior.

The great and striking similarity, however, is between Descartes and Boileau. For it is hardly too much to claim that the metaphysical idealism of Descartes is the exact replica of the aesthetic idealism of Boileau, and that the principal rules of classic art either stem from or completely coincide with the Cartesian logic. The most interesting chapter of *L'art poétique* is the chapter on rules, and it is uniquely remarkable here to note the inspiration and direction of Descartes. To read Boileau is to discover that "reason" is the governing faculty in the art of poetry as it is in the *Meditations* and the *Discourse on Method*. The "beautiful" is a clear and distinct idea like the "true." The criterion of the beautiful is *clarté*. Apply to art the Cartesian rule "never to accept as true anything that is not certainly known to be so," and you arrive at the basic formula of Boileau: "the beautiful is recognizable as that which is reasonable, intelligible, and clear."

There is something monumental about the role of *clarity* in the science, philosophy, and literature of the seventeenth century. The central position of mathematics in science, of clear and distinct ideas in metaphysics, and of elevated simplicity in literature and language shows that the first duty of scientist, philosopher, and artist is to submit to the imperious obligation to be clear. And for science, philosophy, and literature alike, the claim is made that it is from reason and its exercise alone that true clearness springs. There is no room here for the mysteries of Lamartine and Gautier, the romantic ambiguities of Balzac and Baudelaire, the great troubling "contradictions" of Hegel. And it is perhaps even possible to say that this simplicity, this *repugnance for the obscure* is a characteristic of the "gentleman," the "noble personality" — firm in a class hierarchy which must itself be clear as a geometrical demonstration is clear, without those troubling ambiguities of class position and class mobility — already hinted at in some of the comedies of Molière and Beaumarchais — which reached their peak of expression in the industrialization and hopelessly disordered social categories of the nineteenth century.

The philosophy of Descartes is the social expression of an entire culture's "mode of perception," and to recover from his metaphysics the principles of classical aesthetics and from his method the procedures of the great writers of the seventeenth century is not a difficult task. Classical art was rational, and its method was deductive. Like the Cartesian metaphysics, it was dominated by clearness, simplicity, and certainty. The striking and picturesque qualities of Descartes which recommended themselves to his contemporaries were his clear solutions, general good sense, and unusual originality of presentation. Like Descartes, too, the great French writers of the seventeenth century borrowed their matter and created their own form. Descartes used his method with materials borrowed from Augustine, Anselm, and Aquinas, as Racine imposed his on the tragedies of Euripides. Thus in each case both reason and tradition are served. The enormous cultural importance of the Cartesian philosophy is therefore that, although in asserting the subjectivist principle it ushered in a philosophic epoch which lasted until Hegel, and in propounding the ideals of an applied and technological science it invented the modern world, its method and its rational spirit also serve as the epitome of the age in which Descartes lived.

G. E. Moore. Photograph taken at a meeting of the Moral Science Club at Cambridge in 1936 when Moore was sixty-three.

CONTEMPORARY PHILOSOPHY
The Age of the Professional
G. E. Moore

From Descartes to G. E. Moore: Kant

Whereas in 1644 Princess Elizabeth of Bohemia read Descartes with pleasure, it is doubtful if three hundred years later Queen Elizabeth of England read G. E. Moore at all, although in 1951 she honored him with the British Order of Merit. This may be a reflection upon the changes that have taken place in royalty in the last three centuries, but I am inclined to think rather that it is a commentary upon the changes that have taken place in philosophy. For, although the intellectual autobiography of Cartesianism would constitute an exciting adventure in any age, the intensive but cramped attention which Moore pays to "The Nature and Reality of Objects of Perception," "The Status of Sense-Data," and "External and Internal Relations" would, I think, fail to interest any but the professional philosophers who were members of the Aristotelian Society before whom these papers were delivered.

Every culture has its own style of life and thought, its own special "manner" in which knowing and being are socially related, and although it is probably true that philosophy appeals to the restricted audience — the small group — in any age, the nature of this audience and its interests is not irrelevant to the type of philosophizing it stimulates and brings forth. For Plato it was the intimate circle of the Academy, the semi-Pythagorean society of initiation and close fellowship where the chief medium of communication is the esoteric discourse, although its offshoot — the literary dialogue — is capable of capturing a wide audience. For Saint Thomas it was the dedicated group within the church, held together by a common pedagogical aim, and the ideal of the Christian life, whose initial expression was the university lecture

In this chapter I have utilized two of my previous writings on Moore: chapter 11 of my *Philosophy and the Modern World* (Bloomington, 1959), and especially my article in *Mind* (April 1961), "The Trouble with Ethics: Values, Method, and the Search for Moral Norms." There is as yet no biography of G. E. Moore. In addition to Moore's "Autobiography" in P. A. Schilpp, ed., *The Philosophy of G. E. Moore* and memoirs by Braithwaite, Malcolm, and White, I am indebted to some enlightening judgments by Gilbert Ryle and to considerable specific detail and delightful commentary by Casimir Lewy. These and other books by Moore, about Moore, or about the English nineteenth century are listed in the Bibliography.

and the public disputation, but whose crystallization in the *summa* was capable of broad diffusion in the Christian world. For Descartes it was the indefinite group of learned gentlemen and noble correspondents, the "circle of learning" within which the treatise was circulated and letters were exchanged. For G. E. Moore and the modern world it is the restricted group of professionals, "those with the Ph.D degree," the members of the Mind Association, the American Philosophical Association, or the Aristotelian Society, whose accredited media of expression are the yearly association meetings and a handful of professional journals.

For the world of Plato the significant philosophical expression is the *Phaedrus* or the *Republic* or the unwritten "Lecture on the Good." For the world of Saint Thomas it is the *Summa theologica* or the *Disputed Questions on Truth*. For the world of Descartes it is the *Meditations*, together with the "objections" and the "reply to Objections" which it called forth. But for the world of G. E. Moore it is the *Principia Ethica* of 1908, the symposium "Facts and Propositions" taking place before the Aristotelian Society in 1927, the lecture "Proof of an External World" delivered before the British Academy in 1939. And this latter is a world in which not the dialogue, the *summa* question, or the "meditation" is the atom of philosophic reflection, but rather the short-winded, critical article in *Mind* or *Kant-Studien*, or the *Philosophical Review*.

It is obvious that in the ages of the aristocrat, the saint, the gentleman, and the professional the conditions of philosophizing are profoundly different. And yet, in the first three epochs, although I have said nothing about the transition from the ancient to the medieval world, and from the medieval to the Renaissance, natural continuities occur in almost every case. The intellectual crisis registered by the philosophy of Saint Thomas is expressed in the ambiguities attendant upon the rediscovery and reception of Aristotle. The Janus-like face of Cartesianism presents problems which result in the almost unconscious utilization of principles derived from Saint Anselm and Saint Augustine. But although as an undergraduate at Cambridge G. E. Moore heard G. F. Stout's lectures on Descartes and the history of modern philosophy, his philosophy owes little to mathematical reasoning or to the subjectivist principle. Clearly, between Descartes and G. E. Moore an extraordinary change has taken place in the philosophical climate. And if we wish to understand it and, indeed, the meaning of the transition from philosophizing in the age of the gentleman to philosophizing in the age of the professional, we must turn, I think, to the great intermediate figure of Kant. For it is Kant who ushers in the age of which the philosophy of G. E. Moore is an exemplary expression.

In 1644, in his letter to the city of Utrecht, Descartes, as we have seen, referred to himself as "the Gentleman René Descartes, Lord of Perron." A century and a quarter later, in a letter of 28 March 1776 (to Wolke), Kant signs himself "Your sincere admirer, friend, and servant, Immanuel Kant, professor of philosophy." In this shift from "the Gentleman René Descartes" to "Immanuel Kant, Professor of Philosophy" is registered the birth of professionalism in philosophy. There is little doubt that Kant, if not explicitly aware of this change, is at least fully conscious of belonging to the academy, and of the profound contrast between the university to which he belongs and the fashionable world outside. Writing to Marcus Herz in 1781, Kant explains his efforts toward strict systematization and their lesser accessibility to the universe of polite society:

The whole system of this sort of knowledge had to be exhibited in all its articulation. Otherwise I would have started with what I have entitled the "Antinomy of Pure Reason," which could have been done in colorful essays. . . . But the *school's* rights must first be served; afterward one can also see about appealing to the *world.* [Italics added]

Stylistically and in straightforwardness of statement the *Discourse on Method* and the *Meditations* are available to all, but the *Critique of Pure Reason* is formidable in its abstractness and technicality, and, although Kant never specifically lectured on its contents, it was his hope to reduce it to proportions at least academically manageable. In 1783 Kant wrote to Moses Mendelssohn: "I still hope to work out, eventually, a textbook for metaphysics, according to the critical principles I mentioned; it will have all the brevity of a handbook, and be useful for academic lectures."

We have already seen how in the century of Descartes, Leibniz, and Locke the Scholastic tradition was an object of avoidance and contempt. Kant's proud identification with the university is thus a new note in the history of European culture since the Renaissance. For Descartes's dream of the progressively wider circle of the intellectual and social elite, the ideal of the seventeenth-century learned world, had by now revealed its own inherent weakness—

the dangers of dilettantism — and now finally in Kant the invidious contrast between "Scholasticism" and "gentlemanly science" is to find its precise reversal. In a letter to Jacobi in 1789 — the year of the outbreak of the French Revolution — Kant speaks of the philosophical essays of Count von Windisch-Graetz with appreciation, but not without a trace of learned condescension:

Please thank the Count for me and assure him of my respect for his philosophical talent, a talent that he combines with the noblest attitudes of a cosmopolite. In his *Histoire métaphysique*, I observed with pleasure that the Count discusses, with the clarity and modesty of one who is at home in the great world, the same matters with which I in my scholastic fashion have also been concerned.

The irony is gentle, almost indiscernible, but it is clear that the dispraise of the noble amateur was not a momentary response with Kant, but a general attitude. For that cosmopolitanism which the seventeenth and eighteenth centuries affected as the only proper expression of "Enlightenment" also had its negative implications. In an extremely interesting letter to Borowski in 1790, Kant, in a socially critical vein unusual for him, summed up the less desirable aspects of the Cartesian heritage of "gentlemanly scholarship" as it was illustrated in intellectual life toward the end of the eighteenth century.

You ask me what might be the source of the fanaticism that is so rapidly gaining ground and how this disease might be cured. Both of these questions are as difficult for physicians of the soul as was the influenza epidemic that spread all around the world a few years ago for physicians of the body. . . . It seems to me that the universally prevailing mania for reading is not only the carrier that spreads this illness, but also the poison that produces it. The more well-to-do and fashionable people, claiming their insights at least equal if not superior to the insights of those who have troubled to pursue the thorny path of thorough investigation, are content with indices and summaries, skimming the cream off the sciences. These people would like to obscure the obvious difference between loquacious ignorance and thorough science, and this is easiest to do by snatching up incomprehensible things that are no more than airy possibilities and presenting them as facts that the serious natural scientist is supposed to explain. . . . I see only one antidote for this disease: thoroughness must be substituted for dilettantism in education, and the desire to read must not be eradicated but redirected so as to become purposeful.

As a cultural phenomenon the entire Kantian enterprise may be seen as the substitution of thoroughness for dilettantism in philosophy and in education, as a preference for academic lectures and learned treatises over polished essays and gentlemanly conversations, and as an assertion of the priority of the schools above the intellectual preoccupations of the fashionable world. And this same academic professionalism was to stand Kant in good stead when years later, after the publication of his extremely controversial *Religion within the Limits of Reason Alone*, in an order of 12 October 1794 Kant was enjoined by his king, Friedrich William II of Prussia, from further writing and lecturing on religious subjects. For it was then possible to claim the privilege of an exclusively academic environment. Kant defended himself warmly against the charge of distorting the basic teachings of Christianity as follows:

As an educator of the youth, in academic lectures, I have never been guilty of this sort of thing. Aside from the testimony of my listeners, to which I appeal, this is sufficiently demonstrated by the fact that my pure and merely philosophical instruction has conformed to A. G. Baumgarten's textbooks, in which the subject of Christianity does not even occur, nor can it occur. It is impossible to accuse me of overstepping the limits of a philosophical investigation of religion in my teaching.

And he continues:

Nor have I, as an author . . . opposed the highest purposes of the sovereign that were known to me. For since those purposes concern the state religion, I would have had to write as a teacher of the general public, a task for which this book along with my other little essays is ill-suited. They were only written as scholarly discussions for specialists in theology and philosophy, in order to determine how religion may be inculcated most clearly and forcefully into the hearts of men. The theory is one of which the general public takes no notice and which requires the sanction of the government only if it is to be taught to schoolteachers and teachers of religion.

Although his instincts were elitist, Descartes in the *Discourse on Method* at least made the gesture of writing in his native French so as to pretend to reach all men endowed with the natural faculty of reason. Kant simply admits to preoccupations "of which the general public takes no notice," and to the production of "scholarly discussions for specialists in theology and philosophy." But the very concept of "specialists in philosophy" is an invention of the eighteenth century, and it is to be closely associated with the slow intellectual recovery of the German universities and with the new direction of higher education expressed in the founding of Halle in 1693—of the Renaissance of the *libertas docendi* and the establishment of the precedent of lecturing in the German language. Of this new recovery of importance and prestige by the universities in the eighteenth century the Kantian philosophy, like the Wolffian, was an outstanding ornament.

But the association of "specialists in philosophy" with the resurgence of the German university in the eighteenth century, however essential the relationship, is only one in a plurality of cultural elements, and the historian of ideas interested in the origins of philosophic professionalism will be well advised to consider other factors also. The indexes of professionalism in philosophy as it originated between the periods of Descartes and Kant are, I think, fourfold—two internal and two external. The internal are the invention of a technical philosophic vocabulary and an urge toward exact systemization—both characteristics par excellence of the Kantian philosophy. But the external are reflected in two special events—the founding of the first professional philosophic journals and the rising concern of philosophy with its own history—both originating in the seventeenth century but recognizable as specific trends in the eighteenth.

The learned journal, like the scientific society, is one of the major cultural innovations of the seventeenth century, and its prototype was the quarterly *Journal des savants*, founded at Paris in 1665 and devoted to assorted notes on science, literature, and philosophy. Three years later (on 22 October 1668) Leibniz wrote to Emperor Leopold I of Austria, noting that the rival French had inaugurated this important new journal and asking for a similar medium of communication for the German world. He specifically asked for a license to issue just such a periodical, and fifteen years later (things always moving slowly in Austria) the monthly *Acta eruditorum* (1682-1776) was issued at Leipzig. But what had begun in the seventeenth century as a general intellectual endeavor became in the German eighteenth century a specifically philosophical enterprise. A rash of such journals broke out; the *Acta philosophorum* (Halle, 1715-26), the *Philosophische Büchersaal* (Leipzig, 1741-44), and finally the short-lived *Neues philosophisches Magazin* (Leipzig, 1789-90), devoted exclusively to the philosophy of Kant. But more interesting still, this flowering of German professional philosophical journals is matched by a flowering of great German histories of philosophy.

There is one sense in which the area we call the history of philosophy only came into existence with the European Renaissance, when the West rediscovered the biographers and compilers of late antiquity: Plutarch, Sextus Empiricus, Stobaeus, Clement of Alexandria, Eunapius, Philostratus, Diogenes Laërtius, and the rest. These products of the Hellenistic age were also a consequence of the need to deal with and rationalize philosophic plurality, either in the conservative effort to anthologize the fragments or, as in the more dramatic cases of Eunapius, Philostratus, and Diogenes Laërtius, to preserve the lives of the Sophists and the philosophers in such fashion as to assimilate uniqueness of philosophic doctrine to uniqueness of personal life. But, whether in the form of biography or anthology, these conservative efforts were not truly a product of professionalism.

It was only in the seventeenth and eighteenth centuries that the problem of doctrinal plurality was conjoined with a sense of professional responsibility, to create (in the period between Descartes and Kant) the great resurgence of interest in the history of philosophy which produced such works as Jonsius's *De scriptoribus historiae philosophicae* (1649) and Horn's *Historiae philosophicae libri septem* (1645) and was finally to culminate in the great German works of the eighteenth century: Bruckers's *Historia critica philosophiae* (5 vols., Leipzig, 1742-44), Buhle's *Lehrbuch der Geschichte der Philosophie* (8 vols., Göttingen, 1796-1804), Tiedemann's *Geist der spekulativen Philosophie* (7 vols., Marburg, 1791-96), and Tennemann's *Geschichte der Philosophie* (11 vols., Leipzig, 1798-1819). The history of philosophy flourishes, I think, under two conditions: when the retrospective effort to establish the continuity of a tradition requires a reconstitution of the past, or when the need to impose order upon a vast accumulation of historical materials suggests the typologies which will systematize it and give it meaning. But both the urge to reconstitute a tradition and the imposition of order are chiefly the consequence of the definitive narrowing of a field of intellectual concern and the growth of the professional sense in those who feel themselves committed to it.

Kant is certainly no historian of philosophy, although his occasional references to Descartes and Berkeley, Locke and Shaftesbury, Leibniz and Hume show him extremely well read in the texts of modern philosophy, and the "Short Sketch of a History of Philosophy" which appears as section 4 of his late *Introduction to Logic* (1800) also reveals the professional sense of a philosophic tradition with which one must necessarily identify. Kant is well aware that "rational knowledge" is to be distinguished from "Historical knowledge," in philosophy as elsewhere, that one can in a certain sense "learn philosophy" without being able to philosophize, and that one who desires to become a philosopher must, properly speaking, make a free use of his reason, not one which is merely imitative and mechanical. Yet philosophy as "the system of rational knowledge through concepts" or as "the science of the ultimate ends of human reason," has, indeed, a history to which it is well to pay attention. For the chain of original philosophers is in fact continuous.

Despite Descartes's prideful claim to have begun completely anew, every philosophical thinker builds his own work on the ruins of another (as Descartes in fact built upon the ruins of Scholasticism), and Kant himself is fully aware of how much his own attempt to suspend the whole process of "the dogmatic method of philosophizing" and to introduce "the Method of the Critical Philosophy" yet builds continuously upon the Leibnizian and Wolffian ruins. Specific philosophic systems are contingent, but the thread of rationality links them all into a single cognitive unity. "He who desires to learn to philosophize," says Kant, "must regard all systems of philosophy only as *a history of the use of reason,* and as objects for the exercise of his own philosophical ability."

Kant's own "Short Sketch of a History of Philosophy" begins, however, with a consciousness of a distinctly "professional" concern. There is clearly some difficulty in defining the limits where the *common* use of reason ends and the *speculative* begins, or where common rational knowledge becomes *philosophy.* Kant locates this limit in the special efforts toward abstraction and toward formalization: thus his history of philosophy also necessarily begins with the Greeks. It is unnecessary to detail the structure of his brief historical exercise, with its characteristic overelaboration of the ancients, underestimation of the medievals, and association of the modern era with the rise of natural science and particularly of mathematical physics. What counts is the new spirit of philosophic professionalism which attempts its own definition through a survey of the historical materials. Descartes would have

been half incredulous, half embarrassed by the efforts which
Gilson has expended in showing his essential continuity with medievalism, but Kant's deep respect for the history of philosophy is a
mark of the new philosophic self-consciousness of the age. It is
clearly one with the spirit which produced the great sprawling
multivolumed histories of philosophy to which we have alluded —
those of Tiedemann and Brucker, of Tennemann and Buhle, all
of which fall within the generous span of Kant's own lifetime.

But it is as a systematizer and as the inventor of a technical
philosophical vocabulary that Kant's professionalism chiefly reveals itself. And if one wishes to be aware of the full scope of the
changes which have taken place in the mode and manner of
philosophical writing, it is only necessary to contrast the simple,
nonprofessional epistemology of the second Meditation with a
comparable passage from the *Critique of Pure Reason*. Here is
Descartes:

What of thinking? I find here that thought is an attribute that
belongs to me; it alone cannot be separated from me. I am, I
exist, that is certain. But how often? Just so often as I think; for
it might possibly be the case if I ceased entirely to think, that I
should likewise cease altogether to exist. I do not now admit anything which is not necessarily true: to speak accurately I am not
more than a thing which thinks, that is to say, a mind or a soul,
or an understanding, or a reason, which are terms whose significance was formerly unknown to me. I am, however, a real thing
and really exist: but what thing? I have answered: a thing which
thinks.

And here on the identical topic is Kant:

There can be in us no modes of knowledge, no connection or
unity of one mode of knowledge with another, without that unity
of consciousness which precedes all data of intuitions, and by
relation to which representation of objects is alone possible. This
pure original unchangeable consciousness I shall name *transcendental apperception*. That it deserves this name is clear from
the fact that even the purest objective unity, namely that of the
a priori concepts of space and time is only possible through
relation of the intuitions to such unity of consciousness. The
numerical unity of this apperception is thus the *a priori* ground
of all concepts, just as the manifoldness of space and time is the
a priori ground of the intuitions of sensibility. This transcendental
unity of apperception forms out of all possible appearances a
connection of these representations according to laws. For this
unity of consciousness would be impossible if the mind in knowledge of the manifold could not become conscious of the identity

of function whereby it synthetically combines it in one knowledge. The original and necessary consciousness of the identity of the self is thus at the same time a consciousness of an equally necessary unity of the synthesis of all appearances according to concepts.

The pages of the First Critique bristle with just such coinages of professional terminology: the transcendental unity of apperception, the distinction between analytic and synthetic judgments, the transcendental deduction of the pure concepts of the understanding, the distinction of all objects into phenomena and noumena, the schematism of the categories, a transcendental analytic and dialectic, axioms of intuition, anticipations of perception, analogies of experience, general postulates of empirical thought, the amphiboly of reflection, the paralogism and antinomies of pure reason—and the contrast with Descartes's simplicity and dependence upon ordinary language is immediately obvious.

The *Discourse on Method* and the *Meditations* are written in the first person, in the leisurely, intimate, graceful, autobiographical style of the seventeenth-century gentleman, and even Hume's *Enquiry Concerning Human Understanding* presupposes the geniality of the weekend conversation at a landed estate or an eighteenth-century London club; but the *Critique of Pure Reason* resists all gracefulness, geniality, or stylistic charm. It has all the uncompromising difficulty and stiff professionalism of the learned journal and the advanced philosophical seminar.

And yet it would be completely unfair to hold Kant guilty of careless obscurity and willful pedantry. He was conscious that in the *Critique of Pure Reason* he was not working at the traditional metaphysics but, on the contrary, was producing "a whole new science, never before attempted, namely the critique of *an a priori judging* reason." Other men, says Kant, have touched on this faculty, notably Leibniz and Locke, but to no one has it even occured that this faculty is the object of a formal and a necessary science, requiring a manifold of divisions and a unique philosophical vocabulary. Five years before the *Critique of Pure Reason* was published, Kant wrote in this vein to his favorite student, Marcus Herz:

It must be possible to survey the field of pure reason, that is, of judgments that are independent of all empirical principles, since this lies a priori in ourselves and need not await any exposure from our experience. What we need in order to indicate the divisions, limits, and the whole content of that field, according to secure principles, and to lay the road marks so that in the future one can know for sure whether one stands on the floor of true reason or on that of sophistry — for this we need a critique, a discipline, a canon, and an architectonic of *pure reason*, a formal science, therefore that can require nothing of those sciences already at hand and *that needs for its foundations an entirely unique technical vocabulary.* [Italics added]

In 1781 the First Critique appeared, to the initial consternation of the learned world. Kant's rivals were derisive, his friends were perplexed; even Moses Mendelssohn declared himself repelled by the book. Two years later (on 7 August 1783) Kant wrote a long letter to Christian Garve, largely, as he himself said, "in order to clear myself of the charge that my innovations of language and my impenetrable obscurity cause my readers unnecessary difficulty in grasping my ideas." It is in part an indictment of the amateur spirit, in part a simple assertion that difficult ideas require an unavoidable difficulty in treatment. But it is unmistakably a clarion call for professionalism in philosophy.

I am reconciled to the prevailing taste of our age, which imagines difficult speculative matters to be easy (but does not make them easy). . . . You choose to mention, as a just criticism, the lack of popular appeal in my work, a criticism that can in fact be made of every philosophical writing, if it is not to conceal what is probably nonsense under a haze of apparent cleverness. But such popularity cannot be attempted in studies of such high abstraction. . . . People will get over the initial numbness caused unavoidably by a mass of unfamiliar concepts and an even more unfamiliar language (which new language is nonetheless indispensable.)

If the first indication of the new professionalism is Kant's invention of a unique technical philosophical vocabulary, the second is his deep, almost obsessive committment to method and to system — or, as he himself expressed it, not merely to a "critique," a "discipline," and a "canon," but also an *architectonic* of pure reason. This means a formal structural organization whereby the principles of human cognition in every area are rendered compendent, mutually related, and unified. Such ordering and unification belongs to the very definition of what Kant understands by science. In "The Transcendental Doctrine of Method" — the section which concludes the *Critique of Pure Reason*, Kant has made this abundantly clear.

By an architectonic I understand the art of constructing systems. As systematic unity is what first raises ordinary knowledge to the rank of science, that is, makes a system out of a mere aggregate of knowledge, architectonic is the doctrine of the scientific in our knowledge, and therefore necessarily forms part of the doctrine of method.

In accordance with reason's legislative prescriptions, our diverse modes of knowledge must not be permitted to be a mere rhapsody, but must form a system. Only so can they further the essential ends of reason. By a system I understand the unity of the manifold modes of knowledge under one idea. This idea is the concept provided by reason — of the form of a whole — in so far as the concept determines *a priori* not only the scope of its manifold content, but also the positions which the parts occupy relatively to one another. The scientific concept of reason contains, therefore, the end and the form of that whole which is congruent with this requirement.

The internal organization of *The Critique of Pure Reason, The Critique of Practical Reason,* and *The Critique of Judgment* — the cornerstones of Kant's own critical writing — is a monument to this architectonic obsession, and the rationale for their mutual ordering lies in the Kantian conception of *the primacy of logic.* But this primacy is itself dependent upon another conception which is in fact the profoundest and most unique intuition of Kant's whole existence — of his philosophizing and of his life alike — the fundamental importance of *rules,* and therefore the obsessive banishment of every trace of irregularity, human or conceptual.

Everything in nature, according to Kant, whether in the animate or inanimate world, takes place according to rules. Everything in the exercise of our human faculties also takes place according to certain rules. Everything in the linguistic experience of man has its grammatical base, and thus its formal, rule-oriented grounding. But of all our faculties it is the understanding par excellence which is not only governed in its actions by rules, but is to be regarded as the very source and faculty of conceiving rules in general. As the faculty of *thinking,* the understanding is the special rule-giver of all our cognitive operations; it subsumes the intuitions of sense under rules, organizes the construction of objects, and through its very definition of all formal relations makes possible the creation of unified bodies of knowledge. And the rules which it prescribes are universal and absolutely necessary, independent of any particular objects of thought, discernible a priori (that is, independently of all experience) because they constitute the *conditions* of any experience whatsoever. That science, therefore, which has as its subject these universal and necessary rules, may be viewed as the science of the structure of thought, or of the laws of our understanding, or of the topography of our *reason*. It is, in short, simply *logic*.

In the second section of the little *Introduction to Logic,* Kant outlines the chief divisions of the subject. They are: (1) *Analytic,* which is an analysis of the form of the Understanding and of the Reason, containing the necessary rules of all formal truth and therefore constituting a "canon" or criterion for deciding on the formal correctness of our knowledge, (2) *Dialectic,* which is a logic of semblance or sophistry, arising out of an abuse of the Analytic, but useful as an object of study as indicating the pitfalls and dangers into which reasoning may fall, and in its negative or therapeutic use, therefore constituting what Kant terms "a cathartic of the understanding," and (3) *Methodology,* which is the technical or practical part of logic which would arrange its expressions and distinctions in such a way as "to facilitate the action of the understanding."

These three divisions of the Kantian logic are more than a mere formal classification: they are, in fact, the very foundation of the Kantian system, a clue to that rigorous structuralism which he is the first to introduce into philosophy in the modern period. For each of his three critiques is constructed upon an identical logical model. The *Critique of Pure Reason* contains as its chief divisions a "Transcendental Analytic," a "Transcendental Dialectic" and a "Transcendental Doctrine of Method." The *Critique of Practical Reason* contains as its chief divisions an "Analytic of Pure Practical Reason," a "Dialectic of Pure Practical Reason," and a "Doctrine of Method for Pure Practical Reason." The *Critique of Judgment,* which is slightly asymmetrical because of its two diverse topics, contains an "Analytic of Aesthetic Judgment," a "Dialectic of Aesthetic Judgment," an "Analytic of Teleological Judgment," a "Dialectic of Teleological Judgment," and a "Doctrine of Method for Teleological Judgment." Clearly Kant's three major works (produced over a period of at least twenty years) conform to a structural ideal which is a pervasive feature of his mode of perception.

Behind each of the critiques lies the belief in the primacy of rules. The *Critique of Pure Reason* presents the rules of the Understanding. The *Critique of Practical Reason* grounds all morality in a single ethical rule — the Categorical Imperative. And

even the *Critique of Judgment*, in its treatment of aesthetic judgment, provides form and order for the notorious waywardness of
art by defining "genius" as that special quality "which gives the
rules to art." But what is particularly striking is the congruence
between Kant's philosophy and his life—the way in which an
intellectual commitment to an almost Prussian rule-orientation
becomes the foundation of character and personal habit. Ernst
Cassirer, an editor of Kant and a great admirer of his thought,
nonetheless, in comparing his personal and philosophical development with that of Rousseau, was forced to say: "In Kant rule and
method constituted the animating and inspiring principles, and
they gradually acquired such power that they not only mastered
his life in its fullness and variety, but seemed almost to obliterate
that concrete fullness."

That they mastered his life is clear. That they in some sense
compromised its variety and fullness would be true only for a
romanticism which sees an irreconcilable opposition between freedom and order. For Kant was devoted to his profession, and the
extreme regularity which he introduced into his life made possible
both his enormous productivity and the fulfillment of the strictest
obligations of the eighteenth-century academic career. It is true
that some "fullness and variety" is always sacrificed by the very
fact of commitment. Socrates, except for military service, never
left Athens. In 1872 Jacob Burckhardt turned down Ranke's chair
at the University of Berlin to remain in provincial Basel. And
when Descartes in 1649 succumbed to the blandishments of Queen
Christina and came to Sweden, it was a fatal mistake.

There is indeed a certain symbolism in a man's relationship to
place. Kant's entire life is inseparable from Königsberg and its
university. He never went farther than a few kilometers from its
boundaries, and his devotion to the university was lifelong. When
in 1778 Von Zedlitz, Prussian minister of education and a warm
admirer of Kant's offered him the professorship of metaphysics at
Halle at twice his current salary, he refused, saying (somewhat like
Burckhardt) that he preferred a quiet environment for speculation and study. The *Critique of Pure Reason* was at that time
approaching completion, and Kant wrote: "All change makes me
fearful, even if it gives the greatest promise of an improvement in
my condition, and I believe that I must heed this insight of my
nature if I want to extend to its full length the thread which the
Fates have spun very thin and weak." Kant was at this time fifty-
four, and a full quarter of a century lay ahead of him.

Born in 1724, Kant entered the University of Königsberg at sixteen and studied logic, natural philosophy, and metaphysics as well as mathematics and moral philosophy under men who were disciples of the then overwhelmingly popular Leibnizian-Wolffian philosophy. It was an age of deep religious unrest. Kant, Lessing, and Winkelmann were all sent by their parents to the university to study theology, yet none entered the ministry. Kant completed his work at twenty, in 1744, and at once began work on his first book on the mathematics of kinetic forces. (Descartes at this age was riding, fencing, hunting, and pursuing the arts of the gentleman.) Something over seven years of acting as a private tutor followed before Kant rejoined the philosophical faculty of the university as a privatdocent. In the autumn of 1755 he began lecturing, first on mathematics and physics then on logic and metaphysics, to an unusually large audience, in a sizable room of the house in which he lived. This initial popularity was to continue as a lifelong endowment. Herder, who was at Königsberg between 1762 and 1764, heard him with the greatest enthusiasm, and twenty years later, after Kant had become a full professor and a fixture in Königsberg, Hamann wrote (May 1786) that he had to go with his son at six in the morning to Kant's lecture room—a full hour before the lecture—to secure a place.

The hour is not insignificant. Descartes, the gentleman, customarily lay in bed until noon. Kant, the professional, retired promptly at ten, and his servant had strict orders never to let him sleep later than five in the morning. After a breakfast of weak tea and a pipe of tobacco, between five and seven he prepared his university lectures which, year in and year out, he then delivered between seven and nine in the morning. By nine o'clock, therefore, his strictly university duties were over, and from then until one he worked in his study. Lunch at one often lasted three hours, and was followed by his invariable afternoon walk. He then retired for more reading and meditation until his ten o'clock bedtime. All have remarked the almost military order of Kant's life, and some have even discovered a painful anxiety in his strict conformity to rules. The clocklike regularity of his existence surprised even his friends and became a subject of frequent remark, but the image has been permanently crystallized in the words which Heinrich Heine wrote about him in the *Neue Preussische Provinzialblätter* many years later:

It is difficult to write the history of the life of Immanuel Kant, for

he had neither life nor history. He lived the mechanically ordered
and almost abstract life of a bachelor, in a quiet, retired little
street of Königsberg. . . . I do not believe that the large clock of
the cathedral did its daily work with less passion and with greater
regularity than its countryman, Immanuel Kant. To rise, drink,
coffee, write, deliver lectures, eat, take walks, everything had its
appointed time; and the neighbors knew that it was exactly half-
past three when Kant, in his grey coat, stepped out of his door and
walked toward the small Linden Avenue, which is still called after
him, "The Philosopher's Walk."

But Heine exaggerates. Such a life is only cramped, mechanically ordered, or abstract from the point of view of the gentlemanly presuppositions of a Montaigne or a Descartes, where men
are not dependent upon their labor for their income, where travel
is presupposed as a mark of noble decency, and where freedom of
movement and irregularity are the consequence of a supreme lack
of institutional commitment. In some sense the life of Saint Thomas
Aquinas might also be said to have been mechanically ordered
and abstract, for, although it moved between the poles of Paris
and the papal court, it too was governed by rules: by the requirements of the Dominican order and by a supreme dedication to
the institutional tasks of the Roman church. It is true that Kant's
extreme attention to his own health, his enormous satisfaction in
punctuality, the methodical order of his papers, personal habits,
and household arrangements, are especially to be remarked, but I
have been concerned with these brief details of his life less for
psychological than for sociological reasons. The remarkable order
of Kant's life is but an anagram of the remarkable order of his
mind, and the concentration which was its product was responsible for the creation of an architectonic of reason and a unique
technical vocabulary which has added a new dimension to philosophy in the modern world.

But above all, Kant has set a new pattern of professionalism in
philosophy — far from the aristocratic leisureliness of Plato and the
gentlemanly freedom of Descartes — which joins philosophy indissolubly with the ambience of the university and with academic
life. It would have been difficult in the late eighteenth century
and the nineteenth century to find a place more advantageous for
an intellectual than as a teacher at a German university. It is
preeminently "the learned career." Kant's fame as author of the
Critique of Pure Reason, as the greatest of modern epistemologists
and ethicists, has somewhat obscured the fact that he was also a

great professor and teacher of philosophy with profound influence upon his students and upon the life of the University of Königsberg. After 1773 his lectures were the most popular and the most sought after of any at the university. But more strictly administrative duties occupied him also. He became a member of the academic senate in 1780 and remained one until the last years of his life. In addition, he was six times dean of the philosophical faculty and twice rector of the University, posts which he filled in conscientious, if undistinguished, fashion — certainly, as his ethics required, far more out of duty than inclination.

In such a life, apart from the publication of the great works, it is only the academic opportunities gained and missed that are eventful: in both 1756 and 1758 Kant applied unsuccessfully for chairs in mathematics, logic, and metaphysics; in 1769 efforts were made to secure him comparable chairs at Jena and Erlangen; and in 1770, at forty-six, he finally became full professor of logic and metaphysics at Königsberg. If these details seem unromantic compared with Plato's dramatic trips to Syracuse, Saint Thomas's youthful abduction on the way to Paris, and Descartes's unhappy visit to the royal court of Sweden, this is only because in the modern world the philosopher has become a *professional* for whom thinking and being are one, for whom intellect, study, thought, teaching, and the search for method have become the essence of life itself. For Descartes or for Leibniz in the seventeenth century this would not have been strictly true. But for Wittgenstein or Whitehead or G. E. Moore in the twentieth it surely would. The life and work of Kant is the fateful bridge between them.

The Philosopher as Professional

In all the ways which count professionally, G. E. Moore was perhaps the most influential single philosopher of the first half of the twentieth century. Educated at Trinity College, Cambridge, he was successively fellow of Trinity from 1898, university lecturer in the moral sciences, and, from 1925, professor of philosophy in the university until his retirement in 1939. Generations of students and teachers of philosophy have heard his unpublished lectures on psychology, metaphysics, and epistemology at Cambridge for thirty years. He was always a regular attendant at meetings of philosophical societies and an active discussant of other men's papers, and his own papers and his participation in symposia practically dominated the Aristotelian Society from 1904 to 1936. In 1920 he became editor of *Mind*, the most eminent philosophical journal in the English-speaking world, and retained this post for almost three decades, retiring only in 1947, when the editorship passed into the hands of Gilbert Ryle. No philosopher in the Anglo-Saxon tradition since 1900 has been more influential with his students, more respected and admired by his professional philosophical colleagues.

Yet one would be hard pressed to catalog the substantive contributions Moore has made to philosophy in the modern world. A refutation of idealism, a critique of ethical naturalism, an argument for the existence of intrinsic value, a defense of common sense, a proof of an external world, and a series of sustained, but generally partial and inconclusive analyses of sense perception — these are what remain from a lifetime of philosophic preoccupation, and it is, I think, unlikely that any one of these will take its place in that theoretical pantheon which contains the Platonic theory of Ideas, the Thomistic proofs for the existence of God, or the Cartesian elaboration of the immediacy of self-consciousness.

In a sense, however, this is to miss the point. For the meaning of G. E. Moore for philosophy today lies less in substantive achievement than in a particular conception of the philosophic task: a particular sense of what it means to philosophize, the sturdy and continuous exemplification of a very special concept of *philosophical method*. For whatever his intention (and there is some evidence that he *did* want to be), Moore was *not* a constructive philosopher, but a critic and an analyst whose immense influence stems not from the content of his doctrines but from the sincerity, the simplicity, and the directness with which he has subjected the paradoxical theories of other philosophers to the overt criteria of common sense.

Moore's philosophic behavior has proved influential not because of some special application of scientific insight or technicality of logical theory, but because, even though he used an ordinary-appearing method of dealing with matters of meaning, ambiguity, and linguistic usage, it showed itself, nonetheless, to be a specific form of philosophic investigation with obviously high standards of strictness and logical rigor. Unable to be directly informative about the world, it still in some important way paradigmatically clarified those propositions which claim to be informative about the world. And in an age generally dominated by the concept of professionalism, Moore showed what it was to be a "philosopher's philosopher"—to speak to those matters which are of specialized concern without in any sense engaging the passionate interest of the general public. It is therefore little wonder that Queen Elizabeth did not make "The Status of Sense-Data" or "Proof of an External World" her bedside reading.

G. E. Moore is important, I think, as a prime example of what philosophy reduces to in an age of professionalism, where an enthusiasm for the perfection of tools and techniques, the employment of a division of labor which narrows interest and limits the area of legitimate professional concern, and a strong consciousness of purely professional commitment expressed in the professional association and increased reliance on the purely professional media of communication become decisive for the philosophic task. For those who are more traditionally minded—whose interest centers upon "content" or upon "system" and whose hearts therefore lie with Plato or Saint Thomas or Descartes—G. E. Moore's intelligence sometimes seems like a razor sharpened to an exquisite edge and then used to cut butter. Or, like some wonderfully sensitive and complicated mill used to grind out—almost precisely nothing. But this is indeed a kind of special pleading, and for those of this persuasion, philosophical modernism itself will seem like Santayana's definition of fanaticism: an age which redoubles its technical efforts just as it has forgotten its substantive aim.

The association of G. E. Moore and "modernism" in philosophy is paradoxical, for although the degree of his current influence is overwhelming, it is often forgotten that he belongs more to the early years of this century than to its middle; that his own philosophic enterprise originated in a reaction against philosophic impulses which were Victorian, and that his own values and attitudes were Edwardian. And in this reference to temporality and "date" lies much of the explanation of the kind of philosophic current he produced—its mood and spirit.

G. E. Moore was born in 1873 in a suburb called Upper Norwood, about eight miles due south of the center of London. It was the year of Matthew Arnold's *Literature and Dogma* and of Pater's *Studies in the History of the Renaissance*, and about the same time that Ruskin was finishing *Munera Pulveris*. It was also the year of the death of John Stuart Mill. In short, the forces of Victorianism were at high tide, and they were to continue to

nourish the environment in which Moore reached young manhood. His parents were middle class, comfortably well-off and
quietly religious, and the family life itself was happy, middle-
class, suburban. Moore's earliest memories of his physical environment seem to have been of the red brick family house,
standing in a garden of about half an acre with large oak trees, on
a road leading steeply up a hill upon which stood that monument
of Victorianism, the Crystal Palace, which the Queen herself had
opened about two decades before.

The sense one receives is that Moore's early family life was
comfortable, well-regulated, and secure; like the English novel
itself, bourgeois in its origins and solidly anchored in its social
world. The history of the English eighties and nineties was one of
contained and self-contented provincialism, ruled by the Victorian credo of "trade and individualism," which put a premium
upon those who were pedestrian and "sound." That "possessive
individualism" of which John Galsworthy's "Forsytes" are the classic literary embodiment dominated the Victorian imagination
because it was solidly grounded in economic and social actuality.

Between 1870 and 1890 there was general prosperity in England. A rich country, while it remains at peace and its people are
employed, grows increasingly richer. Victorian thrift and energy
were bearing fruit, and the consequences were impressive as a
noticeable improvement in economic and social conditions. The
urban streets were safer. There was a visible improvement in
lower-class manners. Public taxation was relatively light, with
rents and building costs unusually low. Britain's double preeminence — as a producer of cheap manufactured goods and as a
model of constitutional government — secured a high level both of
public safety and of middle class virtue. England's solidly grounded, but flexible, institutions of government and social life — the
monarchy, the parliamentary system, the established church, the
legal structure, the Bank of England, and the universities — all
had achieved stability, and particularly that continuity and
homogeneous interrelationship which preserves any social system.
And the generally surrounding solidity of institutional order was
reflected in the serenity of more intimate institutional life. The
Victorian virtues are those of strong family life — industriousness,
tolerance, self-reliance, earnest endeavor, liberality of mind, fi-
delity to the pledged word, good faith in human relations, and
charity — precisely those which are reflected in Moore's family life
and early upbringing and which were to characterize his own

activities and relations to the world throughout a long and productive lifetime. If late Victorianism looks for a new and more
adequate set of moral values, this will not be noticeable before
Moore's Cambridge days, and above all not before the publication
of chapter 6 of his own *Principia Ethica* in 1903.

When he was eight years old, Moore was sent as a day student to
Dulwich College, a preparatory school at which he remained for
ten years and where almost all of his time was spent in classics,
mainly in translating English verse and prose into Greek and Latin.
He received some private lessons in singing and organ playing and
was introduced to the songs of Schubert (which became a lifelong
amateur passion), but he learned nothing of the natural or social
sciences and had, naturally, no introduction whatsoever to the
sort of technical philosophic questions with which he was for the
greater part of his life to be "chiefly occupied and worried." In
this respect Moore's experience at Dulwich was the precise opposite
of Descartes's at La Flèche, where the latter received a training
in Scholastic philosophy which he was to repudiate, but never really
outgrow.

From one of his masters at Dulwich (C. Bryans) Moore learned
German, "which was very useful when later I wanted to read
German philosophers in the original," and it was this same master
who was (rightfully, I think) very much concerned about the
inadequacy of Moore's English style. He gave Moore Saintsbury's
book of selections from English prose writers to improve his style
of writing, but it must have had little effect, for when Moore went
up to Cambridge his tutor, A. W. Verall, the great classical scholar and authority on Euripides, was equally concerned and recommended that Moore read the speeches of Macaulay, no doubt
for color and expressiveness. Alas, neither Saintsbury nor Macaulay seems ultimately to have had the slightest effect. Moore's
literary style in philosophy remained to the end dry, rhetorically
sparse, compulsively repetitious, and explicit to the point of bore-
dom. From a literary point of view one might call it mean and
poor; and yet, paradoxically, it somehow admirably suited the
expression of Moore's logically stark, literal, exact, and sober
philosophical ideas.

Moore went up to Trinity College, Cambridge, in the autumn
of 1892 and for his first two years continued his work in classics,
largely under Verall. But it was in the contact with other undergraduates and their serious discussions of literature, politics, and
philosophy that Moore's intellectual horizons widened, and it was

especially Bertrand Russell (also a student at Trinity, and two
years older than Moore) who changed Moore's life by encouraging
him to study philosophy. Russell also introduced Moore to the
young philosophy tutor McTaggart, and in this association was
born the direction which was to determine the entire course of
Moore's philosophical life. It is interesting to note the account of it
in his *Autobiography*, written when he was approaching seventy:

What must have happened during this second year in Cambridge,
was that I found I was very keenly interested in certain philosophical statements which I heard made in conversation. One such
occasion I can remember. Russell had invited me to tea in his
rooms to meet McTaggart; and McTaggart, in the course of conversation had been led to express his well-known view that Time
is unreal. This must have seemed to me then (as it still does) a
perfectly monstrous proposition, and I did my best to argue
against it. . . . It must have been owing to what I said on such
occasions as this that Russell came to think I had some aptitude
for philosophy. And I think this example is also typical of what
has always been, with me, the main stimulus to philosophise. I
do not think that the world or the sciences would ever have suggested to me any philosophical problems. What has suggested
philosophical problems to me is things which other philosophers
have said about the world or the sciences. In many problems
suggested in this way I have been very keenly interested — the
problems in question being mainly of two sorts, namely, first the
problem of trying to get really clear as to what on earth a given
philosopher *meant* by something which he said, and, secondly,
the problem of discovering what reasons there are for supposing
that what he meant was true. I think I have been trying to solve
problems of this sort all my life, and I certainly have not been
nearly so successful in solving them as I should have liked to be.

A number of things are worth noting in this recollection. The
first is that Moore's concern with "philosophical statements," later
elevated to the very center of his philosophic professionalism,
seems to have originated at a very amateur level — namely, in the
give and take of undergraduate conversation. And, second, that
from the beginning Moore's concern seems to have had a definite-
ly semantic orientation. The facts of nature, indeed the facts of
human life, seem to have engaged him professionally only at
second remove; what interested him passionately were logical and
linguistic entities — "statements," as he says, made by other philosophers about the world or the sciences. And this concern with
"second order entities," with the *medium* of intellectual exchange

rather than its original content and reference, shows a natural bias toward that professionalism which emphasizes the technical "means" of life and discourse rather than the substantive world of actions and passions, of physical agency and powerful responses, of cause and effect. And finally, although he mentions two sorts of problems in which he has always been "very keenly interested" — problems of *meaning* and problems of *truth*, it is the former which have distinguished his philosophic career.

Confronted with ambiguity, unclarity, and obvious nonsense in the statements of others, Moore seems to have experienced a kind of mental trauma — almost a distinct physical sensation like a moderate stomachache or a painfully irritating itch — and his vehement response, and his efforts to resolve doubt and achieve clarity and belief conformable with common sense, has something in it of Wittgenstein's "philosophical torment." Only Wittgenstein seems to have been tormented by the problems which *he* could not solve, whereas Moore is tormented by the unclarity and absurdity of *others*.

The *Autobiography* from which I have quoted (which constitutes the first entry in the Schilpp volume *The Philosophy of G. E. Moore*) is, as is to be expected, a "professional" autobiography, containing accounts of Moore's education, his publications, his teaching, along with reminiscences of his professional colleagues and teachers — and little else. But particularly in reading about the latter — his teachers — it is astonishing how often his judgment of the men and their worth is dominated by his own master-value, the concept of *clarity*. Of Lendrum, one of his early classical masters at Dulwich College, whose general culture and critical ability so impressed the young student, he adds: "And I was also, no doubt, impressed by the pains he took to be accurate — to get everything *exactly* right." Of Henry Sidgwick, whose lectures he attended for the Moral Science Tripos at Cambridge, he said: "From his published works, especially of course his *Methods of Ethics*, I have gained a good deal, and *his clarity and his belief in Common Sense*, were very sympathetic to me" (italics added). But, strangely, at Cambridge, it was the young McTaggart, the very same whose proposition about the unreality of time seemed to Moore so monstrous, who influenced Moore the most. "He produced the impression of being immensely clever and immensely quick in argument; but I think that what influenced me most was his constant insistence on clearness — on trying to give a precise

meaning to philosophical expressions, on asking the question,
'What does this mean?' " Moore was of course aware that McTaggart did not himself in his own philosophical works always succeed
in being perfectly clear (as, for example, Broad has shown in his
Examination of McTaggart's Philosophy), but Moore adds: "But
how clear he was, as compared to the majority of philosophers!
and what immense pains he took to get clear, even though he did
not always succeed! McTaggart used often to use the word 'woolly'
as a name for a characteristic of some philosophers to which he
particularly objected. 'Wooliness' was, of course, incompatible
with the kind of clarity at which he aimed; and one of his objects
in aiming at clarity was to avoid 'wooliness!' " No one who notes
the use of this term in Broad, Russell, Whitehead, and Moore
himself can fail to recognize the McTaggart influence at Edwardian Cambridge!

As a Cambridge student Moore combined work in the Moral
Science Tripos (which Russell had recommended to him) with work
in the Greek philosophy section of the Classical Studies program. In
the former he attended the lectures of Sidgwick, Ward, Stout, and
McTaggart. From Sidgwick he seems to have derived a permanent interest in the epistemology of moral judgments and the
problem of moral reasoning, and from Ward, (whom he liked,
but found confusing) some knowledge of metaphysics. Stout's
lectures on the history of modern philosophy from Descartes to
Schopenhauer interested him a great deal, although characteristically it was not the historical references as such which appealed
to Moore, but rather Stout's ability to deal clearly and directly
with specific items of philosophical controversy as they appeared
in, but were abstracted from, historical context. From McTaggart, as we have seen, Moore derived a mandate for clearness and
a categorical imperative against "wooliness," but the actual content of McTaggart's interests at this time was completely Hegelian, and there is some irony in the obvious contrast between the
"manner" and the "matter" of McTaggart's philosophizing. "I
think," says Moore, "it can fairly be said that what McTaggart was
mainly engaged with was trying to find a precise meaning for
Hegel's obscure utterances." McTaggart did manage to find such
precise meanings, but it seemed to Moore that this was obviously
more McTaggart than Hegel. About the obscurity and confusion
of the master himself, Moore was in little doubt, and his response
is laconic and characteristic. "After these two years in which I was

obliged to read some Hegel, I never thought it worth while to read him again." It is a sentiment which can be matched in the pages of Whitehead and of Russell also, and it shows how the new winds of analysis were blowing in Cambridge long before they had been liberated at more conservative, Hegelian Oxford.

The historic figures in the philosophic tradition from whom one draws one's sustenance are a matter of some professional importance. Moore's disinterest in Hegel did not reflect his total response to the history of philosophy. Under the guidance of Henry Jackson, director of his studies in Greek philosophy (a man whom Moore characterizes as "of a very marked and forcible personality"), he read some of the chief works of Plato and Aristotle and, according to his own testimony, here his interest was to be continuous. "I have," he says, "at intervals, spent a considerable amount of time in reading various parts of their works and trying to learn from them." And in the summer of 1895, at Ward's suggestion, Moore spent five weeks in Germany at the University of Tübingen where he listened to Sigwart's lectures on Kant. His interest in Kant, particularly in the Kantian ethics, was also to be an enduring preoccupation.

At the conclusion of his formal studies and at Ward's suggestion, Moore decided to compete in the annual fellowship examination in philosophy at Trinity, and to submit a qualifying dissertation on Kant's ethics. Thus, the major portion of the years 1896-98 he spent "puzzling over Kant's three *Critiques*, his *Prolegomena*, and his *Grundlegung zur Metaphysik der Sitten*." During the first year he was particularly concerned to make sense out of the Kantian dualism between the free "noumenal" self and the determined "empirical" self, and the substance of what he wrote about "these extremely mysterious assertions" was published in his 1898 *Mind* article entitled "Freedom." The second year, his preoccupation was more with Kant's First Critique than with his Second Critique, and he attempted to examine the Kantian conception of "Reason." What he says about this concept is typical of the "Moore method" and the kind of response which he was thereafter to make to any ambiguity, whether by the greatest philosophers or by those of second rank:

This was a term which occurred not only in the title of both these works (*The Critique of Pure Reason* and *The Critique of Practical Reason*), but also frequently in the text, and, as it seemed to me, in a very mystifying manner. What on earth did Kant mean by it?

He must be referring, more or less directly to something which was to be found in the world, and which could be described in other terms. But to what exactly? This was what I set myself to think about; and it led me to think first about the notion of "truth," since it seemed to me that, in some of its uses at all events, Kant's term "Reason" involved a reference to the notion of "truth."

At any rate, the substance of Moore's conclusions here won him the prize fellowship for which he was competing, and they were also published shortly afterwards in *Mind* as "The Nature of Judgement." These two *Mind* articles, inspired by Kant yet treating his problem abstractly and in isolation from the context of its historical occurrence, although they are today almost unknown, are nonetheless distinctly prophetic of the contemporary analytic approach to the history of philosophy.

The prize fellowship to which Moore was elected enabled him to remain in residence at Trinity College for a term of six years. Accordingly, from 1898 to 1904 he lived in a set of fellow's rooms on the north side of Nevile's Court, as he himself said: "a very pleasant place and a very pleasant life." But despite his disclaimers, the level of work during these years was intense and of the highest quality, and in the end, it established his philosophical reputation.

The first piece of philosophical work which I undertook during this period was to write some articles for Baldwin's *Dictionary of Philosophy*. I took very great pains over these articles, aiming particularly at analysing out the fundamental notions involved in the use of the terms I was asked to define, and trying hard to make the meaning of everything I said perfectly clear. I certainly learned a good deal myself in this process, and I think my efforts after clear analysis gave the articles a sort of merit which might enable other people to learn something from them.

Moore's efforts here "after clear analysis," at "analysing out the fundamental notions involved in the use of terms," at "trying hard to make the meaning of everything I said perfectly clear," characterized not only the Baldwin dictionary articles, but everything he wrote at this time, including the two courses of lectures he was invited to give at the Passmore Edwards settlement in London. The first course of ten lectures was on Kant's ethics, and the second was on ethics simply, and the preparation of these lectures (which Moore wrote out completely and read afterwards) was the germinating occasion for the development of the ideas later expressed in the famous *Principia Ethica*. The latter part of Moore's six-year fellowship tenure was mainly occupied in the writing of this work, and he took immense pains with it, writing slowly and rewriting frequently. When it finally appeared in 1903 (when Moore was thirty), it was hailed as a philosophic accomplishment of the first order. In fact, 1903 can well be called the *annus mirabilis* of modern Cambridge philosophy, for in this year appeared both Moore's *Principia Ethica* and Russell's *Principles of Mathematics* — utterly different works, but each capable of dominating its chosen subject for decades to come.

Moore's first stay at Cambridge lasted twelve years: as an undergraduate between 1892 and 1896; working for a fellowship between 1896 and 1898; and as a fellow of Trinity between 1898 and 1904. And it is important to understand the immense personal influence which Moore had upon others at Cambridge during these years, the sense in which his intellectual purity became a moral force, and how the deep ties of friendship and intimacy of these Cambridge years exhibit some of the same characteristics which are to dominate a life of narrowly professional philosophizing. In fact, the most interesting psychological problem of Moore's career — the curious intermediate twilight zone of his intellectual life, product of the tension between professional impersonality and the selective intimacy of the personal life — has its origins here. Cambridge, which formed Moore's mind, and where for almost half a century he formed the minds of others, is the center of the paradox. For Cambridge means no less to the mentality of Moore than Königsberg did to the mentality of Kant.

Cambridge is not only an educational institution; it is also a cornerstone of the British Commonwealth. The university has always trained a large proportion of those later to form public opinion and to determine public policy. There have therefore always been close personal ties between the university and those high in the order of public affairs. Cambridge is not merely an ivory tower of the intellectual life, but an active, purposeful environment whose earnestness, security, and strong traditionalism permit one to speak of something like a "Cambridge civilization" — a stability and self-confidence in the pursuit of excellence which has always had profound influence on the British mind. Yet from the perspective of those within the university, students and tutors alike, there is a sense of separateness, of intimacy, of intense intellectual parochialism crucial to the formation of a permanent intellectual elite. And this sense of intimacy and separateness is fed by the existence of cliques of students and of special "secret societies."

One of these latter was the discussion society known as "the

Apostles." Founded in the late eighteenth or early nineteenth century, it came to have a peculiar philosophical flavor and significance. Henry Sidgwick, elected to the society in 1858, in his *A Memoir* speaks of its nature as: "the spirit of the pursuit of truth with absolute devotion and unreserve by a group of intimate friends." Leonard Woolf, a great admirer of Moore, and one of the leading lights of Bloomsbury, says of his undergraduate days: "It came to seem to me that no part of my life at Cambridge was so real to me as the Saturday evenings on which the apostolic debates were held; and the tie of attachment to the society is much the strongest corporate bond which I have known in life." During this time (1902-3) Lytton Strachey and John Maynard Keynes as well as Woolf were members of the Apostles, and Woolf continues: "Perhaps once a century one member dominates the Society. And what Sidgwick did in the fifties of the last century, G. E. Moore was doing when I was elected."

It is not to be denied that toward the end of the nineteenth century there was an extraordinary outburst of philosophical brilliance at Cambridge. In 1902, among the fellows of Trinity were four philosophers: McTaggart, Whitehead, Russell, and Moore — and all of them were Apostles. Whitehead was forty-one, Russell thirty, and Moore only twenty-nine, but of the whole Cambridge philosophical group it was he who had the charisma, the perennial personal fascination. Woolf says (*Sowing: An Autobiography of the Years 1880-1904*):

> I still think that G. E. Moore was a great man, the only great man whom I have ever met or known in the world of ordinary, real life. There was in him an element which can, I think, be accurately called greatness, a combination of mind and character and behavior, of thought and feeling which made him qualitatively different from anyone else I have ever known.

And John Maynard Keynes also, although he called Moore "a puritan and precisian," yet admitted (*Two Memoires*):

> I went up to Cambridge at Michaelmas 1902 and Moore's *Principia Ethica* came out at the end of my first year. I have never heard of the present generation having read it. But, of course, its effect on *us,* and the talk which preceded and followed it, dominated, and perhaps still dominate everything else. . . . It was only for us, those who were active in 1903, that Moore completely ousted McTaggart, Dickinson, Russell. The influence was not only overwhelming; but it was the extreme opposite of what

Strachey used to call *funeste*; it was exciting, exhilarating, the beginning of a renaissance.

Two things are remarkable in all these very similar accounts of Cambridge philosophy, the Apostles, and the influence of G. E. Moore. The first is the sense of intimacy, of primary group loyalty within which the intellectual influence becomes a bond of iron. The novelist E. M. Forster, an intimate of both Cambridge and Bloomsbury, phrased it perfectly. "The great society," he said, "is always the enemy: only the little society, the intimate group of real friends, is worth anything." And the second is the particular fusion of Moore's intellectual insistence and moral passion which made his unconscious pedagogy even as a young man so irresistibly Socratic. Woolf has said that Moore's mind was Socratic, as was his character and his influence upon the young men at Cambridge. What captivated them all was his combination of "clarity, integrity, tenacity, and passion" and particularly "the passionate distress which muddled thinking aroused in him." To a group of highly intellectual and sophisticated young men — the *jeunesse dorée* of Cambridge — Moore offered a glimpse of freshness and simplicity. He asked them to make quite certain that they knew what they meant when they made a statement, and to analyize and examine their beliefs in the escapable light of common sense. But what converted Moore's intellectual method into a moral force was his obvious passion for truth and his relentless insistence upon relevance. For this we also have the authority of Leonard Woolf.

It was, I suppose, in 1902 that I got to know Moore well. He was seven years my senior and already a fellow at Trinity. His mind was an extraordinarily powerful instrument; it was Socratic, analytic. But unlike so many analytic philosophers, he never analyzed just for the pleasure or sake of analysis. He never indulged in logic-chopping or truth-chopping. He had a passion for truth, but not for all or any truth, only for important truths. He had no use for truths which Browning called "dead from the waist down."

Moore was not witty; I do not think that I ever heard him say a witty thing; there was no scintillation in his conversation or in his thought. But he had an extraordinary profundity and clarity of thought, and he pursued truth with the tenacity of a bulldog and the integrity of a saint. . . . He had a genius for seeing what was important and what was unimportant and irrelevant, in thought and in life and in persons, and in the most complicated argument or situation he pursued the relevant and ignored the irrelevant with amazing tenacity.

The real Socrates scorned the professionalism of the Sophists
and instructed the aristocratic youth of Athens like some gifted
amateur. And Plato, although he founded a formal school, yet
cherished and preserved the Socratic ideal of the dialectical community of philosophic friends and intimates. And it is interesting
that G. E. Moore, who became the epitome of philosophic professionalism, yet owed his early fame to institutional circumstances
that are neither un-Socratic nor un-Platonic. In all three cases the
effective causes are dramatic and characterological. Like Socrates
also, Moore was profoundly influential because of his *style*: the
fascinating, spell-binding way in which he conveyed clear, distilled,
purified *thought*. And as the Socratic circle listened enthralled
as the master interrogated Protagoras or refuted Gorgias, so the
Cambridge Apostles thronged about a young philosopher whose
devotion to truth was almost palpable and found it enthralling to
watch him at his dialectical work. The elderly Athenian pursued
the truth with a quiet irony. But when the youthful Cambridge
fellow engaged in argument, his whole frame was gripped by a
passion to confute error and expose confusion so vehement that it
expressed itself in gestures suggestive of Saint Vitus. John Maynard Keynes describes it:

Moore at this time was a master of this method — greeting one's
remarks with a gasp of incredulity — Do you *really* think *that*, an
expression of face as if to hear such a thing said reduced him to a
state of wonder verging on imbecility, with his mouth wide open
and wagging his head in the negative so violently that his hair
shook. *Oh!* he would say, goggling at you as if either you or he
must be mad; and no reply was possible.

In this way personal particularity becomes the foundation of
professional method!

In 1904 Moore's fellowship lapsed and he left Cambridge. The
death of his parents had left him without financial worries, with,
as he said, the ability "to live in moderate comfort without having
to earn anything," and he therefore continued to work at philosophy as he had during the tenure of his fellowship without trying
to obtain paid employment. The next three and a half years were
spent in Edinburgh and the same number subsequently at Rich-
mond, Surrey. During this period of living quietly on inherited
income, as had Descartes in Holland before him, he wrote the
paper on William James and the little book *Ethics*, written for the
Home University Library, which Moore preferred to the much

more celebrated *Principia Ethica*. He felt that it was "clearer" —
more straightforward and systematic in its presentation, less full of
confusions and invalid arguments. Also during this period, in the
winter of 1910-11, Moore was invited to give twenty lectures at
Morley College in London. These lectures, written out completely
and then read as had been the earlier Passmore Edwards series,
dealt with all the subjects for which Moore was later to be famous:
sense-data, propositions, ways of knowing, material objects, existence in time and space, true and false beliefs, universals, relations, properties, existence. And although they were entitled
"Lectures on Metaphysics," their concern was rather logical and
epistemological — what, in fact, has become newly popular under
the rubric: The Philosophy of Mind. Nevertheless, their title was
not completely undeserved, as attention to the first of the lectures,
"What Is Philosophy?" will show. Moore's philosophical endeavors
have always been taken to be narrowly analytic, piecemeal, ad
hoc, and his "realism" has been looked on as a kind of salubrious
withdrawal from the "wooliness" of McTaggart and the ambiguous marshes of holistic idealist metaphysics. Yet if this becomes
truer as Moore grows older and his delight in analysis for its own
sake grows more pronounced, the younger Moore has still some
pretentions in the direction of a systematic metaphysics. "It seems
to me," he said in this early lecture,

that the most important and interesting thing which philosophers
have tried to do is no less than this: namely: To give a general
description of the *whole* of the Universe, mentioning all the most
important kinds of things which we *know* to be in it, considering
how far it is likely that there are in it important kinds of things
which we do not absolutely *know* to be in it, and also considering
the most important ways in which these various kinds of things are
related to one another.

This sketch of a total inventory of existent things and their relations is hardly less than the ambitious project of a complete
descriptive metaphysics, and if it had been carried through we
should have had from Moore an integrated *Weltbild* — if not the
old, "dusty, cluttered Victorian universe" of Bradley, Bosanquet,
and Whitehead, at least something as spare, streamlined, and
functional as the engineer's universe of Quine, Goodman, or
Strawson. At any rate these extremely interesting lectures lay
unpublished for over forty years, only appearing in the Muirhead
Library of Philosophy under the title *Some Main Problems of
Philosophy* in 1953, when Moore was approaching eighty. In

many ways this volume provides the best and most systematic repository of Moore's nonethical philosophical beliefs.

In 1911 Moore was asked to return to Cambridge as a lecturer in moral science, and beginning in October of that year he lectured at Cambridge during every term for twenty-eight years. If one adds to that that even when he retired from his professorship in 1939, at the age of sixty-five, he remained philosophically active in Cambridge, and, except for spending the war years in the United States (October 1940 to May 1944), had constant contact with undergraduates, philosophical colleagues, and interested visiting philosophers, this makes almost forty-seven years of continuous professional philosophical occupation.

Moore lectured continually, some years three days a week, some years five, in psychology, metaphysics, and the philosophy of mind, and he took enormous pains in preparing these lectures. They occupied him constantly during the university term, and since as a rule he prepared new sets of lectures each year, always dissatisfied with what he had previously done, there seemed to be little time for independent publication. But this made for teaching of extraordinary currency and vividness, for each topic considered was something in which Moore himself was keenly interested and which seemed novel to him, and this sense of novelty and personal involvement communicated itself to those who listened. Moore's written works, particularly during his later years, tend to be technical, repetitious, and dry, and they fail to communicate the passionate involvement and rhetorical liveliness of the man in action and of his speaking voice. For his speech, no less than his mind, was studded with italics and exclamation points.

Unlike the Passmore Edwards lectures (*Principia Ethica*) and the Morley College lectures (*Some Main Problems of Philosophy*), Moore did not write out his Cambridge lectures either in preliminary or finished form (and so nothing distinctly publishable resulted from this quotidian pedagogy). But Moore spoke freely from full sets of lecture notes, sometimes referring to them sometimes not, having prepared in such a way that his mind was full of his subject, and his enthusiasm was so apparent that the quest for accuracy in conceptual analysis which the lectures exhibited seemed simply the perfect expression of analytical mind in action.

It is significant that Moore's lectures, like his epistemological views and his written articles on perception, are never primarily important for their substantive content, but are important for their exhibition of a process—an activity. He was, for example, notoriously unable to finally make up his mind on epistemological matters. Although he was adamant in his rejection of the idealist alternative (his famous "The Refutations of Idealism" of 1903 had been devoted to a complicated disproof of the well-known Berke-leyian dictum *esse est percipi*), he always put off or held in suspension an ultimate choice between representationalism, phen-omenalism, and direct realism (that the visual sense-data we immediately perceive are indeed "parts" of the surfaces of mater-ial objects). One or another of his analytical essays may toy with a momentary preference, but it is never definitive, and this curious modesty before categorical assertion in metaphysical and epis-temological matters also characterized his university lectures so as to make their formal titles and their presumed subjects of distinct-ly secondary importance.   Moore's devotion to his teaching was exemplary. He never took sabbatical leave, and he seldom missed a lecture for whatever reason, so that year in and year out any philosopher wishing to know how Moore was thinking could rely on finding him in Cambridge lecturing at least three times a week. And so, as the fame of his analytical method spread throughout the English-speaking world, there was hardly a year in which there were not British or American philosophers, young or not so young, who had come for a year or a term to savor Cambridge analysis and sit at Moore's feet.

The subject of the lectures did not matter: metaphysics or the philosophy of mind, properties and relations, or sense-data and ways of knowing—it was all the same. Whatever the nominal subject matter or lecture titles, what Moore provided were ex-amples of philosophical analysis, and it was *the search for a correct analysis* of the meaning of a "sense-datum" or "propos-ition" or "relation" which counted. After endlessly elaborating and improving one type of analysis for perhaps twenty lectures, Moore would dismiss it as inadequate and would then pass on to another possible type, only to repeat the same process of endless elucidation, criticism, and modification. Braithwaite has de-scribed the process:

In 1922–23 when I attended both courses of Moore's lectures, we hunted the correct analysis of propositions about the self on Monday, Wednesday, and Friday mornings, and the correct analysis of propositions of the form "This is a pencil" on Tuesday, Thursday, and Saturday mornings throughout the year. By the end of May, when lectures had to stop because the triposes started, Moore would have got through about two-and-a-half of the possible kinds of analysis. The lectures were quite inconclusive: Moore saw grave objections to any of the analyses he had discussed being the *correct* analysis, and the audience dispersed to sit their examinations, or to return to their homes across the Atlantic, without any idea as to which of the analyses had the best claim to correctness. Of course Moore was concealing nothing: he himself did not know which solution to prefer.

The conclusion seems a paradox — if not a travesty. So much intellectual effort with so little substantive result! To a society of scarce resources, pressed by problems of social injustice or economic disadvantage or simple lack, such evasion of pragmatic orientation, such total disregard of *truth as product* (which the applied sciences so relentlessly stress) seems something of a scandal. But it tells us something that the year was 1922, the place Britain, and that the mind of the lecturer (who was now fifty) had been formed in a quietly prosperous and stable society. For the legacy of the Edwardian consciousness obviously shines through. It should not be forgotten that Moore's writings were first published in 1897 — the year of Queen Victoria's Diamond Jubilee, before the First World War, before the loss of a confident sense of the rationality and the stability of the social order; and that, born during the ministry of Gladstone, he spent almost his entire life in provincial England. Cambridge, with its bright river and trees beautiful with color, is a town of distinguished peace. It was a fitting setting for unhurried thought, where the *search* for truth could seem more important than its leisurely seizure, and where intellectual tools could be sharpened without a panicky sense that they were urgently needed for immediate use.

Moore took the responsibilities of teaching with extreme seriousness. It is true that the philosophical curriculum at Cambridge is highly specialized — perhaps as specialized as at any university in the world — so that, since only philosophers attended his lectures, by American standards the audience would be relatively small. Yet the lecture system alone does not provide the dialectical encounters of a truly Platonic pedagogy, and Moore felt constrained to follow McTaggart's model and to hold a "conversation class" in connection with each lecture course for at least one hour a week. "This was an opportunity for the audience to ask questions and discuss topics in connection with the lectures of the week; and it seems to me that such discussion classes form a very important and necessary adjunct to any course of lectures on philosophy." This class, held on Fridays between twelve and one, was faithfully attended by those enrolled in his lectures. But, in addition, every Tuesday from five to seven Moore held open house at 86 Chesterton Road, and it was usual for from six to eight persons to attend—often visitors from America or Cambridge colleagues (as for example Casimir Lewy, Rush Rhees, Norman Malcolm, and G. A. Paul), and the talk (mostly on epistemological subjects, since Moore had long since lost his early ethical concerns) was subtle, evocative, and philosophically highly specialized. Since Moore was now considerably older than his students and visitors, the interchange was inevitably muted and respectful, but it is noteworthy that it was at least Moore's intention to recreate or recapture some of the philosophical intimacy of the early Apostles and fellowship days.

In addition to Moore's teaching at Cambridge, two other activities testify to the pervasiveness of his professionalism. One is his editorship from 1920 to 1947 of the technical philosophical journal, *Mind*. The other is his involvement with, and continuing attendance at, the meetings of the most important professional philosophical association in Britain—the Aristotelian Society.

As early as 1912 Moore had been asked to review books for *Mind*, and in 1920, upon the retirement of Stout, his former teacher in the history of philosophy, Moore succeeded him as editor of what is perhaps the most prestigious philosophical journal in the English-speaking world. The rise of the professional philosophical journal is, as we have seen, primarily the child of the German eighteenth century—the age of Kant—but in the last quarter of the nineteenth century this trend also began to dominate the Anglo-Saxon consciousness. *Mind* was founded in 1876, and it marked an important stage in the growth of philosophical professionalism in the English-speaking world. Philosophers like Mill and Huxley and Herbert Spencer, (as well as those like Emerson and William James and even Charles Sanders Peirce) had published their philosophical essays in the more widely read magazines like the *Westminster Review* or the *Fortnightly Review* or *Scribner's* or *Popular Science Monthly*, but from the days of Bradley and Bosanquet, as well as Moore and Russell, philosophers began to publish not for the general public but primarily for other philosophers with a similar professional interest. This new professional practice of submitting problems and arguments to the expert criticism of fellow craftsmen led, as Gilbert Ryle has noted, "to a growing concern with questions of philosophical technique and a growing passion for ratiocinative rigor." There is therefore a certain intrinsic appropriateness in the fact that G. E. Moore, himself a meticulous philosophical craftsman, should preside over a journal dedicated to intellectual excellence and the perfection of the philosophic craft.

But there is one thing more. In an age when professional prestige depends so heavily upon publication in the proper, accredited philosophical journals, and where the space in these journals is necessarily so drastically limited, editorship carries with it both enormous power and enormous responsibility. The right of access and the judgment of rightful access is one that Moore dispensed and exercised for almost thirty years with admirable justice and concern. Not only did he take enormous trouble in corresponding with contributors in his own hand, suggesting improvements in exposition of pieces accepted and in some cases going to some length in helpfully criticizing those rejected, but, unlike some narrowly partisan and fanatically "ideological" editors, under him *Mind* remained catholic in its composition and open to a wide variety of philosophical positions. "I think," said Moore toward the end of his editorship,

that I have succeeded in being impartial as between different schools of philosophy. I have tried, in accordance with the principles laid down when *Mind* was started and repeated by Stout . . . to let merit, or, in other words, the ability which a writer displays, and not the opinions which he holds, be the sole criterion of whether his work should be accepted.

This too is "professionalism" of the highest quality.

Two of Moore's professional activities unfortunately prevented him from writing for publication: the manner in which he meticulously, although informally, prepared his Cambridge lectures and the time-consuming conscientiousness he exercised in editing *Mind*. But the third, his continuous participation in the activities of the Aristotelian Society, fortunately had just the opposite effect.

It must have been about 1898 that I was asked to become a member of the Aristotelian Society of London; and during these six years [of his Cambridge fellowship] I went very often to London to attend their weekly meetings. It is to my membership of this society that the existence of what, I suppose, constitutes considerably the greater part of my published work is due. I was constantly being asked to write a paper or to take part in a "Symposium" for them; and, until very recent years, I did not like to refuse and thought I had no good excuse for refusing: I have always found it very difficult to say "No" to a request. Having promised to write a paper, I had to write one, and, but for this stimulus, I doubt if I should have published half as much as I have published.

As one looks over Moore's bibliography from his first publication in *Mind* in 1897 to the time he retired from his professorship in 1939, one is struck to find that with the exception of *Principia Ethica, Ethics,* and *Some Main Problems of Philosophy,* all of Moore's major essays were delivered before the Aristotelian Society, either as single papers or as contributions to symposia. The first publication itself — "In What Sense Do Past and Future Time Exist?" — was a symposium with Bosanquet and Shadsworth Hodgson. The "Freedom" of 1898, "The Nature of Judgment" of 1899, the "Identity" of 1901, the "Experience and Empiricism" of 1903, the "Kant's Idealism" of 1904, and the celebrated "The Nature and Reality of Objects of Perception" of 1906 were all read at meetings of the society. In 1914 he participated in a symposium "The Status of Sense-Data" with Stout; in 1916 in the symposium "The Implications of Recognition" with Wildon Carr; in 1917 in the symposium "Are the Materials of Sense Affections of the Mind?" with W. E. Johnson, Dawes Hicks, J. A. Smith, and James Ward; in 1919 in "Is There Knowledge by Acquaintance?" with Hicks and Broad; in 1921 in "The Character of Cognitive Acts" with John Laird, Hicks, and Broad; in 1926 in "The Nature of Sensible Appearances" with Hicks, H. H. Price, and Susan Stebbing; in 1927 in "Facts and Propositions" with F. P. Ramsay; in 1929 in "Indirect Knowledge" with H. W. B. Joseph; in 1932 in "Is Goodness a Quality?" with Joseph and A. E. Taylor; in 1933 in "Imaginary Objects" with Braithwaite and Ryle; and in 1936 in "Is Existence a Predicate?" with W. Kneale. The list of fellow participants in these Aristotelian Society symposia from 1914 to 1936 reads like some blue-ribbon *Who's Who* of professional philosophy in the British Isles. And it must be added that in Moore's first important collection of essays, the *Philosophical Studies,* published in 1922; of the eight papers there previously published, six had been read before the Aristotelian Society. It is, therefore completely fair to say that by far the greatest portion of Moore's total publication was written not for the general audience of educated men but for the specialized response of professional

philosophers. Plato wrote for Athens and Saint Thomas for the
clergy of medieval Christendom, but Descartes wrote chiefly for
Mersenne, Chanut, Balzac, Queen Christina, and Princess Elizabeth; and similarly, but with a somewhat different orientation,
it can be said that G. E. Moore wrote principally for Russell,
Wittgenstein, Wisdom, Ryle, Braithwaite, Joseph, Price, and
W. E. Johnson.

The catalog of Moore's own contributions to the proceedings of
the Aristotelian Society is substantial enough, but it gives no hint
of the extent and liveliness of his oral participation in the debates
or of the vividness and vehemence with which he criticized the
presentations of other philosophers. For over three decades Moore
was "the life and soul" of the society, in its own meetings and at
the joint sessions of the Aristotelian Society and the Mind Association, held annually at different universities. And in the exciting
exchanges, Moore treated with the same human excitement and
unabashed criticism the philosophical novice and the mature
scholar of worldwide reputation. Braithwaite remembers:

Moore's interventions were accompanied by gestures of his pipe
and his whole body and with characteristically over-emphasized
words (*Oh!* you *really* think *that?*) which made it impossible for
anyone to take offence. Moore's mere presence raised the tone
of a philosophical discussion; it made flippancy or sarcasm or
bombast impossible. We were compelled, sometimes against our
wills, to be as serious, and to try to be as sincere, as Moore so
obviously was himself.

And G. A. Paul adds:

Moore has conveyed his thoughts as much by speech as writing.
Over a long period he was the life of many of the gatherings of
philosophers in Britain. When Moore was to read a paper or
take part in discussion, one could be sure that things would go.

When one thinks of Plato one remembers Socrates, the love of
beauty, and the fateful trips to Syracuse. When one thinks of
Saint Thomas one remembers the Chapter House on the Rue
Saint Jacques, the pious hymns, and the papal court at Orvieto.
When one remembers Descartes, it is in terms of La Flèche, the
private sojourn in Holland, and his death at the court of Queen
Christina. But G. E. Moore almost seems to have no personal biography. With him one associates the lecture room in Cambridge,
the frequent meetings of the Aristotelian Society, and the journal

Mind. For he is not a public philosopher, or a churchly philosopher, or a private philosopher, but a *philosopher's philosopher* — the perfect distillation of professionalism in the modern philosophic world.

The Professional Ethicist

Kant, the first great professional philosopher, and G. E. Moore, the epitome of philosophy in an "age of professionalism," are alike in at least one respect: their primary philosophical interests are in ethics and epistemology. But whereas Kant begins with an epistemological concern ("How are synthetic a priori judgments possible?") and only subsequently turns to the world of man's obligation and his freedom, Moore's earliest serious work is in ethics. Partly, as we have seen, this is because Moore had, at the suggestion of Ward, himself been reading Kant's ethics for the fellowship competition at Trinity. But it was also, I think, the influence upon Moore of Sidgwick, and particularly of his great book *The Methods of Ethics*, which was decisive. For *Principia Ethica* in fact takes up precisely where *The Methods of Ethics* leaves off, just as almost all subsequent modern ethical theory begins with a criticism of the solutions Moore himself has given. *Principia Ethica* is therefore the great midpoint in that highroad of modern ethical theory which begins with Mill and ends with Pritchard and Ross, Stevenson and Hare.

But by being the "midpoint," it bears a certain special responsibility for the curious, but decisive, change which has taken place in the nature of modern ethical theorizing. Classical ethical theory, whether in the case of Plato, Aristotle, or Saint Thomas, Hume, Kant, or Bentham, tried to be *normative*: it attempted to explore and to map the realm of values, and by so doing to establish their relevance to human life. Its inquiries not only were directed to the analysis of moral notions and to the epistemic questions about what constitutes "moral evidence," but by giving determinate and culturally specific content to the ideas of "the right" and "the good," it constituted a historically conditioned, to be sure, but yet a *specific* blueprint of "how a man ought to live." This is now all changed. Modern ethics no longer is "normative ethics," it is "metaethics;" *logical* and abstract investigations into the concepts of "moral rules" and "moral judgment" have replaced concrete exploration of human values. That sort of casuistry previously understood to be the goal of ethical investigation (of the kind which Aristotle provides in the middle books of the *Nicomachean Ethics* and Kant in his *Lectures on Ethics*) has become in Stevenson's *Ethics and Language* an enquiry into the "rhetoric" of the moral life, as in Hare's *The Language of Morals* it has become an enquiry into its "grammar." There was indeed something prophetic in Moore's statement in *Principia Ethica*: "It is not the business of the ethical philosopher to give personal advice or exhortation."

John Stuart Mill, for all of his confusions, was one of the sages of the moral life, but Stevenson and Hare (if they are heroes) are much more heroes of the battlefield of logic, and if one asks the question: How has the kind of serious substantive concern which informs almost every word of the *Utilitarianism* been transmuted into the substantive neutrality (if perhaps equally serious logical concern) of *Ethics and Language* or *The Language of Morals*? the answer is to be found in no small part in the new direction of Moore's *Principia Ethica*, and of its subsequent enormous influence. It is a movement toward the transformation of moral philosophy from a humanistic search after the wisdom of life into a wholly abstract and a wholly "professional" discipline.

Yet it is perhaps also true that Moore is not completely responsible for the uses to which *Principia Ethica* has subsequently been put. And there is evidence of division within the book itself: division of intention and concern represented by the subject matter of its first five chapters (1. The Subject Matter of Ethics; 2. Naturalistic Ethics; 3. Hedonism; 4. Metaphysical Ethics; 5. Ethics in Relation to Conduct) in contrast with the last (6. The Ideal). Moore, the perfect professional philosopher, was, as I have said, continually haunted by the tension between professional impersonality and the selective intimacy of the personal life. This expressed itself chiefly in the early period in which his influence was so great with Keynes, Woolf, Strachey, and those others destined to become the ruling spirits of Bloomsbury. But it also expressed itself later in the years of the Cambridge professorate when, entrusted so largely with the professional responsibility of training other professional philosophers, he tried in his "conversation class" and in his "at homes" to infuse the spirit of Socratic informality into the starchy atmosphere of institutionalized requirement. *Principia Ethica* itself belongs to this earlier period; it marks the intersection between the future career of the young professional and the genesis of the spirit of Bloomsbury, and it bears the ineradicable marks of this confrontation.

Principia Ethica begins with simplicity. "It appears to me," says Moore, "that in Ethics, as in all other philosophical studies, the difficulties and disagreements, of which its history is full, are mainly due to a very simple cause: namely to the attempt to answer questions, without first discovering precisely *what* question it is which you desire to answer." From the beginning Moore enlists our most ardent sympathy, for he promises, or seems to promise, that by this simple, indeed artless, device we may at last make "many of the most glaring difficulties and disagreements in philosophy . . . disappear." These difficulties and disagreements in ethics, it seems, are the consequences not of a difficult and crucially important subject matter, of disagreements about ultimate values due to profound differences in human experience or to the subtlety and complexity expressed in the structure of the realm of values, but of a fallacy of simple equivocation, committed over and over again in the procedure of moral theorists. It is almost as if in one moment the deepest problems of the moral life had been converted into a failure of the most elementary logic; and it follows, therefore, that to remedy the logical failure is to "solve" the ethical problem.

Unfortunately it does not prove to be so simple. For even after Moore distinguishes clearly *the* questions with which moral philosophers "have always professed to be concerned," although "they have almost always confused them with one another," the answers he provides are distressingly paradoxical—so unsatisfactory, in fact, as to be hardly acceptable to a sophisticated moral intelligence. The questions are three: (1) What kind of things ought to exist for their own sakes? (the question of *intrinsic value*); (2) What kind of actions ought we to perform? (the question of *duty*); and (3) What is the nature of the evidence by which alone any ethical proposition can be proved or disproved, confirmed or rendered doubtful? (the question of *moral evidence*). But it is not so much the mere distinction between these questions that really counts as the relation of the third to the first two, and in asserting the nature of the moral evidence upon which we may rest our judgments of what is intrinsically valuable and what is our duty, Moore makes his most dogmatic and disconcerting claim.

Once we recognize the exact meaning of the two questions [the question of intrinsic value and the question of duty], I think it also becomes plain exactly what kind of reasons are relevant as arguments for or against any particular answer to them. It becomes plain that, for answers to the *first* question [that of intrinsic value], no relevant evidence whatever can be adduced: from no other truth except themselves alone, can it be inferred that they are either true or false. . . . As for the *second* question [that of our duty], it becomes equally plain, that any answer to it *is* capable of proof or disproof — that, indeed, so many different considerations are relevant to its truth or falsehood, as to make the attainment of probability very difficult, and the attainment of certainty impossible.

The conclusion is astounding. In matters of intrinsic value Moore is a dogmatist. In matters of duty he is a skeptic. Propositions about what kinds of things ought to exist for their own sakes are *self-evidently* true or false. As for propositions as to what kind of actions we ought to perform, there is not too little evidence, but too much. So many factors must be considered about the ultimate effects, the remote consequences of our acts, and they are so difficult to foresee exactly or calculate with certainty, that it is almost as if there were no evidence at all. And this painful fact later leads Moore to espouse certain well-established and customary rules of duty which place him closer to the deontological system of Kant than should be the case for the kind of "ideal utilitarian" he is usually assumed to be. For although Moore's third question: "By what evidence do we prove or disprove moral propositions?" seems to be crucial to his system, his dogmatism (doctrine of self-evidence) about matters of intrinsic value and his skepticism about our rational calculation in matters of duty render the problem of "moral evidence" hopelessly irrelevant, if not actually meaningless.

To the usual moralist in the classical tradition this would have been distressing indeed, but it does not seem to have been so to Moore, and the reason, I think, is that for him to solve the moral problem is much less important than "to ask the right question," and that "to utilize the proper principles of moral reasoning" is an absolute imperative, whatever paradoxical consequences may spring from their "proper use." In the preface to *Principia Ethica*, Moore states this explicitly:

One main object of this book may, then, be expressed by slightly changing one of Kant's famous titles. I have endeavored to write "Prolegomena to any future Ethics that can possibly pretend to be scientific". In other words, I have endeavored to discover what are the fundamental principles of ethical reasoning; and the establishment of these principles, rather than of any conclusions which may be attained by their use, may be regarded as my main object. I have, however, also attempted, in Chapter VI, to present some conclusions with regard to the proper answer of the question "What is good in itself?" which are very different from any which have commonly been advocated by philosophers.

To "discover" and "establish" the fundamental principles of ethical reasoning is certainly a worthy ambition and a worthy aim. But why should one then be relatively uninterested in the conclusions which may be attained by their use? "The patient died, but the operation was a great success!" The surgeon may be more interested in the perfection of the surgical technique than in the fate of the patient. And the moralist too, victim of the same "professionalism," may be more interested in the tools of moral reasoning than in their consequences for human life. Here then, in *Principia Ethica* in 1903, is already the first announcement of moral philosophy's contemporary disease. In a theoretical science or an organon like formal logic, Moore's position is justifiable; in a "practical" or "applied" science it is not, and in his disclaimer we have, I think, the first intimations of the mentality which has turned the deepest concerns of moral practice into a matter of propositional relationships and has transformed the field of moral theory itself into a small segment of the all-inclusive field of logic.

But of course, Moore *does* have some real interest in the conclusions to be reached by the use of the proper principles of moral reasoning. His last words above prove it. For those "answers" which he promises to present in chapter 6 to the question of intrinsic value—"What is good in itself?"—and which he tells us are so "very different from any which have been commonly advocated by philosophers," must be of the greatest importance for his whole moral system. Moore may say that he is less interested in conclusions with respect to intrinsic value than in establishing correct principles of moral reasoning, but if his conclusions about intrinsic value are false, or mistaken, or inadequate, or clearly questionable, then this casts the most serious doubt upon the validity or adequacy or utility of his asserted principles of moral reasoning. To this matter we must later turn.

But before doing so, it will be good, I think, to notice again briefly the structure of *Principia Ethica*, and the strange way in

which the estimate of the relative importance of its parts has shifted since the time of its writing. Chapter 1 deals with "The Subject
Matter of Ethics," and it is here that Moore does most of his work
in the construction of theory. Taking his departure from the
standpoint that the most fundamental question in all ethics is how
"good" is to be defined, and that the definition here in question is
not verbal, but real; not, that is, about the customary usage of a
word, but about the actual nature of an idea or concept, Moore
states his most famous principle—that "good" is simply *undefin-
able*, that propositions about the good are all, in Kantian terms,
"synthetic" and not "analytic," that "good" is, like "yellow," a
simple notion which is absolutely inexplicable to one who does not
already know what it means. The implication of this doctrine,
clearly stated, is that there is no term or idea which can be
substituted for that of "good," and from this it follows that any
attempt to equate the good with pleasure, happiness, content-
ment, contemplation, or virtue is simply a mistake; that any
confusion of "good" with any natural object or property, psychological state of consciousness, or relationship between persons
should be termed an instance of *the naturalistic fallacy*.

The next three chapters of *Principia Ethica*, on "Naturalistic
Ethics," "Hedonism," and "Metaphysical Ethics" are simply ex-
cursions into the history of ethical theory which use the apparatus
of the naturalistic fallacy to show that almost all prior moral
philosophers have based their systems upon this formidable mistake. Naturalistic Ethics, of which the evolutionism of Herbert
Spencer is a notable example, holds, for example, that "quantity"
or "breadth and intensity of life" is that natural property by means
of which the good may be defined. Hedonism, on the other hand,
holds not only that "pleasure is the sole good," but that it is
implied in the very meaning of the term "good." And to assert that
"Nothing is good but pleasure," or that "Pleasure alone is good as
an end," is a general form of Naturalism to which both John
Stuart Mill and Henry Sidgwick were committed, although they
expounded this common system with different degrees of methodological sophistication. Moore criticizes both severely, although he
has great respect for Sidgwick's subtlety, and he believes that
Sidgwick was perhaps the first to recognize clearly the intuitional
genesis of all perception of intrinsic value.

Of all hedonistic writers, Prof. Sidgwick alone has clearly
recognized that by "good" we do mean something unanalysable,

and has alone been led thereby to emphasise the fact that, if Hedonism be true, its claims to be so must be rested solely on its self-evidence — that we must maintain "Pleasure is the sole good" to be a mere *intuition*. It appeared to Prof. Sidgwick as a new discovery that what he calls the "method" of Intuitionism must be retained as valid alongside of, and indeed as the foundation of what he calls the alternative "methods" of Utilitarianism and Egoism. And that it was a new discovery can hardly be doubted.

In the chapter on "Metaphysical Ethics," Moore deals with the type of ethical theory exemplified in Spinoza, Kant, and the modern idealistic followers of Hegel like Bradley and T. H. Green, all of whom hold that ethical truths follow logically from metaphysical truths, that ethics *should* be based on metaphysics, and who therefore *describe* the Supreme Good in metaphysical terms. Spinoza's definition of perfection as the unity of absolute substance, Kant's idealization of a "Kingdom of Ends," Green's and Bradley's assertion that the final ethical end is to realize our true selves are examples of this kind of moral theory. But although each of these theories has the merit (not possessed by Naturalism) of defining perfect goodness in other than spatiotemporal terms, they do make claims concerning the nature of "reality," and from these claims they *derive* their assertions about the nature of intrinsic value. But precisely this derivative character of their definition of value also constitutes an instance of the naturalistic fallacy. Thus Spinoza and Kant and Green take their place with Mill and Sidgwick and Herbert Spencer in the pantheon of those whose moral philosophy rests upon a mistake.

Moore's discovery of the naturalistic fallacy is a brilliant turning point in modern ethical theory, but it falls nonetheless within the continuity of a definite moral tradition. Bentham's hedonism is too simple-minded, too materialistic for John Stuart Mill. Mill's remarks on what sort of proof the principle of utility is susceptible of, and its "inadequacy," lead to Sidgwick's Intuitionism. Sidgwick's statement of the intuitional position and his version of hedonism leaves Moore unsatisfied, and in borrowing from the first and in challenging the second, he is led to his discovery of the naturalistic fallacy. And the influence of the naturalistic fallacy upon subsequent ethical theorists has been overwhelming. Quite mistakenly, I think, the discovery of the naturalistic fallacy has been taken to be the heart of Moore's ethical enterprise, and for over half a century it has been impossible for any ethical theorist

in the Anglo-American tradition to proceed without some judgment about its truth or falsity. Intuitionists (like Ross) adopt it as
the cornerstone of their methodology. Naturalists (like Dewey and
Perry), even as they repudiate it, admit that its effects have been
cataleptic. Noncognitivists (like Stevenson and Hare) do their best
to ignore it, but in the end find that they must deal with its
embarrassing power. Moore's statement of this principle, and his
use of it to discredit naturalistic, hedonistic, and metaphysical
ethics is impressive business, and it was well calculated to awe the
"professionals," however much it might bore the "amateurs." But
the interesting, and not sufficiently recognized fact, is that *Principia Ethica's* first and greatest substantive influence was precisely among the "amateurs." These amateurs were, as we shall
see in a moment, just those representatives of *fin-de-siècle* Cambridge civilization who founded Bloomsbury and its brilliant literary and artistic circle. And what they prized in *Principia Ethica*,
and in most cases did not forget as long as they lived, were the
substantive remarks which Moore provided about the nature of
intrinsic value in Chapter VI — "The Ideal."

This chapter is, however, preceded by Chapter V, Ethics in
Relation to Conduct, and if this is, in a sense, transitional between
the technical considerations of Chapter I-IV, and the substantive
values asserted in Chapter VI, it has an intrinsic interest which has
not often been observed. For here the consequences of Moore's
skepticism with respect to the accurate determination of the truth
of propositions concerning our duty (which we have contrasted
with the dogmatism of his statements about the self-evidence of
our propositions about intrinsic values) eventuates in a practical
conservatism concerning personal and social behavior. The intuitionism with respect to ultimate values, the doctrine of valuational self-evidence, which might seem to result (as it did among
the Cambridge circle of Keynes, Woolf, Strachey, and Russell) in
a kind of subjectivism or willfulness in the choice of personal
behavior, is counterbalanced in Moore himself by a rule-orientation almost Kantian in its intensity, and this is surprising in the
extreme in one whose moral theory as "ideal" or "act" utilitarianism has been so often contrasted with deontological moral systems.
But Casimir Lewy and others who have known Moore well have
commented upon his highly developed personal sense of duty, his
respect for moral rules, and the basic conformity of his life to the
norms and the established rules of English upper-middle-class

society. In this respect (but of course without their possessiveness
and highly developed sense of property) Moore could have been in
his personal life one of Galsworthy's famous "Forsytes." But what
is astonishing, although in some ways very satisfying (as in any
evidence of congruence between a man's "theories" and his
"life"), is the fact that this respect for the traditional wisdom of
established societies is already prefigured in *Principia Ethica,*
chapter 5.

There is little doubt that in his fundamental theory Moore is an
ideal utilitarian; one who believes that the rightness of an act
depends immediately and solely upon its consequences in max-
imizing human good. And, whereas the truths about what things
are intrinsically good are intuitively self-evident (and also "objective" in the sense of being strictly universal), when we inquire
about *the rightness of acts,* we are asking about their probable
effects. "To ask," says Moore, "what kind of actions we ought to
perform, or what kind of conduct is right, is to ask what kind of
effects such action and conduct will produce. Not a single question in practical Ethics can be answered except by a causal generalization." Moral laws are therefore merely *predictions* that certain kinds of acts will always, or in general, have good effects. And
in view of the extreme difficulty encountered by any individual in
personally estimating the complex and remote consequences of
alternative lines of conduct, it is the part of wisdom for him simply
to rely upon those rules of conduct which, over the centuries, have
been established, less as scientific principles, to be sure, than as
the maxims of common sense. And surprisingly enough, *these
rules can be defended independently of the correct perception of
what is good in itself, of what is intrinsically valuable.*

If now, we confine ourselves to a search for actions which are
generally better as means than any probable alternative, it seems
possible to establish as much as this in defense of most of the rules
most universally recognized by Common Sense. . . . A similar
defense seems possible for most of the rules most universally enforced by legal sanctions, such as respect of property; and for
some of those most commonly recognized by Common Sense, such
as industry, temperance and the keeping of promises. . . . These
rules, since they can be recommended as a means to that which is
itself only a necessary condition for the existence of any great
good, can be defended independently of correct views upon the
primary ethical question of what is good in itself. On any view
commonly taken, it seems certain that the preservation of civilized

society, which these rules are necessary to effect, is necessary for
the existence, in any great degree, of anything which may be held
to be good in itself.

G. E. Moore is surely the forerunner of professionalism in
modern ethics, of that technical rationality in the philosophical
realm which examines the right and the good in all their propositional forms, logical, grammatical, and rhetorical, without the
slightest obligation to affirm any single value or assert any moral
imperative. But even abstract, technical rationality has its sociological meaning. *Principia Ethica* too has its pretentions to impersonality, its rejection of the obligation to embrace casuistry,
and yet no work in contemporary philosophy could be more
clearly interpreted as an unconscious repository of social values. In
the quotation above are, I think, artlessly and unknowingly embedded (as in one of those blocks of transparent amber in which
ancient insects have been flawlessly preserved since the ice age) all
those values of Moore's Victorian childhood and Edwardian
youth: "respect for property," "industry," "temperance," and
"the keeping of promises." But what is even more striking here is
that tenacious provincialism (not unreinforced by Cambridge)
which sees in the localized virtues of the bourgeois British nineteenth century the permanent deliverances of "common sense,"
evolved through the ages as the very conditions for the preservation of civilized society itself.

It is notable that "common sense" always has for Moore that
kind of preferential solidity, of ultimate dependability, which was
so suspect to the skeptical rationality of the eighteenth century. In
the last section of the *Critique of Pure Reason*, "The Discipline of
Pure Reason," Kant sets within historical perspective his own
efforts in the direction of "Enlightenment."

Prior to our own transcendental criticism it was considered
better (since that principle could not be surrendered) boldly to
appeal to the common sense of mankind—an expedient which
always is a sign that the cause of reason is in desperate straits.

Moore's moral appeal to the common sense of mankind may not
be a sign that the cause of reason is in desperate straits, but it
surely reflects essentially the same institutional conservatism
found in Edmund Burke (also in opposition to the critical rationalism shared with Kant by Bentham, Voltaire, and Hume), although in Moore's case, I think, it is unconscious rather than

deliberate. Yet, paradoxically, this conservatism issues in an underwriting of *moral rules* hardly less stringent than that found in
Kant. "It seems then," says Moore,

> that with regard to any rule which is *generally* useful, we may
> assert that it ought *always* to be observed, not on the ground
> that in *every* particular case it will be useful, but on the ground
> that in *any* particular case, the probability of its being so is
> greater than that of our being likely to decide rightly that we
> have before us an instance of its disutility. In short, though we
> may be sure that there are cases where the rule should be
> broken, we can never know which those cases are, and ought,
> therefore, never to break it. It is this fact which seems to justify
> the stringency with which moral rules are usually enforced
> and sanctioned. . . . The individual can therefore be
> confidently recommended *always* to conform to rules which
> are both generally useful and generally practiced.

The recommendation to conform to rules of common sense and
social establishment is a rigorously conservative requirement, especially since the recommendation is *consciously* made independently of any correct perception of the nature of ultimate values.
And it is somewhat as if this chapter 5 of *Principia Ethica*, "Ethics
in Relation to Conduct," serves as a kind of practical safety
device; a guarantee that social order shall be preserved and
morality continued, even as the chapters which preceded dealt
with abstract moral criticism, and the chapter which follows is to
assert an "unworldly" and idiosyncratic outline of moral value.
And it is slightly reminiscent of Descartes, early in the *Discourse
on Method* and the *Meditations*, asserting his "provisional morality" in order that life shall go on and the social structure be
preserved, whatever the dangerous conclusions of an astringent
and dissolving reason.

When *Principia Ethica* was first published, it was a bombshell
and a revelation—not yet to professional ethicists, but to those
members of the Apostles and a small group of friends in King's
College and Trinity College, Cambridge, for whom its insights
into the nature of intrinsic value came as the validation of their
own intuitions—in fact, as the codification of their own way of
life. On 7 October 1903, John Maynard Keynes wrote to B.
Swithinbank: "I have just been reading Moore's *Principia Ethica*, which has been out a few days—a stupendous and entranc-
ing work, *the greatest* on the subject." It is doubtful if Keynes
and his friends were overly impressed by the naturalistic fallacy.

And it is certain that they skimmed over and ignored the conventional rule-orientation of chapter 5. But the Bible and the
holy scripture of this little group was chapter 6, "The Ideal,"
where Moore presented with conviction and clarity his own "self-
evident intuitions about the nature of intrinsic value — "of those
kinds of things which ought to exist for their own sakes."

In the light of this early judgment by some of Moore's closest personal friends at Cambridge, it is almost incredible how little subsequent attention has been paid to it by professional ethicists themselves. It is as if *Principia Ethica* had only five chapters and the
last had never been written. Later moral theorists have been so
obsessed by the magic of the naturalistic fallacy that they have
forgotten that it is in a consideration of "The Ideal" that moral
philosophy finds its culmination. For "professionals" and "amateurs" alike it is more important to know what is of intrinsic
value than merely where the moral theories of Mill, Sidgwick,
and Kant have gone astray. Moore himself, I think, knew this
even if his successors did not, but *that* they did not is in large
part his own responsibility. For in the end chapter 6 of *Principia
Ethica* is a failure, and it is perhaps a dim recognition of this
which has made it easier for Moore's successors to lose sight of
the substantive task of moral philosophy and rest content with
emulating the critical brillance which the first four chapters of
Principia Ethica so admirably express.

Chapter 6 of *Principia Ethica* is principally concerned with
answering the question: What things have intrinsic value, and in
what degree? And the method Moore uses to come to his conclusions in these matters has already been announced in chapter
3 — it is the famous "principle of isolation." "In order to arrive at
a correct decision . . . it is necessary to consider what things are
such that, if they existed *by themselves*, in absolute isolation, we
should yet judge their existence to be good; and, in order to
decide upon the relative *degrees* of value of different things, we
must similarly consider what comparative value seems to attach
to the isolated existence of each." I do not wish to criticize this
method directly, but rather will let it stand or fall by its fruits.
For we are now upon the threshold of Moore's deepest insights
into intrinsic value — insights which we may rightly call the very
keystone or heart of the entire edifice of *Principia Ethica*.

If now, we use this method of absolute isolation, it appears that
the question we have to answer is far less difficult than the

controversies of Ethics might have led us to expect. Indeed, once the meaning of the question is clearly understood, the answer to it, in its main outlines, appears to be so obvious, that it runs the risk of seeming to be a platitude. By far the most valuable things, which we know or can imagine, are certain states of consciousness, which may be roughly described as *the pleasures of human intercourse* and *the enjoyment of beautiful objects*. No one, probably, who has asked himself the question, has ever doubted that personal affection and the appreciation of what is beautiful in Art or Nature, are good in themselves; nor, if we consider strictly what things are worth having purely for their own sakes, does it appear probable that any one will think anything else has nearly so great a value as the things which are included under these two heads. [Italics added]

Moore goes on to state the consequences that follow from this intuition of the two basic intrinsic values: that it is *only* for the sake of these things that anyone can be justified in performing any public or private duty, or that the virtues exist, and that these two values are not only the rational ultimate end of all human action, but also the *sole* criterion of social progress.

I think that we may now at last understand what Moore meant in his Preface where he warned that his conclusions with respect to intrinsic value would be "very different from any which have commonly been advocated by philosophers," and we can be little short of dumbfounded when he now tells us that his conclusion "appears to be so obvious that it runs the risk of seeming to be a platitude." That "personal affections" and "aesthetic enjoyments" are values, even intrinsic values of great importance, no one, I think, would be prepared to question, but that "they include *all* the greatest, and *by far* the greatest goods we can imagine" is a claim so preposterous that I think we must explain how the youthful Moore ever came to assert it. The answer is twofold, one aspect being local, the other of general nineteenth-century cultural concern: it lies, on the one hand, in the elitist aestheticism of Edwardian Cambridge, and on the other in the general crisis in the assessment of Victorian moral values which came to a head in England sometime around the turn of the nineteenth century.

Is it really the case that "the pleasures of human intercourse" are so much more valuable than "the pleasure of human solitude?" Or that "the *enjoyment* of beautiful objects" is so much more valuable than "the *creation* of beautiful objects?" Or, putting the two together, it is now absolutely and unambiguously clear that the first pair of states of consciousness possess more intrinsic value than the second: that a life of human intercourse and aesthetic appreciation is "intrinsically better" than a life of solitude and artistic creation? I do not think so; nor indeed do I think it will appear indubitable and self-evident to every rational self.

In speaking of the pleasures of human intercourse and the enjoyment of beautiful objects as *the only things* worth having for their own sakes, chapter 6 of *Principia Ethica* exhibits a certain almost inexplicable *value blindness*. For it says nothing of the many other "very greatest goods" which one *can* imagine: the joy of communion with the divine of a Saint Francis or a Saint John of the Cross, the joy of active leadership in a great moral cause like that of Ghandi or Albert Schweitzer, the joy of difficult problem-solving and intellectual contemplation of a Newton or an Aristotle. But this is only to say that whereas Moore is explicitly sensitive to social and to aesthetic values, he is here in *Principia Ethica* neglectful of religious and moral and intellectual ones. And it is this neglect and insensitivity, I think, which, translated into false and partial conclusions, demonstrates the ultimate inadequacy of Moore's moral method. For the mentality which supports a doctrine of moral self-evidence is not likely to be patient in its detailed attention to the nuances of the realm of values or interested in the scrupulous comparison of the varieties of value which experience comprehends, and the mind which is more technically interested in the method to be pursued than in the correct answer to the moral question is not likely to advance our progress through its valuational sensitivity.

Moore's espousal in *Principia Ethica* of the intrinsic values of personal affection and aesthetic enjoyment is the immediate translation of "the aesthetic way of life" practiced by the brilliant group of Cambridge undergraduates of which we have previously spoken, which was to become a few years later the intimate circle of Bloomsbury, including Lytton Strachey, Virginia Woolf, Vanessa Bell, Duncan Grant, Clive Bell, Leonard Woolf, Roger Frye, E. M. Forster, David Garnet, Lowes Dickinson, John Maynard Keynes, and Arthur Waley. Leonard Woolf speaks of the nature of the Cambridge group from 1899 to 1904 as follows:

We were intellectuals, intellectuals with three genuine and, I think, profound passions: a passion for friendship, a passion for literature and music, a passion for what we called the truth.

And John Maynard Keynes corroborates this picture in faithful detail:

The appropriate subjects of passionate contemplation were a beloved person, beauty and truth, and one's prime objects in life were love, the creation and enjoyment of aesthetic experience and the pursuit of knowledge. Of these love came a long way first. But in the early days under Moore's influence the public treatment of this and its associated acts was, on the whole, austere and platonic.

Moore's most important contribution to ethics—the doctrine of the indefinability of good, and the intuitionism upon which this rests—seemed to this Cambridge circle (who, as I have said, appear not to have read chapter 5 of *Principia Ethica* with care) to imply that decisions about what is good (and also what is good to do) depend upon direct personal intuition in each individual case. For Moore himself, as chapter 5 of *Principia Ethica* clearly shows, these doctrines were mediated by the customary imperatives of society and the *rules of traditional morality,* embodying the intuitions of the wise throughout the ages. But at Cambridge, in the inner circle of Woolf, Keynes, and Strachey, it was interpreted as a fairly free license to judge all things individually and anew. Thus, ironically, the popularity of *Principia Ethica* among this group, and their feelings that (as Keynes said) it meant the dawn of a renaissance and the beginning of a new dispensation in morals and in life, was based upon a complete misreading—a crucial misunderstanding of how essentially conservative the treatise really was! For Moore's idiosyncratic and unworldly concentration on these two particular forms of good— personal intimacy and aesthetic experience—was possible only within the framework of a secure society, where other goods like trust, and obligation, and social responsibility were presupposed; just as that elite, aesthetic existence of "those happy few" at King's and Trinity in 1903, itself presupposed the security, good order, and public safety of a peaceful and a prosperous British Empire.

Thirty-five years later, when he was fifty-five, Keynes himself, now economist, statesman, and famous public figure, recognized the aesthetic narrowness, the essential unreality of *Principia Ethica*'s attributions of intrinsic value:

I read again last week Moore's famous chapter on "The Ideal." It is remarkable how wholly oblivious he managed to be of the qualities of the life of action and also of the pattern of life as a whole. He was existing in a timeless ecstasy. His way of translating his own particular emotions of the moment into the language of generalized abstraction is a charming and beautiful comedy.

But by this time Keynes had already recognized the essential shallowness of his former self, and of his brilliant companions of those faraway Cambridge days. "I can see us," he says, "as water-spiders, gracefully skimming, as light and reasonable as air, the surface of the stream without any contact at all with the eddies and currents underneath." Chapter 6 of *Principia Ethica* also seems the valuational conclusions of a water spider, "gracefully skim-ming, as light and reasonable as air" the surface of the social stream, with little , if any, contact with the darker eddies and more ambiguous currents of the moral life.

Sir Roy Harrod, John Maynard Keynes's biographer, sustains the verdict of his subject in an editorial aside. "Moore's book," he said,

only comprises a fragment of the moral story. If his ideals are to retain their place, they must be integrated into a wider philosophy, which, while doing honor to them, would have something more adequate to say about the nature and rationale of the social obligations on which a civilized society rests.

There is surely some truth to this, and yet it too does not pay sufficient tribute to the content of Moore's reflections "Ethics in Relation to Conduct," which constitute *Principia Ethica*, chapter 5. For the fact is that the confrontation of chapter 5 with chapter 6 constitutes a dialectical opposition which is not merely peculiar to Moore's mentality, but reflects a crisis in the very nature of British society itself. "When in the grim, grey, rainy January days of 1901 Queen Victoria lay dying," says Leonard Woolf in his autobiography,

we already felt that we were living in an era of incipient revolt and that we ourselves were mortally involved in this revolt against a social system and code of conduct and morality, which, for convenience sake, may be referred to as bourgeoise Victorianism.

Swinburne and Bernard Shaw, and to some extent, Samuel But-ler, Thomas Hardy, and H. G. Wells were the agents of this revolt, but it had also had earlier roots. For in some sense *the moral way of life*, exemplified in Mill and Carlyle, and Matthew

Arnold (which, even where it castigated the philistinism of Victorian virtue, yet unconsciously emulated its moral seriousness) was opposed as a matter of principle by *the aesthetic way of life* advocated by Ruskin, Pater, and to some extent Oscar Wilde. The "moral way" came to have the flavor of a musty and moribund conservatism, whereas the "aesthetic way" was associated not only with the waywardness of self-determination but with artistic values of such individuality as to be almost synonymous with personal license. At the turn of the century the death of the queen could symbolize the unsuspected fragility of institutional forces and the possible triumph of aesthetic revolt. In an inner inconsistency not previously remarked, Moore's *Principia Ethica* seems to me in chapter 5 to conservatively assert the old moral claims of institutionalized wisdom, whereas in chapter 6 is to be found the momentary possibility of a utopianly motivated aesthetic revolt sublimated into an intuition of intrinsic value.

But if I am correct in my assessment, it is the Moore of chapter 5, the social conservative, who most conspicuously represents the stance of the ethicist in an age of professionalism, where the rigors of the technical task seem to absolve the moral philosopher of substantive responsibility. Moore's early venture into normative ethics (in *Principia Ethica,* chapter 6) quickly faded away. From 1911 to 1942 such thinking as Moore did in moral philosophy was in analytical ethics, influenced largely by Prichard and Ross, and there are no subsequent pronouncements in the area of intrinsic values. The early venture in this domain had been made while Moore was very young, and at Cambridge—influenced, as might be any amateur, by an undergraduate way of life and by the earnest conversations about ultimate values among intimate friends. As Moore grew older, and his professional life as a teacher of philosophy began to dominate his perceptions, his relations with his contemporaries grew more distant, and his relations with his own students, although infinitely cordial, never trespassed on the grounds of intimate feeling and personal philosophy. In all the years of the "conversation class" and the "at homes," technical questions and clarification dominated the discussions. No one seems to have asked the respected master to state or justify the value preferences which sustained his own life.

But there is one thing more. *Principia Ethica* might easily have been given the subtitle of Thomas Mann's famous work of

1918, *Betrachtungen eines Unpolitischen—Reflections of an Unpolitical Man.* For in one sense both Keynes and Harrod are
surely right. *Principia Ethica* is oblivious to the life of action, to
the nature and rationale of social obligations, to that intimate
relationship between ethics and politics about which Moore's
master Sidgwick had some very trenchant things to say, and
which has been a commonplace since the treatises of Aristotle.
For the "unworldliness" of *Principia Ethica* derives not only from
its nonnatural theory of value, which removes values and obligations from the living matrix of natural societies into a timeless
Platonic realm of abstract concepts, but also from a natively
"unpolitical" sense of life.

Moore's philosophical professionalism is based upon a concentration unhampered by passionate political concern. Moore took
no active part in politics. Before 1918 he would, perhaps, have
called himself an Asquithian Liberal, but after the Liberal party
fell, during the interwar period, he voted with Labor like Russell, but without Russell's passionate conviction. And despite his
enormous unconscious sympathy with social order, in the choice
which Liberals faced after 1918 Moore always mildly favored
Labor, never the Conservatives. It is perhaps significant that the
Moores always took the *Manchester Guardian*, never the *Times*.
Before the outbreak of the Second World War, Moore was briefly a supporter of the Republican side in the Spanish Civil War,
and Casimir Lewy remembers that once, in the autumn of 1936,
Moore attended a public meeting to advance the Spanish Republican cause. But these episodes reflect the times rather' than
Moore's temperament. In essence he remained "an unpolitical
man," and his moral theory reflects this quality; some will think
as its greatest weakness, but others perhaps as its greatest strength.

The Professional Epistemologist

In some respects, it can perhaps be said that of all the parts of
philosophy, epistemology is the most "professional" division.
Logic is technical, but it is akin to mathematics; metaphysics too
has important relation to the natural sciences, and ethics is of
interest to all who have experience with human society and individual conduct. The contrast between a Platonic dialogue like
the *Phaedrus* and one like the *Theaetetus* is unmistakable, and it
is exemplified again and again in the history of philosophy—in
the contrast between Aristotle's *De anima* and his *Nicomachean
Ethics,* in Hume's *Treatise* and his *Dialogues concerning Natural*

Religion, in Kant's *Critique of Pure Reason* and his *Metaphysic of Morals.* But in G. E. Moore this contrast is hardly to be remarked. His ethics and his epistemology are in form and ultimate aim almost identical, and one reads them both not as substantive philosophical pronouncements but as examples of a common method of philosophical clarification and analysis.

The consequence is that to one experienced in the tradition of classical epistemology, Moore is a very unsatisfactory epistemologist indeed. One comes away from Hume's *Treatise* with a very clear picture of the ground rules of epistemological skepticism, and from long study of the *Critique of Pure Reason* with a structure that is difficult, but worked out in such brilliant detail that its form remains fixed in the mind like a monument of granite. But after reading all of Moore's major epistemological papers (such as "The Refutation of Idealism" of 1903; "The Nature and Reality of Objects of Perception" of 1905-6; the chapters on "Sense-Data" and "Ways of Knowing" in *Some Main Problems of Philosophy* of 1910-11; "Some Judgments of Perception" of 1918-19; "A Defense of Common Sense" of 1925; and the "Proof of an External World" of 1939), the total substantive impression is of quicksand beneath one's feet. One remembers the fixed elements along the way: those concepts like "sense data," "internal images," "acts of perception," "sensibles," "external facts," "material objects," "the surfaces of material objects," and so on, but *no firm theory ever emerges.* From time to time one does get a certain sense of the epistemological *possibilities* implicit in the relationship of sense-data to material objects, as in "The Defense of Common Sense," where Moore distinguishes what we know from the terminology of others to be "representationalism," "direct realism," and "phenomenalism"; but arguments for and against each of these three possibilities (and others) studded Moore's Cambridge lectures for many years, and, although more of the position of "direct realism" is to be found in his published writings than of the other two options, nothing fixed, final, and definitive ever emerges. Braithwaite has suggested why.

One reason why Moore, in his prime of life, never wrote a book on perception (or indeed on anything else) is, I suspect, that he saw the reasons against any view so clearly that he could never make up his mind which was on the whole the most defensible, especially since he was ingenious in recasting every theory into its least objectionable form.

One consequence of this eternal openness to new analytical

results is that Moore was not only constantly investigating what the epistemological views of other philosophers could mean and whether they were true (as in "Professor James' 'Pragmatism' " of 1907, and "Hume's Philosophy" of 1909), but a considerable amount of permanent skepticism was directed toward his own previous views—as if, by a curious dissociation of personality or suspension of personal identity, they had been uttered by some one else. Miss Stebbing cites an example:

> At a symposium of the Aristotelian Society, on "Internal Relations," the two symposiasts based their remarks on Moore's well-known paper on that subject. Moore expressed genuine surprise that they should do so. He expressed himself as unable to understand what he could *possibly* have meant by the views he had previously stated, and was quite convinced that they were wrong.

This may be admirable in its candor and fluidity, but it is exasperating when the task is not simply to portray the philosopher in the steady pursuit of *methodical questioning and clarification,* but in *the achievement of results.* The only way to portray a Socrates is to have a dramatic genius like Plato for a disciple; but even the Platonic dialogues reveal a body of substantive doctrine as well as a dialectical method. But in considering the body of Moore's epistemological writings as a whole, one chief difficulty emerges: there truly seems to be no distinct and ascertainable development of his epistemological beliefs. And this difficulty is only compounded by the fact that the papers vary in their assertoric weight. Some are relatively explicit and assured. In others the answers he advances are extremely tentative and provisional. And in still others he is explicit and assured in repudiating positions he had previously been explicit and assured in asserting, now finding them doubtful, if not downright false. No Ariadne's thread provides the way out of this epistemological maze.

But there is another possibility for approaching the matter—to seek in Moore's epistemology not fixed dogmas but *directions*; not a permanent content of epistemological belief, but certain *tendencies* or *habits of procedure.* And if we proceed this way, I think we can distinguish three. (1) The general *tendency* of Moore's epistemology is to be "realistic." (2) His major *criterion* for the adequacy of epistemological propositions is that they be in conformity with "common sense." (3) The major *aim* of his epistemological investigations is to achieve analytic "clarity" in philosophical belief. About each of these a word or two should be said.

It is obvious that there is an extremely close relationship between (1) and (2). For the natural epistemology of common sense
is a kind of "naive" realism which knows that the world is furnished with "things"—that is to say, natural objects—and that we
perceive them with our "minds," which, if they are not physical
objects, are at least "attached" to our bodies and our brains. Over
the years Moore's attention shifted somewhat from the espousal of
(1) to the espousal of (2), that is to say, from a direct advocacy of
epistemological realism to a defense of common sense; but this is a
change of formulation, not of belief.

It must, of course, be remembered that as an undergraduate at
Cambridge, Moore's concern with philosophy began with a keen
interest in "certain philosophical statements which I heard made,"
and that from the beginning what troubled him was the unclarity,
if not absurdity, he detected in these utterances. Moore's first
philosophic passion was aroused by the existence of philosophic
"muddle" and philosophic "nonsense." But it must also be remembered that Moore's undergraduate years at Cambridge
(1892-96) saw a great flowering of philosophical Idealism—chiefly at Oxford, to be sure, but also at Cambridge with McTaggart—
and it was in this atmosphere of Idealistic conversation and dialectic that Moore was first moved by an indignation almost phys-
ically painful against the "monstrosity" of Idealistic statements
about mind and about the world. It is therefore not at all surprising that in 1903, the same year in which *Principia Ethica* appeared, Moore published in *Mind* "The Refutation of Idealism"—an
article which was to win him almost as great a reputation in
epistemology as the former did in moral philosophy. Here, ten
years later, was a sober repudiation of all the Idealist claims which
had plagued his Cambridge days. It was characteristically entitled
"The Refutation of Idealism" rather than "The Defense of Realism." Moore's positive beliefs were most often implied in his
attacks.

Modern Idealism, says Moore, if it asserts anything, asserts that
the universe is *spiritual*. And it seems to mean by this that physical
objects like tables and chairs are not as lifeless and unconscious as
they seem to be, but are somehow a part of a nonmechanical,
intelligent, purposeful totality. This makes the world from the
Idealist point of view very different than it commonly seems to be,
containing properties we do not commonly find it to have. But the
metaphysical statements about the *world*, he thinks, somehow
depend upon epistemological statements about *how we know the*

world. Belief that matter is of the nature of mind depends upon the assimilation of matter to mental acts. The whole of his essay is therefore devoted to a refutation of the Idealistic argument made famous by Berkeley: *esse est percipi*—whatever exists is experienced; things *are* mental perceptions. But the error of this is simple. There are minds and there are objects, and minds perceive objects. But the perceptions which are *of* the objects are clearly *not* the objects, for if the object of the Idealist's sensations were, as he supposes, *not* the object, but merely the *content* of that sensation, no Idealist could ever be aware of himself or of any other real thing. The crucial point is to understand that "awareness" of an object is neither the object nor the condition of its existence. Thus "matter" exists as well as "spirit." And "things" exist independently of "minds."

When, therefore, Berkeley supposed that the only thing of which I am directly aware is my own sensations and ideas, he supposed what was false; and when Kant supposed that the objectivity of things in space *consisted* in the fact that they were "Vorstellungen" having to one another different relations from those which the same "Vorstellungen" have to one another in subjective experience, he supposed what was equally false. I am as directly aware of the existence of material things in space as of my own sensations; and *what* I am aware of with regard to each is exactly the same—namely that in one case the material thing, and in the other case my sensation does really exist.

Moore's article "The Nature and Reality of Objects of Perception" of 1905-6 and his "Hume's Philosophy" of 1909 only apply to other cognate problems the explicit Realism of "The Refutation of Idealism." The first deals chiefly with the issue of solipsism: How do we *know* that anything exists except our own perceptions? How do we *know* that other people exist who have sensations similar to ours? And more philosophically: What *reason* do we have for our belief in other persons? The second deals with Hume's skepticism: his doubt that we can *know* any matters of fact which are not the object of direct observation, his claim that we cannot *prove* any real causal connection of objects and events, his belief that "custom" and "habit" are the *only* foundations of true belief. And in both essays, whatever the sophistication of the analytic procedure, the refutation itself reduces always to dogmatic assertion. We *do* know of the existence not only of other persons, but also of the movements of matter in space. The only proof that we know external facts, and indeed facts of external causal relations, lies in the simple fact that we *do* know them.

In both of these essays two very interesting facts emerge. The problems of solipsism, of the existence of other minds, of the nonexistence of genuine causal connections, are philosopher's problems, and as such their puzzle and their perplexity has a certain artificiality. They are not only at variance with what "the common man" believes, but even philosophers themselves cannot believe them and *act* consistently with these beliefs at all times. This is true both of Berkeley's solipsism and of Hume's extreme skepticism, and it raises the very serious question whether these violations of common sense have any claim to legitimacy even as "philosophical" propositions. In "Hume's Philosophy" Moore says:

> The philosopher may believe, when he is philosophizing, that no man knows of the existence of any other man or of any material object; but at other times he will inevitably believe, as we all do, that he does know of the existence of this man and of that, and even of this and that material object. There can, therefore, be no question of making all our beliefs consistent with such views as this, of never believing anything that is inconsistent with them. . . . It is worth while to consider whether they are views which we ought to hold as philosophical opinions, even if it be quite certain that we shall never be able to make the views which we entertain at other times consistent with them. And it is the more worth while because the question how we can prove or disprove such extreme views as these, has a bearing on the question how we can, in any case whatever, prove or disprove that we do really *know* what we suppose ourselves to know.

What is important here is not only the distinction between "philosopher's problems" and "ordinary beliefs," but the insight that in matters of proof, the second have priority over the first. This insight provides the link through which Moore can combine the insistence upon epistemological Realism with a "Defense of Common Sense."

The famous "Defense of Common Sense" of 1925 — which Murphy called "one of the few really decisive contributions to philosophical enlightenment which this century has given us," and for whose theme Malcolm believes Moore owes his chief claim to be remembered in the history of philosophy — sums up the principal doctrines of his epistemology; but it had long been a tenet of his thinking that "common sense" provides the iron-clad criterion against which our epistemological propositions are to be tested. This is implicit in his early epistemological articles, and it is expressly stated in *Some Main Problems of Philosophy*—the lectures of 1910-11. Moore begins these lectures by submitting a series of propositions which belong to common sense, and he states at once the reason why he thinks it important to do so:

And I wish to begin by describing these views, because it seems to me that what is most amazing and most interesting about the views of many philosophers, is the way in which they go beyond or positively contradict the views of Common Sense: they profess to know that there are in the Universe most important kinds of things, which Common Sense does not profess to know of, and also they profess to know that there are *not* in the Universe . . . things of the existence of which Common Sense is most sure. I think, therefore, you will best realise what these philosophical descriptions of the Universe really mean, by realising how very different they are from the views of Common Sense — how far, in some points, they go beyond Common Sense, and how absolutely, in others, they contradict it. I wish, therefore to begin by describing what I take to be the most important views of Common Sense: things which we all commonly assume to be true about the Universe, and which we are sure that we know to be true about it.

The series of propositions he presents includes the following: The universe contains an enormous number of natural objects such as our own bodies, the bodies of other men, plants, stones, minerals, and so on, as well as objects made by men such as chairs, tables, engines, books, and the like. It also contains another class of things which we call "minds" with their numerous acts of consciousness: sensing, judging, feeling, desiring, loving, hating, and so forth. We believe that material objects always exist somewhere in space, that they can and do continue to exist even when we are not conscious of them, and that they are therefore independent of our consciousness. The universe which common sense describes, and in which Moore implicitly believes, is spatiotemporally situated, dualistic, and objectively real. It is the universe of classical naturalism, Cartesian dualism, and scientific realism. But it is not for these technical philosophical reasons that Moore defends it, but because it is the deliverance of that sturdy and dogged common sense which all men share.

Moore understands perfectly well that there are certain critical problems connected with common sense—that it is variable and seems to be related to the scientific knowledge of its time. But what Moore unfortunately does not do is provide a detailed consideration of the relationship of the "common sense" current in any age to the refined scientific theory of its period. For this might have had the consequence of weakening the "universality" and "objectivity" of common sense as an epistemological criterion. I think that when Kant said that to appeal to the common sense of mankind is always a sign that the cause of reason is in desperate straits, this was one of the things he had in mind.

But although Moore appeals to common sense, it must not be thought that he does so with the philosophical naivete of the "man in the street." On the contrary, although he avoids philosophical professionalism in the Kantian sense (being temperamentally repelled by system, and avoiding when possible all resources of technical vocabulary), the arguments in which he utilizes common sense are complicated, highly sophisticated, and technically exact. In his hands, therefore, the appeal to common sense is not the reduction of philosophy to amateurism, but, on the contrary, a highly professional accomplishment. No "man in the street" ever dealt with Moore's problems, for, howevermuch he scorned reconditc and "unbelievable" solutions, Moore's problems too are philosopher's problems; and if, in contrast to Kant, he wrote in the plainest possible English, going to great pains to explain his meanings in the common language of everyday life, no one would ever mistake his meticlous philosophical analysis for philosophical amateurism. His appeal to common sense was not aimed *to outlaw* the practice of philosophy (as were so many of the enterprises of Wittgenstein), or to restore it to the amateur, but *to change its professional practice in the direction of increasing simplicity and intelligibility.*

Professionalism and the Modern World:
The Triumph of Method

The philosophy of G. E. Moore symbolizes the triumph of method as philosophic achievement. For, as we have seen, the substantive results of his years of philosophizing are meager indeed. Yet his influence upon his colleagues and his students has been literally overwhelming. Never in the history of philosophy have *results* counted so little. Never have the passion for clarity and the interest in the practice of analysis for its own sake been so enthroned in the philosophical consciousness. Method has, of course, been an enduring preoccupation throughout the history of philosophy, but it has previously been conceived of as a tool for discovering the *truth* and unraveling the secrets of the universe. The dialectical

method of Plato was meant to secure access to the realm of values
which would indicate how men and societies ought to live. The
Scholastic method of Saint Thomas was meant to demonstrate in
the language of reason the details of the Divine Will. The skeptical method of Descartes was meant to sift the sands of traditional
belief in order to discover the rock upon which the new sciences
could be founded. But in Moore the motivation is neither moral,
religious, nor scientific. It is sui generis. It is no longer a question
of the end justifying the means. The means *are* the end!

Yet there is a paradox here. Although everyone agrees that the
method of analysis is the center of Moore's philosophical enterprise, no one quite knows how to define it, or describe it, or deal
with it discursively. Moore himself, in the few pages he devotes to
"Philosophical Method: Analysis" in his "Reply to My Critics" in
the Schilpp volume, is very vague and unsatisfactory. He does
make it clear that his analysis is always meant to be of "an idea or
concept or proposition, and not of a mere verbal expression," and
that it always attempts to define a concept, not a word, but about
how his *definition* of a concept differs from classical strategies of
definition (as it clearly does) he has nothing to say.

Others have succeeded little better. Alan White writes:

Moore's main interest lies in investigating neither the *truth* nor
the *meaning* of statements of ordinary life . . . which as such
he believes to have a well-known meaning and to be in many
cases certainly true, but in giving an *analysis* of their meaning.
He investigates the views of other philosophers to see what these
views could mean and whether they are true, because they are
often attempted analyses whose results deny the commonly accepted truth and meaning of what they analyse.

It is true that Moore has spent much of his life discovering and
pointing out the confusions into which other philosophers have
fallen, and trying to determine "what they mean," but his theory
of meaning is unorthodox and quixotic, since he believes that the
question "whether we understand a meaning" is entirely different
from the question "whether we *know what it means* in the sense
that we are able *to give a correct analysis* of its meaning." What
exactly "a correct analysis" of any meaning meant for Moore is a
mystery, and since he was so meticulous in his analytic demands,
so uncompromising in his quest for exactitude, his results are
scandalously inconclusive. No one has pointed up the paradox
better than his great admirer, Morton White.

Because he was so cautious about saying that one expression meant the same as another, Moore seemed to be left with a set of unanalyzable concepts in one hand, and in the other a set of concepts about whose analysis he was never certain. The result was that one of the greatest philosophical analysts of our age found it hard to point, in all honesty, to a single successful analysis of an important philosophical idea.

If this were all that could be said, the admission would be devastating. But Morris Lazerowitz has perhaps seen best the two criteria which govern Moore's "clarificatory analysis." One of Moore's chief aims is to bring to light hidden contradictions in philosophical theories. Another is to bring philosophical theories into direct confrontation with matters of fact for the purpose of testing their truth value. "For this Moore used a technique which he called 'translation into the concrete.' A philosophical view which on translation into the concrete turned out to be inconsistent with a truism of Common Sense was condemned as an unquestionable falsehood." Internal contradiction and incompatibility with the deliverances of common sense are thus the two criteria utilized in Moore's analytical method.

But even this insight is in the end only an approximation. For it remains true for any great philosopher (whether a Socrates or a Plato, a Moore or a Wittgenstein) that there is a mystique of method illustrated not in its description or in its preaching, but only in its practice. No text can recapture the Socratic genius in action. Moore's method remains embalmed in the philosophical papers he published, but it has eternal life in the living memory of those who were spectators in his Cambridge classroom or participants in the meetings of the Aristotelian Society where his presence was so vitally felt.

I have said that the philosophy of G. E. Moore symbolizes the triumph of method as philosophical achievement. But it is certainly no accident of history that the reputation of Moore's analytic method has proved so influential to contemporary philosophy, for it is simply an expression of that professionalism which arose in the eighteenth century and has dominated philosophizing since the late nineteenth. Moore said in *Principia Ethica* that "the establishment of the fundamental principles of ethical reasoning, rather than of any conclusions which may be attained by their use" was his main object. And the sentiment only echoes Kant. In section 3 of his *Introduction to Logic*, Kant had also said: "We must, therefore, for the sake of exercise in independent thought or philosophizing, look more to the *method* of employment of reason than to the propositions themselves, at which we have arrived by its means." But the emphasis of method over content, of technique over substantive results, is only one consequence of that *déformation professionnelle* which has produced the doctor's doctor, the lawyer's lawyer, and the philosopher's philosopher.

It is perhaps a little unfair to speak here of a professional "deformity," for what we have again is only the consequence of a general cultural situation. Social fragmentation and an extensive division of labor breed increasing specialization. The gentleman and the saint are in firm possession of values which are in their nature of great generality, and which govern not only "occupation," but citizenship, moral obligation, and family life as well. But *the professional ideal* is the fruit of specialization— it is the product of technology in the moral and spiritual order, as industrialization is the product of technology in the material order; and its range is comparably limited.

But there is one thing more. The fragmentation of Western culture, discernible since the dissolution of the medieval synthesis, has meant not only increasing secularization but a shrinkage in the domain of shared (and assured) values. And in almost every area of the cultural spectrum this has stimulated the development of a virtuosity of style and technique to compensate for an impoverishment of assured belief. This holds not only for philosophy— for a Moore, a Wittgenstein, and a Quine—but for the arts and literature as well: for a Joyce, a Pound, and a Gertrude Stein, for a Mondrian, a Jackson Pollock, and a DeKooning, and for a Schönberg, a Webern, and a Stockhausen. In every domain and branch of culture we are confronted by *the triumph of technique over content*.

But for philosophy proper, the characteristics of a professional age are, I think, three: (1) a concern with the *procedural* rather than the substantive—a care for *methods* rather than results; (2) a *specialization* of interest rather than a general cultural concern, so that much devotion is lavished upon the perfection of professional *tools*—upon logic, technical vocabulary and symbolism, and analytic method; and (3) modes of communication which have become adjusted to the *needs of a professional elite*—careful departmentalization within the university, local and national philosophical associations, periodic world congresses, and a limited number of reputable professional journals with a narrowly restricted audience.

These can only be seen as general tendencies: certainly not as cultural rules without exception. For example, the relationship between (1) and (2), between concern for method and narrowing of vision, although probable, is neither universal nor necessary. A recognition of the primacy of methodological considerations in philosophy can, but need not, lead to a narrowing of cultural focus, and a progressive disinterest in substantive problems of metaphysical doctrine, aesthetic measure, and moral and political concern. Certain philosophers of the first half of this century like Santayana, Bergson, Whitehead, and Dewey have not found it necessary to sacrifice breadth of orientation to exclusively methodological concern. But then both Bergson and Santayana were atypical—men lightly associated with university life, who in the end made themselves independent of its rigorous professionalism. And Dewey and later Whitehead, though always conscious of the fundamental importance of logical theory, were yet too deeply involved by background and temperament in the immediate problems of contemporary society and the valuational dilemmas of modern civilization as a whole to invert the relationship between the establishment of the conditions of rationality and its substantive use.

Yet these philosophers were influential a generation ago rather than today. They belong almost to a prepositivistic and a preanalytical period. And if G. E. Moore was in fact their contemporary, it is still his influence rather than theirs which has largely prevailed. For it is Moore and Wittgenstein, Carnap and Quine, J. L. Austin and Gilbert Ryle who so largely constitute the modern philosophic temper, who represent so clearly the nature of philosophic achievement in a professional age. It is for this reason that, forced by the definition of my enterprise to settle on a single figure, I have chosen G. E. Moore to represent "philosophy in the age of the professional."

Through this choice Moore is meant to provide a contrast with Plato, Saint Thomas, and Descartes which (I hope) illuminates not merely valences in philosophic style and temperament but also deeper variations in sociological presupposition and cultural need. The ambiences of post-Periclean Athens, medieval Paris, and seventeenth-century France and Holland, although they haunt our memory and even to some extent the pages of our histories of philosophy, are gone, never to return. And it is for this reason that the concept of "the isolated philosophical classic," and of the timeless debate of philosophic minds across the centuries, although it has its inevitable charm, and even its pedagogical utility, cannot stand against the reality of "dated thought" and the mute insistency of time.

Thus finally, though one may regret the absence of a Plato, an Aquinas, or a Descartes in the twentieth-century Anglo-American world, it is necessary to recognize the social conditions and the cultural situation which made a Plato, an Aquinas, or a Descartes possible. Neither Plato, Aquinas, nor Descartes lacked concern for the utilization of a rigorous method, and *dialectic, disputation,* and *doubt,* clearly formulated and vigorously applied, provided eminently suitable procedures for dealing with the respective problems of the Hellenic, the medieval, and the seventeenth-century situation. But in each case method was a means, not an end in itself.

Dialectic was for Plato the heart of that elitist education which, by guaranteeing access to true values, was to effect an aristocratic restoration in the Greek world. Scholastic method was for Aquinas that mold of reason which, whether in oral or written disputation, should cause God's truth to prevail within the organic community of medieval culture. Analysis (as opposed to synthesis), with its initial component of doubt, was for Descartes the organon which would permit the firm establishment of natural science, and hence its saving fruits of human technology and control for the aspiring early modern period. Only Moore, deeply cushioned within the peace of Cambridge, seems to have lacked the sense of social urgency — to have valued clarity as an intrinsic good in his professional life (if not in his moral theory), and to have obsessively pursued his own version of the method of philosophical analysis in splendid isolation from any specific considerations of societal, religious, or scientific need.

6

CONCLUSION
Philosophy's Historic Fate
Museum Pieces, Messages, and Classics

Philosophy, Mirror of Its Time: Summary

In emphasizing the nature of philosophy as "social expression," I have meant to consider my chosen examples: Plato, Saint Thomas, Descartes, and G. E. Moore not simply as philosophers, but as epoch-making and epoch-expressing figures; "culture images" as surely as a sculpture by Myron, a Madonna of Giotto, a Rembrandt portrait, or a drawing by Picasso. For—to follow a Spenglerian metaphor—it could almost be said that they work in the "expression medium" of philosophy as others worked in art, or politics, or science. Thus from this perspective it was important to at least partially delineate the surrounding culture of each—to briefly examine fourth-century Athens, medieval Paris, seventeenth-century Holland, and Edwardian and early twentieth-century Cambridge as *horizons* in which, respectively, politics, religion, science, and analysis loom large.

To view philosophic achievement as the cognitive correlate of a certain cultural "life-style," means to ask the questions: What sort of society was the author writing for? What were the conventions of communication current in his day? What were the philosopher's class affiliations, his place in the social hierarchy of his time? and perhaps most important of all, What were his ideals, his basic philosophic intentions? For in this mode of writing the history of philosophy, the elements of social context, semantic convention, class affiliation, and guiding motivation are dimensions in terms of which the philosophic texts are themselves to be construed. Thus Plato's *Republic* reveals what it *means* to philosophize like an aristocrat, the *Summa theologica* what it *means* to philosophize like a saint, the *Discourse on Method* what it *means* to philosophize like a gentleman, and *Some Main Problems of Philosophy* what it *means* to philosophize like a professional.

But whether or not one holds that there is a morphological relationship that inwardly binds together all the expression forms of a culture, there is a similar problem of unification for a culture and for a philosophy. For the thesis that every culture has its characteristic philosophy—a symbolic expression and a way of posing problems closely related to architecture and the other "arts of form"—has its analogue in the Hegelian effort to identify in any philosophy the fundamental themes which inform its diverse details and render them coherent. And if what is important here is less the range of answers than the choice of questions, then the fundamental nature of ancient, medieval, modern, and contemporary philosophy can best be recognized by identifying the root questions of their leading and their characteristic representatives. For the Platonic philosophy this question is: *How can aristocracy be restored?* For the Thomistic philosophy it is: *How can the Roman church prevail?* For the Cartesian philosophy it is: *How can science be progressive and certain?* And for the philosophy of G. E. Moore it is: *How can we be absolutely clear about what we mean?* Thus a comparative cultural biography of the great philosophers reveals not only a Platonic, a Thomistic, a Cartesian, and a Moorean character, but the serial prominence of political, religious, scientific, and semantic considerations as we pass from the ancient to the contemporary world.

If we see Plato as the great philosopher and educator of an aristocratic restoration in Greece, interested in reinstating in a somewhat more sophisticated form the aristocratic virtues of the Greek heroic age, and directing his cultural criticism against the "degenerate" democracy of Athens, product of Periclean imperialism and "leveling," then his major values and his major philosophic enterprises become intrinsically intelligible. The passion for excellence; the enthronement of a principle of hierarchy in his sociology, his psychology, and his cosmology and of a principle of permanence in his metaphysics; his belief in the supreme value of the few; and his permanent and rancorous mistrust of the many all take their place as parts of a coherent political vision of the world. Then the trips to Syracuse as an effort to secure the monarchical principle, the founding of the Academy as a training center for the new class of aristocratic administrators, and the writing of the dialogues for the Academy, for Athens, and for the Hellenic world to secure the Socratic ideal of the dialectical community in living memory, to provide the principles and examples of academic instruction, and to rationally construct and codify the value system for an aristocratic change of heart in the Hellenic world all seem ingredients in a single but comprehensive enterprise. And if the dialogues continually revere the memory of

Socrates, continually attack the poets, the rhetoricians, and the Sophists, this is because Plato recognized that the instruction of the young is central to the accomplishment of a desirable social change. The anti-Sophistic bias is directed against the influence of the democratically inclined customary educators who have led Athens astray; the Socratic myth is a fantasy constructed to enthrone the aristocratic influence of a martyred teacher. And if the Academy, as a product of alienation and disgust, exists within the very polis it despises, this is but a foretaste of that isolation and retreat which is to characterize the curious political anomalies of the Hellenistic world.

The internal political conflict, mirror of a conflict of basic values, which infected the Greek city-state in the time of Plato, had sixteen hundred years later been supplanted by a remarkably organic unification in the medieval Christian world. The church had provided an institutional framework and the modes of ideological support which made possible a stable theocratic social order in which no function—political, cultural, or intellectual—was isolated from the central driving force of Christian belief. Thus in the thirteenth century philosophical preeminence and the performance of ecclesiastical tasks were inseparably conjoined. The history of philosophy during this period is very largely bound up with the Franciscan and Dominican orders and with the University of Paris, intellectual center of the medieval world—in fact with those few philosophers of genius, Franciscan or Dominican, who occupied the chairs of theology at the University of Paris. Thus Saint Thomas Aquinas, greatest of medieval philosophers, spent his life obediently fulfilling the philosophic tasks set for him by his superiors in the church and the Dominican order, and his philosophy can be rightly understood only if he is seen as the great bringer of Christian enlightenment and doctrinal clarification in institutional support of the Roman church.

But in the Middle Ages the philosophic forms also reflected the institutional realities. The methods of teaching at the medieval university were decisive for determining the literary forms into which philosophical treatises were cast: commentaries on a text expressive of classroom exegesis, and the great series of disputed questions, quodlibetal questions, and summas, reflecting the notable occasions of public disputation. The summas of Saint Thomas are great philosophical works in their own right, but they were also codifications of Christian doctrine intended to serve as training manuals for a knowledgeable and militant clergy.

But there is a sense in which Saint Thomas, no less than Plato, was an aristocrat—that curious medieval anomaly, a saint of noble birth—and the content of his philosophic work also expresses the gradations of the medieval order built into the epistemology and the metaphysics. His cosmic gradations are mirrors of feudal class division, and God's supreme creation—the creatural hierarchy—expresses a sense of the order of rank, indigenous to a characteristic medieval mind. The grades of knowledge present a rationalization of feudal order in the epistemology, as the "order of Being" reflects that order in the metaphysics. For in Aquinas, Plato's rather simply tripartite divisions are expanded into a cosmology full enough to encompass every minute distinction within "the great chain of Being." And behind all of this infinite cosmological elaboration lies a permanent dedication to the institutional task. Thomism, even as an abstract philosophic construction, is eternally expressive of Christian piety and churchly concern.

By the seventeenth century this Christian piety and churchly concern was no longer the source of preeminent philosophical activity. A dogmatic, frozen, and illiberal Scholasticism had captured the universities, so that whereas in the thirteenth century the University of Paris was the avant garde of intellectual fermentation, the seventeenth-century Sorbonne was a kind of Scholastic graveyard. Philosophy had passed from the hands of the scholarly saint into the hands of the noble gentleman like Montaigne, functioning wholly outside the university milieu and writing neither for students nor the clergy as such, but for a mature, although restricted, upper-class audience. It is in this light that the writings of the gentleman, René Descartes, Lord of Perron, also are to be understood.

But this change of philosophic location from the institutionally anchored saint and professor of the Middle Ages to the independent and self-reliant seventeenth-century gentleman brought with it a new subjectivism and a new self-preoccupation. The chief subject of philosophizing is no longer God and his creation, but the personal self and its self-knowledge, its mind and its mental functioning: in short, epistemology. But what has not always been remarked is that this new epistemological preoccupation is largely the consequence of the gentlemanly milieu itself: its idleness,

tranquillity, and economic independence. Attention to the functioning of "materials" is the natural habit of the artisan, and
attention to the relentlessness of "things" that of the practical man
who must earn his living by his work, but Descartes's *Cogito ergo
sum* is an upper-class proposition, a product of privacy and abstraction. And the entire Cartesian metaphysics is, in fact, the
consequence of the gentlemanly way of life: of its withdrawal,
self-reliance, solitude, quiet, and the concentrated contemplation
which is its fruit.

Descartes's search for tranquillity and solitude is symbolized by
the more than two decades of his sojourn in Holland. Whereas
France in this period was a country of pomp and circumstance,
monarchical grandeur and theatrical gestures, grandiloquence
and exaggerated etiquette, the Dutch Republic lent itself to ideals
of a very different nature: mildness, tolerance, a strong sense of
justice, a distrust of sonorous phrases and political rhetoric, and a
love of industrious orderliness expressed to perfection in the serenity of that peaceful country life which Descartes himself lived for
almost a quarter of a century. It is the contrast between a land-
scape of Ruisdael or van Goyen or one of Vermeer's quiet interiors
and the bombastic royalism of Velaquez, Bernini, and Vandyke.
For in speaking of the "gentlemanliness" of Descartes, I have not
meant to suggest the heroic swashbuckling of *The Three Muske-
teers*, or the Spain of Calderón, or even the England of Cavaliers
and Roundheads. For there was, in addition, the celebrated *noblesse de robe*—gentlemen of the pen, rather than of the sword.
Surely there was little wildness or fierceness in the character of
Descartes. Brilliant, unheroic, prudent: these he undoubtedly
was, and perhaps this, as well as its renowned tolerance, made the
Dutch Republic of the seventeenth century so comfortable for
him, so satisfying and secure as a philosopher's abode.

The Dutch Republic provided the background, and it is perhaps one reason why Descartes's philosophy is a philosophy of
privacy in a double sense: it originated in tranquillity and independence, and it stresses the centrality of the tranquilly thinking subject—the *res cogitans*. But if Cartesianism began in subjectivism, it does not end there. Its real motive is the secure
founding of the natural sciences; the great new preoccupation of
the seventeenth century. And if the Cartesian rationalism had a
highly aristocratic flavor, even more original was the fashion in

which Descartes transformed mathematical interest and physical and physiological experiment into an upper-class fashion. The "enoblement" of science, by virtue of which the inquiry into and the search after natural knowledge achieved status as worthy of serious upper-class concern, was the Cartesian heritage to the generation which was to follow.

By the eighteenth century, and particularly with reference to the eighteenth century in Germany, all of this had again changed. Partly this was because the gentlemanly association of philosophy and science with upper-class amateurism, symbolized by Montaigne and reaching its culmination after the death of Descartes, revealed its weakness — dilletantism and superficiality. And partly it was because with the founding of the University of Halle in 1693, the *libertas docendi* was restored, the dead Scholasticism of the sixteenth and seventeenth centuries was replaced by a new liberal spirit, and the universities, now under secular rather than ecclesiastical control, began once again to assert that independence which made Oxford, Paris, and Bologna the ornaments of medieval culture.

But the German eighteenth century also brought two changes which were of the greatest importance for shifting philosophy from a "gentlemanly" to a "professional" preoccupation — the rise of the highly specialized philosophical journal, and the new academic concern of philosophy with its own past which was to produce the great scholarly multivolume histories of philosophy which were published at Leipzig, Marburg, and Göttingen toward the end of the eighteenth century. Of this new philosophical professionalism Immanuel Kant at Königsberg is the classic transitional figure, and his own major contributions to this trend — the passion for philosophical system and the invention of a highly technical philosophical terminology — influenced philosophical writing profoundly for the next two hundred years.

By the end of the nineteenth century philosophical professionalism had been established, and its great representative for our time is G. E. Moore. Coming from a middle-class, comfortably well-off English bourgeois background, Moore's nonprofessional ethical values, sense of moral responsibility, respect for established moral rules, and general conformity to a conventional upper-middle-class way of life are displayed in his everyday behavior when they do not appear in the structure of his moral theory (as, for example, in the much neglected chapter 5 of *Principia Ethica*). But it is the quiet influence of Edwardian Cambridge, with its peace, prosperity, and intellectual isolation, which is decisive for his intellectual formation. Here his passion for clarity exercised itself against the dominant Hegelianism which had reached its peak and was now overripe; and that Germanic fondness for a special philosophic vocabulary, classically expressed in Kant and spilling over from Hegel into Bradley, Bosanquet, and McTaggart, produced its counterbalance: a faith in the possibility of using ordinary language, with rigorous standards of logical exactness and clarity, to express philosophical ideas and clarify their conceptual ambiguities.

Moore's analytical method was meant to produce a correct analysis of meanings or concepts, and yet the close attention to "meanings" inevitably required concentration upon the words or linguistic expressions through which these meanings were conveyed. This too is symptomatic of the modern movement in philosophy, where the primarily metaphysical interests of Plato and Saint Thomas and the primarily epistemological interests of Descartes have been transformed into a primarily semantic interest — that is to say, where the world and mind are less important than the correct interpretation of "statements" about the world and mind, and where attention to linguistic mechanisms and to analytical methods per se has replaced the substantive interest in illuminating the structure of the cosmos and the mind's role in its ultimate understanding.

For all of this there is a certain sociological explanation. For if the general peace and prosperity of the British Empire during the late nineteenth and early twentieth century permitted just that comfortable quiet and isolation in which the analytic enterprise could flourish, cut off from the pragmatic requirements of economic necessity and the urgencies of political crisis, the general situation with respect to values made the abandonment of primary substantive concern inevitable. Western culture since the seventeenth century has become progressively less religious and progressively more secular in its orientation. Plato, Saint Thomas, and Descartes all have a place for God in their philosophical systems. Moore does not. But the difference is cultural and not personal

For as philosophy progressively detaches itself from politics, theology, and, finally, psychology to become a separate subject of study within the university, technical considerations become increasingly important, and philosophical professionalism and general cultural secularization go hand in hand. The breakdown of the organic pattern of Christian belief shattered the medieval synthesis into a thousand fragments, and today, in every cultural area, literature, painting, music, or philosophy as the case may be, virtuosity of style and the hyperdevelopment of technical accomplishment are used to compensate for a drastic impoverishment of commonly held values and shared belief. The philosophy of G. E. Moore marks the triumph of method in modern philosophizing, and in so doing, represents one of the chief characteristics of philosophy in a "professional" age. For such an age means for philosophy a care for methods rather than results, a specialization of interest requiring increasing concentration upon perfecting professional tools, and finally, modes of communication (like the philosophical association and the specialized philosophical journal) which have become carefully adjusted to the needs of a professional elite. It is G. E. Moore's particular achievement that to his followers, as to his colleagues at large, that passion for clarity which produced his analytic method has functioned not only as a technical mechanism but as a moral force.

In considering the course of philosophy in the ages of the aristocrat, the saint, the gentleman, and the professional, it is obvious that no two cultural ages have exactly the same qualities and characteristics. And it follows that the philosophic intentions of Plato, Saint Thomas, Descartes, and G. E. Moore are also quite different. But although a philosophy may be *typical* of its century, it need not be its exact mirror. For in considering the total body of Saint Thomas's works, or of the complete canon of the Platonic dialogues, it seems as if each of these thinkers had absorbed *the entire content* of the Hellenic and the medieval epochs. Whereas in the case of Descartes or of G. E. Moore, the cultures out of which they spring are already too heterogeneous and splintered to permit more than the typicality I have mentioned. And this makes it extremely difficult to discern a clear structure in the sequence of philosophical experience, just as it is extremely difficult to discern such a logic in the sequence of history itself. If one wishes to ask: Is there a logic of philosophical experience? Is there, beyond all the casual and contingent events in the history of philosophy, something we may call "a metaphysical structure" of the historic sequence of diverse philosophies? the answer must inevitably be skeptical. But this is only a natural consequence of the very standpoint we have previously adopted. There are perhaps two kinds of a priori for philosophical creation, one *intellectual* and one *cultural*—one based upon the *logical* possibilities available to the human mind, the other based upon the *historical* requirements of the period in which the philosophy originated. In committing ourselves to the way of history rather than the way of logic, we have only contingently avoided the issue of *a comparative morphology of philosophical knowledge*, not outlawed it. But from the historical approach it is also clear that there are culturally conditioned styles of philosophizing, and this raises the very question with which I wish to deal very briefly in the next section: Is disagreement in philosophy primarily a matter of truth, falsity, and logical error, or is it due rather to preferences of an essentially aesthetic or temperamental sort, exercised in the confrontation of a plurality of philosophical styles?

However, even from the four studies which compose the body of this book certain striking generalization do, I think, emerge. One is the essential elitism, the *exclusiveness* of the philosophical enterprise. Another is the pervasiveness of *the concern with method* throughout the history of philosophy. And a third is the way those virtues which characterize and are embedded in the content of any philosophy take their color and their quality from the prevailing characteristics of its age.

It seems clear that despite its "democratic" commitment to a rationality which is universal, the actual practice of philosophy as represented by the tradition is limited to the small group, the restricted audience in any age. The Platonic society of aristocratic young men embarked upon an aristocratic education is constructed upon the Pythagorean model of a truly intimate circle or coterie, bound together by life-ties and even a formal initiation. The Platonic Academy is only this little society formalized and embodied, where the medium of the esoteric discourse and the internal lecture produced (rather as a centripetal force) those literary dialogues written for Athens and the Hellenic world. The medieval community of saints and saintly educators, never far from the isolation of the monastery and monastic life, a dedicated group within the medieval university (itself a form of secular

monastery) produces its modes of philosophic argument (*lectio,
ordinatio, disputatio, questiones quodlibetas*, etc.) within the
small group of those bound together by the exertions of the
Roman church and the cementing influence of a commonality of
Christian belief. The seventeenth-century "circle of learning," the
exclusive and independent group of learned gentlemen, no longer
concentrated in an Academy or a University (in short, no longer
merely local, but as wide as Europe itself, although no less small
and exclusive for this fact) communicates *at a distance* through the
exchanged letter, and the circulated treatise with its "objections"
and "answers to objections," without losing its sense of a community of the intellectually "chosen." And the comtemporary intercourse of professional philosophers, "those with the Ph.D. degree," who communicate at the professional association meetings,
attend world congresses of philosophy, and write articles for *Mind*
and the *Journal of philosophy*, although it approaches the size of
an unruly crowd, and at some professional meetings even a swirl-
ing mob, yet in fact comprises a relatively modest number, and
actually manages to emphasize its singularity by the unconscious
snobbery of its exclusions. Whether in ancient Athens, medieval
Paris, seventeenth-century France, England, or Holland, or in
contemporary Oxford, Cambridge, or Chicago, the practice of
philosophy is inbred, restricted, and drastically limited.

   Although obsessive concentration upon techniques of philosophizing is the hallmark of philosophy today, Plato, Saint Thomas, and Descartes, no less than G. E. Moore, felt that some set
ritual of disputation, demonstration, inquiry, discovery, or proof
was the necessary precondition of philosophic accomplishment. It
is therefore certainly no accident that each of these thinkers is
associated with a particular philosophic method. First there is *the
dialectial method* of Plato, a formalization of conversation and
dialogue within an elite group of aristocratic truth seekers, where
"division" and "analysis" are utilized to track down the essential
nature of ideas and ultimately to provide real definitions for
crucial metaphysical and moral concepts. This method—a purposive sublimation of the Greek contest system in the intellectual
domain—presupposes the existence of an intellectual and social
elite philosophizing—first publicly with Socrates in the agora,
then privately with Plato in the Academy. Second there is *the
Scholastic method* of Saint Thomas, originating in the living

actuality of formal disputation, the set ritual of systematic statement, counterstatement, rebuttal, and decision, peculiar to the
closed university atmosphere with its small, but profoundly influential society of clerks and clerics, and finally becoming crystallized
in the demonstrative procedure of the summa "question." Third
there is *the skeptical method* of Descartes, the meditative cogita-
tions of the private thinker steeped in mathematics and natural
science, who subjects the whole spectrum of traditional beliefs to
the test of indubitability in an attempt to found the sciences of the
natural world upon an ultimate and unshakably rational basis,
and who then communicates his results at a distance to the circle
of savants and learned noblemen. And finally there is *the analytic
method* of G. E. Moore, the details of which are difficult to
pinpoint, but which utilizes the criteria of noncontradiction and
conformity with common sense in taking infinite pains to establish
an exactitude of meaning, and which expresses the natural pursuit
of the professional philosopher functioning in the university classroom, the meetings of the learned society, and in the pages of the
professional philosophical journal. These methods, dialectical,
Scholastic, skeptical, or analytic, as the case may be, attest to a
permanent philosophic concern with effective approaches and an
accredited procedure for the achievement of philosophic truth.

If, as I have tried to show, philosophies are produced as a
response to the needs of their time, and (often unconsciously)
reflect its mood and spirit, then that part of philosophizing which
shows the greatest immediate sensitivity to current custom and
standards of valuation — moral philosophy — should be the firmest
witness to the value configuration of any historical epoch. But
even where there is no such one-to-one correlation, or where the
philosophy is primarily metaphysical or epistemological and has
no well worked out ethics, the philosopher's own life and philosophic procedures may nonetheless express the influence of the
dominant ideals of his age. In the age of the aristocrat, the virtues
are "aristocratic" virtues, and for Plato so are the civic requirements of courage, temperance, justice, and wisdom. Throughout
the dialogues, the ancient influence of Homer and Simonides
spills out between the lines. In the age of the saint, the virtues are
"saintly" virtues, and so are devotion to God, purity, obedience,
love, spirituality, and self-denial in the life and work of Aquinas.
Here the New Testament and the Rule of Saint Benedict find

constant expression. In the age of the gentleman, the virtues are "gentlemanly" virtues, and for Descartes so are moderation, reserve, nobility, resignation, fineness of feeling and conservatism. In his letters to Queen Christina and Princess Elizabeth of Bohemia, the seventeenth-century equivalent of Stoic nobility is enshrined. In the age of the professional, the virtues are "professional virtues; and although, as I have tried to show, in the pages of *Principia Ethica* is to be found a profound conflict between a bourgeois and conservative conformity to social rules and the glimmerings of aesthetic revolt, this is but an early eccentricity in the thought of G. E. Moore. In his philosophic life he is himself a perfect example of the professional virtues of conscientiousness, analytic precision, steadfastness of application, logical rigor, and passionate devotion to the truth.

It should certainly be clear that the method of writing the history of philosophy which I have here adopted is meant not to supplant the more usual procedure of descriptive exposition and logical criticism, but to supplement it with considerations which are cultural and, to some extent, sociological. Above all, it is not meant as a substitute for any close reading of the textual sources themselves. My hope, rather, has been to increase the intelligibility of the basic texts by constructing a few simple hypotheses about their cultural role and social functioning. Nor has my purpose been in any sense to minimize or deny the crucial nature of the individual philosopher's creativity: the power of the personal agent or reflective mind striving to communicate method, argument, and vision through those basic texts which are our primary philosophic sources. Rather, I have tried to show for Plato, Saint Thomas, Descartes, and G. E. Moore how we can appreciate more deeply the nature of philosophic theories by observing their authors working within the horizon and resources of their own unique stage in human history and responsive to its peculiar quality and moral demands. For I believe that, despite the fiction of "logical inevitability," there is always an important element of "contingency" and "historicity" at the heart of any system.

Examining a philosopher's doctrines simply in terms of internal logical development and consistency is valuable, but it neglects one key resource—the historical matrix within which theory is always embedded. Individual philosophic statements are crucial, but the habit of seeing them always as "placed" and "dated" permits us to furnish an anchorage in history for the complex reality of the philosopher's intent. Such historical anchorage does not compromise the availability of former doctrines to contemporary critical judgment, but it enhances the accessibility of their meaning.

The Uses of the History of Philosophy

Although the whole thrust of *Philosophy as Social Expression* has been to show that the works of the great philosophers are not simply expressions of their culture, or of the historic moments in which they were produced, it is true that it has emphasized their responsiveness to the challenges of culture and the way in which they reflect a dominant ideal or way of life. And this poses a certain question for the historian of philosophy: In exactly what way are philosophical ideas which were developed in part to satisfy local and historical needs available to other ages? What are the possible responses of a contemporary thinker to those great works which have become part of the tradition of the history of philosophy? What has been the historical fate of Platonism, of Thomism, of Cartesianism?

Two possible answers immediately become apparent. One is that any philosophy which attempts to answer certain questions for one age will again be useful when a later age faces similar problems. Any antidemocratic impulse might take its arguments from Platonic organicism and class stratification. Any conservative counterrevolution might find its rationale in the divine ordering of the Thomistic cosmos. Or, put in a less tendentiously political idiom, any recrudescence of the aristocratic ideal might find its inspiration in Platonism, even if it refused to accept the details of the Platonic metaphysics; any commitment to modern professionalism might find its inspiration in G. E. Moore's methodical search for clarity, even if it found his early Realism unsympathetic, and his reliance upon common sense unsophisticated and provincial.

The second answer is that however anchored in history a particular philosophy or *Weltanschauung* may be, it at the same time contains "timeless" or "rational" or "logical" elements eternally ripe for appropriation and elaboration. Thus the Thomistic and the Cartesian proofs for the existence of God are available whenever theological questions are of current interest, and Whitehead, no antidemocrat but a good late-nineteenth-century liberal, can make the chief elements of the Platonic philosophy (the ideas, the numbers, the eros, the receptacle, the harmony, etc.) the foundation stones of his own philosophy of organism.

What is at stake here is the meaning of philosophic tradition — the ideological relationship between past and present — and this has clearly a twofold application. On the one hand the details of the contemporary philosophical situation (the dominance of professionalism) condition our understanding of the history of philosophy, and this seriously compromises the making of any hard and fast distinction between a "faithful" and a "distorted" — that is to say, a legitimate or an illegitimate — interpretation of the philosophic past. And the consequence is a serious tension between any desire to understand the past on its own terms and an equally legitimate desire to find it *usable* for solving current philosophical perplexities. On the other hand, even the dedicated attempt to arrive at a fuller comprehension of the doctrines held by Plato or Saint Thomas or Descartes will lead to some judgment about their adequacy, and this alone turns us in the direction of the "reasons" which might lead us to accept or reject them.

The balance between the claims of logic and of time, with which my initial chapter dealt, is a delicate one indeed. The historian of philosophy, no less than the constructive metaphysician, is eternally confronted with the need to deal both with *the historical roots* and *the permanent importance* of any philosophical position. And since the estimate of "permanent importance" is itself a variable one, this returns the act of judgment to the level of date, essential temporality, and historical fate. In his *History of Philosophy and Philosophical Education*, Etienne Gilson wrote: "The history of philosophy cannot be a graveyard for dead philosophers, because in philosophy there are no dead." Unfortunately this is far from the truth, and we had better reverse the witticism of Mark Twain ("Reports of my death are highly exaggerated") to reply to Gilson that reports of the life of, say, Herbert Spencer's *System of Synthetic Philosophy* or Avenarius's *Kritik der reinen Erfahrung*, or even so recently decased a work as Samuel Alexander's *Space, Time, and Deity*, are highly exaggered indeed. A judgment I think is much truer than Gilson's has been given by Merleau-Ponty in the introduction to his *Signs*:

The history of thought does not summarily pronounce: This is true, that is false. Like all history, it has its veiled decisions. It dismantles or embalms certain doctrines, changing them into "messages" or museum pieces. There are others, on the contrary, which it keeps active. These do not endure because there is some miraculous adequation or correspondence between them and an invariable "reality" — such an exact and fleshless truth is neither sufficient nor necessary for the greatness of a doctrine — but because, as obligatory steps for those who want to go further, they retain an expressive power which exceeds their statements and propositions. These doctrines are the *classics*. They are recognizable by the fact that no one takes them literally, and yet new facts are never absolutely outside their province but call forth new echoes from them and reveal new lusters in them. . . . Are you or are you not a Cartesian? The question does not make much sense, since those who reject this or that in Descartes do so only in terms of reasons which owe a lot to Descartes.

Merleau-Ponty's distinction between "museum pieces," "messages," and "classics," is, I think, of the very greatest importance. Only it is necessary to add that these distinctions themselves are not eternal and unchangeable categories but historically variable and interchangeable, so that the message of one age may be the museum piece of the next. Or even that at the same time a certain philosophic position may function as a message in one tradition and as a museum piece in another. To understand what a museum piece is, is to recognize what Anaximines or Carneades or Panaetius or Wolff or Lotze or Haeckel or James Mill means to us today. And to understand what a message is, is to recognize what Hume meant to Hans Reichenbach or Hegel to Herbert Marcuse. But at the same time, if Hegel is a message to a revisionist Marxism, he is the deadest of museum pieces to a militant Postivsim or a Logical Empiricism. And classics too may undergo the same fate of historical transformation. It is as possible to speak of a "downfall" of Cartesianism in the late seventeenth century as it is to speak of a "revival" of Thomism in the late nineteenth. The death and resurrection of the classics of philosophy is as mysterious, and sometimes as incomprehensible, as is the central mystery of the Christian religion.

Merleau-Ponty's analysis of philosophy's historical fate is an important contribution to the problem of the relationship of former achievement to contemporary creation — of past to present. And its solution is essentially the same as that of T. S. Eliot. What counts is not the "pastness" of the past but its *presence*, and whereas museum pieces function as pure past (a collection of memorials or mummy cases), messages and classics share a present—the one ephemeral, the other as a permanent possibility of inspiration which is powerful in its effect. And although we should probably agree that there is something ineradicably contingent and unforeseeable about the messages prevailing in any age, the classics have just that transcendant permanence to which Merleau-Ponty calls attention. Plato and Aristotle, Saint Thomas and Saint Augustine, Descartes and Spinoza, Locke and Hume, Kant and John Stuart Mill remain active philosophically because, although no one today can possibly be a complete Platonist, or Cartesian, or Kantian, yet the stages which they register in the philosophic tradition are critical, and their resonance remains such that the process of their adaptation and assimilation is endless. The classics are therefore those philosophers and those philosophic works which are *eternally relevant.*

Yet to put it this way is not really to contradict the claim we have made that classics too undergo "historical transformation." Every age learns (positively or negatively) from Plato, but it is not always the same Plato. Every age learns (positively or negatively) from Descartes, but it is not always the same Descartes. A former generation read Descartes as the indispensable preparation for the French materialism of the eighteenth century or (since Gilson) as the not always willing heir of Saint Augustine and the entire medieval tradition. Today we read another Descartes for whom we have been prepared by Ryle and Wittgenstein: a Descartes whose dualism ("the ghost in the machine") is laughable and whose subjectivism ("Cartesian privacy") was (without once mentioning his name) the target of Wittgenstein's most sustained polemic!

But there are a third and a fourth Descartes also. For his dualism lives on (approvingly) in Strawson's "individuals"—"things" and "persons," and the subjectivism also lives on (lovingly) in the appropriations of contemporary existentialism and phenomenology. Sartre, in addition to utilizing the concept of "Cartesian freedom," has in his *Transcendence of the Ego* taken over the Cartesian notion of the "pre-reflexive Cogito" to found his own epistemology. And Husserl in his *Cartesian Meditations* (1929) has followed the Cartesian example of a meditative philosophic procedure in which one begins radically anew, undertakes a radical "suspense of judgment" in a process of rigorous questioning to discover "the unquestionable basis" of human knowledge, and at last finds this basis in the peculiar qualities of the personal subject. Husserl's great idols were Plato and Descartes. Already in 1892 at Halle and in 1916 at Göttingen, he had reflected deeply on Descartes's *Meditations*, and in the unpublished lectures "Phenomenological Method and Phenomenological Philosophy," which he delivered at the University of London in June 1922 (the last of which was chaired by G. E. Moore), he demonstrated the historical connection between Descartes's arrival at the *ego cogito* as a result of a methodological negation of the world of sense experience, and his own method of "the phenomenological reduction."

An entire dissertation could be written on the Cartesianism of Husserl, but that is not of overriding importance here. What I have wished to indicate is the multiple uses of Descartes, and how the phenomenological and existentialist utilization of his results is, on the whole, in striking contrast to their "analytic" rejection. But also, as we have seen, something very similar is true of the contemporary uses of Plato. Whitehead, like Plato a great mathematician and philosopher and perhaps the last great representative of the Platonic tradition in Anglo-Saxon philosophy, builds his comprehensive metaphysics upon consciously adopted Platonic foundations, while John Dewey (who once asserted nevertheless that Plato was his favorite philosophical reading) criticizes the Platonic abstraction, mentalism, and aristocratic distaste for association with common everyday "materials" (whether nonliving or human) as a step in the establishment of his own practical and ordinary "arts of control." But even here it is possible to find certain social correlations. Whitehead, although no British nobleman (he stems from essentially the same upper-middle-class background as G. E. Moore) is yet in some sense a contemporary of that nineteenth-century aristocratic Oxford and Cambridge espousal of Greek culture expressed by Jebb and Jowett and later by Verall and Gilbert Murray, whereas Dewey's nineteenth-century rural New England background, with its town-meeting, farmer-shrewdness atmosphere, prepared him for precisely that apotheosis of the quotidian which his pragmatism so completely expresses.

In the Platonism of Whitehead, the Cartesianism of Husserl and Sartre, and the Thomism of Gilson and Jacques Maritain, we have evidence of how the philosophical classics are transformed into "messages," just as in the virulent anti-Platonism, anti-Thomism, and anti-Cartesianism to be found in the camp of the Pragmatists, Logical Empiricists, and Analytic Philosophers we see them being converted into museum pieces, if not worse. What is now perhaps the next task for the historians of philosophy is to begin with Merleau-Ponty's important distinction between museum pieces, messages, and classics and to direct their efforts toward a search for the logic which governs their cultural incidence and their transformations.

BIBLIOGRAPHY

Chapter Two

Adkins, Arthur W. H. *Merit and Responsibility: A Study in Greek Values*. New York and London: Oxford University Press, 1960.

Burnet, John. *Greek Philosophy: Thales to Plato*. London: Macmillan, 1950.

Cherniss, Harold. *The Riddle of the Early Academy*. Berkeley: University of California Press, 1945.

Field, G. C. *Plato and His Contemporaries*. London: Methuen, 1948.

Havelock, Eric A. *Preface to Plato*. New York: Grosset and Dunlap, 1967.

Landsberg, Paul. *Wesen und Bedeutung der platonischen Akademie*. Bonn: F. Cohen, 1923.

Ritter, Constantin. *Neue Untersuchungen über Platon*. Munich: Beck, 1910.

Robinson, Richard. *Plato's Earlier Dialectic*. New York and London: Oxford University Press, 1953.

Ross, David. *Plato's Theory of Ideas*. London: Oxford University Press, 1951.

Ryle, Gilbert. *Plato's Progress*. New York and Cambridge: Cambridge University Press, 1966.

Taylor, A. E. *Plato: The Man and His Work*. New York: The Dial Press, 1929.

Shorey, Paul. *The Unity of Plato's Thought*. Hamden, Conn.: Shoe String Press, 1968.

— — —. *What Plato Said*. Chicago: University of Chicago Press, 1933.

Wilamowitz-Moellendorff, Ulrich von. *Platon*. 2 vols. Berlin: Weidmann, 1920.

Chapter Three

Adams, Henry. *Mont-Saint-Michel and Chartres*. New York: Anchor Books, 1959.

Bourke, Vernon J. *Aquinas' Search for Wisdom*. Milwaukee: Bruce, 1965.

Chenu, M. D. *Toward Understanding St. Thomas*. Chicago: Regnery, 1964.

De Wulf, Maurice. *Philosophy and Civilization in the Middle Ages.* Princeton: Princeton University Press, 1922.

Gilson, Etienne. *La philosophie au moyen age.* Paris: Payot, 1947.

— — —. *The Philosophy of St. Thomas Aquinas.* Cambridge: Cambridge University Press, 1929.

Glorieux, Palémon. *La littérature quodlibétique.* Paris: J.Vrin, 1935.

Grabmann, Martin. *Die Geschichte der scholastischen Methode.* Graz: Akademische Druck u. Verlagsanstalt, 1957.

Mandonnet, P. "Chronologie des questions disputées de saint Thomas d'Aquin." *Revue thomiste* 23 (1928).

Panofsky, Erwin. *Gothic Architecture and Scholasticism.* New York: University Publishers, 1951.

Rashdall, Hastings. *The Universities of Europe in the Middle Ages.* London: Oxford University Press, 1936.

Sertillanges, D. *Les grands philosophes: St. Thomas d'Aquin.* Paris: F. Alcan, 1910.

Thompson, James Westfall. *An Economic and Social History of the Middle Ages.* New York and London: Century Co., 1928.

Ueberweg, Friedrich. *Die patristische und scholastische Philosophie.* Edited by B. Geyer. Basel-Stuttgart: Benno Schwabe, 1961.

Chapter Four

Adam, Charles. *Vie et oeuvres de Descartes.* Paris: L. Cerf, 1910.

Alquié, Ferdinand. *La découverte métaphysique de l'homme chez Descartes.* Paris: Presses universitaires de France, 1950.

Baillet, Adrien. *La vie de Monsieur DesCartes.* Paris, 1691.

Brunschvicg, Léon. *Descartes et Pascal, lecteurs de Montaigne.* New York and Paris: Brentano's, 1944.

Gilson, Etienne. *Discours de la methode: Texte et commentaire.* Paris: J. Vrin, 1939.

— — —. *Etudes sur le rôle de la pensée médiévale dans la formation du système cartésien.* Paris: J. Vrin, 1930.

Gouhier, Henri. *La pensée religieuse de Descartes.* Paris: J. Vrin, 1924.

— — —. *Essais sur Descartes.* Paris: J. Vrin, 1949.

Guérard, Albert Léon. *France in the Classical Age.* New York: Harper and Row, 1965.

Gueroult, Martial. *Descartes selon l'ordre des raisons.* 2 vols. Paris: Aubier, Montaigne, 1953.

Krantz, Emile. *Essai sur l'esthétique de Descartes.* Paris: G. Ballière, 1882.

Lefebvre, Henri. *Descartes.* Paris: Editions Hier et Aujourd'hui, 1947.

Roth, Leon. *Descartes' Discourse on Method.* London: Oxford University Press, 1948.

Treasure, G. R. R. *Seventeenth Century France.* New York: Barnes and Noble, 1966.

Chapter Five

Ambrose, Alice, and Lazarowitz, Morris, eds. *G. E. Moore: Essays in Retrospect.* New York: Humanities Press, 1970.

Ensor, R. C. K. *England 1870-1914.* London: Oxford University Press, 1960.

Harrod, R. F. *The Life of John Maynard Keynes.* London: Macmillan, 1951; New York: St. Martin's Press, 1963.

Keynes, John M. *Two Memoires: "Doctor Melchior, a Defeated Enemy," and "My Early Beliefs."* Clifton, N. J.: Augustus M. Kelley, 1970.

Klemke, E. D. *Studies in the Philosophy of G. E. Moore.* Chicago: Quadrangle Books, 1969.

Moore, G. E. *The Commonplace Book.* Edited by Casimir Lewy. New York: Humanities Press, 1962; London: Allen and Unwin, 1963.

— — —. *Ethics.* London: Oxford University Press, 1912; paperback edition, New York: Oxford University Press, 1965.

— — —. *Lectures on Philosophy.* Edited by Casimir Lewy. New York: Humanities Press; London: Allen and Unwin, 1966.

— — —. *Philosophical Papers.* London: Allen and Unwin, 1959; New York: Macmillan, 1962.

— — —. *Philosophical Studies.* London: Routledge and Kegan Paul, 1922; paperback edition, Totowa, N. J.: Littlefield, Adams and Co., 1968.

— — —. *Principia Ethica.* Cambridge and New York: Cambridge University Press, 1929, 1959.

— — —. *Some Main Problems of Philosophy.* London: Allen and Unwin, 1953; New York: Macmillan, 1962.

Schilpp, P. A., ed. *The Philosophy of G. E. Moore.* Evanston, Ill.: Tudor, 1942.

Thomson, David. *England in the Nineteenth Century.* Baltimore: Penguin Books, 1950.

White, Alan R. *G. E. Moore: A Critical Exposition.* New York: Humanities Press, 1958.

Woolf, Leonard. *Sowing: An Autobiography of the Years 1880-1904.* New York: Harcourt Brace Jovanovich; London: Hogarth, 1961.

INDEX

Abelard, Peter, 23, 24, 102, 105, 106, 107, 111, 122, 123, 125, 126, 132, 146, 163

Academy, the, 36, 42, 43, 46, 47, 48, 59, 61, 71, 72, 73, 76, 77, 78, 79, 80, 83, 87, 89, 91, 95, 99, 112, 122, 123, 165, 167, 233, 302, 303, 308, 310

Adams, Henry, 161

Adelard of Bath, 105

Adkins, Arthur, 54, 55

Aeschylus, 54

Agathos, 54, 56

Albert the Great, 8, 104, 108, 109, 110, 117, 122, 133, 134, 146, 156, 157, 160, 171

Alexander of Hales, 108, 109, 122, 146

Ambrose, Saint, 132

Amsterdam, 184, 185

Analysis, 4, 22, 265, 295, 296, 300, 307

Analytic philosophy, 7, 265, 317

Anaxagoras, 83, 98

Anselm, Saint, 5, 111, 112, 122, 123, 132, 159, 231, 234

Anselm of Laon, 105

Antinomies of bourgeois thought, 20, 32

"Apostles," 260, 261, 281

Aquinas, Saint Thomas, 2, 5, 9, 10, 27, 30, 35, 44, 101-62, 165, 167, 168, 170, 171, 176, 180, 226, 231, 233, 234, 248, 251, 270, 271, 296, 300, 301, 303, 304, 307, 308, 310, 312, 314, 316

Archytas of Tarentum, 48

Aristocracy, 39, 62, 65

Aristocratic restoration, 80, 83, 91, 94, 113, 226, 300, 302

Aristotelian Society, 267, 268, 269, 297

Aristotle, 1, 2, 9, 11, 14, 18, 24, 37, 42, 43, 48, 49, 51, 55, 74, 75, 76, 103, 108, 109, 119, 120, 121, 123, 132, 133, 134, 139, 141, 144, 158, 160,

161, 167, 180, 194, 197, 234, 257, 271, 272, 284, 288, 315

Arnauld, Antoine, 165, 170, 225

Arnim, von, 49

Arnold, Matthew, 249

Athens, 14, 47, 48, 52, 55, 70, 74, 76, 91, 98, 99, 226, 301, 302, 303, 309

Atomism, 15

Augustine, Saint, 9, 32, 103, 108, 110, 112, 120, 121, 122, 132, 139, 144, 150, 158, 180, 231, 234, 316

Austin, J. L., 1, 4

Averroës, 108, 133, 139, 144, 158, 161

Avicenna, 108, 132, 133, 158, 160

Bacon, Francis, 171, 194, 198

Bacon, Roger, 146, 171

Baillet, Adrien, 30, 180, 181, 182

Balzac, Guez de, 167, 172, 183, 184, 229, 270

Bartholomew of Lucca, 140

Bayle, Pierre, 171

Being, 62

Benedict, Saint, 132

Bentham, Jeremy, 24, 39, 271, 277

Berkeley, George, 164, 239, 292, 293

Bernard, Saint, 101, 102, 106

Bérulle, Cardinal de, 183

Bloch, Ernst, 145

Bloomsbury, 260, 261, 272, 284

Boethius, 132, 154

Boileau, 230

Bonaventura, Saint, 27, 37, 104, 108, 109, 111, 122, 134, 136, 145, 146, 160, 171, 214

Bosanquet, B., 263, 267, 269, 307

Bourgeois consciousness, 21

Bourke, Vernon J., 130

Bradley, F. H., 3, 263, 267, 277, 307

Braithwaite, R. B., 265, 270, 289

Bréhier, Emile, 1, 16, 17, 20, 26, 27, 28, 29, 30, 33